AF872356

Causal Artificial Intelligence

Scrivener Publishing
100 Cummings Center, Suite 541J
Beverly, MA 01915-6106

Leading-Edge Breakthroughs in Artificial Intelligence

Series Editor: Dr. S. Balamurugan, Director, Intelligent Research Consultancy Services, Coimbatore, Tamil Nadu, India (Email: sbnbala@gmail.com)

The world is on the cusp of several breakthroughs in artificial intelligence (AI), rapidly transforming industries and the research field. The "Leading-Edge Breakthroughs in Artificial Intelligence" book series is dedicated to exploring the most pioneering developments in artificial intelligence. The series aims to highlight both theoretical and practical advancements, offering insights into several cutting-edge advancements in AI and how the same could be deployed to solve complex problems in fields such as healthcare, finance, manufacturing, robotics, marketing, energy management, agriculture, autonomous systems, and many more. It also addresses critical issues like AI governance, ethics, trust, security, transparency, and societal impacts, making it an essential resource for researchers, engineers, and industry leaders looking to leverage AI for future breakthroughs.

Managing Editors

1. **Dr. T. Ananth Kumar,** Associate Professor & HoD, Department of Computer Science and Engineering, IFET College of Engineering, Tamil Nadu, India

2. **Dr. K. Suresh Kumar,** Assistant Professor, Department of Computer Science and Engineering, Sri Eshwar College of Engineering, Coimbatore, Tamil Nadu, India

3. **Dr. R. Karthick Manoj,** Assistant Professor, Department of Electrical and Electronics Engineering, Academy of Maritime Education and Training (AMET), Deemed to be University, Chennai, Tamil Nadu, India

Publishers at Scrivener
Martin Scrivener (martin@scrivenerpublishing.com)
Phillip Carmical (pcarmical@scrivenerpublishing.com)

Causal Artificial Intelligence

Fundamentals and Applications

Edited by

Rajdeep Chakraborty
Dept. of CSE, Institute of Engineering and Technology, SAGE University, Indore, Madhya Pradesh, India

Aleem Ali
Dept. of CSE, Chandigarh University, Sahibzada Ajit Singh Nagar, Punjab, India

Amit Paul
Dept. of Computer Science & Engineering, St. Thomas' College of Engineering and Technology, Kolkata, West Bengal, India

Nawaf R. Alharbe
College of Computer Science and Engineering, Department of Artificial Intelligence and Data Science, Taibah University, Madinah, Kingdom of Saudi Arabia

and

S. Balamurugan
Intelligent Research Consultancy Service (iRCS), Coimbatore, Tamil Nadu, India

Scrivener Publishing

WILEY

This edition first published 2026 by John Wiley & Sons, Inc., 111 River Street, Hoboken, NJ 07030, USA and Scrivener Publishing LLC, 100 Cummings Center, Suite 541J, Beverly, MA 01915, USA
© 2026 Scrivener Publishing LLC
For more information about Scrivener publications please visit www.scrivenerpublishing.com.

All rights reserved. No part of this publication may be reproduced, stored in a retrieval system, or transmitted, in any form or by any means, electronic, mechanical, photocopying, recording, or otherwise, except as permitted by law. Advice on how to obtain permission to reuse material from this title is available at http://www.wiley.com/go/permissions.

Wiley Global Headquarters
111 River Street, Hoboken, NJ 07030, USA

For details of our global editorial offices, customer services, and more information about Wiley products visit us at www.wiley.com.

The manufacturer's authorized representative according to the EU General Product Safety Regulation is Wiley-VCH GmbH, Boschstr. 12, 69469 Weinheim, Germany, e-mail: Product_Safety@wiley.com.

Limit of Liability/Disclaimer of Warranty
While the publisher and authors have used their best efforts in preparing this work, they make no representations or warranties with respect to the accuracy or completeness of the contents of this work and specifically disclaim all warranties, including without limitation any implied warranties of merchantability or fitness for a particular purpose. No warranty may be created or extended by sales representatives, written sales materials, or promotional statements for this work. The fact that an organization, website, or product is referred to in this work as a citation and/or potential source of further information does not mean that the publisher and authors endorse the information or services the organization, website, or product may provide or recommendations it may make. This work is sold with the understanding that the publisher is not engaged in rendering professional services. The advice and strategies contained herein may not be suitable for your situation. You should consult with a specialist where appropriate. Neither the publisher nor authors shall be liable for any loss of profit or any other commercial damages, including but not limited to special, incidental, consequential, or other damages. Further, readers should be aware that websites listed in this work may have changed or disappeared between when this work was written and when it is read.

Library of Congress Cataloging-in-Publication Data

ISBN 978-1-394-40399-8

Cover image: Created by AI Using Adobe Firefly
Cover design by Russell Richardson

Set in size of 11pt and Minion Pro by Manila Typesetting Company, Makati, Philippines

Printed in the USA

10 9 8 7 6 5 4 3 2 1

We dedicate this book to our families and friends.

Contents

Series Preface

This book provides the foundation of causal AI for understanding cause-and-effect reasoning in AI. It also describes how Causal AI can be implemented in the real world so that AI systems can deliver a high degree of explainability, robustness, and trust in their decision-making processes. As part of the *Leading Edge Breakthroughs in Artificial Intelligence* series, the volume addresses a critical limitation of traditional AI—its inability to reason about causality. It presents cutting-edge approaches that enable AI to incorporate causation into inference, including structural causal models, counterfactual reasoning, and intervention-based learning. *Causal Artificial Intelligence: Fundamentals and Applications* emphasizes the development of fair, transparent, and resilient systems capable of reasoning under uncertainty. In doing so, it aligns closely with the series' mission to highlight transformative advances that strengthen the trustworthiness and real-world impact of AI.

Dr. S. Balamurugan
Director, Intelligent Research Consultancy Services, Coimbatore, Tamilnadu, India
Series Editor - Leading Edge Breakthroughs in Artificial Intelligence

Managing Editors
Dr. T. Ananth Kumar
Associate Professor, Computer Science and Engineering, IFET College of Engineering, Tamilnadu, India
Dr. K. Suresh Kumar
Assistant Professor, Computer Science and Engineering, Sri Eshwar College of Engineering, Coimbatore, Tamilnadu, India
Dr. R. Karthick Manoj
Assistant Professor, Department of EEE, Academy of Maritime Education and Training (AMET), Deemed to be University, Tamil Nadu, India

Preface

This book provides a comprehensive exploration of how causal reasoning can enhance the transparency, reliability, and ethical foundations of artificial intelligence systems. Addressing both theoretical and practical dimensions, it examines structural causal models, explainable AI, and privacy-preserving learning frameworks across diverse fields, including healthcare, climate science, manufacturing, automotive safety, and cybersecurity.

The book highlights innovative research in areas such as CNN-based causal inference for signal detection, explainable mobile AI for disease prediction, image processing for Ayurvedic material identification, and AI-driven systems for driver fatigue and collision detection. It also examines cyber resilience in electric vehicles and Industry 4.0 environments, with particular attention to causal ML-based defenses against data manipulation and service attacks. Further discussions address federated learning for distributed healthcare systems and adversarial robustness in causal AI.

By bridging theoretical foundations with real-world applications, this book serves as a valuable resource for researchers, practitioners, and policymakers committed to developing transparent, secure, reliable, and ethically aligned intelligent technologies.

Part I: Fundamentals

This part introduces the foundations and applications of Causal Artificial Intelligence, progressing from core concepts and causal models to deep learning and explainable AI applications.

Chapter One introduces causal reasoning as a means of improving the transparency, reliability, and ethical foundations of AI. It examines structural causal models, explainable AI, and privacy-preserving learning across fields including healthcare, climate science, manufacturing, automotive safety, and cybersecurity. Chapter Two explores how structural causal models identify cause-and-effect relationships rather than correlations. Using software bug resolution as an application, the chapter demonstrates how causal analysis can improve decision-making, interpretability, and reliability.

Chapter Three presents a convolutional neural network for classifying gravitational-wave signals amid complex detector noise. The framework demonstrates the potential of deep learning to automate signal detection and support advances in astrophysical research. Chapter Four examines machine learning for mobile disease prediction and prevention. It addresses data privacy, security, interpretability, and scalability while highlighting the potential of explainable AI and federated learning to improve mobile healthcare applications.

Part II: Applications

This part presents ten applications of AI, machine learning, and Causal AI across fields including Ayurvedic medicine, healthcare, road safety, manufacturing, cybersecurity, and privacy-preserving systems, with an emphasis on using causal methods to explain how outcomes are reached.

Chapter Five, by Ankit Raj, Subhajit Chanda, Ashutosh Dubey, Dyuti Mitra, and Debraj Chatterjee, presents a supervised machine learning approach for identifying Ayurvedic medicinal plants from the color and texture of leaves and fruits. It also examines image-processing methodologies and the advantages and challenges of automated plant identification. Chapter Six, by Aakansha Khanna, Inderdeep Kaur, Inzimam Ul Hassan, and Ratyansh Singh, examines the use of AI and machine learning to improve healthcare diagnosis, treatment planning, resource allocation, and predictive analytics. It also addresses challenges involving data privacy, algorithmic bias, regulatory compliance, and equitable access to AI-driven healthcare.

Chapter Seven, by Sumanta Chatterjee and Amit Majumder, proposes a real-time, non-intrusive AI system for detecting driver fatigue through facial analysis and physiological signals. The system provides timely alerts while addressing data privacy, algorithmic fairness, and variations in driving conditions and individual behavior. Chapter Eight, also by Sumanta Chatterjee and Amit Majumder, explores neural network-based collision detection as an alternative to conventional rule-based systems. By integrating artificial neural networks with LiDAR, radar, and cameras, the proposed approach aims to improve real-time automotive safety under diverse driving conditions.

Chapter Nine, by Esha Kundu and Arijit Ghosal, applies causal AI and deep learning to facial emotion detection. Using the FER-2013 dataset, the chapter examines feature extraction and CNN-based classification while demonstrating the potential of causal approaches to model relationships underlying emotional expressions. Chapter 10, by MD Masud Rana, presents a machine learning approach for predicting temperature profiles in friction-stir additive manufacturing. Using experimental data to train an artificial neural network, the method predicts parameters such as temperature and cooling rate, with the goal of reducing the cost and complexity of real-time manufacturing processes.

Chapter 11, also by MD Masud Rana, examines cybersecurity vulnerabilities in electric vehicles, particularly false data injection and denial-of-service attacks on CAN bus communication. It evaluates machine learning models for detecting these threats and considers the potential of edge computing to strengthen vehicle safety and resilience. Chapter 12, by MD Masud Rana, addresses cyber resilience in Industry 4.0 and smart manufacturing environments. Using a digital twin simulation platform, it evaluates machine learning techniques for real-time anomaly and cyberattack detection and provides recommendations for strengthening manufacturing system resilience.

Chapter 13, by Amit Chakraborty, Chirantana Mallick, Saptarshi Das, Madhvi Chakraborty, and Abhijnan Chakraborty, explores privacy-preserving federated learning for fine-tuning large language models across distributed healthcare infrastructure. The approach combines federated learning and TinyML to protect sensitive patient information while reducing dependence on centralized computing resources. Chapter 14, by Sakshi Thakur, Mohit Singh Bisht, and Dinesh Singh Dhakar, examines the robustness of causal AI systems against adversarial threats, including data poisoning, model evasion, and confounder exploitation. It presents a hybrid causal defense architecture combining machine learning, deep learning, data sanitization, adversarial training, and explainability to support more trustworthy and resilient AI systems.

In closing, we extend our thanks to Martin Scrivener and the team at Scrivener Publishing for their efforts in bringing this work to publication.

Acknowledgement

We sincerely acknowledge our workplaces and universities, the series editor, the authors, and our colleagues for their support in bringing this book to its current form.

Part I

FUNDAMENTALS

1

Causal Artificial Intelligence: Fundamentals and Applications

Barnali Gupta Banik[1]* and Geeta Ambildhuke[2]

[1]*Department of Emerging Technologies, Mahatma Gandhi Institute of Technology, Hyderabad, Telangana, India*
[2]*Department of Computer Science and Engineering, Gokaraju Rangaraju Institute of Engineering and Technology, Hyderabad, Telangana, India*

Abstract
Causal artificial intelligence (causal AI) studies cause-and-effect relationships. It helps make better decisions. It is used in many ways, i.e., suggesting personalized treatments. It can predict what happens after certain actions. It also improves fairness and transparency in AI. Causal AI lets systems think about the results of actions. It predicts outcomes in different situations. It decides based on how one change affects others. Causal AI is better than traditional AI in many ways. Traditional AI only finds patterns in data. But causal AI explains why things happen. It also shows what will happen if we change something. This leads to smarter decisions. It is useful in real-life cases, like treating patients or setting business plans. It also helps make fair rules. Causal AI makes AI more reliable. It solves complex problems better. Causal artificial intelligence can be used in many different applications by helping to understand and predict the effects of actions. In healthcare, it can suggest better treatments by knowing what causes improvement in patients. In business, it helps companies test what strategies lead to more sales or better customer satisfaction. In policymaking, it shows how a new law might affect people's lives. It can also improve fairness in AI systems by finding and removing biased causes in decisions. Causal AI has the potential to play a significant role in the path toward artificial general intelligence (AGI). It understands the actual cause-and-effect relationship that mirrors how humans learn from experience and make inferences about unseen scenarios. The Causal AI is not sufficient to achieve AGI; however, it is likely to be a foundational component in creating systems with deeper and more human-like understanding. In this chapter, it will be discussed how causal AI overpowers traditional AI and

**Corresponding author*: barnali.guptabanik@ieee.org

Rajdeep Chakraborty, Aleem Ali, Amit Paul, Nawaf R. Alharbe and S. Balamurugan (eds.) Causal Artificial Intelligence: Fundamentals and Applications, (3–18) © 2026 Scrivener Publishing LLC

how it can solve various problems better than traditional AI. Moreover, the future applications of causal AI will also be discussed.

Keywords: Causal AI, cause and effect, machine learning, decision support

1.1 Introduction

Artificial intelligence is driving the world by using huge amounts of data from various platforms and algorithms to make decisions in different areas, but the machine learning model used is mostly based on predictive analysis that works on past information. This traditional approach relies heavily on correlation for developing predictive models. The difficulty derives from the basic shortcoming of conventional AI systems, which is their incapacity to comprehend cause and effect. One major obstacle to the deployment of AI in enterprises is the lack of knowledge about "why" AI makes particular judgments. A groundbreaking method that is revolutionizing artificial intelligence's reasoning, learning, and decision-making is called causal AI, and causal inference tries to overcome traditional AI with a simple principle: "Correlation is not causation". Traditional AI is very good at identifying correlations and patterns in data, but causal AI takes a step further by comprehending cause-and-effect linkages, just the way the human brain does. There are many different types of models in the field of artificial intelligence (AI), as shown in Figure 1.1, and each has special features.

The capacity of causal AI and generative AI to closely resemble human behavior makes them stand out among the others as being especially intriguing and promising. Generative AI is a kind of artificial intelligence. It learns from training data. Then it creates new content, like text, images, audio, and videos. It finds patterns in the data. Using these patterns makes original content. The new content is not an exact copy but follows the same patterns. Causal AI has shaped many new prospects. It can find the root cause of the diseases. This improves medical diagnosis. Then, the doctors can provide more targeted treatments. Causal AI in finance provides investment strategies, insights, and helps identify the drivers of market trends. By identifying the causal relationships between machine behavior and failures, it allows proactive maintenance in the manufacturing sector. Additionally, by decomposing causal chains, causal AI enables social scientists to understand the consequences of action and policy. Causal AI allows companies to make important decisions and find new depths of knowledge in complex systems by transcending correlation and uncovering

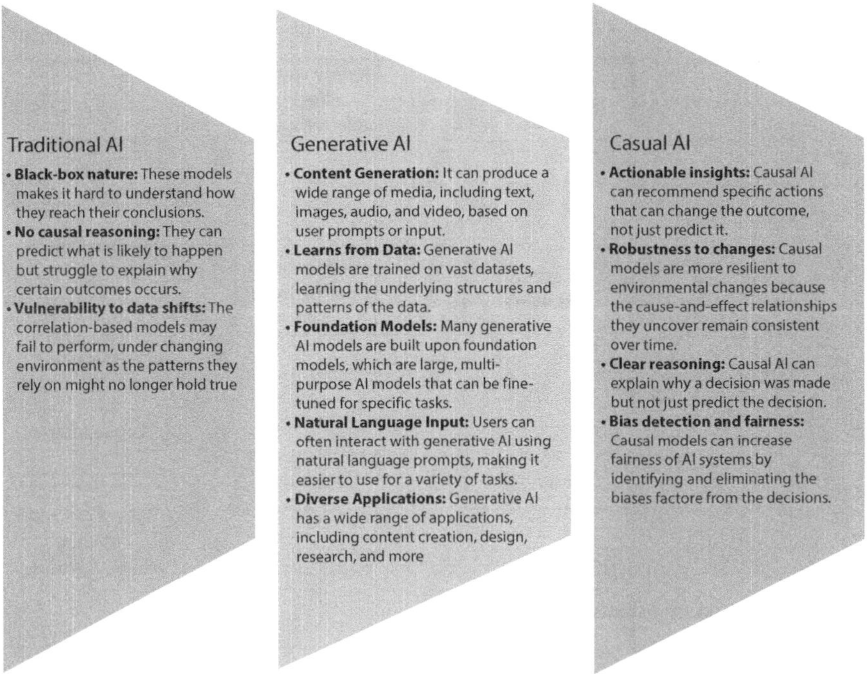

Figure 1.1 Types of models in AI systems.

cause-and-effect relationships. Causal AI utilizes a number of techniques, such as causal graphs and simulation, that assist in exposing causal relationships and enhancing decision-making. These techniques not only enhance decision-making but also enable causal AI to more precisely plan interventions and respond to intricate "what if" situations, revolutionizing strategic planning and operational efficiency across sectors.

1.1.1 Features of Causal AI

As shown in Figure 1.2, the features of causal AI enable it to operate under different circumstances or in changing scenarios by identifying causal relationships between variables and assessing how changes in one variable affect another, thereby helping organizations make more informed plans and anticipate the possible consequences of their decisions.

1.1.1.1 Causal Inference

Traditional AI just finds patterns by correlating data points to predict outcomes, but causal AI makes use of techniques to interpret how one thing

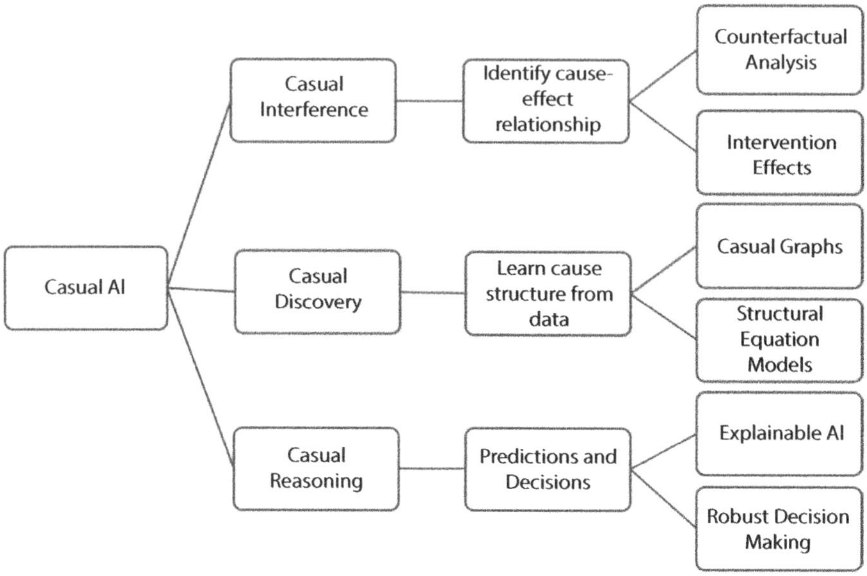

Figure 1.2 Structure of causal AI.

affects another or how one variable depends on another. This process makes causal AI more accurate and reliable, as it does not just depend on patterns but tries to get insight from the data on how variables will change or behave based on other variables and in different circumstances.

Let us take a situation-based example: Can energy drinks increase student performance during exam times?

1.1.1.2 Structural Causal Models

Causal AI mainly uses structural causal models. These models can simulate different situations. That shows how altering one variable affects others. It helps in planning actions and predicting results. It also solves "what if" questions that traditional models cannot handle.

1.1.1.3 Counterfactual Reasoning

It means thinking about what might happen in different situations. It is not only about what has already happened. Causal AI can tell the difference between things that just happen together and things that actually cause each other. It helps in making better and more accurate predictions. It shows what might happen if something changes. Causal AI builds models of these "what-if" situations. It predicts possible outcomes. This helps organizations plan better and see how their choices affect the future.

1.2 Literature Survey

When human lives or financial stability are on the line, stakeholders need to know how and why a model produced a particular prediction, which is lacking in traditional AI models, as they just predict the result based on previous information and patterns. The extended features of explainability and transparency make AI models more popular and suitable in sectors like healthcare and finance, where ethical decision-making, accountability, and compliance are crucial.

In [1], a new approach is introduced to "catch" failures before they occur by combining causation and correlation, or a causation-based AI, and shows how it is superior to the "classic" correlation-based methodology.

One of the main ideas and concepts of causality, causal discovery, and causal inference is presented in the article [2] from an engineering perspective and demonstrates the benefits of using causal AI in data generation for engineering problems and discusses two of the primary theories of causality—the Pearlian and the potential outcome approaches before investigated through engineering cases.

The chapter in [3] explores the philosophical underpinnings of causality in AI and resolves the related puzzles. It looks at moral, social, and philosophical issues. These issues come up when AI systems are given the ability to understand causality. The chapter asks us to think about these important matters. They shape how AI develops. This development depends on philosophy, cognitive science, and AI research.

This paper [4] explores how generative AI, like LLMs (large language models), can be used to improve causal inference when dealing with unstructured data such as text and proposes a method to use internal representations from LLMs to estimate causal effects more accurately, bypassing traditional limitations in causal modeling. It is especially relevant for applications where content generated by users (e.g., reviews, social media) is used to infer behavioral patterns.

In [5], the author highlights the use of AI and causal modeling to improve human understanding. Traditional methods like linear regression struggle with complex and changing data, especially when trying to connect technical food measurements with how consumers perceive taste and quality. The authors propose a technique to better identify true cause-and-effect relationships in food using causal models with Bayesian networks and deep learning.

1.3 Basics of Causal AI

Causal AI enables machine learning to explain predictions with reasoning. It aims at uncovering the "why" and "how" behind outcomes. It uses available data to curate explanations for decision-makers. It needs causal knowledge that is proposed by human intelligence. This knowledge helps in understanding events. These events can strongly affect the future [6]. In machine learning, causal learning finds how one variable affects others. Then the variable being studied is the result. The variable that is changed is the treatment. Confounders affect both the treatment and the result. Covariates are background features or variables.

Pearl's Causal Hierarchy

Pearl's causal hierarchy organizes causal reasoning into three levels. Each level shows increasing cognitive ability. This model is key to understanding and applying causal reasoning in AI. The model, as shown in Figure 1.3, consists of three levels. Those levels are the association, which detects patterns and statistical links in data; the next level is the intervention, which predicts the effects of actions; and the last level is the counterfactuals, which discovers "what-if" scenarios.

Each level builds on the previous one. That ensures deeper and more advanced reasoning.

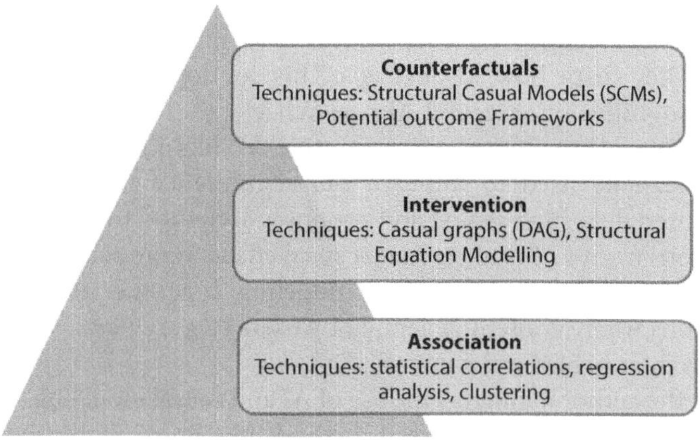

Figure 1.3 Causal hierarchy pyramid.

Components of Causal AI

1.3.1 Causal Graphs and Models

In causal AI, the cause-and-effect relations can be described by a causal graph. They are also called directed acyclic graphs (DAGs). A causal graph can be drawn with arrows and nodes. The nodes show different things, like an action or an effect. The arrows indicate that something has an output. No loops are allowed in causal graphs to keep them unambiguous and systematic. The graph can be used to understand the effect of what if something is done differently. A causal graph in Figure 1.4 shows how things affect each other. In this example, we look at how study time affects exam performance. If a student studies more, they usually do better in exams. But studying too much can reduce sleep quality. Inadequate sleep also makes it more difficult to perform. The study hours have a direct effect on marks in the examination, as well as an indirect effect through sleep. This helps us view the whole picture. This is how we realize that good sleep is also a necessity in test performance.

1.3.2 Structural Equation Modeling (SEM)

Structural Equation Modeling (SEM) is a mathematical tool. It measures cause-and-effect relationships from causal graphs. SEM combines statistics and causal theory. This helps to create models that can be tested in real life. SEM uses mathematical equations to show how variables are related and measures how strong causes affect results. It shows both direct and indirect effects. SEM can also work with hidden factors known as latent variables.

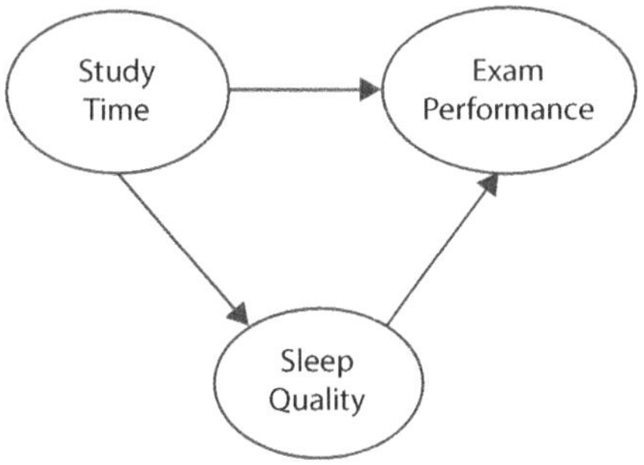

Figure 1.4 Causal graph representing the direct and indirect effects of study time on exam performance *via* sleep quality.

We use statistical tests to check if the model matches real data. For example, let us model how student motivation and study habits affect exam scores. The variables are listed in Table 1.1.

This method enables us to test and show causal relations.

Then, in SEM, this condition can be expressed as:

1. SH = a × M + error
→ a is the strength of the effect of Motivation (M) on Study Hours (SH).
2. CA = b × M + error
→ b is the strength of the effect of Motivation (M) on Class Attendance (CA).
3. ES = c × SH + d × CA + error
→ c: Effect of Study Hours (SH) on Exam Score (ES)
→ d is an effect of Class Attendance (CA) on Exam Score (ES).

In structural equation modeling (SEM), "error" refers to that component of a variable that is unaccounted for by virtue of the model. The "error" captures such factors as time availability, distraction from work, health, or routines of an individual, which also affect Study Hours but are unaccounted for in the model.

1.3.3 Do-Calculus and Interventions

Do-calculus is a mathematical tool created by Judea Pearl. It helps AI understand cause and effect. This makes it very useful for decision-making. Do-calculus has special rules for studying changes. It answers questions like "What happens if we do this?" It works with normal observed data—no experiments needed. It can also answer "what if" questions about past events. The rules of do-calculus confirm the root causes of the effect. It gives a reliable mathematical way to test actions and their effects.

For example, you want to know: "Will increasing study hours improve exam performance?"

Table 1.1 Variables for the example scenario.

Variables	
Observed variables	**Latent variable**
1. Study Hours (SH) 2. Class Attendance (CA) 3. Exam Score (ES)	Motivation (M)

Using do-calculus, we would like to view whether challenging a student to work harder will raise his score.

This is given as:

P(ExamScore | do(StudyHours = high)) The "do" is that we're actually intervening—imposing the study hours to be high.

The simple observation is that students who study more tend to get better scores. But "intervening" (the "do") says that if we force a student to increase the study hours, it causes better exam scores.

1.3.4 Causal Discovery Algorithms

The causal discovery algorithms are aimed at finding causal relationships. These relationships are drawn from the observed data. The algorithms are useful for recognizing patterns in large and complex datasets. It reduces the time for processing and manual errors.

The causal discovery algorithms derive cause-and-effect relationships from observed data. They work even when we don't know the connections beforehand. These algorithms look for patterns to see which variables affect others. They do not need experiments and can use regularly observed data. Some common techniques are the Peter-Clark algorithm (PC algorithm) and fast causal inference (FCI algorithm). We use these when we must learn a system's structure from data by itself. The PC algorithm is a method used to discover causal relationships by checking for conditional independence in the data. It is good when all important variables are observed. The FCI algorithm is similar to the PC algorithm but can also handle hidden (unseen) variables and selection bias. Selection bias happens when the data you are using is not a true or full picture of the real world. This can lead to wrong conclusions. FCI is better when some variables might be missing or hidden.

Let us take an example where you want to find out what affects exam performance. You collect data on: Study Hours, Class Attendance, and Exam Scores. If we run the PC algorithm, and it tells you:

Study Hours → Exam Score
Class Attendance → Exam Score

Now, imagine you missed collecting data on Student Motivation (a hidden cause). Motivated students are more likely to attend classes and score well. If you use the PC algorithm, it might wrongly show:

Class Attendance → Exam Score

But that's not the full truth — Motivation (hidden) is causing both. If we use FCI, it can detect the possible hidden variable and show:

Class Attendance $\leftrightarrow$ Exam Score

This means there's a connection, but it might be due to a hidden cause.

1.3.5 Structural Causal Models (SCMs)

Causal Graphs: Directed acyclic graphs (DAGs) of causally connected variables are the building blocks of SCMs. It was originally suggested by Judea Pearl. Structural equations are mathematical functions. It expresses how each variable is generated from its direct causes and a noise term.

Counterfactual Reasoning: This technique uses the do-operator (do $(X = x)$) to simulate "what if" scenarios.

For instance, lung cancer is caused by tar and other hidden factors.

An SCM might be defined in the following Equation 1.1 if we have variables such as smoking (S), tar (T), and lung cancer (L):

$$T = f1(S, U1)$$
$$L = f2(T, U2)$$

where U1 and U2 are unobserved factors like genes, pollution, or workplace exposure.

1.3.6 Potential Outcomes Framework

The potential outcomes framework (POF), or Rubin causal model, is another way to study cause and effect. It evaluates potential results under alternative treatments or actions. POF looks at treatment effects like what happens if someone gets treatment ($Y(1)$) versus no treatment ($Y(0)$). It uses counterfactuals. That would imply that the effect is just a difference between such possible results. This approach depends on some key assumptions.

Ignorability means there are no hidden biases. The Stable Unit Treatment Value Assumption (SUTVA) means one person's treatment does not affect others. Randomization makes the comparisons fair.

For instance:

The observed result for a binary treatment D is:

$$Y = D \times Y(1) + (1 - D) \times Y(0)$$

Table 1.2 Comparison between SCMs and POF.

Feature	SCMs	POF
Originator	Judea pearl	Donald Rubin
Representation	Graphs + equations	Counterfactual outcomes
Focus	Mechanisms and interventions	Treatment effects
Counterfactuals	Derived *via* do-calculus	Defined directly
Assumptions	Graph-based (e.g., d-separation)	SUTVA, ignorability
Flexibility	Rich modeling of complex systems	Strong in randomized experiments

The comparison between structural causal models (SCMs) and the potential outcomes framework (POF) has been shown in Table 1.2. SCMs use graphs and do-calculus to study causal mechanisms. The POF is built on SUTVA and ignorability.

1.4 Applications of AI

Causal AI is making waves across industries by helping organizations move from predictive insights to actionable interventions. Figure 1.5 shows its application areas in real-world scenarios.

1.4.1 Churn Analysis and Customer Retention

Several businesses benefit from causal AI by understanding the real reasons why customers leave or stay. This means they can take specific actions—like improving customer service or offering loyalty programs that truly make a difference. It leads to better means of customer retention by offering more personalized support.

1.4.2 Decision Support in Healthcare

With the help of causal AI, healthcare professionals can understand how different treatments affect patients' health. It finds that what actually makes

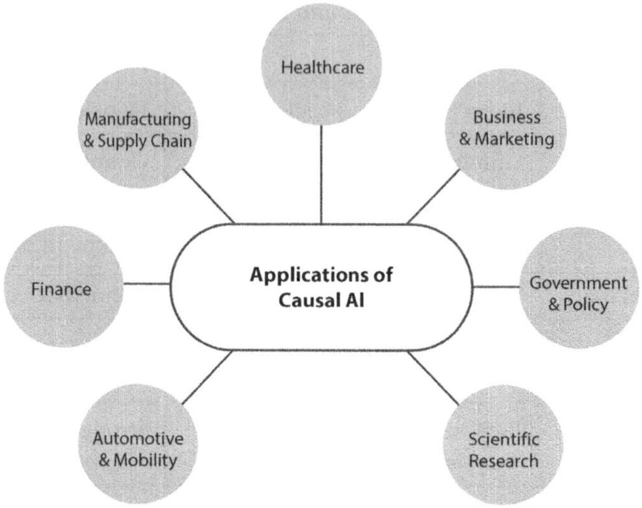

Figure 1.5 Application areas of causal AI.

the difference is more than just searching for patterns and making predictions. In this way, improved treatment can be planned for a patient in a better way.

1.4.3 Fraud Detection in the Finance Sector

Causal AI helps financial institutions to find fraudulent transactions by identifying the real reasons behind suspicious actions, not just spotting patterns. It leads to more accurate fraud detection and reduces the number of false alarms.

1.4.4 Marketing Campaign and Its Optimization

Causal AI expresses kinds of campaigns that affect customer behavior. It looks at actions, for example, purchases, clicks, or sign-ups, not just patterns. It can test strategies like timing, channel, or messaging. This finds that the strategy works best. On this basis, the marketing agents can plan smarter campaigns. They look for better ROI and target customers.

1.4.5 Optimization of Supply Chain

Causal AI discovers the real causes of delays, bottlenecks, or inventory problems in the supply chain. It finds more than study patterns—it shows those actions or events cause disruptions or improvements. It can test scenarios, for example, changing suppliers or adjusting order volumes to see the real impact. The causal AI made the supply chain solution easier than before.

1.4.6 Risk Management and Compliance

The Causal AI contributes to identifying risks and compliance failures. It goes beyond the threat. It helps in proactive risk control. Therefore, it gives better compliance with regulations. It supports better decision-making.

1.4.7 Innovation and Product Development

Causal AI shows the product features to improve satisfaction or performance. It looks outside the surface preferences. It reveals the real impact of design or function changes. It can test new ideas before launch. This reduces trial and error.

1.5 Benefits, Limitations, and Challenges

The intelligent system is transformed with causal AI. It not only predicts that the incident may occur. It also explains why things happen. It shows how to influence outcomes. Like any powerful tool, it has strengths. It also has challenges.

1.5.1 Benefits of Causal AI

Causal AI gives many benefits. It finds the root causes of problems. This makes decisions smarter and more effective. It eases the "what if" questions for planning and policy. The models are effective in providing a solution. It adapts well when data changes because it looks at deep causes. It helps use money and resources in the right places, like marketing or healthcare. It also finds true causes of risks. This allows early action to reduce them.

1.5.2 Limitations of Causal AI

The limitations of causal AI are dependency on huge amounts of good-quality data to work well. In case of missing or biased data, the results tend to be wrong. Building causal models is complex requires expert knowledge. If the wrong assumptions are made, the conclusions can be misleading. Causal methods also require a lot of computer power. Many industries are still new to this, and not many companies use it yet. Moreover, a status quo may come into play in the case of transforming from regular prediction models to causal AI.

1.6 Conclusion and Future Scope

Causal AI is a new transformation in intelligent system. It supports reasoning, trust, and meaningful action. High-stakes decisions often rely on algorithms. Causal models provide interpretability and robustness. But improvements are still needed. We need shared benchmarks and datasets to test models. Autonomous systems should use causal reasoning for smart real-time decisions. Counterfactual simulations should be used more in planning and risk management. This helps strategies adapt to changing situations.

AI disclosure statement: The author confirms that no artificial intelligence (AI)-generated content or AI-assisted writing tools were used in the preparation of this chapter (including summaries and the abstract). All text, analysis, and conclusions are the result of the author's original work.

References

1. Zaman, N., Apostolou, E., Li, Y., Conroy, P., Real-time Diagnosis Of Physical Failures Using Causation-based AI. *PHM Soc. Eur. Conf.*, 6, 1, 7, 2021, DOI https://doi.org/10.36001/phme.2021.v6i1.2831.
2. Naser, M.Z., Causality and causal inference for engineers: Beyond correlation, regression, prediction and artificial intelligence. *Wiley Interdiscip. Rev.: Data Min. Knowl. Discovery*, 14, 4, e1533, 2024.
3. Vallverdú, J., Causality and artificial intelligence, in: *Causality for artificial intelligence: From a philosophical perspective*, pp. 13–23, Springer Nature Singapore, Singapore, 2024.

4. Imai, K. and Nakamura, K., Causal Representation Learning with Generative Artificial Intelligence: Application to Texts as Treatments, arXiv preprint arXiv:2410.00903, 2024.
5. Kurtanjek, Ž., Causal Artificial Intelligence Models of Food Quality Data. *Food Technol. Biotechnol.*, 62, 1, 102–109, 2024.
6. Miller, T., Explanation in artificial intelligence: Insights from the social sciences. *Artif.l Intell.*, 267, 1–38, 2019.

2

Unveiling the Power of Causal AI: From Structural Causal Model to Bug Resolution Analysis

Reshmi Maulik[1]*, Subhajit Datta[2], Subhashis Majumder[3] and Soumen Santra[4]

[1]Department of Computer Application, Meghnad Saha Institute of Technology, Kolkata, West Bengal, India
[2]Department of CSE (Data Science), Heritage Institute of Technology, Kolkata, West Bengal, India
[3]Department of Computer Science and Engineering, Heritage Institute of Technology, Kolkata, West Bengal, India
[4]Department of Master of Computer Applications, Techno International New Town, Kolkata, West Bengal, India

Abstract

Understanding cause-and-effect linkages in data is the focus of the cutting-edge artificial intelligence field known as "causal AI."

The goal of generative AI is the creation of new content, whereas predictive AI aims to forecast future events. However, causal AI seeks to understand the causal relationships that drive these events, providing deeper insights and more actionable information. Causal AI aims to uncover the hidden in-depth truth behind the cause-and-effect relationships in data through human-machine interaction. Instead of considering only the correlations as done by classical AI, causal AI strives to identify the underlying causal mechanisms behind the possible outcomes. We have studied the causal analysis on the Django dataset using structural causal models (SCMs). SCMs are made up of two parts—one showing the causal linkages between variables using the directed graph and the other part describing the relationships that appear in the data using a series of equations. This technique helps with a more accurate and understandable forecast while simulating the outcomes of possible solutions. Causal AI helps to understand the crucial factors

**Corresponding author*: reshmi.maulik@msit.edu.in

Rajdeep Chakraborty, Aleem Ali, Amit Paul, Nawaf R. Alharbe and S. Balamurugan (eds.) Causal Artificial Intelligence: Fundamentals and Applications, (19–44) © 2026 Scrivener Publishing LLC

influencing their outcomes, which in turn helps the organization to make better decisions. The mystery of the factors behind the quick bug resolution time remains unsolved. Some of the identified factors that may affect the bug resolution time are software type, the frequency of code modifications, the involvement of multiple developers, and the level of experience of developers. Absence of proper regression testing may give rise to new bugs, thereby making problem-solving more challenging and time-consuming. Our study reveals that the bug resolution time is more affected by the number of developers than by their experience level or the frequency of system modifications. The goal of causal AI is to enhance the trustworthiness, interpretability, and actionable insights of the software ecosystems to obtain a more effective solution.

Keywords: RCA, bug resolution, ATE, causal model, Django, DAG

2.1 Introduction

Causal AI is a new field in artificial intelligence. It seeks to find and comprehend cause-and-effect relationships through the variables used in the model. The models from causal AI represent this in a coherent manner and make sense. This plays a role in holding the production model based on causal AI accountable and trusted. The AI models that exist today rely on relationships between the variables, while causal AI attempts to uncover the causal and driving force [1]. The robustness of causal AI to data distribution is how it builds trust. For decision-making, the potential outputs of models obtained from causal AI are evaluated to inform early decisions. Causal AI was applicable in virtually every field, from economics to medicine and social sciences, marketing, and many others. Therefore, it is useful to make us know the causal relationship of variables in a complex system more accurately. Here, we used the 'DoWhy' Python package and structural causal models (SCMs) to estimate potential outcomes of an intervention [2].

In many ways, as mentioned below, causal AI breaks the existing conceptual barrier, with certain advantages that other types of AI targeting specific use situations do not have [3].

- Deeper explainability: Causal AI provides a deeper understanding of complex systems by revealing the reasons behind outcomes, not just correlations.
- Reduced bias: Causal AI diminishes the bias present in machine-learning datasets by detecting real causal relationships rather than relying on shallow correlations, resulting in more accurate and fairer final outputs.

- Answering counterfactual questions: Data scientists can predict what would have happened otherwise if they had intervened in a certain way before applying that intervention to real-world scenarios with the help of causal AI and "what-if" queries.
- Enhanced optimization: Causal AI isn't just about predictive analytics. Enabling applications in areas such as scenario analysis and root cause identification enables enhanced optimization and decision-making across numerous domains.

Contemporary software systems consist of various interdependent modules, libraries, and frameworks that interact in intricate and dynamic ways. Diagnosing the root cause of a bug often entails navigating through multiple layers of abstraction, which significantly complicates the debugging process and makes fixing the bug challenging. Trial-and-error methods are required, as developers need to check ambiguous data and rebuild it again with little information. Faulty software may result from poor programming practices, miscommunication among developers, insufficient time for debugging, conflicts between hardware and software, or the presence of one or more defects. In some specific cases, where certain bugs only occur with some hardware configurations or under certain conditions, debugging may be more complex. Bugs can manifest in various ways, affecting a software product and/or its operability, including by causing the failure of a specific feature or capability, or even of the entire system. This is leading to a loss of reputation, money, and time. One of the most famous cases is when millions were stolen along with private details from the Aadhaar website due to security vulnerabilities [4].

In spite of the rapid evolution of the industry, numerous flaws still hamper the software development lifecycle. It is necessary to address these issues in a timely manner for user satisfaction and program reliability. That calculates to a whopping 40% of development costs budgeted toward maintenance, emphasizing the money that can be saved by useful bug resolution. Much of the work currently in print is more about correlation and not about causative mechanisms that impact defect resolution.

Root cause analysis, or RCA, is a method that is used to address a problem in terms of sorting out its causes. It entails going backwards in time to trace a series of events, starting from the initial causes and ending with the final observable result. RCA provides essential insights that contribute to effective problem-solving as well as preventing a recurrence by systematically identifying when, why, and how an issue took place. In this way, root cause analysis diagnoses where the problem originated. With the help of causal inference techniques of prediction models, there can be a separation between meaningful causal effects and spurious correlations, which results in more reliable and applicable defect prediction.

The following research questions have been the focus of our investigation.

RQ1: Does the recent experience level of the developer affect how long it takes to fix bugs?

RQ2: Does the system-level experience of the developer affect the time taken to fix bugs?

RQ3: Does the number of developers have an impact on the time needed to fix bugs?

RQ4: Is bug resolution time impacted by frequent code changes?

RQ5: Is bug resolution time impacted by the number of systems and the number of files?

To examine the system, let us formulate our null hypothesis as follows:

H0: Bug resolution time is not causally impacted by the number of developers, their level of experience, or the frequency of code changes.

H1: The overall number of developers, their level of experience, the frequency of code changes, and the time it takes to fix bugs are all causally related.

The structure of the paper is as follows. In Section 2.2, we have done the literature review. In Section 2.3, the dataset is defined along with the model variables. Section 2.4 presents the conceptual paradigm, which views the causality-driven approach to bug resolution time as a causal inference problem. The estimands and optimal values are discussed in Section 2.5. The sensitivity analysis is performed in Section 2.6. The threats to validity have been discussed in Section 2.7. Finally, Section 2.8 presents the conclusion, and Section 2.9 discusses the future scope.

2.2 Literature Review

Chadbourne and Eisty made the causal investigations to identify the code segment that generates the error, thereby reducing the bug resolution time and improving the software problem resolution and overall quality of the software [5].

Maulik *et al.* had used causal inference techniques on two real-world datasets, namely, TensorFlow and VSCode, to identify the factors that influence the bug resolution time. The study shows that the bug resolution time is directly related to both the number of developers involved in the resolution process and the frequency of modifications made to the system files [6].

Peralta *et al.* had used causal inference models such as Bayesian networks and linear non-Gaussian acyclic models to investigate key determinants of the bug-fixing time. The study reveals that the key indicators behind bug-fixing time are reporter reputation, severity of the problem, and blocker status. The bug-fixing time is independent of the reporting done by the user or developer. For quicker bug-fixing time, it is necessary to understand the underlying complexities in the software development ecosystem rather than focusing on the comprehensive bug reports [8].

Maulik *et al.* had used causal discovery techniques such as the GES algorithm on Eclipse data to identify the factors that affect the bug resolution time. According to the study, factors likely to impact bug resolution time include the types of interactions among developers, the workload and experience of the developers owning the bug, and the number of developers working on the bug [7].

Tunde-Onadele *et al.* had provided a cross-layer causal analysis framework named ClearCausal for microservices to identify the root cause service and the root cause function required by causal analysis of application function traces and infrastructure metrics [11]. Johnson *et al.* had used counterfactual analysis on the Defects4J benchmark to identify the root causes of defects that supplement existing testing and debugging tools [9].

Baah *et al.* used a statistical causal inference technique to differentiate correlation from causation, which enhances the accuracy of the fault localization in the software development environment. This advanced fault localization technique will help in the creation of more reliable software systems [10].

Siebert examined 32 papers that were published between 2010 and 2022. Siebert found that the papers emphasize the growing use of causal inference techniques in software engineering [12].

Through the proposal and validation of a causal model of bug resolution time and the identification of causal effects, our research adds to these previous investigations.

2.3 Methodology

The causal AI works in the following way:

- Data collection: Compile a large amount of observational data that includes pertinent metrics, behaviour, and occurrences.

- Causal discovery: Potential causal linkages in the data are found using algorithms.
- Building causal models: To depict the identified causal linkages, create models such as structural causal models.
- Integration of domain expertise: Use domain experts' ideas to improve causal models.
- Causal effect estimation: Calculate the effects of hypothetical interventions using counterfactual analysis.
- Intervention testing: To forecast the efficacy of possible interventions, model them, or carry out small-scale experiments.

The methodology is described in Figure 2.1.

2.3.1 Data Specification

To start the investigation, a simple statistical method is used to assess the data and determine its distribution. The Django dataset consists of 26360 rows and 18 columns. For our study purpose, we have omitted four variables, namely, 'unnamed_column', 'fix', 'contains_bug', and 'author_date_unix_timestamp'.

2.3.2 Model Variables

We have not considered the variables 'fix' and 'contains_bug' to build up the directed acyclic graph (DAG) using the GES algorithm.

The model variables of our study are defined as follows [13]:

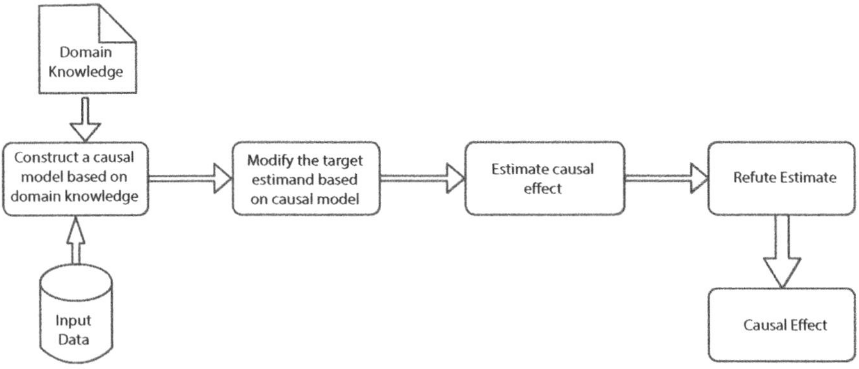

Figure 2.1 Types of research methodology.

- ***ns:*** The total number of altered subsystems.
- ***nd:*** The quantity of altered directories.
- ***nf:*** The quantity of altered files.
- ***entropy:*** Distributing the updated code to every file.
- ***la:*** Additional lines of code.
- ***lt:*** Code lines in a file prior to modification.
- ***ld:*** Code lines removed.
- ***ndev:*** The total number of developers involved in the modification or alteration of files.
- ***age:*** It is the time difference between the most recent change and the present.
- ***nuc:*** The quantity of unique changes made to the altered files.
- ***exp:*** Overall developer experience.
- ***rexp:*** Recent developer experience.
- ***sexp:*** Developer experience in a subsystem.
- ***days_to_first_fix:*** The first day on which the bug was fixed after its discovery.

2.3.3 Causal Discovery

The area of artificial intelligence called "causal discovery" aims to identify and understand the effective structure of causal relations among the variables of a dataset. Contrary to classical statistical methods, which often rely on simple correlations, causal discovery searches for an underlying cause-and-effect process that gives rise to observed outcomes [7]. Causal discovery is the process of uncovering and interpreting cause-and-effect relationships among variables based on empirical data. These causal insights help us in deepening our comprehension of complicated systems, improving prediction accuracy, and guiding better decision-making.

We have used a widely used technique named the greedy equivalence search (GES) algorithm to determine causality. GES is a valuable method for determining causation in observational data. GES balances edge addition and removal based on the scoring system to identify the optimal causal structure. GES is considered one of the best methods for dealing with complex systems when actual experimentation may be difficult or even immoral, although there are some drawbacks associated with it [7].

GES is preferred for the following reasons:

- ***Efficiency:*** GES is appropriate for huge datasets since it is built to search across the space of potential causal structures with efficiency.
- ***Score-Based:*** It assesses and contrasts various causal structures using a score-based methodology, usually the Bayesian Information Criterion (BIC).
- ***Flexibility:*** GES is adaptable for a range of applications due to its ability to handle both continuous and discontinuous data.
- ***Optimality:*** By iteratively adding and deleting edges according to the score, the method seeks to determine the best causal structure while maintaining a balance between model complexity and data fit.

The existence of these characteristics enables GES as an effective method for identifying causal links in intricate data sets, providing more insightful and useful data [7, 30].

In our dataset, there are 18 columns, but 4 columns of less importance are dropped, and a graph has been built consisting of 14 variables.

Figure 2.2 shows the causal network as the outcome of running GES on the Django dataset. We have used Python's *DoWhy* (https://www.pywhy.org/dowhy/) and *causal-learn* (https://github.com/py-why/causal-learn) libraries to build the causal discovery model [6, 7].

A causal graph given nodes X and Y is defined by the following three parts, each of which holds a distinct meaning: (1) X causes Y if and only if there exists a directed link from X to Y; (2) X causes Y or X is caused by Y if and only if there exists an undirected link from X to Y; and (3) if X and Y do not cause each other directly, then there is no link between X and Y [7, 14].

We comprehend Figure 2.2 using the notation already presented. The arrows leading to the vertex representing bug resolution time (days_to_first_fix) indicate that the lines of code in a file prior to the change (lt), the number of modified subsystems (ns), the updated code across files (entropy), and the number of developers who have altered the modified files (ndev) all influence bug resolution time. All the updated code to each file (entropy), the number of additional lines of code (la), the lines of code in a file prior to modification (lt), the lines of code removed (ld), the count of altered files (nf), the count of altered directories (nd), and the count of developers who made changes to the modified files (ndev) all have an

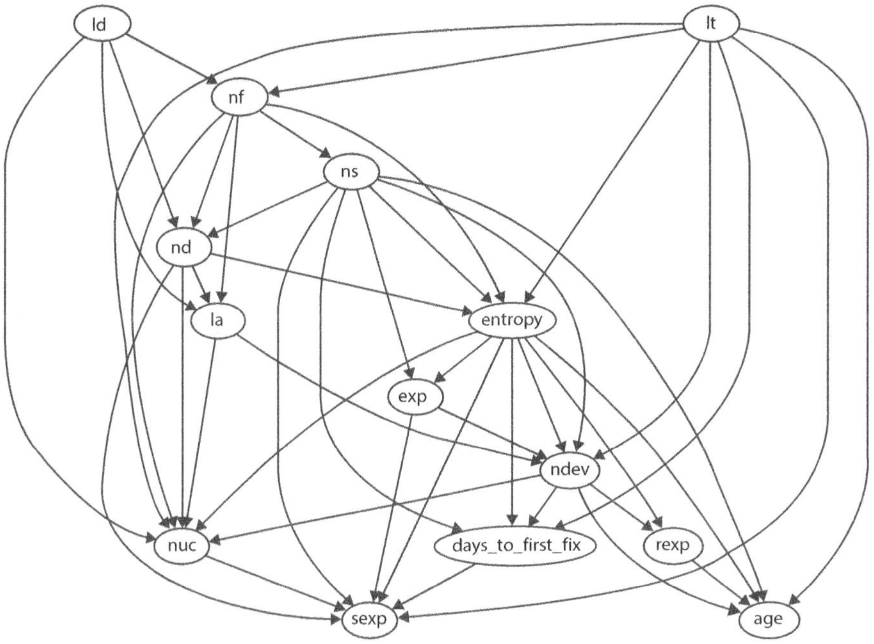

Figure 2.2 Causal structure derived from the Django dataset on the application of the GES algorithm.

impact on the number of distinct modifications made to the altered files (nuc). Furthermore, our analysis reveals that nuc, nd, ns, lt, exp, entropy, and days_to_first_fix all have an impact on sexp.

Given the complexity of the causal discovery graph, using all variables may lead to overfitting, false correlations, higher computational complexity, dimensionality concerns, and difficulty in practical interpretation. We will leverage our human knowledge and insights from previous research to consider only the relevant links. More accurate and meaningful results can be obtained by focusing only on the critical links that can directly impact the bug resolution time.

2.4 Model Construction

2.4.1 DAG and SCM

A directed acyclic graph (DAG) is a visual representation of the relationships among the variables. A structural causal model (SCM) is a combination of a DAG and statistical models that measures the causal relationships among the variables. A DAG only helps in understanding and visualizing the causal connections, whereas an SCM is used for estimation of causal effect and making predictions based on causal relationships [6, 17].

The structural causal model (SCM) from the Django dataset is shown in Figure 2.3. We have used our domain knowledge and have considered only the relevant variables that have a direct impact on the bug resolution time. The *causal faithfulness* assumption postulates that the observed independence relations in a dataset reflect the true underlying causal mechanism and not just random parameter choices. By contrast, the Markov property states that a variable is independent of all its non-descendants, given its parents, in a causal graph [15]. The faithfulness assumption refines the Markov property by guaranteeing that the only conditional independencies that may hold are the ones that are implied by the causal structure [16]. As a result, it prevents false dependence and ensures that the learned model has no spurious associations.

Including all variables of a dataset to construct a causal model may result in problems such as overfitting, complexity in computation, spurious correlations, assumptions being violated, and dimensionality, as well

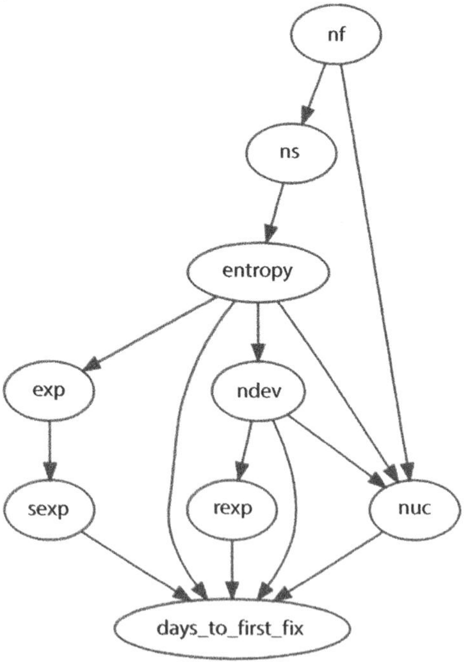

Figure 2.3 DAG for the Django dataset.

as interpretability issues. Selective choosing of those related variables is critical in solving these problems and obtaining successful causal-related modeling [6, 18]. We have omitted irrelevant variables such as 'lt', 'ld', 'la', 'nd', and 'age' from our causal analysis.

We had made the following assumptions based on our domain knowledge, and the graph was obtained through causal discovery using the GES algorithm. We have tried to identify only those variables that affect the bug resolution time:

exp → sexp: The system-level experience of developers is influenced by their total experience.

rexp → days_to_first_fix: The developer's experience determines how many days are needed to initially address the bug.

ndev → nuc: The number of unique changes made to the file depends on the number of developers.

sexp → days_to_first_fix: The level of subsystem experience of the developers affects the bug resolution time.

ndev → days_to_first_fix: The involvement of multiple developers in a file impacts the time required for bug resolution.

nf → nuc: The quantity of unique changes made to the altered files is impacted by the number of files modified.

nf → ns: The number of files modified affects the number of subsystems.

nuc → days_to_first_fix: The bug resolution time is influenced by the number of unique changes made to a file.

entropy → days _to_first_fix: The time it takes to fix bugs is also impacted by how the changed code is distributed throughout each file.

ns → entropy: The number of subsystems present determines how the changed code is distributed throughout each file.

DAG is the graphical part of the entire causal modeling infrastructure, which we call the graphical causal model (GCM). The Markov equivalence class of GCM is a group of DAGs that have the same conditional independence between variables and thus are statistically equivalent from the observational data point of view [20]. The Local Markov Condition (LMC) is an alternative criterion for the causality of a relationship in a GCM. LMC says that a variable is independent (in the probabilistic sense) of its non-descendant when we condition on their parents. Based on the above notions, we will use various statistical measures to estimate how well the GCM fits these. Such metrics consist of those based on Kullback-Leibler (KL) divergence, the number of violated LMCs, and the percentage of permutations belonging to the same Markov equivalence class as a given GCM [19].

We can track the overall number of conditional dependencies that are not satisfied by counting the number of LMCs that are broken. The validity of the graph could be estimated by comparing it with a massive sample of random graphs and then checking if the number of such violations does not exceed some limit [21].

LMC describes how the variables in the large dataset are locally dependent on each other for the purpose of extracting the pattern and the relationship between the variables. On the other hand, the KL distance is the method used to determine the similarity between the already observed data distribution and the modelled data distribution using the GCM [6, 22]. LMC and the KL distance are used to determine the similarity between the data distribution and the modelled data distribution using the GCM.

Total Positivity (TP) is a property of the joint distribution of variables in the model [23]. Within causal analysis, it requires that every individual have a nonzero probability of exposure to any level of treatment [24, 25]. If a violation of the total positivity condition occurs, this would result in incorrect causality inferences, which would suggest that the model does not provide an adequate description of the variables' interdependencies [6, 26]. Thus, it can be concluded that the validity and accuracy of our GCM can be measured with the help of total positivity and LMC [6, 26].

The performance of the GCM is presented in Figure 2.4. The evaluation indicates that it outperforms 96.0% of the permuted DAGs (pvalue = 0.04), while the pvalue for TP is 0.0. Given the specified significance level (0.2) and the informativeness of the DAG, we do not reject it. This is evaluating the effectiveness of the causal mechanisms, which are the procedures or models that explain how changes in one variable lead to changes in another. This may entail assessing their dependability, correctness, and capacity to represent the actual causal linkages.

The strength of the causal association between variables in a graphical causal model is referred to as the "arrow strength" in causal modeling.

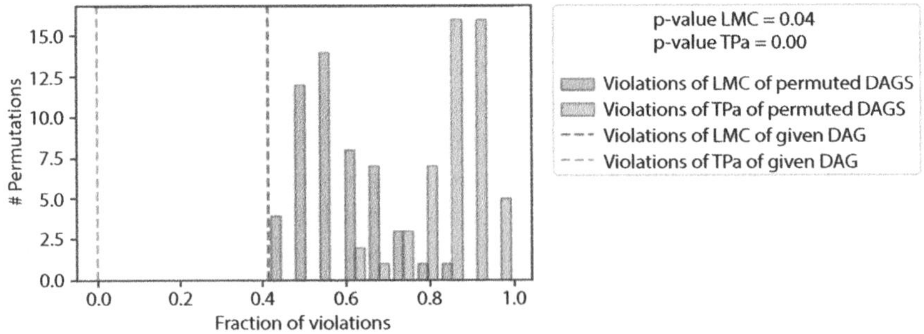

Figure 2.4 Evaluation of the performance of the causal model.

In these models, the arrows (or edges) show the intensity and direction of the causal relationship between two variables. Arrows indicate the direction of causality. An arrow from variable A to variable B (A → B) suggests that changes in A cause changes in B. The magnitude of the causal effect is represented by the strength of an arrow. A more significant impact of one variable on another is indicated by a stronger arrow. Quantitatively, this can be represented by the coefficients or weights in the model. The strength of the causal influence can be graphically represented in graphical models by the arrows' thickness or color intensity. Stronger relationships are usually indicated by thicker or darker arrows. Figue 2.5 shows that the number of unique commits, the system-level experience of the developers, and the number of developers have a significant effect on the bug resolution time. The causal graph shows that *nuc*, *ndev*, *rexp*, *sexp*, and *entropy* all directly affect the *days_of_first_fix*. However, the direct arrow strength algorithm, which measures the causal influence of a particular arrow in the graph, can be used to determine which of these factors contributes the most to the variance. From Figure 2.5, the number of developers has the highest contribution towards the variance in the bug resolution time. In causal analysis, confounders are variables that have an impact on both the treatment (or exposure) and the outcome. If they are not appropriately considered, they may cause a misleading association. Here, entropy is a confounder. So, its effect could not be found on the *days_to_first_fix*, and it was not possible to estimate the causal effect.

2.4.2 Causal Inference

The backdoor criterion is a notion used in causal inference that aims to find a group of variables that, when considered, help estimate the causal effect of one variable on another without introducing bias. The intended causal measure (ATE) is estimated by first developing a suitable estimator that considers the selected adjustment set and then applying the estimator to the data. At this point, the inferred causal estimate is made for the designated causal measure (ATE), and a causal test result with 95% confidence intervals is generated [27].

Given the observed confounders, the assumption of non-confoundedness guarantees that the assignment of treatment *(ndev)* is not affected by the possible results (*days_to_first_fix*).

This makes it possible to estimate the causal relationship between the number of developers and the length of days to first fix objectively. The "backdoor" estimand is used to find the relationships among variables

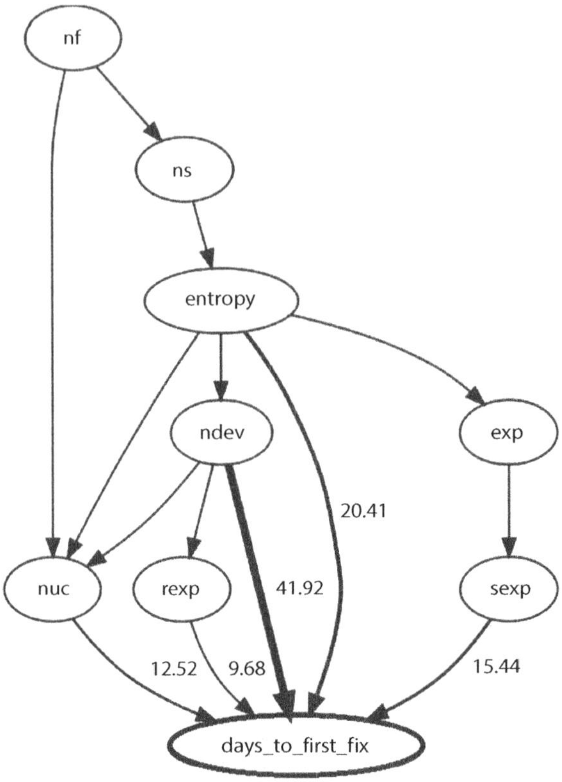

Figure 2.5 The arrow strength of the causal model.

when the confounding variables are present. In Figure 2.6, we calculate the derivative of the expected *days_to_first_fix*, based on *entropy*, in relation to the number of developers. In causal inference, this measure shows how much the number of developers impacts the expected *days_to_first_fix*, considering *entropy*. The *Unconfoundedness* assumption states that if an unobserved confounder (U) affects both *ndev* and *days_to_first_fix*, then conditioning on *ndev* and *entropy* should make the dependency on U irrelevant. This ensures that the causal effect can be estimated without bias from U.

In Figure 2.7, the realized estimand equation suggests a linear regression model where *days_to_first_fix* is influenced by several variables:

$$\text{days\_to\_first\_fix} \sim \text{ndev} + \text{entropy} + \text{ndev} \times \text{exp} + \text{ndev} \times \text{sexp}$$

```
### Estimand : 1
Estimand name: backdoor
Estimand expression:
  d
────────(E[days_to_first_fix|entropy])
d[ndev]
Estimand assumption 1, Unconfoundedness: If U→{ndev} and U→days_to_first_fix
then P(days_to_first_fix|ndev,entropy,U) = P(days_to_first_fix|ndev,entropy)
### Estimand : 2
Estimand name: iv
No such variable(s) found!
### Estimand : 3
Estimand name: frontdoor
No such variable(s) found!
### Estimand : 4
Estimand name: general_adjustment
Estimand expression:
  d
────────(E[days_to_first_fix|entropy])
d[ndev]
```

Figure 2.6 The code snippets showing the identified estimand obtained after controlling the number of developers.

This model aims to estimate the causal effect of *ndev* on *days_to_first_fix*, adjusting for entropy and considering interactions of the number of developers with overall experience (*exp*), as well as between the number of developers and system-level experience (*sexp*). If the backdoor criterion is satisfied, the model should provide an unbiased estimate of the causal effect.

According to the estimate derived using the backdoor criterion, the mean value of the causal effect of the number of developers *(ndev)* is -0.7301.

With a p-value of 3.46179525e-114, we have a 95% confidence interval [-0.7751, -0.6850] for the causal influence of *ndev* on bug resolution time. The fact that a greater number of developers are participating in bug fixes could be the cause of this reduction in bug resolution time.

2.4.3 Testing the Validity of Causal Claims

The process of assessing a claim using statistical techniques to see whether the evidence supports or contradicts it is known as statistical refutation.

```
Estimate of causal effect: *** Causal Estimate ***
## Identified estimand
Estimand type: EstimandType.NONPARAMETRIC_ATE

### Estimand : 1
Estimand name: backdoor
Estimand expression:
  d
———— (E[days_to_first_fix|entropy])
d[ndev]
Estimand assumption 1, Unconfoundedness: If U→{ndev} and U→days_to_first_fix
then P(days_to_first_fix|ndev,entropy,U) = P(days_to_first_fix|ndev,entropy)
## Realized estimand
b: days_to_first_fix ~ ndev + entropy + ndev*exp + ndev*sexp
Target units:
## Estimate
Mean value: -0.7301556332321582
p-value: [3.46179525e-114]
95.0% confidence interval: (np.float64(-0.7705032315914764), np.float64(-
0.6840094178424749))
```

Figure 2.7 The code snippets showing the causal estimate.

Here, three types of refutation techniques have been introduced, namely, random common cause, data subset refuter, and placebo treatment. The random cause refutation methodology introduces a random, meaningless variable and determines whether it incorrectly appears to have a causal influence to assess the robustness of a causal inference model. If the random variable shows an effect, it suggests the model is picking up noise rather than true causality. If the random variable has no effect, it adds confidence that the causal relationships identified are valid. Figure 2.8 shows the result obtained when one refutes the causal effect of *ndev* on bug resolution time

```
Refute: Add a random common cause
Estimated effect: -0.7301556332321582
New effect: -0.7301667090809727
p value:0.86
```

Figure 2.8 The refute obtained after adding a random common cause.

and finds that the model is robust, as the new estimate, -0.73016, is close to the estimated effect, -0.73015.

A randomly chosen subset of the original dataset is utilized to rerun the study to evaluate the robustness of causal estimates using a subset of data refutation techniques. This aids in determining whether the causal effect is consistent across samples. Figure 2.9 shows that our result is consistent, as the new effect is almost close to the estimated causal effect, -0.7301.

The placebo refutation technique substitutes a random, independent variable with no discernible causal effect for the actual treatment variable to assess the validity of causal estimates. According to the theory, the estimated effect of the placebo variable should be zero or negligible if the causal model is appropriately defined. If the placebo variable shows a significant effect, it suggests that the original causal estimate might be biased or picking up spurious correlations. If the placebo variable has no effect, it strengthens confidence in the validity of the causal inference. From Figure 2.10, it can be seen that the new effect on placebo treatment is negligible.

Similarly, one can estimate the causal effect of *nuc*, *sexp*, *rexp*, *exp*, *ns*, and *nf* on *days_to_first_fix*. The results are summarized in Table 2.1.

The backdoor estimand is used where the number of files (*nf*) is controlled to find its causal effect on the *days_of_first_fix*. The backdoor estimand assumes that once a condition is put on *nf*, the outcome *days_to_first_fix* is independent of any unobserved confounders *U*. However, since the entropy is a confounding variable, the direct estimation of the effect of *nf* on *days_to_first-fix* is biased due to confounding. In this case, the front-door estimate will be considered as *nf* satisfies the front-door criteria. Front-door adjustment is a technique in causal inference employed

```
Refute: Use a subset of data
Estimated effect: -0.7301556332321582
New effect: -0.7316372451404777
p value:0.94
```

Figure 2.9 The refute obtained after using a subset of data.

```
Refute: Use a Placebo Treatment
Estimated effect: -0.7301556332321582
New effect:0.0013063549602574654
p value:0.8999999999999999
```

Figure 2.10 The refute obtained after using a placebo treatment.

Table 2.1 Results of analysis for Django (p-values in bold imply statistical significance).

Treatment variable	Estimate		Refute		
	Mean	**p-value**	**RCC**	**DSR**	**PT**
nuc	-0.0279	**0.0018**	-0.0279	-0.0288	0.0006
ndev	-0.7301	**3.46e-114**	-0.7301	-0.7316	0.0013
sexp	0.0166	**6.24e-43**	0.0166	0.01659	-0.0001
rexp	0.0045	0.150	0.00455	0.00430	0.0019
exp	0.0062	**1.46e-28**	0.00016	0.00016	1.2093
ns	24.244	**6.37e-14**	24.247	24.244	0.0610
nf	-0.2086	**0.0024**	-0.20864	-0.2114	0.0154

to estimate causal effects when conventional methods, such as backdoor adjustment, are inapplicable.

Estimating the impact of *nf* modifications on the expected value of *days_to_first_fix* is done using the estimand. The estimand by front-door criteria is based on certain assumptions:

Assumption 1: Full-Mediation, which states that certain variables (*entropy, ndev, rexp, sexp, exp, nuc*, and *ns*) block all directed paths from *nf* to *days_to_first_fix*. This assumption is crucial in causal mediation analysis, ensuring that the mediator fully captures the causal effect.

In causal inference, full mediation means:

a. The treatment (*nf*) affects the mediator (*entropy, ndev*, etc.).
b. The mediator then influences the outcome (*days_to_first_fix*).
c. There is no direct effect of *nf* on *days_to_first_fix* outside of the mediator.

Assumption 2: First-stage-unconfoundedness ensures that the mediator variables (*entropy, ndev, rexp, sexp, exp, nuc*, and *ns*) are conditionally independent of the unobserved confounders (U) given the treatment (*nf*). It can be explained briefly as:

a. $U \rightarrow \{nf\}$ and $U \rightarrow \{entropy, ndev, rexp, sexp, exp, nuc, ns\}$ indicate that the unobserved confounders U influence both the treatment (*nf*) and the mediators.

b. The assumption states that P (mediators | *nf*, *U*) = P (mediators | *nf*), meaning that upon putting a condition on *nf*, the mediators are no longer affected by *U*.
c. This also allows us to estimate the causal effect of *nf*→ mediators without bias, as the relationship between *nf* and the mediators is not confounded.

Assumption 3: Second-stage-unconfoundedness ensures that the outcome (*days_to_first_fix*) is conditionally independent of unobserved confounders (*U*) given the mediators (*entropy, ndev, rexp, sexp, exp, nuc, ns*) and the treatment (*nf*).

Interpretation:

- *U*→ {*entropy, ndev, rexp, sexp, exp, nuc, ns*} and *U*→ *days_to_first_fix* indicate that unobserved confounders *U* influence both the mediators and the outcome.
- The assumption states that P (*days_to_first_fix* | mediators, *nf*, *U*) = P (*days_to_first_fix* | mediators, *nf*), meaning that once a condition is put on the mediators and treatment, the outcome is no longer affected by *U*.
- This ensures that the relationship between mediators → *days_to_first_fix* is not confounded, allowing us to estimate the causal effect of mediators → outcome without bias.

All these assumptions are crucial in causal mediation analysis, ensuring that the mediators correctly capture the causal pathway from *nf* to the outcome.

The results of causal inference are summarized in Table 2.1.

2.5 Discussion

The process of assessing a proposition using statistical techniques to see whether the data support or contradict it is known as statistical refutation. Unless specified otherwise, we calculate the likelihood of the observed data under the null hypothesis. If the likelihood is below a threshold, we reject the null hypothesis in favor of the alternative hypothesis. A rebuttal evaluates the results and the goodness of fit of the model based on that.

The results and the strength of the model are evaluated in a refutation. For this purpose, the dataset must have an independent random variable as a common cause. The estimates should be close if the assumptions are correct. We first consider the treatment effect of the number of developers on the bug resolution time. A p-value of 0.86 supports our inference that the estimated effect (-0.73015) is close to the new impact (-0.73016). We conclude that there is no significant difference between the original and the new effects.

The revised effect, which was estimated using a subset of the data, was -0.731637, which is almost near the original estimate of -0.730155. With the strong p-value of 0.94, it can be confidently stated that our estimate is stable and dependable. Therefore, the alternative hypothesis is chosen, and the null hypothesis is rejected. Using the provided dataset, let us conduct the placebo test. The estimate should not alter if the assumptions are accurate. We used the placebo test to corroborate our findings, and the results showed that the new effect was 0.001306, the estimated effect was -0.730155, and the p-value was 0.89. Our estimate is found to be consistent with the data after refutation. Therefore, we choose an alternative hypothesis and reject the null hypothesis.

Table 2.1 shows that *sexp* and *exp* have a significant causal effect (0.0166 and 0.0062) on increasing the bug resolution time, with p-values of 6.24e-43 and 1.46e-28, respectively. Furthermore, with a p-value of 6.37e-14, our analysis shows that the number of subsystems (*ns*) has a high positive causal effect (24.44) on the bug resolution time. Additionally, as the p-value (0.0018) and causal effect (-0.0279) show, limiting the number of unique commits will also shorten the time it takes to fix bugs. If the number of files (*nf*) is managed properly, the bug resolution time can be significantly decreased, with a causal effect (-0.2086) and p-value (0.0024). The presence of the confounding variable *entropy* makes it impossible to estimate the effect of *nf* on *days_to_first_fix* with any degree of accuracy. Upon performing the mediation analysis, the causal effect is estimated to be -18.9061. This shows that the number of files, if properly treated, can significantly reduce the bug resolution time.

2.6 Sensitivity Analysis of Treatment Variables

This study has also done the sensitivity analysis of the above treatment variables and summarized it in Table 2.2 below.

As per Table 2.2, the study has shown the sensitivity analysis of the variables with their interpretations. Figure 2.11 has been generated from Table 2.2, which explains the graphical visualization of the sensitivity of the treatment variables. Figure 2.11 shows that the variable *exp* has the highest sensitivity among the others. The high sensitivity variable has crossed the

Table 2.2 Results of sensitivity analysis of treatment variables.

Variable	Interpretation	Estimate stability (RCC vs DSR)	PT (perturbation term)	Sensitivity assessment
nuc	Negative effect (small)	RCC: -0.0279, DSR: -0.0288	0.0006	Low sensitivity
ndev	Strong negative effect	RCC: -0.7301, DSR: -0.7316	0.0013	Low sensitivity
sexp	Small positive effect	RCC: 0.0166, DSR: 0.01659	-0.0001	Low sensitivity
rexp	Small positive effect, not significant	RCC: 0.00455, DSR: 0.00430	0.0019	Moderate sensitivity
exp	Small positive effect	RCC: 0.00016, DSR: 0.00016	1.2093	High sensitivity
ns	Strong positive effect	RCC: 24.247, DSR: 24.244	0.0610	Low sensitivity
nf	Moderate negative effect	RCC: -0.20864, DSR: -0.2114	0.0154	Low-moderate sensitivity

threshold limit, and it has been identified, which indicates that the proposed model is scalable as well as robust with the appropriate data variables.

2.7 Threats to Validity

The following *threats to the validity* of our results are identified and addressed.

- **Construct validity:** Construct validity is the capacity to precisely determine and compute the variables pertinent to a study. According to Section 2.1, data gathered from peer-reviewed sources [28] and [29] were used to define and

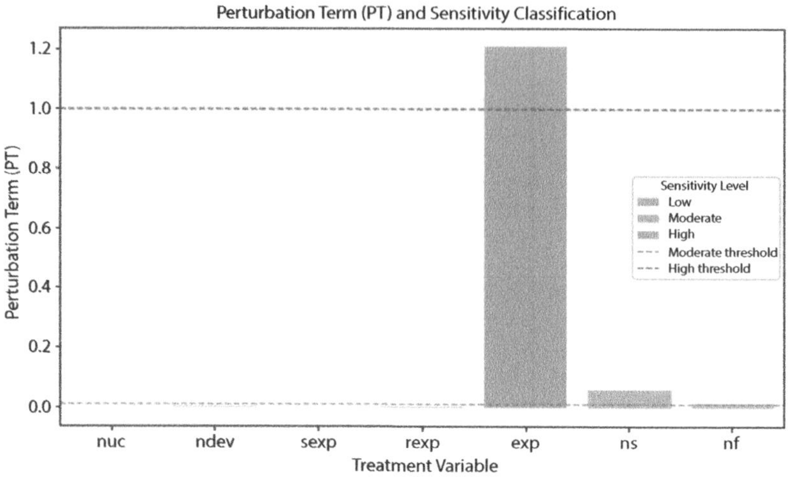

Figure 2.11 Graphical representations of sensitivity analysis of treatment variables.

compute each model variable. However, we acknowledge that the limitations imposed by the data available for the building of our causal model pose a threat to the construct validity of the study's findings. Only the variables found in the Django dataset could be included in the causal model. However, a few factors that we were unable to incorporate into our model, such as bug complexity, priority, developer knowledge with the bug type, and team staffing levels, can affect bug resolution. We emphasize that our model provides valuable insights in our study environment, even as we acknowledge these risks to construct validity.

- **Internal validity:** Problems like selection bias and maturation effects can jeopardize the internal validity of a study's findings. We used historical data in this investigation. Consequently, neither selection bias nor maturation effects poses a significant concern.
- **External validity:** The generalizability of a study's findings is one factor that poses a threat to its external validity. In this study, we have looked at data from a single system. We therefore make no claims regarding the generalizability of our findings. Nonetheless, practical lessons can be extracted for both the advanced usage and the exercise of software engineering.

- **Reliable:** The results are reliable if the key findings of the study are reproducible. A publicly accessible dataset has been used in this investigation. To help replicate our findings, we have provided a replication package along with the code and data (https://github.com/ReshmiMaulik/Causal-AI/blob/main/django.py).

2.8 Conclusion

In conclusion, the use of Greedy Equivalency Search (GES) has enabled us to recognize the signs of the relationships that may impact bug-fixing time. Our study revealed that the time to bug resolution is significantly affected by the number of developers and their experience. This growth of developers causes an increase in the time to solve bugs, which could be a result of efforts being split and skill shift. The most senior developers are bound to be working more often with complex or important problems, which could potentially lead to slower bug fixes. The architecture gets complicated whenever the number of subsystems is increased, and as a consequence, the bug-fixing time can also tend to increase. Correct handling of code in multiple files allows for a faster bug-fixing time. Correctly assessing cause-and-effect relationships is key to optimal bug-fixing that eventually leads to more productive and more effective development teams.

2.9 Future Scope

Causal inference is a hot topic that applies to various domains such as econometrics, business analytics, social science, computer science, and other disciplines like medicine and psychology. The potential of causal AI is here to stay since it lays out a compelling platform to model and solve difficult problems in system logic. In contrast to the traditional correlation-based analyses, causal AI allows the identification of the underlying causal relationships between variables that may not be immediately apparent through association. When it is not practical to carry out direct experiments, causal inference provides a well-informed basis for decision-making. It estimates the potential outcome based on the effect of a treatment or intervention and helps practitioners anticipate and prevent undesirable outcomes. Ultimately, it helps us to determine whether a population should receive a certain treatment or not.

AI disclosure statement: The author confirms that no artificial intelligence (AI)-generated content or AI-assisted writing tools were used in the preparation of this chapter (including summaries and the abstract). All text, analysis, and conclusions are the result of the author's original work.

References

1. Carloni, G., Berti, A., Colantonio, S., The role of causality in explainable artificial intelligence. *Wiley Interdiscip. Rev.: Data Min. Knowl. Discovery*, 15, 2, e70015, 2025.
2. Lokala, U. and Roy, K., Tutorial: Causal AI for Web and Health Care, in: *Companion Proceedings of the ACM Web Conference*, 2023. https://aiisc.ai/causalai/.
3. What is causal AI?, https://www.infobip.com/glossary/causal-ai. Accessed: 2024-01-28.
4. Maulik, R., A Review on Mitigating Security Threats in Aadhaar. *Indian J. Comput. Sci. Eng.* (IJCSE), ISSN: 0976-5166, 15, 3, 252–260, 2024, https://doi.org/10.21817/indjcse/2024/v15i3/241503027.
5. Chadbourne, P. and Eisty, N.U., Applications of casualty and causal inference in software engineering, in: *2023 IEEE/ACIS 21st International Conference on Software Engineering Research, Management and Applications (SERA)*, IEEE, pp. 47–52, 2023.
6. Maulik, R., Datta, S., Majumdar, S., The Causality of Bug Resolution: A Tale of Two Systems, in: *33rd ACM International Conference on the Foundations of Software Engineering (FSE Companion '25)*, Trondheim, Norway, June 23–28, 2025, ACM, New York, NY, USA.
7. Maulik, R., Datta, S., Majumdar, S., The Effects on Bug Resolution Time: A Causal Discovery Perspective, in: *Human-centered Data Analytics: Technology for Sustainable Development: Third Analytics Global Conference, AGC 2025, Kolkata, India, March 8–9, 2025, Revised Selected Papers*, pp. 172–183, Springer Nature, Cham, Switzerland, https://link.springer.com/book/10.1007/978-3-032-09153-6.
8. Peralta, S.R.O., Washizaki, H., Fukazawa, Y., Noyori, Y., Nojiri, S., Hideyuki, K., Unraveling the Influences on Bug Fixing Time: A Comparative Analysis of Causal Inference Model, in: *Proceedings of the 28th International Conference on Evaluation and Assessment in Software Engineering*, pp. 393–398, 2024.
9. Johnson, B., Brun, Y., Meliou, A., Causal testing: Understanding defects' root causes, in: *Proceedings of the ACM/IEEE 42nd International Conference on Software Engineering*, pp. 87–99, 2020.
10. Baah, G.K., Podgurski, A., Harrold, M.J., Causal inference for statistical fault localization, in: *Proceedings of the 19th International Symposium on Software Testing and Analysis*, pp. 73–84, 2010.

11. Tunde-Onadele, O., Qin, F., Gu, X., Lin, Y., ClearCausal: Cross Layer Causal Analysis for Automatic Microservice Performance Debugging, in: *2024 IEEE International Conference on Autonomic Computing and Self-Organizing Systems(ACSOS)*, IEEE, pp. 175–180, 2024.
12. Siebert, J., Applications of statistical causal inference in software engineering. *Inf. Software Technol.*, 159, 107198, 2023.
13. Fukushima, T., Kamei, Y., McIntosh, S., Yamashita, K., Ubayashi, N., An empirical study of just-in-time defect prediction using cross-project models, in: *Proceedings of the 11th Working Conference on Mining Software Repositories*, pp. 172–181, 2014.
14. Neapolitan, R.E., *Learning bayesian networks*, vol. 38, Pearson Prentice Hall, Upper Saddle River, NJ, 2004.
15. Zhang, J. and Spirtes, P., The three faces of faithfulness. *Synthese*, 193, 1011–1027, 2016.
16. Uhler, C., Raskutti, G., Bühlmann, P., Yu, B., Geometry of the faithfulness assumption in causal inference. *Ann. Stat.*, 436–463, 2013.
17. Eapen, T., Structural Causal Modeling Using DAGs, 2018, Available at SSRN 4588545.
18. Babyak, M.A., What you see may not be what you get: a brief, non-technical introduction to overfitting in regression-type models. *Biopsychosoc. Sci. Med.*, 66, 3, 411–421, 2004.
19. de Cristo, F.S., Eisenbarth, J.-P., Meira, J.A., State, R., Causal AI for XRPL/GossipSub network configuration, in: *20th International Conference on Network and Service Management (CNSM)*, IEEE, pp. 1–5, 2024.
20. Hauser, A. and Bühlmann, P., Characterization and greedy learning of interventional Markov equivalence classes of directed acyclic graphs. *J. Mach. Learn. Res.*, 13, 1, 2409–2464, 2012.
21. Spirtes, P.L., Directed cyclic graphical representations of feedback models, arXiv preprint arXiv:1302.4982, 2013.
22. Wildberger, J.B., Guo, S., Bhattacharyya, A., Schölkopf, B., On the interventional Kullback-Leibler divergence, in: *Conference on Causal Learning and Reasoning*, PMLR, pp. 328–349, 2023.
23. Fallat, S., Lauritzen, S., Sadeghi, K., Uhler, C., Wermuth, N., Zwiernik, P., Total positivity in Markov structures. *Ann. Stat.*, 1152–1184, 2017.
24. Frydenberg, M., The chain graph Markov property. *Scand. J. Stat.*, 333–353, 1990.
25. Neal, B., Introduction to causal inference, Course Lecture Notes (draft), pp. 20–22, 2020.
26. Eulig, E., Mastakouri, A.A., Blöbaum, P., Hardt, M., Janzing, D., Toward falsifying causal graphs using a permutation-based test, arXiv preprint arXiv:2305.09565, 2023.
27. Clark, A.G., Foster, M., Prifling, B., Walkinshaw, N., Hierons, R.M., Schmidt, V., Turner, R.D., Testing causality in scientific modelling software. *ACM Trans. Software Eng. Methodol.*, 33, 1, 1–42, 2023.

28. Song, L. and Minku, L.L., A procedure to continuously evaluate predictive performance of just-in-time software defect prediction models during software development. *IEEE Trans. Software Eng.*, 49, 2, 646–666, 2022.
29. Tabassum, S., Minku, L.L., Feng, D., Cross-project online just-in-time software defect prediction. *IEEE Trans. Software Eng.*, 49, 1, 268–287, 2022.
30. Huang, B., Zhang, K., Lin, Y., Schölkopf, B., Glymour, C., Generalized score functions for causal discovery, in: *Proceedings of the 24th ACM SIGKDD International Conference on Knowledge Discovery & Data Mining*, pp. 1551–1560, 2018.

3

Exploring Causal AI through Deep Learning: A CNN-Based Framework for Signal Detection in Climate and Space Sciences

Aditya Sharma and Inderdeep Kaur*

Department of Computer Science & Engineering, Channdigarh University, Mohali, Punjab, India

Abstract

The gravitational waves that are ripples in the spacetime generated by powerful events in the universe, like black hole mergers, neutron star mergers, and supernovae, offer a radical way of investigating the universe. According to the general theory of relativity developed by Einstein, such waves carry crucial information about their astrophysical source and the essential characteristics of gravity. Their identification and categorization are, however, very difficult since the distortions produced by them are so small and the noise environments of the interferometric detectors, such as LIGO and Virgo, are of a highly complex nature. This research is of high relevance as it deals with an urgent challenge of representing the gravitational wave signals by using their correct classification labels because, today, there are 22 possible different types of gravitational wave events defined, including astrophysical signals, instrumental glitches, and noise artifacts, and the use of the Gravity Spy dataset. The convolutional CNN architecture that will be proposed uses convolution layers, max pooling, and dropout regularization, as well as dense layers, to pull out a hierarchy of spatial features based upon time-frequency representations of gravitational wave data. The model improves generalization in a broad pattern of signal shapes with the help of data augmentation, including rotation and scaling. The training and validation were performed on a carefully curated dataset that was balanced to reduce bias and optimized through an Adam optimizer with categorical cross-entropy loss. Early stopping was used to provide

**Corresponding author*: inderdeep.sgtb@gmail.com

Rajdeep Chakraborty, Aleem Ali, Amit Paul, Nawaf R. Alharbe and S. Balamurugan (eds.) Causal Artificial Intelligence: Fundamentals and Applications, (45–72) © 2026 Scrivener Publishing LLC

a good convergence that avoids overfitting. It also had such a high validation accuracy of 94.63% and almost the same curve of training and validation, thus illustrating its capability in generalization. The performance could be observed by analyzing the confusion matrices because the precision was high, which made it possible to discriminate slight differences between classes when there were weak variables in some categories that had noise. It is a demonstration of how deep learning can transform gravitational wave astronomy. This high rate of accuracy enhances the detection of the scientifically relevant occurrences like the merging of black holes and star collisions, which will allow prompt follow-ups using the electromagnetic telescopes. The CNN model maximizes the accuracy of large-scale data analysis at observatories by not only minimizing false positive rates but also automating the entire classification pipeline, which will allow making discoveries in multi-messenger astrophysics. Moreover, it is depicted in the study that the model can test the predictions of Einstein in extreme circumstances and explore phenomena that have not been observed before, e.g., primordial gravitational waves of the early universe.

***Keywords*:** Gravitational waves, convolutional neural networks (CNN), gravity spy dataset, signal classification, deep learning, astrophysical phenomena

3.1 Introduction

Gravity is observed as distortions in spacetime, arising from the acceleration of massive bodies such as merging black holes or colliding neutron stars. First mentioned by Albert Einstein [1] when he published his theory of relativity in 1916, these phenomena reflect the idea that physical objects such as stars and constellations change the geometry of spacetime, like a weight placed on an object.

Therefore, any change in the motion or speed of these entities can cause this structure to be distorted, which is expressed externally in the form of gravitational waves, where the cosmic speed limit (e.g., the speed of light) describes how matter and energy affect the curvature of spacetime. In linearized gravitational wave theory, which is applicable to weak gravitational fields and low speeds, the waves can be described by linearized Einstein field equations [2]. GW waves are shown in 3D in Figure 3.1.

Gravity does not transfer energy from its source and causes oscillations in spacetime as it propagates. However, since its effects are very small, controlling it requires the use of sensitive equipment. Interferometers such as the Virgo interferometer and the Laser Interferometer Gravitational Wave Observatory (LIGO) [6] are promising tools for this task. When a

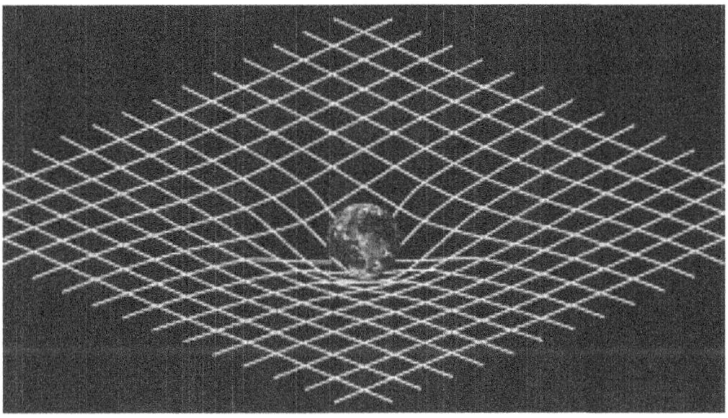

Figure 3.1 Gravitational waves 3D view [8].

gravitational wave passes through an interferometer, it causes a slight difference in the arms, causing a change in the interference of the interferometer. Gravity is an entity. Drawing inspiration from the hierarchical organization of the visual cortex in biological systems, CNNs are good at learning spatial features from input data [3].

This makes them ideal for tasks that involve waveform or image analysis, such as identifying gravitational wave signatures in noise data obtained by interferometers. A different method. Detection of gravitational waves has become critical in current astrophysics to give an insight into the most energetic phenomena in nature [4]. However, because these conditions are complex and variable, there is no correct classification of the conditions.

The finding provides a unique peephole into the most energy-intensive processes in the universe, such as black hole mergers, neutron stars colliding, and supernova blasts [5]. A proper categorization of these gravitational events is, however, vital in bringing out scientific implications and enhancing the comprehension of astrophysical processes. The idea motivating this work is the recent progress in deep learning and image classification, so we suggest a neural network (CNN) model to be applied to the Gravity Spy dataset.

To capture the good features and enhance better performance in this model, it utilizes the convolutional method, max pooling, and continuous throughput. The database consists of an array of gravitational wave image types collected into 22 different categories, consisting of a variety of astrophysical events, e.g., glitches, signals, and whistles. According to the experiment results, there is a great improvement in the care outcomes.

Algorithm 3.1 Training a Convolutional Neural Network.

Step 1: Environment Setup and Data Acquisition
Step 2: Data Preparation
Step 3: Model Architecture Design Initialize a Sequential model. For each layer configuration, do
Add Conv2Dlayers with varying numbers of filters and kernel sizes, applying the convolution operation:

$$C(i,j) = \sum_{m}\sum_{n} I(i+m, j+n) \cdot K(m,n)$$

Include MaxPooling2D layers after Conv2D layers for down-sampling, using the max pooling formula:

$$M\,(i, j) = \max(I(i + p, j + q))$$

Insert Dropout layers for regularization, with the dropout.
end for otherwise

Flatten the output from the convolutional base. Add Dense layers for classification.
Add a final Denselayer with Softmax activation for output probabilities, calculated.
Step 4: Model Compilation
Specify the optimizer (e.g., Adam), with its update rule. Define the loss function (e.g., categorical cross-entropy).
Step 5: Model Training
Step 6: Model Evaluation
Step 7: Performance Visualization

Algorithm 3.1 shows a systematic procedure that can be used to create a convolutional neural network (CNN) and its evaluation in classification problems, like the detection of gravitational waves.

Step 1: Data Capture Environment Setup
The workflow starts by preparing the computing space, which entails the installation of the requisite libraries (e.g., TensorFlow, Keras, NumPy) and preparing the GPU support in case it is available. This is followed by data gathering of what is reported on the target source, and it must

be representative of the problem domain. In the case of gravitational waves, this may include time-series detector data, e.g., LIGO or Virgo spectrograms.

Step 2: Preparation of Data

The obtained information is washed, standardized, and redirected to a format suitable for the CNN input. This involves transformations to make images or spectrograms fit into the demands of the task, scaling, and possibly augmenting them to improve the generalization of the models.

Step 3: Model Architecture Design

The sequential model structure is set up.

i. Convolutional Layers (Conv2D): Conv layers use convolution to extract spatial information from the input data. The model can identify patterns of various sizes with different filters and kernel sizes.
ii. MaxPooling2D Layers: These compress spatial dimensions in a pooling window, that is, the maximum value in that pooling window, as assumed by the formula.
iii. The characteristics of this operation are the ability to preserve the dominance, minimize the computation, and lessen the overfitting.
iv. Dropout Layers: These apply regularization, randomly removing (during training) some of the neurons, thereby avoiding having an overfitted model by promoting more generalized learning.
v. Flatten Layer: Converts 2D feature maps to 1D vectors to perform the subsequent dense layers.
vi. Dense Layers: Completely connected layers that interpret the features extracted and translate those to the classification.
vii. Softmax Layer: This layer gives the probabilities of each class so that multi-class classification becomes possible by normalizing the outputs to a probability distribution.

Step 4: Compilation of Models

The model is assembled with a chosen optimizer like Adam that has an effective and adaptive rule of learning rate update. The multi-class mode of operation is selected, and the loss criterion—categorical cross-entropy is used so that the model learns to optimize the likelihood of class prediction.

Step 5: Training of Models
The model is prepared beforehand and trained on the preprocessed dataset. It means that input data can be fed in batches across many epochs, and the weights are updated depending on the gradient of the loss. The validation metrics are also used to help avoid overfitting.
Step 6: Model Evaluation
The model is then evaluated on a test dataset after the training. The effectiveness in terms of recognizing target patterns can be measured by such metrics as accuracy, precision, recall, F1-score, confusion matrices, and so on.
Step 7: Visualization of Performance
The information concerning the learning behavior and its convergence, and areas that may be improved, can be obtained by visual analysis using loss and accuracy curves, ROC curves, and other plots.

In recent years, DL approaches, particularly CNNs, have revolutionized image classification tasks across various domains. As admirers of the success of CNNs in the task of image classification, we consider a system based on CNNs to classify images based on their content in the Gravity Spy dataset.

The rest of this work is structured as follows. In Section 3.2, a detailed literature review will be provided in accordance with this topic (gravitational wave detection and application of advanced computational methods). Section 3.3 expounds more on the nature of gravitational waves and how they are detected, the associated principles, advanced concepts in detecting gravitational waves, and their prospects. The results and discussion, including the dataset, preprocessing, proposed approach, and evaluation and performance analysis; comparison and validation; and accuracy are expressed in Section 3.4. Section 3.5 is devoted to the performance analysis, such as measuring accuracy and loss, the confusion matrix, interpretations of performance in detail, and the explanation of the importance of the attained accuracy. At the end, there is the conclusion, which sums up the most important findings as well as the implications of the research.

3.2 Literature Review

The recent breakthroughs in gravitational wave detection and classification techniques, with the usage of DL solutions in particular, have resulted in enhanced efficiency and accuracy of automated detection systems.

Wang *et al.* (2020) [6] is one of the publications in this direction, more specifically in the area of classifying signals within a convolutional neural network (CNN). They prove that the use of CNNs is highly advantageous in recognizing the complicated patterns in GW data, one of the valuable properties of automatic detection systems. Proving the CNN's usefulness and ability to learn and analyze such complex patterns.

This is necessary to enable early identification of the big astronomical processes like the merger of black holes and collisions between neutron stars. Large gravitational wave datasets can be of good use to scientists who could use the power of CNNs in order to identify certain events of interest much faster and more accurately than before. Observation of the stage of achievements. Their work opens the doors to the future of advanced automatic detection systems that will be able to respond in real-time capacity using the power of CNNs applied to known patterns. These machines are very promising for speeding up wave research so that scientists can easily observe and analyze most events in the heavens.

The very work of CNN in the undertaking of the process of classification of the signal of gravitational wave even has a blueprint for the future advancement of the automatic vacuum system. Their work has assisted gravitational wave astronomy because, by the way, they have demonstrated that CNNs will be able to reliably and quickly recognize occurrences in the gravitational field; they have made gravitational wave astronomy a viable pursuit. With the field continuing with its progress, the methods and concepts suggested in the plan by Wang *et al.* will be used in the endeavor to unzip the mysteries of the universe due to the advent of gravitational wave astronomy.

The study of Krastev [7] throws some light on the significance of gravitational wave (GW) astronomy, which emphasizes the significance of detection during flight with the aid of artificial neural networks (ANN). In his speech, Krastev dwelt on applications of these networks, mainly the speed in capturing the event of the wave as well as BNSM, among others, and insisted on the necessity of speed in capturing the gravitational wave.

Such valuable measurements have now become very essential as a way to enable prompt observations using other astronomical tools and, in the process, get to know more about what happens in the universe. The inclusion of CNN into the search line is ongoing. Due to this cooperation, the study of gravitational waves will be a significant step forward because the process of perceiving and studying high-speed events will become as accurate as ever before. Having the computing capabilities of neural networks, scientists may analyze huge amounts of information about gravitational waves in real-time and, therefore, determine and classify various events. The usefulness of the electrons in fast-moving radio waves, which is shown in the work by Krastev, is based on the purpose of BNSM and, as it appears, can, with the help of such networks, transform the sphere of GW astronomy. The application of ANNs, and in particular CNNs, despite speeding up and optimizing the detection of waves, also unravels new means of studying the phenomenon of time in space. The contribution made in this study implies the urgency of analysis that should be made in order to enable us to observe the universe in time and gain more knowledge about it. They could show the value of fast recognition further with the help of neural networks. The methods and ideas that the research carried out by Krastev revealed will certainly have a significant place in the future developments of the field, especially as it is still in its developmental process.

The discoveries of the gravitational wave detectors themselves have played a significant role in helping classify the faint signals of the faraway events in the cosmos. The Harry G. M. and the LIGO scientific collaboration progress lies at an exciting stage in the history of GW astronomy through the knowledge transfer of the technological aspect of the instrument in the gravitational field (GW) [8]. This paper takes an in-depth look at the development of these detectors, showing how much progress has been made over the years, a fact that has brought worthy changes in sensitivity and accuracy. The sensitivity of such devices allows them to tune in to low-level messages of remote events in the cosmos with extraordinary precision. The more sensitive and accurate these machines are, the more significant the data of the gravitational wave is, not only the correction of the gravitational wave signal but also the level of importance of the gravitational wave data. Useful information can be derived by using a parallel gravitational wave dataset in order to come up with useful information and distinguish important cosmic events with unbelievable efficiency. Machine learning incorporated in the process of gravitational wave detection technology has a lot of potential in enhancing our knowledge about the universe and bringing out more information about it. Partnership research gives an in-depth review of the world. The study sheds light on the development of detectors and how they influenced the study of gravitational waves, paving the way for more research and advancement in this area.

Moreno and associates [9] present a novel technique for magnetic field (GW) detection that uses iterative autoencoders, exhibiting a more versatile and flexible approach to deep learning models at various layers. By suggesting the use of effective iterative autoencoders in processing adjacent data, this work offers an update to the central convolutional network (CNN) for GW detection. Its location-independent nature makes it possible to detect gravitational wave signals without being aware of their past history, which makes it significant. This differs greatly from conventional techniques, which typically depend on particular information to ascertain the nature of gravity. The study broadens the scope of the observed phenomena and creates new avenues for the study of cosmic time by employing a source-independent methodology. Based on the characteristics of the GW signal, it offers a distinct dominance sequence of data. Recurrent autoencoders are well-suited for the study of GW symbols most frequently found in physical structures because they are adept at capturing physical features in data sequences, unlike CNNs, which are primarily made for image processing. The CNNs and the recurrent autoencoders complement each other in GW. Iterative autoencoders do provide another option, though, where the temporal aspect is highlighted despite the realization made in CNNs that they can successfully extract the features of GW data. This DL model combination boosts the power of the gravitational wave detection system generally and its performance. This technique has contributed to gravity detection, which has seen another breakthrough when using cyclic autoencoders. This paper discusses the phenomena in space and expands our knowledge of the universe by demonstrating how simple and rich deep learning models are. It is always expected that the fusion of recurrent autoencoders and CNNs will advance the opportunities of gravitational wave observatories and spread fresh data as researchers keep trying to find new methods to spot gravitational waves.

The convolutional neural network (CNN) architecture holds a strong power in the complex gravitational wave (GW) sensing environment, as demonstrated by Duraisamy *et al.* [10]. They applied their work to see how CNNSs perform various signal detections with continuous wave noise and highlight the specific challenges in recognizing waves whose nature and competitiveness are different due to their strength and pulse noise. That is why evaluating the potential of CNNs to discriminate these signals against the background should help to cope with this challenge. The CNN can also continuously detect the real gravitational waves. This demonstrates the efficiency and the accuracy of CNN structures in the challenging sensing environment in which the accuracy of detection is critical to the strengthening of our understanding of the world. Duraisamy *et al.* demonstrate the performance in the form of continuous gravitational wave signals.

CNNs' capacity to distinguish signals from noise effectively creates new opportunities for improving gravitational wave observers' sensitivity and dependability, which will aid in the detection of unfavorable cosmic events. Solving the crucial signal detection problem will help gravitational wave astronomy progress. This work offers crucial information that can direct the creation of more effective detection techniques and algorithms by concentrating on persistent GW signals and assessing CNN performance in challenging environments. The study highlights the accuracy and resilience of CNN architectures in hard-to-detect areas, marking a significant advancement in GW detection. The findings of this study show the development of more effective and dependable detectors, which will ultimately advance our comprehension of the world as researchers continue to look for novel ways to detect gravitational waves.

3.3 Gravitational Waves and Their Detection

In this section, there are four subsections. In Section 3.3.1, the detection of gravitational waves is described, giving the basic principles and difficulties relevant to the task. Section 3.3.2 presents advanced features and methods promoting the accuracy of detection. Section 3.3.3 provides a set of milestones in gravitational wave astronomy, which point out scientific breakthroughs. Section 3.3.4 is devoted to the future expectations, paying attention to the emerging streams and directions of research and advancing detection technologies.

Large things speed up and produce gravitational waves ripples in spacetime. The waves propagate out from their source, at the speed of light, carrying with them information about their origin and about gravity itself. They were anticipated by Albert Einstein's general theory of relativity in 1915.

Characteristics of Gravitational Waves: Gravitational waves are created by the interactions of massive celestial objects. Some main ones include:

a) Weaver Black Hole Merger: Gravitational waves emanating from a pair of black holes, orbiting each other, and bashing into each other. The amount of energy involved in all of this is just staggering [11].
b) Neutron Star Mergers: Analogous to merging black holes, when neutron stars spiral toward each other, they release gravitational waves, eventually fusing and emitting a similar kind of waves.
c) Supernovae: The deaths of massive stars can be very hard by providing the meanest figure of detection in terms of accretion caused by the explosion [12].
d) Early Universe: Gravitational waves may also be traces of the early universe, offering information about the circumstances immediately following the Big Bang. As these waves travel through spacetime, they compress and stretch it, but the effect is so small that it is very difficult to detect.

3.3.1 Detection of Gravitational Waves

Measuring the minute distortions that gravitational waves produce in space-time is necessary for their observation. Sensitive devices that can identify changes in dimensions smaller than a proton's diameter are needed for this [13]. An interferometer is the primary tool used for this. Laser interferometry is the basis for the operation of interferometers such as Virgo and LIGO. Here's a thorough examination of how they work:

a) Laser Source: A powerful laser beam is divided into two perpendicular beams using a beam splitter.
b) Perpendicular Arms: These beams travel down two long vacuum arms, typically several kilometers in length. At each arm's end, mirrors reflect the beams back to the beam splitter.
c) Interference Pattern: When the beams recombine at the beam splitter, they create an interference pattern. Under normal conditions (without gravitational waves), the beams are set up to interfere destructively, resulting in minimal light detected by a photodetector.

A gravitational wave compresses one arm and slightly expands the other as it travels through the detector, changing the interference pattern. A variation in the photodetector's light intensity is indicative of this change, which suggests the existence of a gravitational wave.

3.3.2 Advanced Features and Techniques

a) Fabry-Pérot Cavities: Enhance sensitivity by reflecting the laser beams multiple times within the arms, effectively increasing their length and thus the precision of the measurement.
b) Suspended Mirrors: The mirrors at the arm's end are suspended to isolate them from ground vibrations and other noise [14].
c) Elimination of Noise: This requires less ambient noise and enhances the sensitivity of the detectors, and there are several tactics that are used, which include temperature control and seismic isolation.

3.3.3 Milestones in GW Astronomy

Gravitational Wave Detection: The first direct detection of gravitational waves was announced by LIGO on February 11, 2016 [15]. The merger of the two black holes that are around 1.3 billion light-years apart was a historic event. Since then, LIGO has collaborated with Virgo to measure a series of gravitational wave events, including the mergers of neutron stars and black holes, and the merger of black holes and Neutron star mixed systems.

Scientific Implications: Gravitational wave astronomy provides a new perspective of the universe to scientists by allowing them to observe and explore the cosmic events, which otherwise remain unseen to the traditional electromagnetic telescope. Some important scientific discoveries have been made, namely:

a) Black Hole Properties: Accurate measurements of black holes' spins and masses.
b) Characteristics of Neutron Stars: The chaos of neutron star mergers imparts data on the composition of the matter in nuclear densities.
c) Cosmology: The merging of the neutron stars is a source of information on the properties of matter in nuclear densities.
d) A test of General Relativity: Trying out Einstein under hard conditions.

3.3.4 Future Prospects

Gravitational wave astronomy shows promise of a bright future as there are plans to upgrade existing instruments and build new ones like the Einstein Telescope in Europe and the LISA (Laser Interferometer Space Antenna) in space [16]. This will enhance the next understanding of the absorption qualities of the water that will allow us to travel further in space and understand the concept behind the cosmos completely [17].

They are detected with the help of a sophisticated instrument called an interferometer. Besides confirming the predictions of the relationship, the study of those waves represents a revolutionary means of accessing worldwide exploration that has never provided an insight into the greatest events and disasters in history.

3.4 Results and Discussion

This section is organized into 6 subsections. Section 3.4.1 presents the dataset used in the study, whereas Section 3.4.2 demonstrates the preprocessing procedure carried out to prepare the data. The described method is presented in Section 3.4.3, and Sections 3.4.3.1 and 3.4.3.2 describe the architecture design of the model and model compilation and training process, respectively. Evaluation and performance are given in Section 3.4.4, while Section 3.4.5 discusses the comparison of results to existing benchmarks, and Section 3.4.6 gives the final accuracy attained.

3.4.1 Dataset

The study relied on carefully collected data to classify the images of gravitational waves into 22 different groups, whose number was selected to capture the specifics and intricacy of the data on the Earth. Such images of gravitational waves are created with the advanced instruments and detectors that use state-of-the-art technology to discover invisible signals of cosmic events, improving signals and reducing noise, and developing models so as to analyse them efficiently. Figure 3.2 represents the classification of total images in the dataset.

```
... label
    Blip                    1821
    Koi_Fish                 706
    Low_Frequency_Burst      621
    Light_Modulation         512
    Power_Line               449
    Extremely_Loud           447
    Low_Frequency_Lines      447
    Scattered_Light          443
    Violin_Mode              412
    Scratchy                 337
    1080Lines                328
    Whistle                  299
    Helix                    279
    Repeating_Blips          263
    No_Glitch                150
    Tomte                    103
    None_of_the_Above         81
    1400Ripples               81
    Chirp                     60
    Air_Compressor            58
    Wandering_Line            42
    Paired_Doves              27
    Name: count, dtype: int64
```

As you can see, the most common type is 'Blip'. Here is what such an image looks like

Figure 3.2 Classification of total images in the dataset.

Moreover, such data contains various kinds of events of gravitational waves, in each of which a different name of a specific class is assigned, based on which they are classified and analyzed [1]. Other data is transformed by means of mechanisms such as rotation, measurement, and the information obtained with the various modifications of the gravitational wave image is amplified to ensure the possibility of clear and ubiquitous use of deep learning models.

The division of data also ensures the even distribution of classes across the subsets. We want to provide scientists, researchers, and agents with a better possibility of answering what the future of colliding waves is, and that is made possible by critically selecting and presenting the data in a sequential manner.

3.4.2 Preprocessing

Each of the gravitational wave images in the dataset has already been allocated one of 22 possible categories [18]. Such topics denote types of gravitational wave events or phenomena, such as the so-called Levels: Blip, Chirp, Low Frequency Burst, Koi Fish, etc. Figure 3.3 represents the most common blip image.

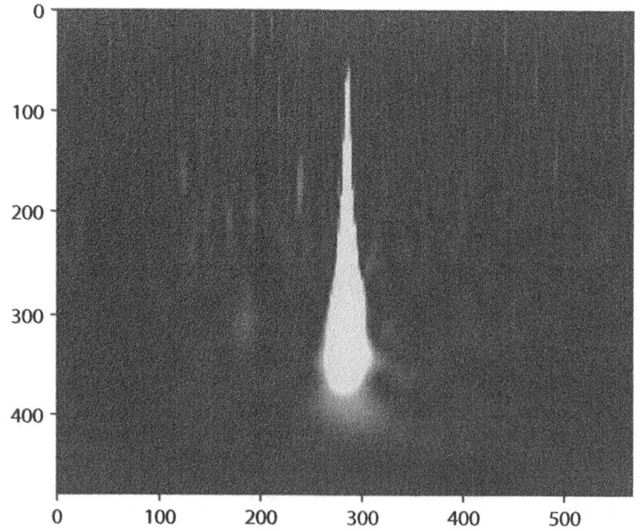

Figure 3.3 Most common blip image.

3.4.3 Proposed Approach

This analysis develops the gravity spy deep learning model through a CNN architecture to that effect: the formerly formal method of determining the type of gravitational wave images is structured to classify the latter into 22 distinct categories by means of the former. The procedure is explained in detail below:

3.4.3.1 Model Architecture Design

A specific architecture of CNN was developed to learn the images of gravitational waves more efficiently and classify them. Several layers consisting of the architecture were designed and arranged to prevent overfitting and feature highly relevant spatial features of input images.

3.4.3.2 Model Compilation and Training

The Adam optimizer and the categorical cross-entropy loss were used to compose the desired CNN model [18]. The dataset of Gravity Spy was then used to train the model. Training involved training the iterative process to refine the parameters of the model to maximize classification and reduce the loss function. Early stopping criteria were adopted to avert overfitting and create a favorable model convergence.

```
Epoch 1/40
32/32 [------------------------------] - 28s 547ms/step - Loss: 2.3082 - accuracy: 8.3745 - val_loss: 2.8955 - val_accuracy: 8.5342
Epoch 2/40
32/32 [------------------------------] - 17s 547ms/step - Loss: 1.4960 - accuracy: 8.6045 - val_loss: 1.2310 - val_accuracy: 8.7012
Epoch 3/40
32/32 [------------------------------] - 17s 553ms/step - Loss: 1.0407 - accuracy: 8.7461 - val_loss: 1.1953 - val_accuracy: 8.7140
Epoch 4/40
32/32 [------------------------------] - 17s 551ms/step - Loss: 8.0951 - accuracy: 8.7637 - val_loss: 8.8661 - val_accuracy: 8.7900
Epoch 5/40
32/32 [------------------------------] - 17s 550ms/step - Loss: 8.7591 - accuracy: 8.8115 - val_loss: 8.8537 - val_accuracy: 8.7959
Epoch 6/40
32/32 [------------------------------] - 17s 546ms/step - Loss: 8.6565 - accuracy: 8.8227 - val_loss: 8.6283 - val_accuracy: 8.8506
Epoch 7/40
32/32 [------------------------------] - 17s 550ms/step - Loss: 8.5050 - accuracy: 8.8564 - val_loss: 8.5440 - val_accuracy: 8.8594
Epoch 8/40
32/32 [------------------------------] - 18s 557ms/step - Loss: 8.5132 - accuracy: 8.8602 - val_loss: 8.5681 - val_accuracy: 8.8201
Epoch 9/40
32/32 [------------------------------] - 17s 552ms/step - Loss: 8.4355 - accuracy: 8.8877 - val_loss: 8.4144 - val_accuracy: 8.8994
Epoch 10/40
32/32 [------------------------------] - 17s 553ms/step - Loss: 8.3688 - accuracy: 8.8877 - val_loss: 8.4849 - val_accuracy: 8.8906
Epoch 11/40
32/32 [------------------------------] - 17s 549ms/step - Loss: 8.4610 - accuracy: 8.8799 - val_loss: 8.5148 - val_accuracy: 8.8496
Epoch 12/40
32/32 [------------------------------] - 17s 550ms/step - Loss: 8.3373 - accuracy: 8.8994 - val_loss: 8.3373 - val_accuracy: 8.8945
Epoch 13/40
---
Epoch 35/40
32/32 [------------------------------] - 17s 549ms/step - Loss: 8.1906 - accuracy: 8.9541 - val_loss: 8.2788 - val_accuracy: 8.9229
Epoch 36/40
32/32 [------------------------------] - 17s 552ms/step - Loss: 8.1003 - accuracy: 8.9463 - val_loss: 8.2818 - val_accuracy: 8.9160
```

Figure 3.4 Epochs during the model training.

3.4.4 Evaluation and Performance Analysis

To evaluate the CNN model, validation and test datasets were formed after training. Figure 3.4 shows the no.of Epochs during the model training. The evaluation measures, such as accuracy, loss, and the analysis of the confusion matrix, are applied in the determination of the performance of the model [19, 20]. The accuracy score was used to evaluate the results of classification by the model, and the confusion matrix unveiled its competence in distinguishing among different gravitational wave types.

3.4.5 Comparison and Validation

The work of the CNN model was critically evaluated, including verification against the known standards and rigorous comparison to those performed. Such a detailed analysis has been done (as shown in Table 3.1) to give a detailed analysis of the usefulness and generalizability of the model as applied to different datasets.

In such a vigorous assessment procedure, the potential and weaknesses of a model were well-considered, ensuring a good understanding of the performance territory.

Table 3.1 Table for comparison and validation.

Aspect	Description
Model evaluated	Convolutional neural network (CNN)
Evaluation approach	Critical evaluation, verification against known standards, and rigorous comparison with existing methods
Purpose of Evaluation	To assess the usefulness and generalizability across different datasets
Assessment focus	Identification of strengths and weaknesses; understanding performance boundaries
Accuracy achieved	**94.63%**
Key outcome	High resilience and ability to detect fine-grained patterns in complex data
Significance	Demonstrates strong detection capability for gravitational wave events after thorough validation

This accuracy rate was astonishingly high and resulted in 94.63% of detection of the occurrence of the event of gravitational waves after the process through which the established CNN architecture was subjected to these rigorous assessment practices. Such a remarkable achievement showed that the model was resilient and had the capacity to detect fine-grained patterns within complex datasets.

3.4.6 Accuracy

Accuracy is one of the key metrics that helps in evaluating the ability of the gravity spy deep learning model to correctly label the figure of gravitational waves as belonging to the correct category [21]. The accuracy rate in the model of this study was astounding, as it had 94.63% in detecting the gravitational waves. This accuracy rate depicts the model as an indication of the achieved level of accuracy, reflecting excellent precision and exactness in distinguishing among the distinctive realities of gravitational wave developments, and thereby confirming the model's reliability in capturing complex spacetime phenomena.

Interpretation of Accuracy:

a) Training Accuracy: This metric evaluates the performance of the training defined by the accuracy of the model when using the training dataset. The more the training accuracy, the better able the model is [22].
b) Validation Accuracy: This is a measure of how the model looks towards generalizing it to new data, or rather, the validation data [23]. It makes sure that this model is not overfitted to the training set and may generalize well to new samples. The model is able to generalize, and therefore, its validation accuracy was 94.63%.

Accuracy Improvement and Impact:
The supplied code also makes accuracy much better when it reaches 94.63 per cent on the validation set. Such enhanced precision can signify a number of things:

The CNN model has improved the precision in detecting the gravitational wave events and classifying them more precisely. This is critical in the proper sniffing of different types of gravitational wave signals that can make available significant information on astrophysical events. A higher accuracy rate minimizes the likelihood of false positives occurring with the model classifying the non-existent gravitational wave events as events that do exist.

This reduces the chances of false interpretation, besides enhancing the reliability of the detection system. More accurately, scientists will be able to dedicate more time and effort to the analysis of real gravitational wave signals.

This will ensure that time is only spent on productive data, resulting in more sensible astronomical findings. Overall, with the enhanced efficiency of the CNN model, the gravitational wave detection equipment becomes more reliable and effective, and we tend to understand the basic scientific processes better and add to the knowledge concerning the nature of the universe.

The first one is to import the needed libraries and set up the environment to receive a dataset. The next step is to download the dataset available on Kaggle and unzip it. Subsequently, the code establishes training, validating, and testing directories and imports useful libraries. Data generators are created with the ImageDataGenerator class of TensorFlow. It prepares and generates sets of image data to test, validate, and train.

The number of classes in the training data is determined, and after that, example images of each of the classes are visualized [24]. The Sequential model from Keras is used to build a custom CNN model that includes fully connected layers, activation functions, convolutional layers, max-pooling layers, and dropout layers.

The model compilation includes the appropriate optimizer, loss function, and assessment metrics [25]. The training and validation generators are used to train the CNN model, and early stopping is employed to prevent overfitting. Accuracy and loss plots are generated to illustrate the model's performance during training. To evaluate the model's classification performance, a confusion matrix is created. Predictions based on test data are made using the trained model, and [26]. The model's overall accuracy is computed.

3.5 Performance Evaluation

This section has four subsections. Accuracy and analysis of loss are displayed in Section 3.5.1 to assess the learning behavior of the model. In Section 3.5.2, the confusion matrix is given as an evaluation of classification in detail. Section 3.5.3 is the detailed discussion of the model performance using various measures of evaluation. Section 3.5.4 lays out the importance of the accuracy obtained, considering the story of gravitational wave detection.

The gravity spy deep learning model, which is based on convolutional neural networks (CNNs), performs exceptionally well in classifying gravitational wave images into 22 separate categories. Using a comprehensive dataset and advanced deep learning techniques, our model achieves an astonishing 94.63% accuracy rate.

3.5.1 Accuracy and Loss Analysis

After 40 epochs of training the model, we saw a consistent improvement in both validation and training accuracy, with the training accuracy peaking at 94.63% and the validation accuracy peaking at 91.60%. Figure 3.5 shows the loss observed by the proposed model.

This high level of accuracy suggests that the model learns to categorize gravitational wave images and generalizes well to new data, preventing overfitting. However, in our example, the near alignment of the training and validation accuracy curves indicates that the model is not overfitting and yet has high generalization capabilities.

The model's performance during training and validation across epochs is visualized using the accuracy and loss charts. The accuracy curves in these plots are rising while the loss curves are falling, which is a typical pattern in deep learning training. In particular, as training progresses, training accuracy rises steadily, indicating that the model is efficiently assimilating the training set. Confirming the model's outstanding generalization ability, the validation accuracy curve very closely tracks the training accuracy

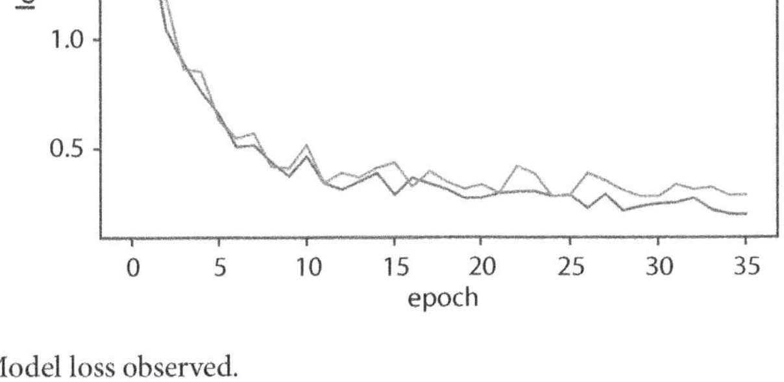

Figure 3.5 Model loss observed.

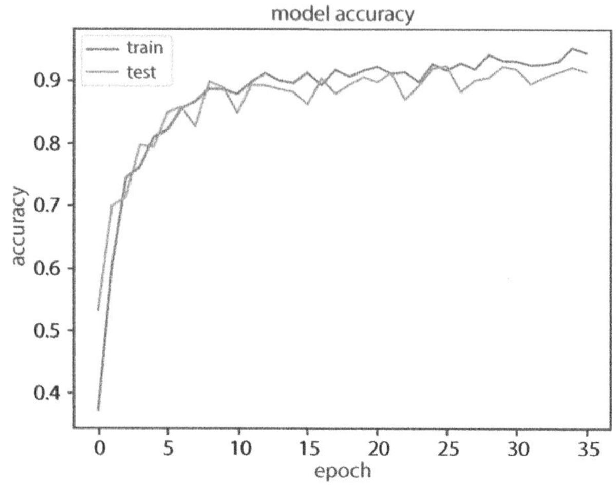

Figure 3.6 Model profit observed.

curve. This implies that improvements in training data performance of the model are practically carried over to validation data. Figure 3.6 shows the profit observed by the proposed model.

Furthermore, the loss curves for both training and validation data decrease with epochs. The constant decline in the training and validation loss indicates the growth in the ability of the model to diminish errors in predicting the outcome over time. It also means that the learning process is not changing too much and that the model is learning. One of the unique features of the VA curve is its proximity to the TA curve. This good fit is important in that it indicates that the model is not just learning the training set, but learning to apply a pattern in new, previously unseen data. The closeness of the training and validation accuracy indicates that there is a good fit, that is, the model has both suitable bias and variance to allow good generalization to new observations.

The validation loss curve can also be used to determine the performance of the model. In our case, the validation loss is also a decreasing one over epochs, which is positive. As the validation loss decreases, it will show that the model is learning not only about the training data to make the correct prediction but also about the data in the validation set, to make correct predictions. Judging on this ever-decreasing value of validation loss and correspondingly increasing value of validation accuracy, the model appears to be learning the underlying pattern in the data successfully and getting more precise in its predictions.

These outcomes mean that the model is properly trained with high learning abilities and good data generalization. The model is doing fine because the training and validation loss curves are consistently going down, the training and validation accuracy lines are very close to one another, and overall training accuracy is steadily going up. Also, the accuracy and loss curves in a model normally show an upward trend and a downward trend, respectively, which denotes successful training in deep learning. The effectiveness of the model architecture and the quality of the training process are shown by the fact that the model does not overfit and has remarkably high accuracy on the validation and training sets. In conclusion, the 40-epoch training process produced a model that performed very well on validation and had high training accuracy. The model is generalizing and training accurately, as seen in the similar trend of training and validation accuracy and the gradual dropping of losses in both datasets. These findings demonstrate the level of success that this model may have in classifying the images of gravitational waves and that it has the potential to be applied to models to make projections of new, untested data. Such good results are needed in real-life contexts where the ability to achieve successful generalizations is required to deliver accurate predictions. There is also a steady drop in the validation loss graph over epochs, which shows that the model can reduce the errors of prediction.

3.5.2 Class Correlation Matrix

Figure 3.7 represents a correlation (similarity) of classes, or how well related various categories are to one another. Unlike a confusion matrix, which reveals the actual occurrence of proper and erroneous predictions, the correlation matrix indicates how closely the predictions of each class are to each other by means of their feature representation [27]. The perfect self-correlations are reflected by the diagonal elements (in teal), since each class is always maximally similar to itself. The higher the diagonal values, the more the separability of that class, and off-diagonal values characterize any possible overlaps or similarities between classes. These off-diagonal areas give hints on the categories that might be similar to each other and thus present more difficulty in separating them, which leads to the model.

3.5.3 Analyzing Model Performance

The calculation of the correlation matrix should help in establishing interclass relationships that may influence model performance. Though the classifier can have a high overall accuracy, tables containing stronger correlations (those squares that are lighter) denote those regions where the model tends to mix things up, confusing one category with another [28]. As an example, two categories of sound or types of signals that are highly correlated with each other in training indicate that they have extensive overlap of features, and the classifier can fail to identify these data points correctly in the field.

This is an especially helpful tool in troubleshooting the classification pipeline weaknesses [29]. In the case of classes with high similarity, feature engineering can be used, as well as data augmentation or superior model architectures, such as transfer learning or ensembles. Correlation with such insights leads to such corrections as combining highly similar categories, rebalancing the data distribution, or the selection of features [30]. In short, although the diagonal elements validate high levels of self-class

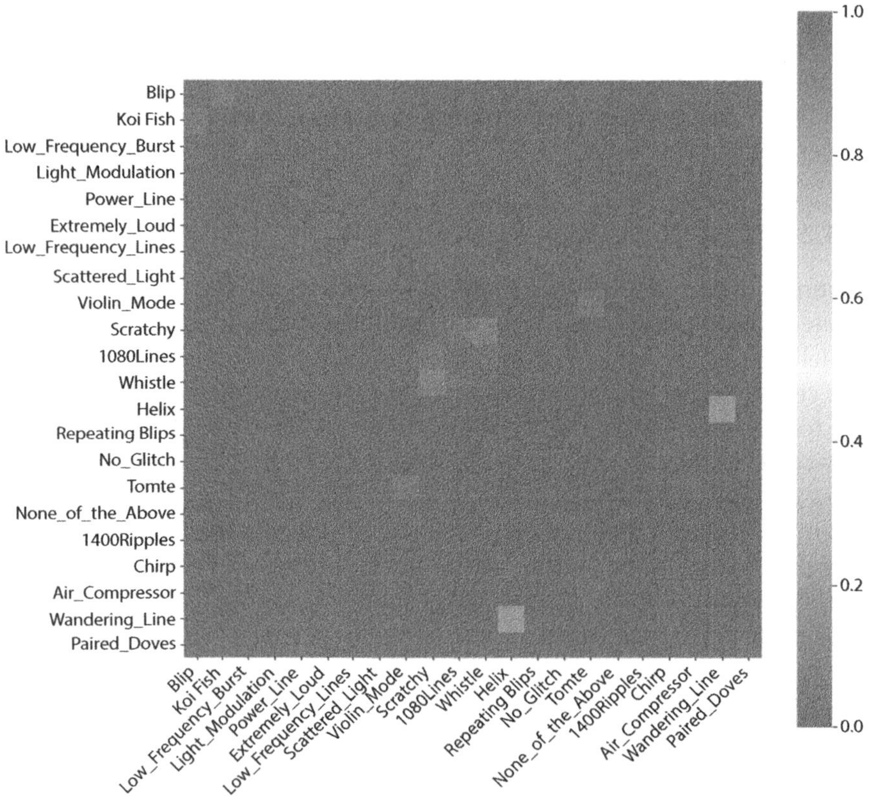

Figure 3.7 Correlation matrix.

identification, the off-diagonal correlations provide nuanced details of similarities that may be used to facilitate classifier robustness and accuracy [31]. The correlation matrix (Figure 3.7), therefore, helps to get more insight into the relatedness of the classes as shown in the confusion matrix.

3.5.4 Significance of Achieved Accuracy

It will produce the best accuracy of 94.63%, which will make a big difference in gravitational wave astronomy. Figure 3.8 shows the accuracy achieved by the proposed model. The importance of having a high level of accuracy in classifying gravitational wave signals is that scientists can successfully isolate and prioritize scientifically meaningful events. The possibility to conduct more specific follow-up observations and analysis is crucial since, in this way, it can be guaranteed that the most significant and possibly the most revolutionary things will be noticed as they should be. Proper classification of gravitational wave signals is important to the success of observational campaigns. The researchers have the freedom to concentrate on events that have the best chance of providing valid scientific findings since they are assured that their models will detect the signals in the most appropriate manner, hence using their resources effectively. This issue of setting up the priorities is exceptionally critical in areas where there is too much information, since the likelihood of rapidly and accurately locating some crucial events could result in a discovery.

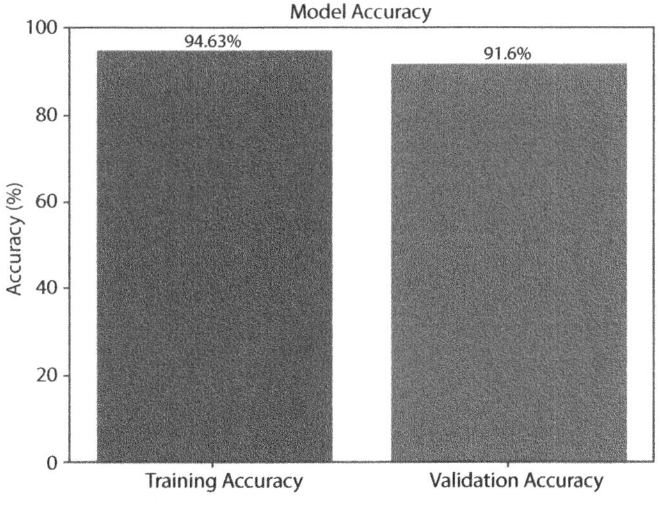

Figure 3.8 Accuracy achieved.

Also, the fact of the high level of precision of our model simplifies the process of data analysis to a great extent [32]. The observatories that detect gravitational waves, like LIGO and Virgo, produce masses of data, which should be processed and analyzed to identify and group or categorize signals. An accuracy of 94.63% is achieved in a model that can be used to process such large sets of data in a repeatable and scalable way. It will be required to ensure that observatories run smoothly at a stable speed, and they should not have any delays in generating or analyzing the incoming data without any bottlenecks. The effects of such a high-performance model go beyond processing existing data. The approach boosts pipeline reliability in data processing generally because it removes the blind spot of error in signal classification. The results of the model will be less uncertain and reproducible scientific research. According to the researchers, this will make them more confident in the results.

3.6 Conclusion

To tag about 22 gravitational wave image groups, we have developed a CNN gravity spy deep learning model. The model, based on a large dataset and the latest deep learning algorithms, gives a remarkable accuracy of 94.63% in differentiating between different types of gravitational wave signals. The fact that our model is so accurate shows that it can be used in gravitational wave astronomy for practical purposes. The discovery rate in our field will become higher due to the possibility of fast analysis of even more incredibly large data being gathered by gravitational wave observatories because the proposed model will perform a fine-grained classification of gravitational wave events. In general, by demonstrating the feasibility and effectiveness of the deep learning approach to signal classification, the present work paves the way for breakthroughs in gravitational wave astronomy, offering new opportunities for accurate detection, improved interpretation, and deeper insights into the dynamics of spacetime. To obtain a better insight into the gravitational wave phenomenon and obtain new knowledge about the dynamics of the universe, we anticipate our model to be further optimized and refined, as well as be incorporated into existing data analysis structures.

AI disclosure statement: The author confirms that no artificial intelligence (AI)-generated content or AI-assisted writing tools were used in the preparation of this chapter (including summaries and the abstract). All text, analysis, and conclusions are the result of the author's original work.

References

1. Anwar, R.W., Abrar, M., Ullah, F., Transfer learning in brain tumor classification: Challenges, opportunities, and future prospects, in: *2023 14th International Conference on Information and Communication Technology Convergence (ICTC)*, IEEE, pp. 24–29, 2023.
2. Arya, A.D., Verma, S.S., Chakarabarti, P., Chakrabarti, T., Elngar, A.A., Kamali, A.-M., Nami, M., A systematic review on machine learning and deep learning techniques in the effective diagnosis of Alzheimer's disease. *Brain Inf.*, 10, 1, 17, 2023.
3. Badaut, J., Hippauf, L., Malinconi, M., Noarbe, B.P., Obenaus, A., Dubois, C.J., Endocannabinoid-mediated rescue of somatosensory cortex activity, plasticity and related behaviors following an early in life concussion, bioRxiv, 2024–01, 2024.
4. Benedetto, Gissi, F., Ciaparrone, G., Troiano, L., AI in gravitational wave analysis: An overview. *Appl. Sci.*, 13, 17, 9886, 2023.
5. Boyd, M., Resolving the extra dimensions for gravity, Authorea Preprints, 2024.
6. Wang, H., Wu, S., Cao, Z., Liu, X., Zhu, J.-Y., Gravitational-wave signal recognition of LIGO data by deep learning. *Phys. Rev. D*, 101(10), 104003, 2020, https://doi.org/10.1103/PhysRevD.101.104003.
7. Krastev, P.G., Real-Time Detection of Gravitational Waves Using Deep Learning. *Phys. Lett. B*, 803, 135330, Mar. 2020, doi: 10.1016/j.physletb.2020.135330.
8. Harry, G.M. and for the LIGO Scientific Collaboration, Advanced LIGO: The Next Generation of Gravitational Wave Detectors. *Classical Quantum Gravity*, 27, 8, 084006, Apr. 2010, doi: 10.1088/0264-9381/27/8/084006.
9. Moreno, A., Rodriguez, S., Gomez, M., Torres, L., Iterative Autoencoders for Generalized Gravitational Wave Detection. *IEEE Access*, 10, 89562–89573, 2022, doi: 10.1109/ACCESS.2022.3208347.
10. Duraisamy, P., Natarajan, Y., Niranjani, V., Parvathy, K., Optimized detection of continuous gravitational-wave signals using convolutional neural network, in: *2023 3rd International Conference on Artificial Intelligence and Signal Processing (AISP)*, pp. 1–5, 2023.
11. Kumar, P., Javeed, D., Kumar, R., Islam, A.K.M.N., Blockchain and explainable AI for enhanced decision making in cyber threat detection. *Softw.: Pract. Exper.*, 2024.
12. O'Shea, E.D., Gravitational waveform modelling with machine learning and for eccentric binary systems, PhD thesis, Cornell University, 2021.
13. Patole, P., Sarawate, M., Joshi, K., A communication translator interface for sign language interpretation. *Int. J. Res. Appl. Sci. Eng. Technol.*, 11, 4546–4558, 2023.

14. Saleem, M., Gunny, A., Chou, C.-J., Yang, L.-C., Yeh, S.-W., Chen, A.H.Y., Magee, R., Benoit, W., Nguyen, T., Fan, P., *et al.*, Demonstration of machine learning-assisted real-time noise regression in gravitational wave detectors, arXiv preprint arXiv:2306.11366, 2023.
15. Vajente, G., Huang, Y., Isi, M., Driggers, J.C., Kissel, J.S., Szczepańczyk, M.J., Vitale, S., Machine-learning nonstationary noise out of gravitational-wave detectors. *Phys. Rev. D*, 101, 4, 042003, 2020.
16. LIGO Scientific Collaboration and Virgo Collaboration. Observation of gravitational waves from a binary black hole merger. *Phys. Rev. Lett.*, 116, 6, 061102, 2016. https://doi.org/10.1103/PhysRevLett.116.061102.
17. Aguiar, O.D., Ain, A., Ajith, P., Alemic, A., Allen, B., Zuraw, S., Zweizig, J., Search for gravitational wave ringdowns from perturbed intermediate mass black holes in LIGO-Virgo data from 2005–2010. *Phys. Rev. D*, 89, 102006, 2014.
18. Abbott, B.P., Abbott, R., Abbott, T.D., Abernathy, M.R., Acernese, F., Ackley, K., Adams, C., Adams, T., Addesso, M.E., Zuraw, S.E., Zweizig, J., Binary black hole mergers in the first advanced LIGO observing run. *Phys. Rev. X*, 6, 041015, 2016.
19. Astone, P., Cerdá-Durán, P., Di Palma, I., Drago, M., Muciaccia, F., Palomba, C., Ricci, F., New method to observe gravitational waves emitted by core collapse supernovae. *Phys. Rev. D*, 98, 122002, 2018.
20. Baker, P.T., Caudill, S., Hodge, K.A., Talukder, D., Capano, C., Cornish, N.J., Multivariate classification with random forests for gravitational wave searches of black hole binary coalescence. *Phys. Rev. D*, 91, 062004, 2015.
21. Dou, X.-L., Kuang, X.-Y., Xia, X.-X., Ju, M., Exploration of the structural and optical properties of a red-emitting phosphor. *Chin. Phys. B*, 28, 1, 017107, 2019.
22. Gebhard, T.D., Kilbertus, N., Harry, I., Schölkopf, B., Convolutional neural networks: A magic bullet for gravitational-wave detection. *Phys. Rev. D*, 100, 063015, 2019.
23. Harry, G.M., for the LIGO Scientific Collaboration, Advanced LIGO: The next generation of gravitational wave detectors. *Classical Quantum Gravity*, 27, 8, 084006, 2010.
24. Harry, I., Privitera, S., Bohé, A., Buonanno, A., Searching for gravitational waves from compact binaries with precessing spins. *Phys. Rev. D*, 94, 024012, 2016.
25. He, K., Zhang, X., Ren, S., Sun, J., Deep residual learning for image recognition, in: *2016 IEEE Conference on Computer Vision and Pattern Recognition (CVPR)*, pp. 770–778, 2016.
26. Kaur, I. and Ali, A., An in-depth exploration of machine learning algorithms and performance evaluation approaches for personalized diabetes prediction, in: *2024 International Conference on Emerging Innovations and Advanced Computing (INNOCOMP)*, Sonipat, India, IEEE, pp. 532–538, 2024, https://doi.org/10.1109/INNOCOMP63224.2024.00093.

27. Kaur, I. and Ali, A., A Complete Study on Machine Learning Algorithms for Medical Data Analysis, in: *Fog Computing for Intelligent Cloud IoT Systems*, C. Banerjee, A. Ghosh, R. Chakraborty, A.A. Elngar (Eds.), Wiley Online Books, 2024, https://doi.org/10.1002/9781394175345.ch7.
28. Kaur, I. and Ali, A., Unveiling the power of prediction: A comprehensive guide to learning techniques, from data preparation to model interpretability for early prediction of diabetes and effective management, Taylor & Francis, 2025, https://www.taylorfrancis.com/chapters/edit/10.1201/9781003592969-1/unveiling-power-prediction-inderdeep-kaur-aleem-ali.
29. Sehgal, D., Kaur, I., Sharma, V., Gautam, B., Singh, A., Kumar, N., AI-Driven Early Diabetes Prediction, in: *2024 IEEE 3rd World Conference on Applied Intelligence and Computing (AIC)*, Gwalior, India, pp. 40–48, 2024, doi: 10.1109/AIC61668.2024.10730970.
30. Haq, I.U., Rather, A.H., Rufai, S.Z., Shah, A., Sheetal, Khanday, A.M.U.D., Transparency in Disease Diagnosis: Leveraging Interpretable Machine Learning in Healthcare, in: *Explainable Artificial Intelligence in the Healthcare Industry*, pp. 105–130, Elsevier, 2025.
31. Haq, I.U. and Khanday, A.M.U.D., Exploring the Role of Explainable AI in Women's Health: Challenges and Solutions, in: *Explainable Artificial Intelligence in the Healthcare Industry*, pp. 283–306, Elsevier, 2025.
32. Kaur, I. and Ali, A., WoS Driven Bibliometric Analysis of Diabetes Mellitus Prediction Using Machine Learning and Deep Learning, in: *2025 4th OPJU International Technology Conference (OTCON) on Smart Computing for Innovation and Advancement in Industry 5.0*, Raigarh, India, pp. 1–6, 2025, doi: 10.1109/OTCON65728.2025.11070435.

4

Predictive Health Mate: An Explainable AI for Disease Prognosis and Prevention on Android Device

Abhishek Roushan, Gurmeet Kaur, Inderdeep Kaur*, Vatsala Singh, Harsh Yadav and Yash Srivastava

Department of Computer Science & Engineering, Chandigarh University, Mohali, Punjab, India

Abstract

The incorporation of machine learning algorithms into Android apps in recent years has transformed the healthcare industry, as it has allowed predicting diseases and preventing them early and with high precision. The present paper provides the idea of a machine learning application in predicting diseases among Android applications in a detailed manner. We discuss the different steps involved in the creation and implementation of these applications, including data collection, pre-processing, feature extraction, model training, evaluation, prediction, and continuous learning. Also, we comment on the challenges and opportunities related to adopting machine learning algorithms in mobile health applications that comprise data privacy, security, model interpretability, and scalability. *Via* a critical review of the literature and case studies, we point out the usefulness of machine learning-based disease prediction models in improving patient outcomes, elevating patient engagement, and providing proactive management of healthcare. Moreover, we pinpoint research opportunities and future perspectives, including federated learning, explainable AI, and multimodal data fusion, to overcome the existing constraints and likely expand the scope of the realm of disease prediction in Android applications. On the whole, the paper can be included in the list of materials that can be used by researchers, developers, and healthcare experts in order to utilize the power of machine learning to predict diseases using mobile health applications.

**Corresponding author*: inderdeep.sgtb@gmail.com

Rajdeep Chakraborty, Aleem Ali, Amit Paul, Nawaf R. Alharbe and S. Balamurugan (eds.) Causal Artificial Intelligence: Fundamentals and Applications, (73–98) © 2026 Scrivener Publishing LLC

***Keywords*:** Machine learning, GNN, XAI, LSTM, SHAP

4.1 Introduction

The machine learning techniques have been actively used in the healthcare field to predict disease, diagnose it, and treat it. The techniques are applicable to large and complex medical records to identify hidden patterns, correlations, and risk factors relative to various conditions [1]. Predicting the disease incidence will enable the health workers to come up with preventive measures plans based on a given patient, with the assistance of predictive models. It is a preventive measure that is used to aid in early diagnosis, in addition to cost savings of treatment and survival rate. This has led to the emergence of machine learning as one of the disruptive trends in the healthcare sector that can guide the application of data in decision-making and the enhancement of patient care outcomes. Machine learning algorithms have been proven to be exceptionally promising in disease prediction since they can be applied to analyze patient data and identify the likelihood of being exposed to particular medical issues [2]. Such models can process structured (e.g., lab results, demographic details) and unstructured data (e.g., clinical notes, imaging). By correctly defining high-risk individuals, healthcare practitioners can provide interventions and individual treatment plans on schedule. In addition, continuous monitoring of health and contact with patients with the assistance of machine learning can allow people to become more active in health management and take informed lifestyle choices. The book chapter establishes a comprehensive overview of the role of machine learning in the prediction of diseases in Android-based healthcare applications. It talks about the major stages in the development, which include preprocessing of information, model selection, integration, and deployment in mobile environments [3]. In addition, the chapter covers the problems associated with mobile health systems, such as privacy of data, limited computational resources, and the ability to interpret the model. The findings of the deeper investigation of the recent literature and case studies of interest in the context of the current paper allow the researcher to admit the augmented relevance of machine learning models in enhancing the efficiency, accessibility, and personalization of healthcare services.

Furthermore, the chapter shows the prospect of introducing the most recent technologies to mobile health applications like graph neural networks (GNN) and explainable artificial intelligence (XAI). GNNs demonstrate particularly positive outcomes in the description of complex relationships among patient features, and XAI provides a greater degree of transparency to the model and provides interpretable predictions [4]. In this chapter, a mobile app is presented that is based on Android and utilizes the technologies to deliver personal health insights based on the medical history and lifestyle of the users. GNN and XAI increase predictive accuracy and also allow users to discover contributing factors to their health [5]. The proposed application architecture and the performance analysis can also reflect how the new ways of machine learning can change an existing model of healthcare delivery and transform it into a smarter, more accessible, and patient-centered system. Interpretability and predictive modeling make the system correct and reliable, a fact that should be considered to implement the system in the actual medical world [6]. Lastly, the research will be able to contribute to the current body of knowledge regarding AI-based healthcare and form a foundation for developing new disease prediction systems that are transparent, efficient, and effective in the future.

4.2 Literature Review

There are a few studies carried out in this field, and different machine-learning algorithms have been applied to anticipate sicknesses. Nevertheless, classical machine learning models like logistic regression, decision trees, random forests, etc., are limited in their capacity to handle complex data formats, e.g., graphs. Graph neural networks (GNNs) come in here and have proven to be much more effective with respect to graph-related tasks [7].

Besides GNN, there is another technology that should be mentioned, explainable artificial intelligence (XAI), which has also become popular over the past few years [8]. XAI is concerned with the creation of machine learning models that would allow clear and comprehensible outcomes to the user [9]. It may be particularly helpful in the medical field, where patients should be made aware of the contributing factors that led to their health conditions [10].

A number of studies have examined the application of GNN and XAI in healthcare. The paper by Kipf and Welling introduced a Graph Convolutional Network (GCN) model as the backbone of semi-supervised classification of graph-related data [11]. They demonstrated that a two-layer GCN with simple node features and graph connectivity demonstrates high levels of performance on citation and knowledge-graph benchmarks, and scales linearly with the number of edges, making GNNs now practical in most downstream tasks with relationships between nodes (e.g., between patients and diagnoses and treatments) becoming important. The major weakness of the paper is that relatively small citation/benchmark graphs had been experimented with; more research was required to test scalability and robustness on noisy and heterogeneous clinical EHR graphs.

Lipton wrote about the mythos of model interpretability and classified interpretability goals [12]. Their evaluation is broadly referenced in the literature on healthcare ML since it explains why black-box models (as well as deep GNNs) require mechanisms of careful explanation in clinical conditions. One of the lessons is that interpretability is multi-dimensional in nature—technical explainers (feature attributions, attention maps) are not always the answer to clinically required transparency or lawful explainability. Limit: conceptual and not an empirical study—it draws outlines of what should be done, but not a turnkey approach to clinical XAI.

Tang *et al.* suggested a multimodal spatiotemporal GNN (MM-STGNN) to forecast 30-day readmission in the hospital using a patient graph by incorporating both structured EHR fields and temporal signals [13]. The model outperformed the traditional feature-based baselines of predicting readmissions because the model explicitly models patient and event time dynamics and relationality. Weaknesses are that it depends on curated time series (not all hospitals have timestamps that are consistently available), and its results might be sensitive to the choice of graph construction (its definition of edges can have a significant impact).

Boll *et al.* presented the results of a systematic review of graph neural networks in clinical risk prediction with the use of electronic health records (EHRs) [14]. Their summary of the state of GNNs in patient relationships (co-morbidities, shared procedures) showed that they tend to perform better than flat tabular models on cohort-based problems (mortality, readmission). The review mentions the common restrictions: heterogeneity of EHRs, a variety of approaches to graph construction, and deficient external validation across hospitals.

The article by Linardatos *et al.* facilitated a review and taxonomy of XAI methods of the ML models [15]. They contrasted model-agnostic explainers (SHAP, LIME), inherent interpretability (simple trees, attention), and global and local explanation, and assessed their relevance to high-stakes settings, such as healthcare. Their production makes trade-offs understandable: lots of *post-hoc* explainers give convincing reasons that can fail to keep up with small changes of inputs into them, a crucial drawback when clinicians use explanations to make decisions.

Kumar *et al.* outlined an end-to-end Android application, where users input (symptoms, demographics) and pretrained models (in their solution logistic regression) are deployed in Firebase to predict COVID-19, heart disease, and diabetes risk in real time [16]. The article shows a demonstration of practice with mobile implementation and integration with cloud inferences, yet the article reports insufficient performance measures (some of the accuracy values are not available) and uses classical models; therefore, it does not test modern deep or graph models or even offer widespread medical validation.

Moreno-Sánchez *et al.* examined the advances in heart-failure survival prediction and underscored interpretable models and survival analysis [17]. They combined the ML algorithms with the explainability analyses to create models that can be checked by clinicians, and they claim that discrimination gains, but calibration and explainability should be assessed simultaneously. Limitations: a fraction of model gains were particular to the dataset and must be externally validated; also, explainers must be clinically tested to be based on medically significant aspects.

Visco *et al.* designed an explainable predictive model of worsening heart conditions that explained the features of using both ML risk models and *post-hoc* explainability to focus on contributing features in individual patients [18]. Their empirical findings demonstrate that they not only have better clinician trust in pilot assessment but also note that some explanations were too technical to be understood by non-expert patients, and some feature importance differed in different subpopulations (which is problematic in terms of fairness). This highlights the fact that XAI will have to be audience-specific (clinicians vs. patients).

Pharmacat: The open-source Android + web healthcare application Pharmacat performs symptom analysis using ML interpreting and proposing a list of likely illnesses, providing such helpful features as chat and booking a doctor appointment [19]. Pharmacat is useful as a development baseline, demonstrating the ability of a combination of symptom-based ML and product features, but again, it is community work, not peer-reviewed research; thus, its predictive capabilities, clinical validation, and regulatory compliance are not reported in the literature. This points to the insufficiency between prototype apps and tested clinical tools. It is an open-source healthcare app that uses the power of machine learning to diagnose diseases based on symptoms. It has a large number of features, such as live chat with medical professionals, appointment booking, medication recommendations, and contact with specialists. The application is aimed at reducing the workload of hospitals and doctors by detecting frequent diseases and helping to schedule online appointments. The Pharmacat project is designed to serve as a basis for a complete healthcare service, created with the assistance of medical workers.

Android Disease prediction and medical prescription application: This is a project that provides various healthcare services, such as disease prediction, identification of hospitals, ordering medicines, identification of the nearest medical shops, vitamins/supplements, and feedback on the ordered medicines [20]. It will be particularly beneficial during emergencies when the patient is distant from the hospital, and a doctor is not available in that area. By giving out their symptoms, the patient can easily diagnose the disease they are possibly infected with, and the application can produce the correct diagnosis. The Android application for the disease prediction and medical prescription project does not refer to the accuracy of the disease prediction algorithm. Android application disease prediction based on Machine Learning: The app is aimed at analyzing the symptoms entered by the user and giving the most probable disease result. It not only presents information regarding the predicted disease but also presents the measures to be undertaken by users who have a given predicted disease [20]. Naive Bayes Classifier is used to undertake the analysis.

The Naive Bayes classifier, as utilized in the disease prediction Android application using machine learning, might not be the best disease prediction algorithm.

A number of groups have used GNNs to predict readmission outcomes and others on MIMIC/MIMIC-IV EHRs, demonstrating state-of-the-art performance in terms of patient-event and temporal information on patient-event graphs. All these studies promise, but all require further robust external validation, explainability integration (XAI) to make use of it in clinical practice, and consideration of data shift when transferring models between hospitals.

Author(s)	Year	Technique used	Key results (summary)	Main limitations
Kipf *et al.*	2016	Graph convolutional network (GCN)	Strong semi-supervised node classification on citation/ knowledge graphs; established GCN as practical for graph tasks.	Benchmarks were small and non-clinical; needs evaluation on noisy/ heterogeneous EHR graphs.
Lipton (Z.C.)	2016	Conceptual XAI analysis	Clarified interpretability taxonomy (transparency vs. *post-hoc*); influenced healthcare XAI discourse.	Conceptual — not an empirical clinical solution; does not provide operational explainers.
Tang *et al.*	2023	Multimodal spatiotemporal GNN (MM-STGNN)	Improved 30-day readmission prediction vs. feature baselines by modelling temporal + graph signals.	Requires well-timestamped EHRs; results are sensitive to graph construction choices.
Boll *et al.*	2024	Systematic review of GNNs for EHR risk prediction	Found GNNs frequently outperform tabular models for relational clinical tasks.	Heterogeneity in methods; inconsistent external validation across sites.

(*Continued*)

(*Continued*)

Author(s)	Year	Technique used	Key results (summary)	Main limitations
Linardatos *et al.*	2020	XAI methods review (SHAP, LIME, intrinsic models)	Taxonomy of explainers; discussion of local vs. global explanations and pros/cons for healthcare.	Stability and fidelity of *post-hoc* explainers remain concerns for clinical adoption.
Kumar *et al.*	2021	Mobile app + logistic regression (cloud model)	Demonstrated Android app pipeline for predicting COVID/heart/diabetes risk using cloud-hosted pretrained model.	Missing/limited accuracy reporting; classical models only; limited clinical validation.
Pharmacat (rajlm10)	2020	Symptom-based ML (open-source Android + web)	Prototype symptom prediction + telehealth features; good developer baseline for app integration.	Lacks peer-reviewed performance metrics, clinical validation, regulatory/privacy documentation.
Moreno-Sánchez *et al.*	2023	ML + explainability for heart-failure survival	Improved discrimination; argued for paired evaluation of calibration + explainability.	Dataset-specific gains; needs external validation; explainers require clinical testing.

(*Continued*)

(*Continued*)

Author(s)	Year	Technique used	Key results (summary)	Main limitations
Visco *et al.*	2024	Explainable ML for worsening heart outcomes	Pilot showed increased clinician trust when explanations were provided.	Explanations sometimes too technical; fairness/ subpopulation variability observed.
Multiple groups	2024–2025	GNNs on MIMIC/ MIMIC-IV + XAI hybrids	Many report SOTA gains on readmission/ mortality tasks when modelling patient graphs and temporality.	Often single-center data, varying graph heuristics, and lacking standardized XAI evaluation.

4.3 Model Architecture

4.3.1 Graph Neural Networks (GNNs)

These are considered one of the most recent advancements in today's machine learning. They are a special kind of neural network that operates on graph-structured data that is fundamentally different from the vectors or matrices that are operated on by traditional neural networks, as shown in Figure 4.1. In traditional data structures, data are modeled as tabular or in a grid format, in which individual features are modeled as entities, and the relationship between features is not formally encoded [21]. Nevertheless, lots of real-world data, especially in areas like healthcare, social networks, chemical modeling, and biology, are inherently in the form of graphs. These datasets consist of entities, which are connected with each other in complicated forms, and the connections between entities are as significant as the entities themselves. In data with a graph structure, the elementary units are nodes (also known as vertices) and

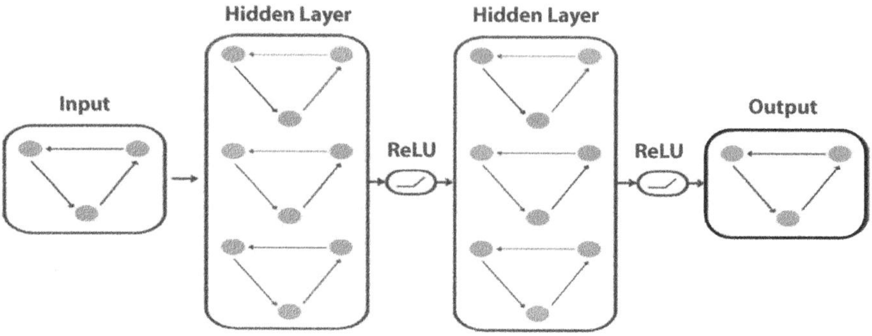

Figure 4.1 GNN architecture [11].

edges. The entities are represented as nodes and can be an individual in the social network, an atom in a molecular structure, or a patient in a healthcare dataset. The relations or the interaction between these nodes is defined by the edges. The nature of these relationships can be very diverse based on the domain, as in a social network, the edges can be a friendship or a communication; in biology, the edges may be a chemical bond or a protein-protein interaction; and in the healthcare sector, the edges may be a symptom-symptom correlation, a diagnosis-diagnosis correlation, or a patient-patient similarity [22]. Such relational information has a vital meaning, and the capacity of GNNs explicitly to represent it is one of the main strengths of this class of AI.

The fundamental idea of GNNs is to create node representations to reflect the features of a specific node as well as the graph structure around the node. In these representations, the local information, which includes properties of the node and of its immediate neighbors, is encoded, as well as global information created by the larger graph structure. GNN learning entails the information flowing iteratively on the graph. At every step, a node obtains the information received by its network neighbors and processes this information to make updates to its internal state. This is repeated with a number of layers, and the network is able to progressively add more information about the graph.

As an illustration, in a healthcare scenario, the nodes in the graph could be patients, symptoms, diseases, and results of lab tests. Both sides between these nodes are the relationships, including the frequency of a certain symptom in patients with a specific disease or the correlation between lab test results and diagnosis [23]. An applied GNN to such a graph may learn complicated patterns that relate symptoms and test outcomes to diseases;

nonetheless, these patterns may be indirect or include many steps in the graph. This feature, to apply both direct and indirect relationships, provides a great advantage over other traditional machine learning approaches, which tend to process features at a time and are not intrinsically structured to handle this type of relationship complexity.

The flexibility of GNNs has been identified as one of its main strengths. They are able to work with large and small graphs with any structure without necessarily restructuring the data. The conventional models are often rigid in terms of the size of inputs and cannot adapt to new structures. Conversely, GNNs are adaptive in nature, i.e., they can be applied to graphs of varying sizes (number of nodes and connections) without deterioration. They are used in dynamic datasets where new data points or relationships are being added continuously, e.g., real-time patient monitoring systems, knowledge graphs being built, or adaptive recommendation systems.

The other major strength of GNNs is that they are able to generalize across graphs. After being trained, a GNN may be used on new, unseen graphs with a similar structure, without having to be retrained. It is especially useful in healthcare and biology, where models must be able to learn new biological data with different patient populations or new biological data. Consider the case of a GNN that has been trained on a set of patients in one hospital and used to predict the outcomes of their diseases in another hospital, in case the underlying relational patterns are comparable.

GNNs have already shown excellent results in numerous fields. They are applied in social networks in friend recommendation, community detection, and link prediction. GNNs are now used in chemistry and biology as a tool in drug discovery and molecular modeling, to predict molecular properties, discover potential drug candidates, and model protein structures. GNNs are becoming actively used in the field of healthcare to predict a disease, analyze patient similarity, and create an individual treatment plan. As a case in point, a GNN can be used to estimate the probability of an individual developing a particular disease in the future and do so with a high level of accuracy by modeling a health profile of a patient as a node, and linking it to other nodes that represent symptoms, lab results, and past diagnoses.

The performance of GNNs is not the only reason why they have become a matter of interest, due to the fact that they can reveal the interpretability of data relationships. Although deep learning models have been criticized as black boxes, GNNs provide a certain level of transparency through the possibility of researchers inspecting the relationships between learned node embeddings and edges. The book chapter provides a general framework for the use of machine learning in predicting diseases in Android-based healthcare apps. It discusses the significant phases in the development, which comprise preprocessing of information, model selection, integration, and implementation into the mobile environment [3]. Besides this, the chapter addresses the issues that are related to the mobile health systems, like data privacy, inadequate computational capabilities, and the capability to understand the model. The results of the further analysis of the recent literature and case studies of interest in the framework of the present paper enable the researcher to acknowledge the increased relevance of the machine learning models in terms of improving the efficiency, accessibility, and individualization of healthcare services.

Moreover, the chapter demonstrates the possibility of bringing the newest technologies to the mobile health applications, such as graph neural networks (GNN) and explainable artificial intelligence (XAI). GNNs show very promising results when it comes to describing complex relations among characteristics of patients, and XAI offers a higher level of clarity to the model and even offers understandable predictions [24]. The researcher in this paper proposes a mobile application, which is anchored on Android and uses the technologies to provide personal health insights on the basis of the medical history and lifestyle of the users. GNN and XAI are more accurate predictors, and users can also learn the factors of their health. The offered application architecture and the performance analysis can also indicate how the new forms of machine learning can transform an already existing model of healthcare delivery and convert it into a smarter, more accessible, and patient-centered system. The system is correct and predictable, a fact that should be taken into consideration to introduce the system into the real medical world. Finally, the study will have an opportunity to become a part of the existing knowledge in AI-based healthcare and establish a base for creating new disease prediction models that will be transparent, efficient, and effective in the future.

In the past few years, it has been shown that GNNs are capable of outperforming classic machine learning algorithms in a range of tasks that have a graph-like character in the domains of healthcare. They especially serve well in situations where interrelations between variables are as important as the variables themselves. As graph-based data representations continue to gain popularity in healthcare systems, the GNNs will exert an even greater impact on the future of medical AI. Due to the individualized risk of illnesses in the exploration of drug spans and tracking of the well-being of the population, the use of GNNs is continually increasing.

In summary, graph neural networks can be regarded as a powerful advance in machine learning. Having the very potential to model complex relationships, problem-adaptive properties in different graph structures, and their generalization over data sets, they are in a unique position to undertake such tasks that need relational data. GNNs, as further integrated into healthcare, will become an intrinsic aspect of a modern disease prediction system to enable the creation of smarter, more understandable, and more precise healthcare solutions.

4.3.2 A Long-Short Term Memory Augmented LSTM

LSTM Framework is an advanced machine-learning model that offers an opportunity to change the paradigm of disease prediction in Android apps. With the assistance of an LSTM neural network with attention mechanisms, this structure will be capable of identifying patterns and correlations between patient data and the presence of diseases, as shown in Figure 4.2.

In order to use this framework, medical workers can collect patient data and enter it into the model.

The Augmented Long Short-Term Memory (LSTM) Framework is a new type of machine-learning technology that has remarkable opportunities for revolutionizing the manner in which diseases are predicted, especially

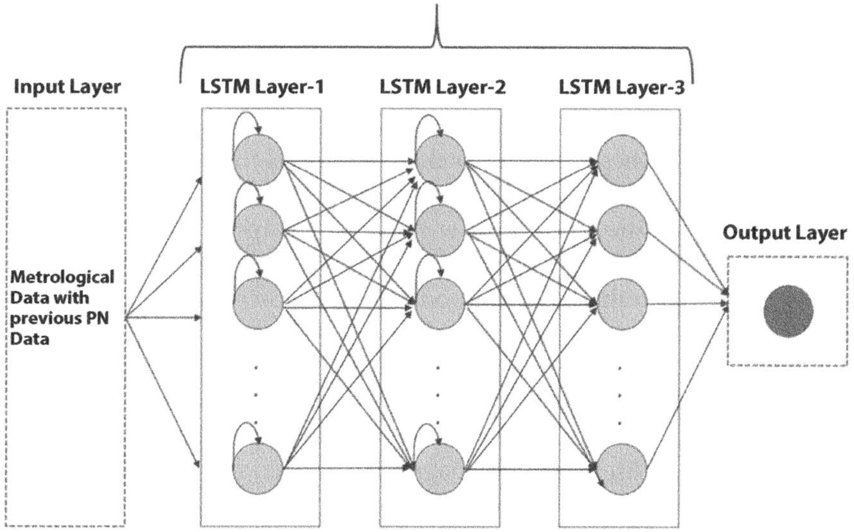

Figure 4.2 LSTM architecture [12].

in Android-based health programs [25]. The type of recurrent neural network (RNN) that is capable of processing and analyzing sequential data is the LSTM network, which stores the information over time. The latter can be particularly handy in the healthcare sector, where the data about patients is often time-sensitive and can include sequential behavior, e.g., vital signs measured in days, weeks, or months, or chronological order of symptoms and treatments. This framework can identify subtle time trends and significant features of the patient data more effectively and predict the patient with a higher degree of accuracy by combining LSTM networks with attention mechanisms.

A selective attention mechanism is attained by integrating the attention mechanisms in the LSTM structure that is adopted to give predictions on the most relevant portions of the input sequence [26]. Attention allows the network to give weighted averages of the different inputs; this is according to their relevance to the task that is being performed. This becomes highly necessary in medical datasets due to the importance of not all the data points in the prediction of diseases. When it comes to data of a patient tracking his health over time, certain changes in blood sugar levels or pulse rate may turn out to be more indicative of heart disease or diabetes than others. Augmented LSTM Framework uses attention to provide priority to these important signals, therefore improving interpretability and performance.

In order to apply this framework in a healthcare environment, patient data will need to be collected and arranged. This includes the demographic information, medical history, laboratory test outcomes, a record of the symptoms, and even the lifestyle information, such as diet, physical activity, and sleep behavior. The mobile application may be used to input this information into the system by patients or healthcare providers. The processing of these time-series data then takes the Augmented LSTM Framework that identifies the temporal dependencies and correlations that could not be identified by any other means of analysis. The model is also able to establish whether a patient is experiencing symptoms of a certain illness, and it is also able to make good predictions of occurrence due to the identification of patterns over time.

Personalized and early diagnosis, among others, is one of the best advantages of the augmented LSTM framework. One of the most important points in the effective treatment and improved patient outcomes is an early diagnosis of diseases. Early diagnosis has been useful in chronic diseases such as diabetes, cardiovascular diseases, and certain types of cancer because early diagnosis will assist in averting the development of the disease and reducing the number of complications. This is facilitated by the

Augmented LSTM Framework that continues to interpret patient data and determine patterns that can be used to demonstrate the presence of signs of a disease long before it even manifests itself in a clinical environment. This will allow the healthcare providers to prescribe preventive interventions based on the risk profile of the individual. It is even more helpful based on the application of the Augmented LSTM Framework with an Android application. The mobile platforms facilitate easy access to healthcare services, and the patients, as well as the healthcare providers, can access the system at any location and at any time. The users, with the assistance of the Android app, will be able to insert their data and receive real-time analysis and actionable insights regarding their health data. An integration of this type of power of machine learning, combined with mobile accessibility, can radically streamline the healthcare delivery process. It allows one to constantly monitor, tailor alerts, and dynamically suggest and recommend, thereby making healthcare proactive rather than reactive. The scalable and adaptable augmented LSTM Framework is also scalable [27]. It can be scaled to a large number of healthcare applications, not only in predicting the occurrence of chronic diseases but also in predicting acute medical events, such as linking the occurrence of a heart attack or respiratory failure. The framework can continuously evolve due to the constant update of new information, and the structure can change according to new patterns of diseases and more effectively predict diseases over time, as shown in Figure 4.3. It can enable it to be an invaluable asset to the healthcare practitioners who desire to expand their diagnostic abilities and deliver quality care.

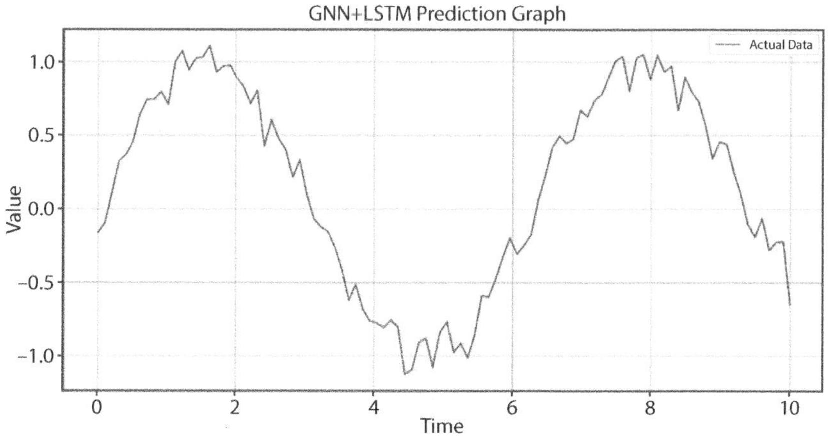

Figure 4.3 GNN+LSTM prediction graph.

Lastly, the augmented LSTM Framework is not only a predictive model but also a transformative framework, which integrates better sequential modeling and intelligent attention mechanisms. It enables healthcare providers to deliver effective and efficient healthcare through accurate, interpretable, and personalized prediction of diseases through mobile platforms. That is why it is a massive investment for any healthcare system, which tends to improve the degree of diagnostic accuracy, patient outcomes, and effectiveness of the healthcare in general.

4.3.3 Explainable Artificial Intelligence (XAI) and SHAP

This type of artificial intelligence is the best-known as explainable artificial intelligence or XAI and is, by far, one of the most valuable advancements of contemporary AI, especially in such a sensitive field of its use as healthcare. Traditional AI systems, particularly those based on deep learning, are generally considered to be black boxes—they can produce extremely precise predictions, but they cannot provide any information as to how such predictions were derived [28]. Lack of transparency is a major barrier to adoption in healthcare, where the decisions reached about the issue may impose huge implications on the patients. The doctors, the patients, and the bodies that control them must not only possess the right predictions but also a clear understanding of how the predictions can be the way they are. At this point, XAI is highly essential.

XAI refers to a set of tools and methods to ensure that the decision-making process of the AI systems can be made transparent to humans. It minimizes the gap that exists between machine learning models and human cognition and enables end-users to trust and certify AI-based systems. XAI improves accuracy and interpretability as it provides additional information on what causes a prediction in the disease prediction situation. This form of clarity is essential to healthcare professionals since it helps them identify whether the rationale model and clinical knowledge, or patient-specific considerations, are in line with each other. Predictions of diseases are informed by disease prediction models that rely on machine learning algorithms to process voluminous and complex data. Such data typically has a variety of patient-specific data, such as demographic data, medical history, lab results, genetic profile, lifestyle, etc. Even though such models are able to reveal the pattern and correlation in such datasets, the complexity of the algorithms may tend to obscure the derivation of the predictions. XAI tries to overcome this problem by giving the explanations in a way that can be understood by clinicians, hence making their output interpretable. This not only creates trust but also helps in the clinical decision-making process so that predictions can be effectively applied in patient care [28].

One of the most powerful and widely used XAI methods in disease prediction is SHAP (short for Shapley Additive Explanations) [29]. SHAP is based on the concept of Shapley values, which originate from cooperative game theory, as shown in Figure 4.4. In this context, each feature of a dataset is treated like a player in a game, and the value of each feature is determined by its marginal contribution to the prediction outcome. SHAP assigns an importance value to every feature for a given prediction, quantifying its impact compared to a baseline prediction. This allows users to see not only which features influenced the prediction but also how much influence each feature had. SHAP has a significant strength in the ability to offer local interpretability. Local interpretability refers to the ability to explain individual predictions, and not just the behavior of the model as a whole. To illustrate, when a model predicts that a given patient has a high likelihood of getting diabetes, SHAP can decompose the factors that led to the prediction (e.g., high levels of fasting glucose, BMI, or blood pressure) and decompose the contribution of each factor. Such insight is priceless to clinicians, as it will allow them to confirm the prediction with their clinical intuition and be able to talk to the patient about it in language she can comprehend. In addition to local interpretability, SHAP has global interpretability, which is the ability to aggregate the explanations

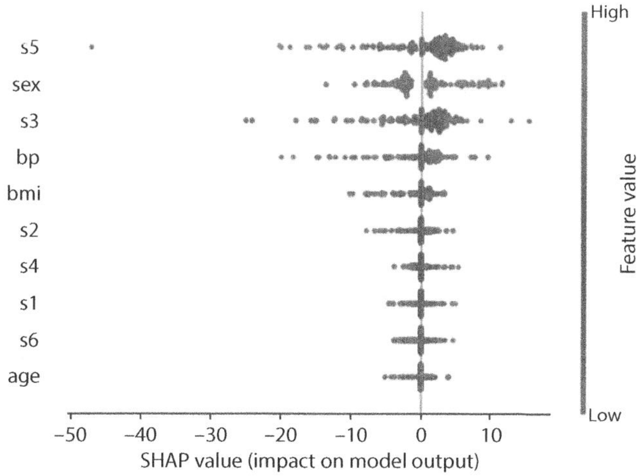

Figure 4.4 SHAP summary plot.

over a large number of instances [30]. Explaining the average significance of each feature on a dataset will help healthcare providers to learn about the overall behavior of the model. The global understanding can be used to determine the strongest variables that cause a specific disease in a group of patients, which may be used in the development of public health programs and medical practices.

SHAP is model-agnostic, i.e., it can be used on everything without considering the algorithm. This flexibility allows it to be used especially in healthcare, where a variety of different models can be used, such as decision trees, random forests, gradient boosting, and neural networks. There are variants of SHAP (including Tree SHAP) designed to optimize the performance of tree-based models, such that faster and more efficient interpretability is achievable without compromising accuracy. In addition to that, SHAP has the ability to produce visual explanations such as summary plots, dependence plots, and force plots, thereby making it easier to use by clinicians. These kinds of visualizations allow visual intuitive comprehension of the interactions between complex features, which is highly important in a clinical practice where time and clarity are critical. The XAI methods that can be used, like SHAP, on Android apps will become productive and lucid healthcare tools [31]. The algorithm normally initiates with the retrieval of the data, which entails different sources, e.g., electronic health records, wearables, patient questionnaires, and other health databases. These raw data are then preprocessed in order to remove noise, standardize formats, and utilize missing data to determine the accuracy of the predictions. It is followed by feature selection, the job that suggests the selection of the best features to be used on the model. The reason is that the quality of the features selected will determine the quality of the model and its readability.

When the data is ready, the model is then trained, which means that the model will be trained to learn to predict using the features as the input. After this is the prediction phase of the model that is deployed to predict the risk of disease based on new patient data. At this point, interpretation using XAI methods such as SHAP is used. SHAP determines the input of each feature towards a particular prediction, and it goes into some detail to tell why the model has reached a particular outcome. The interpretive layer is then made available to clinicians in the form of visualizations in the Android application to enable them to navigate through the predictions. The proposed model is shown in Figure 4.5. Having such clear explanations, XAI can enable the creation of confidence in medical systems based on AI. It allows clinicians to verify the rationale of predictions, and it complies with the practice of medicine, not to mention that the patients are

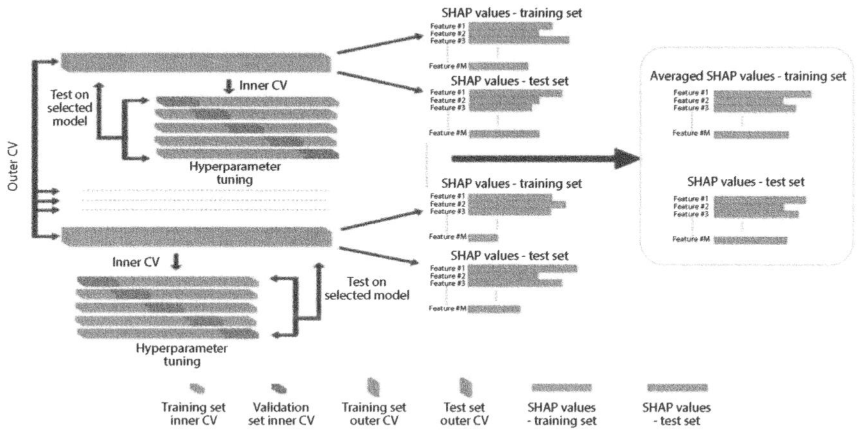

Figure 4.5 The layered architecture of the proposed model.

given the power to have a clearer understanding of their health status. The accuracy comparison of the proposed model with the decision tree model is shown in Figure 4.6. Lastly, XAI is not only more precise in creating a better disease prediction model but also more transparent, trustworthy, and ethical. It is this transparency that is required in the wider application of AI to healthcare, and XAI is an inevitable part of the existing systems of predicting diseases.

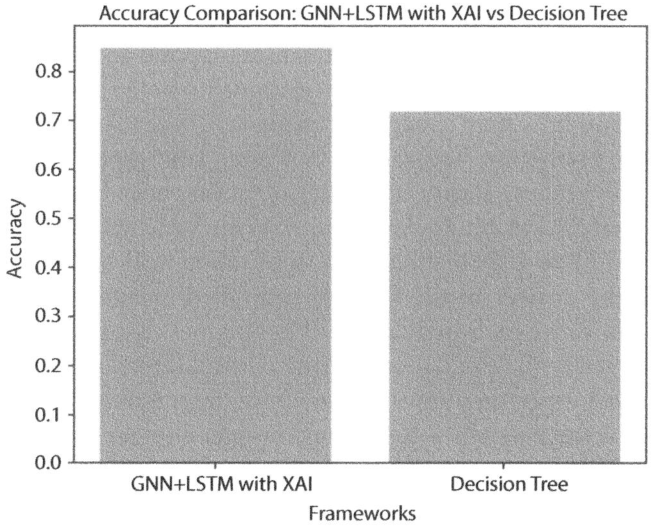

Figure 4.6 Accuracy comparison.

4.4 Conclusion

In conclusion, it can be stated that using graph neural networks (GNN), Long Short-Term Memory networks (LSTM), and explainable artificial intelligence (XAI) algorithms during the development of an Android application to predict a disease is a significant technological breakthrough in the healthcare sector. The two, combined with the sophisticated machine learning approaches, combine the merits of relational modelling, sequencing data analysis, and interpretability, creating a system that is not only very accurate but also transparent and trustworthy. This category of application can transform the relationship between the healthcare provider and the disease patient using healthcare prediction tools and make healthcare proactive, customized, and efficient.

The GNN-LSTM model introduces a fresh algorithm that can successfully acquire the complex character of the associations and time-related reliance of medical information. GNNs are suitable for modeling graphically structured information; that is why, with the assistance of this application, patients, symptoms, medical history, and the elements that surround them can be represented in the network. Local and global patterns of relational modeling are critical in the setting of healthcare, in which diseases would be the outcome of an intricate relationship among a collection of variables. Meanwhile, the LSTM component assesses the effectiveness of understanding the dynamics of alterations in the health indicators of the patient in terms of time series. This will allow time-sensitive and dynamic predictions that will adapt to the varying patient information. GNN and LSTM are complete predictive models that can be applied to collect extremely good results by considering both the relationship between medical factors themselves and how they change over time.

However, prediction accuracy is not adequate, especially in medical practice, where trust, clarity, and interpretability are also crucial. It is at this point that XAI technologies come in. With XAI and, more specifically, SHAPley Additive Explanations, the application will be able to provide users with the answer in the form of simplified explanations of the factors that motivated each prediction. This openness enables medical practitioners to verify the predictions by the clinical knowledge and gives the patients power, since they are able to observe the reasoning behind the risk prediction of their patients. XAI, thus, bridges the gap between detailed machine learning models and reality-based, human-friendly healthcare decision-making. The combination of GNN-LSTM and XAI, however, makes the prediction more accurate and understandable than otherwise.

It also promotes tailor-made healthcare. The recognition of the most important factors leading to a prediction will assist the system in guiding the patients and their medical practitioners to preventive measures and early treatment. The impact of such individualized care may be tremendous in terms of patient outcomes, reduction of healthcare costs, and even life-saving. In this regard, an example, in case the system has identified the high risk of a chronic disease, e.g., diabetes, the application will be able to recommend lifestyle modifications, dietary modifications, or even further diagnostic tests depending on the profile of a person.

An elaborate Android application like this must be developed in a well-thought-out way. Being among the initial and the primary ones is cautious data collection based on reliable medical history and patient feedback, thorough preprocessing to determine the quality of data, intelligent selection of features to focus on the variables that are the most relevant, and intelligent training of the model to produce a well-performing system. Besides the model development, results interpretation, and visualization are also essential steps that can help achieve the enhanced user experience and confidence. The model is supposed to be an Android platform, and they ought to have straightforward user interfaces that can perform within short time periods. The rigorous testing and verification introduce dependability and accuracy before the practical scenarios are exposed.

But in the long run, the Android disease predictor app can be a groundbreaking healthcare tool, provided it is used with GNN-LSTM and XAI techniques in place. It can deliver accurate, readable, and timely forecasts, allow patients to make better decisions about their health, and assist medical staff in delivering more accurate care. Such a system is a step in the right direction of applying artificial intelligence to enable proactive healthcare and the enhanced management of diseases, which have become more manageable, and ultimately leads to healthier people.

4.5 Future Scope

The combination of the new and different sources of data can be regarded as one of the most promising directions for improving the disease prediction application. The classical medical prediction models are mainly founded on clinical and demographic information (medical histories, laboratory results, and simple patient data). Though these could be very informative, they are more likely to represent a segment of the entire picture of the wellness of a patient. As the number of more diverse sources of information (genetic information, information about wearable devices, even information about social media) grows, prediction algorithms can become much more precise and can tell a lot more about the factors that influence the development of a disease. The genetic information may provide information about the predisposition to certain disorders, wearable technology may provide real-time and instant tracking of such physiological data as the heart rate, sleep, the level of physical activity, and the social media information may provide indirect information about the lifestyle, mood, and stress level. This more inclusive health and illness data, which is facilitated by the model, is more holistic. In addition to making them more predictive, this integration enables more individualized recommendations to be given to patients. The application may generate tailored recommendations when a prediction model is used to identify a patient's risk of a particular disease. This can include dietary adjustments, proactive testing, lifestyle modifications, or a personalized treatment plan. By offering precise and useful guidance, the app will not only empower patients to take proactive health-related actions but also improve patient-provider interactions, improving health outcomes and reducing the strain on healthcare systems.

AI disclosure statement: The author confirms that no artificial intelligence (AI)-generated content or AI-assisted writing tools were used in the preparation of this chapter (including summaries and the abstract). All text, analysis, and conclusions are the result of the author's original work.

References

1. Kaur, I. and Ali, A., A Complete Study on Machine Learning Algorithms for Medical Data Analysis, in: *Fog Computing for Intelligent Cloud IoT Systems* C. Banerjee, A. Ghosh, R. Chakraborty and A.A. Elngar (eds.), Wiley Online Books, 2024. https://doi.org/10.1002/9781394175345.ch7
2. Kaur and Ali, A., Unveiling the Power of Prediction: A Comprehensive Guide to Learning Techniques, from Data Preparation to Model Interpretability for Early Prediction of Diabetes and Effective Management, Taylor & Francis, 2025, [Online]. Available: https://www.taylorfrancis.com/chapters/edit/10.1201/9781003592969-1/unveiling-power-prediction-inderdeep-kaur-aleem-ali.
3. Sehgal, D., Kaur, I., Sharma, V., Gautam, B., Singh, A., Kumar, N., AI-Driven Early Diabetes Prediction, in: *Proc. 2024 IEEE 3rd World Conf. Applied Intelligence and Computing (AIC)*, Gwalior, India, IEEE, pp. 40–48, 2024, doi: 10.1109/AIC61668.2024.10730970.

4. Khanna, A., Singh, P., Inzimam-Ul-Hassan, Kaur, I., Predictive Analytics for Cardiovascular Health: A Machine Learning Approach, in: *Proc. 2024 Int. Conf. Advances in Modern Age Technologies for Health and Engineering Science (AMATHE)*, Shivamogga, India, IEEE, pp. 1–6, 2024, doi: 10.1109/AMATHE61652.2024.10582101.
5. Sharma, M., Kaur, I., Saini, G., Thakur, V., Mishra, A., Predictive Modeling for Stroke Risk Assessment Using Machine Learning, in: *Proc. 2024 Int. Conf. Intelligent Systems for Cybersecurity (ISCS)*, Gurugram, India, IEEE, pp. 1–6, 2024, doi: 10.1109/ISCS61804.2024.10581155.
6. Pradhan, R., Devi, M., Kaur, I., Mogha, H., Singh, S., Deepfake Forensics: Detection and Analysis, in: *Proc. 2025 4th OPJU Int. Technol. Conf. (OTCON) on Smart Computing for Innovation and Advancement in Industry 5.0*, Raigarh, India, IEEE, pp. 1–6, 2025, doi: 10.1109/OTCON65728.2025.11070410.
7. Kaur and Ali, A., Swarm Intelligence Optimization for Feature Selection: Techniques, Applications, and Challenges for Enhanced Machine Learning Performance, in: *Metaheuristic Algorithms and Optimizing Neural Networks for Biomedical Image Processing*, P., Balaji, *et al.*, (Eds.), pp. 67–100, IGI Global Scientific Publishing, 2026, doi: 10.4018/979-8-3373-0523-3.ch003.
8. Kaur and Ali, A., An In-Depth Exploration of Machine Learning Algorithms and Performance Evaluation Approaches for Personalized Diabetes Prediction, in: *Proc. 2024 Int. Conf. Emerging Innovations and Advanced Computing (INNOCOMP)*, Sonipat, India, IEEE, pp. 532–538, 2024, doi: 10.1109/INNOCOMP63224.2024.00093.
9. An, Q., Rahman, S., Zhou, J., Kang, J.J., A comprehensive review on machine learning in healthcare industry: Classification, restrictions, opportunities and challenges. *Sensors*, 23, 9, 4178, 2023, https://doi.org/10.3390/s23094178.
10. Javaid, M., Haleem, A., Singh, R.P., Suman, R., Rab, S., Significance of machine learning in healthcare: Features, pillars and applications. *Int. J. Intell. Networks*, 3, 58–73, 2022, ISSN 2666-6030, https://doi.org/10.1016/j.ijin.2022.05.002.
11. Kipf, T.N. and Welling, M., Semi-supervised classification with graph convolutional networks, in: *Proc. Int. Conf. Learn. Representations (ICLR)*, Toulon, France, 2017.
12. Lipton, Z.C., The mythos of model interpretability, in: *Proc. ICML Workshop on Human Interpretability in Machine Learning (WHI)*, New York, USA, pp. 96–100, 2016.
13. Tang, Zhang, X., Zhang, L., Sun, Y., MM-STGNN: A multimodal spatiotemporal graph neural network for hospital readmission prediction, in: *Proc. IEEE Int. Conf. Bioinformatics and Biomedicine (BIBM)*, Shanghai, China, pp. 4212–4219, 2023.
14. Boll, S., Müller, M., Wolf, F.D., Graph neural networks for clinical risk prediction using electronic health records: A systematic review, in: *Proc. IEEE Int. Conf. Healthcare Informatics (ICHI)*, Orlando, FL, USA, 2024.

15. Linardatos, P., Papastefanopoulos, V., Kotsiantis, S., Explainable AI: A review of machine learning interpretability methods, in: *Proc. 11th Hellenic Conf. Artificial Intelligence (SETN)*, Athens, Greece, pp. 1–10, 2020.
16. Kumar, A., Kumar, S., Anand, R.S., Efficient automated disease diagnosis using machine learning models, in: *Proc. IEEE Int. Conf. Computational Intelligence and Data Science (ICCIDS)*, Gurgaon, India, pp. 1–6, 2021.
17. Moreno-Sánchez, Pérez-García, L., Ortega, F., Explainable survival prediction models for heart failure patients using machine learning, in: *Proc. IEEE Int. Conf. Engineering in Medicine and Biology Society (EMBC)*, Sydney, Australia, pp. 1847–1851, 2023.
18. Visco, M., Lombardi, R., Rossi, G., Designing explainable predictive models for worsening heart conditions: Integrating ML risk models and *post-hoc* explainability, in: *Proc. IEEE Int. Conf. Healthcare Informatics (ICHI)*, Orlando, FL, USA, pp. 1–8, 2024.
19. Pharmacat, Pharmacat: An open-source Android and web healthcare application for symptom analysis and disease prediction, GitHub Repository, 2023, [Online]. Available: https://github.com/pharmacat/Pharmacat.
20. Android Application Disease Prediction Projects, Android disease prediction and medical prescription application, Project Report, 2022, [Online]. Available: https://github.com/ML-AndroidHealth/DiseasePredictionApp.
21. Kaur and Hassan, I.U., A Bibliometric Analysis and Management of Big Data and Machine Learning Research, Taylor & Francis, 2025, [Online]. Available: https://www.taylorfrancis.com/chapters/edit/10.1201/9781003512585-11/bibliometric-analysis-management-big-data-machine-learning-research-inderdeep-kaur-inzimam-ul-hassan.
22. Si, C., Chen, W., Wang, W., Wang, L., Tan, T., An Attention Enhanced Graph Convolutional LSTM Network for Skeleton-Based Action Recognition, in: *Proc. IEEE/CVF Conference on Computer Vision and Pattern Recognition (CVPR)*, Long Beach, CA, USA, pp. 1227–1236, 2019.
23. Lu, Z., Lv, W., Xie, Z., Du, B., Huang, R., Leveraging Graph Neural Network with LSTM for Traffic Speed Prediction, in: *Proc. IEEE SmartWorld/UIC/ATC/SCALCOM/IoP/SCI*, 2019.
24. Kuo, P.C., GNN-LSTM Based Fusion Model for Structural Dynamic Response Prediction. *Eng. Struct.*, 2024.
25. Wang, J., Wang, Y., Zhang, Q., LSTM-Based Graph Attention Network for Vehicle Trajectory Prediction. *Eng. Appl. Artif. Intell.*, 2024.
26. Orji, U., Güven, Ç., Stowell, D., Enhanced Load Forecasting with GAT-LSTM: Leveraging Grid and Temporal Features, in: *Proc. ACM International Conference on Future Energy Systems (eFutures)*, Rotterdam, Netherlands, 2025.
27. Hooshyar, D. and Yang, Y., Problems with SHAP and LIME in Interpretable AI for Education: A Comparative Study of *Post-hoc* Explanations and Neural-Symbolic Rule Extraction. *IEEE Access*, 2024, doi:10.1109/ACCESS.2024.3463948.

28. Van den Broeck, G., Lykov, A., Schleich, M., Suciu, D., On the Tractability of SHAP Explanations, in: *Proc. 2020 Conference on Uncertainty in Artificial Intelligence (UAI)*, 2020.
29. Rathi, S., Generating Counterfactual and Contrastive Explanations using SHAP, in: *Proc. 2019 Conference on Fairness, Accountability, and Transparency (FAT/XAI Workshop)*, 2019.
30. Weerts, H.J.P., van Ipenburg, W., Pechenizkiy, M., A Human-Grounded Evaluation of SHAP for Alert Processing, in: *Proceedings of the 2019 ACM Conference on AI, Ethics, and Society (or relevant workshop)*, 2019.
31. Schlegel, U., Arnout, H., El-Assady, M., Oelke, D., Keim, D.A., Towards a Rigorous Evaluation of XAI Methods on Time Series, in: *Proc. 2019 International Conference on Advanced Visual Interfaces (AVI)*, 2019.

Part II
APPLICATIONS

5

A Machine Learning-Based Approach for Identifying Ayurvedic Medicinal Raw Materials *via* Image Processing

Ankit Raj*, Subhajit Chanda, Ashutosh Dubey, Dyuti Mitra and Debraj Chatterjee

Computer Science & Engineering Department, Techno International New Town, Kolkata, West Bengal, India

Abstract

Ayurveda has been part of human life for thousands of years. Instead of being limited to a single type of treatment, it has offered ways to manage many different illnesses. Its influence is still visible in traditional healthcare practices that survive today. The choice of appropriate medicinal plants was once determined manually, depending largely on experiential wisdom. However, automating this identification process has become essential due to the increasing demand for mass production. In our study, we present a type of supervised machine learning technique that relies on features such as the color and texture of leaves and fruit to accurately classify medicinal plants.

The paper also reviews recent studies and methodologies used in the field of image processing, ranging from traditional machine learning approaches to identifying plants, several diseases associated with them, and geographic object-based analysis, and imposes a contrast on the various approaches taken in our project.

The paper also discusses the advantages and the various challenges imposed as a result of image-based identification.

**Corresponding author*: ankit.raj.cse.2021@tint.edu.in

Rajdeep Chakraborty, Aleem Ali, Amit Paul, Nawaf R. Alharbe and S. Balamurugan (eds.) Causal Artificial Intelligence: Fundamentals and Applications, (101–122) © 2026 Scrivener Publishing LLC

***Keywords*:** Machine learning, medicinal plants, Ayurveda, image processing, plant classification, feature extraction, automation

5.1 Introduction

Ayurvedic herbs have been a crucial component of traditional global healthcare systems for centuries. They contain numerous natural treatments for ailments. Ayurveda, which is the world's most trusted system of treatment, relies on herbs. Identification of these species is very important for their proper use and preservation of biodiversity. There are traditional approaches to plant identification that emphasize physical inspection and comparison of morphological characteristics. Such approaches are time-consuming and require a lot of expertise and can thus prove to be difficult to apply in remote or low-resource settings.

In our modern world, advancements in artificial intelligence (AI), especially in fields like machine learning and computer vision, have brought up new possibilities for automating the identification of plants and similar operations. Techniques of image identification and characteristics, which include the training of machine learning models in order to recognize patterns and such characteristics in digital images of plants, having achieved tremendous success in various domains such as object detection, medical imaging, and face identification, are now being leveraged to revolutionize automated species classification and biodiversity monitoring. This study attempts to use cutting-edge technology to create an automated system for recognizing medicinal plants based on photos of their leaves or fruits.

The model in this project uses modern technologies and libraries such as OpenCV, NumPy, TensorFlow, Keras, and scikit-learn to harness the strength of deep learning algorithms and vast data sets of labeled plant images. The proposed method has several advantages over traditional means of plant identification.

First, it would significantly shorten the time and labor needed for human identification, allowing one to process volumes of information in an effective way. Second, it can increase precision and accuracy by eliminating the human bias and subjectivity present in human identification methods. Third, to allow experts in evaluating and verifying plant species and characteristics from anywhere in the world without the physical presence of the specimens, remote identification is included.

In general speaking, such an automated system has varying results and consequences for both the promotion and preservation of Ayurveda and its medical knowledge, including the future applications of medicinal plant resources. By improving our ability to accurately identify the thousands of medicinal plants used in traditional practices, this research can help conserve biodiversity, document traditional knowledge, and discover new natural remedies with potential therapeutic uses.

In conclusion, this study investigates the application of modern computer vision and machine learning techniques, utilizing strong tools such as NumPy, OpenCV, TensorFlow, Keras, and scikit-learn, to solve the essential problem of medicinal plant identification. The proposed system has the potential to transform traditional practices, promote sustainable resource management, and open up new avenues for global advancements in traditional medicine and healthcare practices, particularly in regions with a rich medicinal plant heritage, such as India's Ayurvedic system.

5.2 Literature Survey

Ref. no.	Aim of the work	Methodology	Dataset used	Outcome, limitations & future scope
1.	The present review work investigates some of the deep convolutional neural networks applied to medical image processing for retrieval, segmentation, abnormality detection, and diagnosis. It also intends to present recent advances in this area, underlining both the potential and challenges of deep learning in effective data extraction from medical images. The paper also discusses clinically important performance metrics and provides insight into what it could mean for the integration of these approaches within the future of medical image analysis [1].	This paper throws light on deep learning for medical applications using the "deep medic" model based on a convolutional neural network. Lisa Pereira, in her study, discussed the CNN models, SegNet, and 3DNet, and narrowed her discussion to how such networks can be utilized for medical image analysis. These have proved their utility in various medical imagery applications, improving accuracy and efficiency, and are part of the broader movement toward deep learning–based diagnostics [1].	Clinical diagnosis and prognosis utilize a wide range of medical imaging modalities. Handcrafted features, which may perform commendably with expert knowledge, are not suitable for certain tasks like the analysis of a medical picture. Deep convolutional neural networks enable an end-to-end learning process in which complex structures can be acquired by the model, enhanced representation, and data-driven features. Retrieval, diagnosis, and segmentation are among the many successful medical image tasks achieved through DCNNs. Examples are the identification of the nucleus of colorectal adenocarcinoma, lung disease classification, and brain tumor segmentation. Accuracy rates as high as 98.88% were recorded for the classification of Alzheimer's disease using datasets consisting of 80,000 images, outperforming the performances of older approaches [1].	This review outlines the promises and challenges of deep learning in medical image analysis. Recognizing the challenges that include high processing power requirements and the need for labeled data, possible solutions such as transfer learning and GANs for sparse data are put forward. Challenges notwithstanding, CNNs are finding greater acceptance, overcoming problems at either end through augmentation of data and transfer learning. The study envisions advancements in computer-aided diagnosis systems with an evolution of technology and substantial contributions from deep learning in unexplored imaging modalities [1].

(*Continued*)

(Continued)

Ref. no.	Aim of the work	Methodology	Dataset used	Outcome, limitations & future scope
2.	The present study focuses on the automation of identifying medicinal plants, putting great emphasis on leaf form, color, and texture features. Given both sides of a leaf, along with morphological information, this paper will determine an optimal combination of features that yields the best recognition rate. This investigation improves community understanding of medicinal plants and allows taxonomists to accurately identify plant species, with implications for developing pharmaceutical drugs from these plants. This paper proposes a system that takes into consideration the necessary features required for plant identification in herbal, ayurvedic, and folk medicine, working toward the goal of accurate, automatic identification of medicinal plants [2].	This work uses deep learning and, specifically, the most accurate Densenet121 CNN architecture for challenging datasets. In order to develop the model, the research will take as a basis well-acknowledged libraries such as Theano, Tensorflow, Caffe, and MxNet, giving priority to Keras for training and designing purposes. The main topic of this study is the identification of medicinal leaves. Botanists, taxonomists, and pharmaceutical experts need to correctly recognize various plants. Correct classification not only contributes to medicine production but also to enhancing its quality and reducing unwanted side effects [2].	With 60 photos per species, showing both faces of the leaf, at least 30 leaves are sampled from each of 50 medicinal plant species. Samples collected excluded leaves showing severe damage during simple hand sampling. Hence, the resulting dataset is useful in providing data for a comprehensive study of medicinal plant attributes in tabular form [2].	From generation to generation, communities looked upon herbs for healing, sometimes relying on them to survive. On the contrary, today's advances in analytical science allow much more accurate identification of these plants, overcoming a lot of the guesswork and limitations of older approaches. The proposed computational and statistical approach offers a rapid and trustworthy method, advantageous mainly to those who cannot invest in costly equipment. This study recognizes current difficulties in plant identification, such as when the subject plants are small or do not have leaves, and discusses possible future work, including portable applications. Advanced machine learning classifiers are called for to further enhance accuracy and overall performance in plant identification and help develop robust identification tools [2].

(Continued)

(*Continued*)

Ref. no.	Aim of the work	Methodology	Dataset used	Outcome, limitations & future scope
3.	The purpose of this research paper is to develop a robust AI system for the categorization and identification of wild plants using the SVM, RF, and AlexNet CNN models on different datasets. Focusing on datasets of wild plants, the identification process should be as straightforward as possible, including taking photographs only. Advanced technologies in machine learning and image recognition will be integrated to enable a single central electronic herbarium system for wild plants, which will make the entire process easier [3].	The performed study presents the application of deep learning in plant image classification, where the dataset has been extended from 51 to 3954 images. Divided into training-3164 and testing-790 sets, it focuses on the Apiaceae and Brassicaceae families and the individual species in these families. Feature extraction includes a Histogram of Oriented Gradients (HOG) and a CNN model. The results obtained were with the fine-tuning of AlexNet, DLeaf, and AyurLeaf, among others, with diverse classifiers, obtaining an accuracy of 96.76%. By using transfer learning, models like SVM, ANN, K-NN, NB, and CNN improve to reach an accuracy from 90% up to 98%. Various neural networks improve the classification, with the maximum reaching 95.28% with the improvement of AMSCNN. Thus, this study explores distinctive features of plants; a dataset was presented about citrus fruits, and methods of recognition were reviewed [3].	The original dataset, which includes 51 images of 17 species belonging to two families, has been augmented to 3954 images. For the process of identification of plants, four plant species have been reserved as test sets. By creating and applying the dataset with lower and upper leaf images and fruit images, the key contribution has been made in this study. Feature extraction relies on the HOG descriptor, enhanced based on the CNN model [3].	The machine learning tools used in the study involved a convolutional neural network, a random forest, and a support vector machine for the classification of plants (wild), both in family and species distinction. RF achieved the highest accuracy in binary classification with 99.7%, followed by SVM with 99.5% and CNN with 99%. While the CNN developed in this study had an accuracy of 98.2% during categorical classification, that of SVM was 96.7%, and RF was 96%. Future recommendations include increasing the dataset and developing a digital library to help in the better collection of wild plant samples. The limitations identified would be to refine the challenges of species classification and then use more datasets for comprehensive analysis [3].

(*Continued*)

(*Continued*)

Ref. no.	Aim of the work	Methodology	Dataset used	Outcome, limitations & future scope
4.	This work applies various AIT techniques, SVM, naive Bayes, random forest, KNN, and neural networks, to automatically identify a plant from its leaf. In this work, 22 VF features were extracted from a dataset of 637 healthy leaves and were grouped into four categories: texture, color, dimension, and pattern. The classification accuracy achieved from the SVM model was 92.91%. Feature selection using CFS showed 16 efficient VF features. When these selected features were applied to the SVM model, it recorded an accuracy of 94.49%. For the identification of a leaf in a damaged condition, this work achieved an accuracy of 92.53%. This work highlighted that P5 is the most effective feature group and proved that well-modeled AIT will yield good performance in plant identification in practical scenarios [4].	During feature selection, the algorithm used is that of Correlation-based Feature Selection, CFS. Starting with n = 1, a feature is chosen for which the relevance metric, rcf¯, and redundancy metric, r¯ff, are calculated. Vs values are calculated for each feature, and a feature with the highest Vs value is picked out. This process is iteratively done for n = 2 onwards, wherein multiple features are combined and Vs values are computed for optimal double and increased combinations. By using the CFS algorithm, each feature's contribution towards classification is checked to select 16 of the most useful features out of 22 [4].	The process described involves the extraction of feature data from the image of leaves for the purpose of AIT. The set of leaves for identification includes images of 32 plant species. Image The preprocessing steps that will be employed are resizing, grayscale and binary conversion, and morphological operations to further enhance the images. Dimensions include length, width, perimeter, and area; color features from RGB values; texture features through gray-level co-occurrence matrix; and pattern features extracted from leaf edges and centroids. These features will lead to a more complete dataset and enhance the robustness of the identification. Fullness, color mean values, and various texture and pattern features are extracted; thus, a detailed assessment for an effective plant identification through AIT is provided [4].	This study looks into leaf classification using AIT, applying 22 visual features in color, texture, dimension, and pattern parameters extracted from the leaf images. Consequently, SVM was the highest-rated classifier, with an accuracy of 94.2% in the Comb_1 group. The study identified pattern features as the most important factors for any improvement in the accuracy of classification. It also recommends future work to explore larger data sets in order to achieve better general performance. Limitations include the different processing times of each AIT and additional validation on a variety of botanical data. Despite some setbacks, the study was able to indicate how AIT has remarkable potential in plant applications [4].
5.	Identification of medicinal plants using the machine learning approach, where most plants are identified using their leaves [5].	The common ways to classify the leaves of a plant are capturing images, noise removal, resizing, extracting features, and finally identifying or recognizing the plant. The random forest algorithm is used and includes the use of a confusion matrix for system performance [5].	Leaves of medicinal plants—aloe vera, coriander, drumstick, hibiscus, mint, neem, papaya, peepal, rui, and Tulsi_Basil [5].	The random forest algorithm-based method for identifying medicinal plants has produced encouraging results. With the use of color, texture, and geometric characteristics, leaves could be identified with 94.54% accuracy. The project can be expanded to include more plant species and examine the algorithm's suitability for a wider variety of medicinal plants, improving its accuracy and application in various contexts. Potential limitations on the selected features (color, texture, and geometrical aspects) and the importance of being cautious when applying the method to a greater variety of plant species are among the drawbacks [5].

(*Continued*)

(*Continued*)

Ref. no.	Aim of the work	Methodology	Dataset used	Outcome, limitations & future scope
6.	Use of Geographic Object-Based Image Analysis (GEOBIA) to analyze high-spatial resolution remote-sensing imagery and discuss the new development in GEOBIA and talk about possible avenues for future growth [6].	1. Data integration a. Large-area coverage b. Closing the gap in historical data. c. Combining or integrating data from several sensors with complementary properties. 2. Image segmentation a. Scale parameter determination. b. Semantic segmentation. 3. Object-based feature extraction a. Novel object-based features. b. Feature space reduction. 4. Geo-object-based modeling frameworks [6].	Optical Imagery from Satellites or Airborne Sensors, UAS (Drones) Imagery, Hyperspectral Imagery, LiDAR (Light Detection and Ranging) Data, Historical Aerial Photos, Multisource Data Integration [6].	The paper includes certain limitations, such as boundary delineation challenges, data resolution selection, and novice-GEOBIA user systems. This in turn also draws attention to a number of opportunities and increasing tendencies in Geographic Object-Based Image Analysis(GEOBIA), such as tackling huge data difficulties, investigating novel kinds of image objects, creating solutions for inexperienced GEOBIA users, and integrating knowledge for other disciplines [6].

(*Continued*)

(*Continued*)

Ref. no.	Aim of the work	Methodology	Dataset used	Outcome, limitations & future scope
7.	Deep convolutional neural networks are used to recognize the species of plants shown in an image and to assess many elements influencing the networks' performance through transfer learning parameter optimization [7].	This study's methodology centers on deep neural network training for plant identification, utilizing a range of techniques to maximize model performance. The training goal is to use stochastic gradient descent (SGD) optimization to minimize the average loss, which includes both prediction loss and regularization. By contrasting training from scratch with fine-tuning pre-trained models, transfer learning is investigated. Using the dataset of LifeCLEF plant identification of 2015 for training and assessment, data augmentation is carried out during the training and testing stages to improve model generalization. To increase overall system accuracy, the outputs from separately optimized deep neural networks are finally combined using a fusion approach [7].	Training Dataset (LifeCLEF 2015 Plant Task): Has 91,758 photos with labels. Features pictures of different plant parts, like fruits, flowers, leaves, and stalks. Includes 1000 species of ferns, plants, and trees. Images were collected from different photographers and locations, with varying backgrounds, poses, colors, and illumination conditions. Testing Dataset (LifeCLEF 2015 Plant Task): 1. Comprises 21,446 images. Ground-truth labels were recently released. Challenging due to variations in image conditions from different photographers and locations. Validation Dataset: Generated from the training dataset using proportionate stratified random sampling. Divided into training and validation subsets. One-fifth of the samples from each class that are available are included in the validation set. Training set: 70,904 images. Validation set: 20,854 images [7].	Deep convolutional neural networks (CNNs) enhanced plant species recognition performance through transfer learning. The whole system outperformed prior benchmarks by about 15% by merging predictions from the top classifiers, demonstrating its efficacy in handling the LifeCLEF 2015 plant identification job. Additional investigation into deep learning architectures and optimization techniques may result in even better performance. Accuracy could be further improved by scaling up computer resources to investigate greater batch sizes and more iterations. The observations made in this study could serve as a valuable reference for similar visual recognition problems, offering guidance on effective model selection and training strategies. While transfer learning and fine-tuning improved performance, there might still be limitations in handling diverse conditions and variations in plant images, such as extreme lighting conditions or occlusions. The study's conclusions are based on the LifeCLEF 2015 dataset, and the generalization of findings to other datasets or domains should be further investigated [7].

(*Continued*)

(Continued)

Ref. no.	Aim of the work	Methodology	Dataset used	Outcome, limitations & future scope
8.	This work aims to develop an automatic vegetation monitoring and management system using aerial images captured by unmanned aerial vehicles (UAVs) [8].	1. Optimization of NDVI: Use of Numpy arrays to perform operations and use of bit-saving strategies and image copy saving for optimization. For faster processing, use slicing syntax instead of loops. 2. Optimization with K-means: For a quicker way to determine the centroid, use the color histogram. Use of Cython to improve the K-means algorithm for faster processing. 3. Taking and Preparing Images: Pictures were taken with a UAV-mounted digital camera that is not covered by an infrared filter. Orthomosaic pictures for examination were created. 4. System Development: Software used to divide photos into management zones according to color areas and compute NDVI. Addition of a geolocation feature to the map so points of interest can be identified. 5. System of Coordinate Capture: Made effective use of management zone maps when capturing coordinates along with a user-friendly interface for picture movement and zooming. 6. Portability: Developed a single-board computer called Tinker to create a portable embedded system combining the functions of an LCD touch screen and a digital camera to capture and display images, and implemented a graphical user interface for user interaction [8].	The dataset includes different images: 1. Infrared Images: Captured by a digital camera without an IR filter. 2. Orthomosaic Images: Generated by stitching together multiple images captured by the unmanned aerial vehicle (UAV). Management Zone Maps: These are derived from the segmentation process applied to the infrared images [8].	To facilitate automatic and quick processing for flexible analysis, the study created a system for segmenting and geolocating management zones in aerial photos taken by UAVs. The technique successfully identified areas of sugarcane crops with low vigor by using the NDVI vegetation indicator. To facilitate the direct administration of suitable treatments based on geo-referenced data, additional improvements are planned to improve the identification and treatment of areas with low vigor. Even though the system processed data quickly, scalability to larger datasets or new crop varieties would present difficulties. Treatment recommendations based on geo-referenced data may or may not be successful, and their applicability in real-world settings may necessitate additional validation [8].

(Continued)

(*Continued*)

Ref. no.	Aim of the work	Methodology	Dataset used	Outcome, limitations & future scope
9.	The project's goal is to create an automated system that uses image processing techniques to accurately detect and classify citrus plant illnesses, allowing for earlier intervention and better crop management [9].	1. Image enhancement 2. Color-based transformation 3. Noise reduction 4. Segmentation 5. K-means clustering 6. Thresholding 7. Edge detection 8. Disease detection using color features 9. Disease detection using shape features 10. Deep learning Preprocessing, segmentation, feature extraction, and classification are the four main stages of the survey. Each stage's methods are thoroughly compared according to performance, benefits, and drawbacks. According to the report, K-means is the most effective approach for segmenting sick plants. The survey highlights the significance of texture in illness representation in photos, which may be effectively classified using support vector machines (SVM) and neural networks (NN) [9].	A dataset of 600 disease-infected plants is used [9].	The survey summarizes the methodologies for plant disease identification using image processing with steps like preprocessing, segmentation, feature extraction, and classification. The major implications of the review are that the quality of preprocessing is crucial to segmentation precision, K-means performs well in segmentation, and texture features *via* SVM and NN enable useful representation of diseases. Limitations of the survey include a deficiency in detailed insights into methodologies under discussion, which cannot allow for adequate examination of the applicability of the latter. Lack of quantitative measures may raise doubts over the validity of reached conclusions, while the exclusion of issues of implementation challenges raises questions over the feasibility of the approaches proposed. The survey provides a basis for further research, despite these limitations. Algorithm improvement in preprocessing, segmentation, [9].
10.	Convolutional neural networks are used in precision agriculture to recognize and classify plant images [10].	CNNs may be trained from scratch on enormous datasets or fine-tuned using pre-existing models. Fine-tuning entails moving learned weights from the first layers of a pre-trained network to a new one. CNNs efficiently learn general picture characteristics, and their last layer may be deleted to use the previous layer's activations as features, transforming the network into a feature extractor rather than a classifier for a variety of computer vision applications [10].	The model handles 224 x 224 RGB images that are fixed in size and performs center normalization on the training images immediately. The CNN architecture is made up of 13 filter layers. The paragraph underlines that convolutional neural networks outperform smaller datasets when trained on bigger ones [10].	Off-the-shelf ConvNet representations were used to determine plant health on a maize plantation, with a 99.58% average prediction accuracy. Because of the model's versatility, it may be modified for a variety of places with differing soil composition, climatic conditions, and other characteristics, allowing for informed decision-making in plantations across different geographical areas [10].

(*Continued*)

(Continued)

Ref. no.	Aim of the work	Methodology	Dataset used	Outcome, limitations & future scope
11.	This research will look at the usefulness of artificial intelligence approaches combined with visual cues for automatically classifying plant species based on leaf photos [11].	1. Image Resizing: All leaf images are downsized to the same dimensions to guarantee uniformity in the subsequent processing steps. 2. Grayscale conversion: Each pixel in the leaf photos has its RGB values established, and the images are converted to grayscale format. 3. Otsu's technique is used to convert grayscale pictures to binary images (black/white), which employ a threshold value to distinguish foreground (white) from background. 4. To remove noise or unwanted artifacts, the "bwareaopen" tool eliminates tiny objects from the binary image [11].	The collection contains 32 plant species, each with 20 distinct photos. The leaf photos were taken in broad daylight with a full HD resolution camera [11].	The study shows that artificial intelligence techniques (AIT) combined with diverse feature groups may effectively classify plant leaves. A study found that SVM consistently produces the highest accuracy rates across multiple feature groups after experimenting with various feature combinations and AIT. In the future, there are many avenues of further exploration and development. One might be to investigate new groups of features or to hone existing ones for still greater classification accuracy [11].

(Continued)

(Continued)

Ref. no.	Aim of the work	Methodology	Dataset used	Outcome, limitations & future scope
12.	The purpose of this research is to examine and document the Maasai population of southern Kenya's traditional medicinal knowledge of plants used to treat malaria and malaria-like symptoms [12].	Interviews and Plant Collection: In order to find out about plants that can treat malaria and its symptoms, we spoke with three herbalists from the Maasai tribe in southern Kenya. Plants mentioned in the interviews were harvested with permission from Kenya's Ministry of Education, Science and Technology. The taxonomic identification of the obtained plants was verified. Preparation of Crude Extracts: Dried plant material was pulverized and extracted using methanol, hexane, and chloroform. Bioassays were performed on chloroform extracts that did not include tannins. The extracts were concentrated and stored for future use. 3. Antimalarial Activity Determination: The D6 clone of Plasmodium falciparum was used for *in vitro* testing. Test chemicals were dissolved in DMSO and tested at various concentrations. Parasite vitality was assessed by measuring [3H]. hypoxanthine incorporation and calculating IC50 values [12].	The Maasai Medicinal Plant Dataset offers information on 21 plant species gathered from conversations with Maasai herbalists. Each entry in the dataset has the following fields: Voucher number, species, and family Maasai name Part utilized therapeutic formulations and pharmaceutical applications. Crude Extracts Dataset: It includes data about the preparation and testing of crude extracts from collected plant samples. Each member of the collection features data on the method of extraction, such as the type of extract used (methanol, hexane, or chloroform), and *in vitro* antimalarial activity and cytotoxicity test results [12].	The study chronicles the Maasai community's traditional medical knowledge of plants used to treat malaria and associated symptoms, finding various plant species with possible antimalarial characteristics *via* literature searches and *in vitro* testing. More than half of the 21 studied species had antiplasmodial action, Confirming Maasai herbalists' expertise. Limitations are the use of *in vitro* testing, which might not totally validate *in vivo* efficacy, as well as differences in preparation procedures and synergistic action with other plants. Nevertheless, the research underscores the possibility of ethnomedical research as a means of discovering antimalarial drugs, offering interesting leads for prospective drug development endeavors in spite of modest means [12].

(Continued)

(*Continued*)

Ref. no.	Aim of the work	Methodology	Dataset used	Outcome, limitations & future scope
13.	Certain Tanzanian plants that are typically used to treat fungal infections were evaluated for their toxicity to brine shrimp [13].	Each plant sample was crushed and allowed to air dry. Using Whatman number 1 filter paper, around 400 grams of the plant material were filtered following a 24-hour maceration in 80% methanol at room temperature. The procedure was carried out three times to ensure that every fragment of plant debris was removed. The extracts were mixed and concentrated, and the solvent was removed at low pressure and 40°C using a rotor vapor evaporation process. The extracts were freeze-dried and kept in a freezer at -20°C until they were needed. For the lethality test of brine shrimp [13].	Between February and March of 2004, 65 plant pieces from 56 different species were gathered from four different locations in Tanzania [13].	Concerns about accessibility and cost are addressed by the research findings, which also identify herbal remedies for fungal infections in HIV/AIDS patients. Brine shrimp cytotoxicity tests confirmed that nine of the plants are toxic, which was evidence of anticancer activity and validated traditional healers' assertions regarding Jatropha multifida and Euphorbia heterophylla. However, considering the preliminary nature of these findings, further studies must be undertaken to ascertain absolute safety, specifically for animal toxicity tests. The study brings to the fore the necessity of extensive research on the antifungal and anticancer action of these plants, acknowledging the shortcomings of insufficient testing and inconsistency of results [13].

(*Continued*)

(*Continued*)

Ref. no.	Aim of the work	Methodology	Dataset used	Outcome, limitations & future scope
14.	The goal is to address the difficulty of recognizing Ficus species, a diverse genus with over 900 species, using traditional manual approaches. In light of the restricted availability of herbarium specimens and the complex taxonomy of Ficus, the research suggests employing pattern recognition methods, particularly by making use of leaf morphological characteristics. The objective is to create an automated identification system using image processing to train classification models such as artificial neural networks (ANN) and support vector machines (SVM) for three species of Ficus: F. benjamina, F. pellucidopunctata, and F. sumatrana. [14] As scientists work to address the rising crop waste brought on by illnesses, image-based plant disease identification is becoming more and more popular. It is essential to implement application-based disease identification in agriculturally dependent countries like South Asia [14].	1. To improve image quality, the image preprocessing step tackles shadow issues under non-flat leaves by using techniques such as RGB to HSV conversion, high-contrast channel selection, grayscale conversion, histogram-based contrast enhancement, and Canny edge detection for efficient leaf segmentation. 2. After processing leaf images, feature extraction converts them into descriptive parameters such as textural features using the Histogram of Oriented Gradients, Hu moment invariants, and morphological features. These 158 traits improve the ability to discriminate between various leaves and offer a thorough representation for further examination. 3. In the training stage of the investigation, two machine learning models—ANN and SVM—are used. SVM makes use of the radial basis function kernel, whereas ANN makes use of a three-layer feedforward network with 158 input nodes, 10 hidden nodes, and three output nodes. Robust model building and evaluation are ensured for the automatic identification system by the random allocation of training and testing datasets [14].	The pictures used in this project's dataset were obtained from the Rimba Ilmu Botanic Garden's University of Malaya Herbarium (abbreviated KLU). Three different species of Ficus (F. benjamina, F. pellucidopunctata, and F. sumatrana) were represented by a total of 54 sheets of herbarium specimens. These Specimens were painstakingly identified and annotated. They were gathered between 1961 and 2010, mostly from Kuala Lompat, Pahang, with some F. benjamina specimens from Kluang, Johor [14].	This study uses herbarium leaf photos and a pattern recognition approach to introduce automated identification procedures for three species of Ficus. The models' ability to generate satisfactory results through the use of machine learning techniques, particularly ANN and SVM, demonstrated their effectiveness in tasks involving species identification. This automated approach is not meant to take the place of knowledgeable taxonomists, but it offers a quick and easy way to identify plants with a respectable degree of accuracy. It can be enhanced in the future by including additional Ficus species, and it is particularly beneficial for people who are not taxonomy experts [14].

(*Continued*)

(Continued)

Ref. no.	Aim of the work	Methodology	Dataset used	Outcome, limitations & future scope
15.	Researchers are focusing more attention on image-based plant disease identification as a way to reduce the growing amount of agricultural waste caused by illnesses. Using characteristics like leaf size, color, and development patterns, application-based disease identification is becoming essential in agriculturally reliant regions like South Asia to provide farmers with timely and accurate information. This paper investigates the integration of artificial intelligence, specifically deep learning through convolutional neural networks (CNNs), to achieve a commendable 90.4% accuracy in classifying 38 diseases across 14 crops in the Plant Village dataset. This is achieved by leveraging the widespread use of smartphones and basic internet access [15].	The picture preprocessing technique used in this study entails resizing input images to various dimensions, using appropriate optimization and prediction, and normalizing the results to improve training performance. Calculating the mean and standard deviation, transforming the training set into a normalized distribution, and using techniques like rotation, shearing, zooming, and flipping to avoid overfitting are all part of the normalization process. A simple convolutional neural network (CNN) model comprising convolution, pooling, and fully connected layers is used by the training procedure. For non-linear saturation, the ReLU activation function is employed, and max pooling maximizes the output size. The research also uses transfer learning by switching last layers and modifying weights, as well as early halting to combat overfitting [15].	The Plant Village dataset is accessible through Kaggle and is offered for open access. About 50,000 photos of both fully healthy and diseased crops are included in the Plant Village collection, which has 38 classifications already categorized [15].	With a peak validation accuracy of 81.4%, the study assessed the accuracy of a naive network with different depths and found improvement up to 10 convolution layers. Nevertheless, because of a lack of data, deeper networks over ten layers had worse accuracy, which is why transfer learning using pre-trained ImageNet models was used. At 93.5% accuracy, the VGG16 model produced the best results, proving that transfer learning may improve outcomes even in the case of sparse data. The study team adjusted the parameters of well-known models such as Inceptionv3, ResNet50, VGG19, and VGG16 to create a highly effective deep learning model. Following the adjustment, the VGG model demonstrated its importance in disease categorization with an astounding 93.5% accuracy on available validation data [15].
16.	Machine language for the identification of healthy and diseased leaves [16].	1. Hu-moments 2. Texture of Haralick 3. Histogram in color There are actions that need to be taken in order to determine whether the leaf is infected or healthy, that is, earlier processing, extraction of features, classifier training, and classification [16].	One hundred sixty papaya leaf pictures were used to train the model [16].	As of right now, the model's accuracy rate is 70%. Increased training volume and the use of additional local features in addition to global features, such as SURF, DENSE, and SIFT, in addition to BOVW, can improve accuracy [16].

5.3 Methodology

First, 24 plant classes are created and given both common and scientific names. These are stored in the class names list. Each image is read by OpenCV. It then changes the image from BGR to RGB and resizes it to 150 by 150 pixels. Specific folders represent different classes and are used to input training data. These folders contain preprocessed images, tagged according to their titles. One test image has been processed *via* the same approaches. All pixel values have been matched to the [0,1] range by dividing by 255.0.

The manually defined model architecture includes:

- Three convolutional layers with ReLU activation and max pooling layers
- A flatten layer for feature extraction
- A fully connected (dense) layer with 512 neurons
- A dropout layer to reduce overfitting
- A softmax output layer for multi-class classification

The sparse categorical cross-entropy loss function and Adam optimizer are used to construct the model.

For data augmentation, the ImageDataGenerator applies:

- Rotation (40 degrees)
- Width and height shift (20%)
- Shearing (20%)
- Zooming (20%)
- Horizontal flipping with 'nearest fill' mode

By hand, the dataset is divided into 20% validation and 80% training. For training, a batch size of 64 is employed.

Early stopping is used to track validation loss and halt training after three epochs in which there is no improvement. When performance stalls, ReduceLROnPlateau dynamically lowers the learning rate, and ModelCheckpoint retains the top-performing model according to validation accuracy.

The optimal model is loaded and utilized for inference following 50 training epochs. The model's ability to infer is demonstrated by classifying the test image by choosing the label with the highest probability. For further use, the finished trained model is stored in .keras format. Figure 5.1 shows the validation and training accuracy of our ML model.

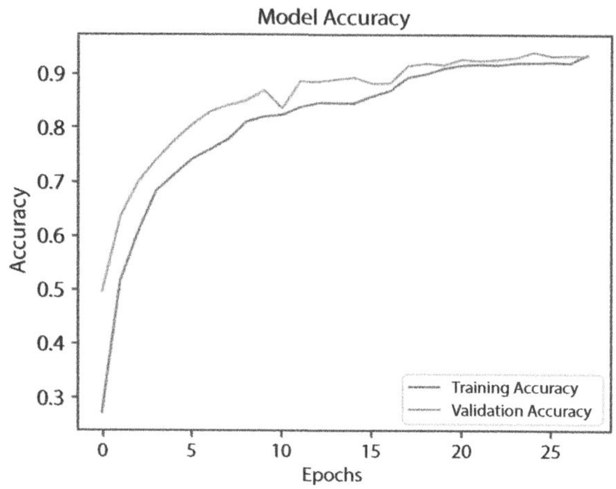

Figure 5.1 Accuracy graph.

5.4 Results and Discussions

The process for constructing the plant categorization model consists of three important steps:

Data Preprocessing: OpenCV was used to convert images of diverse plant species to RGB and resize them to 150x150 pixels. The resultant dataset was then partitioned in a way to include training, validation, and testing.

Training data was fetched and loaded by iterating over the directories, among them, each representing a distinct plant class. Then, images were preprocessed, tagged, and then arranged and shuffled to ensure random distribution.

To create a convolutional neural network (CNN), we have used the hyper-parameter tuning function of Keras Tuner, and to improve the validation accuracy, we have used several dense layer units, kernel sizes, filter topologies, and learning rates that were tested.

Then, to train the model, selecting the optimal hyper-parameters and training with enhanced data were used. The data augmentation techniques we used include zooms, shears, rotations, shifts, and flips. To prevent the model from overfitting the data, we used early stopping.

The model's overall performance was verified and checked on the validation data for evaluation, where both loss and accuracy were taken down. A single test image was then arranged by the model, followed by the same process that was applied during the training part.

Result: The overall execution successfully trained a convolutional neural network model to successfully recognize plant species from images without errors. Hyper-parameter adjustment and data augmentation led to improvement in the model's pliability and scope. The resultant model was then preserved for future use.

5.5 Key Findings

5.5.1 Algorithm Performance

The technique, in general, has the necessary skill to automate the traditional labor-driven process to identify plants and their species. It allows distinct identification, also reducing the overall time and the effort required for identifying and enhancing the accuracy by eliminating human intervention and biases.

5.5.2 Technological Integration

The study shows that artificial intelligence (AI) has all the potential to revolutionize redundant and traditional approaches, especially in places with a very long history of using medicinal plants and their derivatives, by necessarily integrating modern tools and libraries to produce very dependable systems.

5.5.3 Difficulties

The need for and availability of huge datasets, the complexities and problems of distinguishing distinct plants among various species, and potential biases and irregularities caused by a lack of training data are the most common difficulties.

5.6 Future Scope

5.6.1 Dataset Expansion

- Improve the system by cooperating with professionals like the botanists, ethnobotanists, and pharmacologists, which will help to meet the needs of both, the practitioners of traditional medicine and the modern pharmacological research.
- Applying this framework along with current agricultural technologies to further improve plant health monitoring as well as crop disease management.

5.6.2 Enhanced Feature Extraction

- The benefits that are possible from using advanced AI techniques like deep reinforcement learning and GANs are considered to see how they could further enhance both model performance and robustness.
- The system's dependence on large datasets in transfer learning methods can be reduced by retaining models that have previously gone through training for similar tasks.

5.6.3 Practical Applications

- Our system ensures that it supports sustainable harvesting, as it identifies not only the species but also the plant's maturity and the environmental impact of the extraction.
- It will contribute to the conservation of endangered medicinal plants with the development of a digital herbarium that can be used to preserve them.

5.6.4 Interdisciplinary Integration

- Improve the system by cooperation with professionals like the botanists, ethnobotanists, and pharmacologists, which will help to meet the needs of both the practitioners of traditional medicine and the modern pharmacological research.
- By combining this approach with modern agricultural technologies, it will be easier to carry out research on plant health monitoring and crop disease control.

5.6.5 Algorithm Enhancements

- The potential advantages we can get from the cutting-edge AI methods, such as deep reinforcement learning and generative adversarial networks (GANs) for enhancing model performance and adaptability, are currently being investigated.
- Transfer learning is a method that can be used to lessen reliance on big datasets by refining models that have previously been trained on relevant tasks.

5.6.6 Ecological and Ethical Considerations

- We will be ensuring that the system supports sustainable harvesting techniques through recognizing not just the species but also the maturity of the plant and the environmental effects of its extraction.
- We can develop a digital herbarium related to endangered medicinal plants; this will help contribute to their conservation.

5.6.7 Longitudinal Studies

- Longitudinal studies are being conducted to investigate the long-term impact of artificial intelligence–based plant identification on biodiversity conservation and traditional medical practices.
- Monitoring the system's efficacy in various geographical areas and under varied environmental circumstances.

AI disclosure statement: The author acknowledges the use of AI-based tools for minor language editing or grammatical correction. However, all intellectual contributions, analyses, and conclusions presented in this chapter are entirely the author's own.

References

1. Anwar, S.M., Majid, M., Qayyum, A., Awais, M., Alnowami, M., Khan, M.K., Medical Image Analysis using Convolutional Neural Networks: A Review. *J. Med. Syst.*, 42, 11, 226, 2018, doi:10.1007/s10916-018-1088-1.
2. Rao, R.U., Lahari, M.S., Sri, K.P., Srujana, K.Y., Yaswanth, D., Identification of Medicinal Plants using Deep Learning. *Int. J. Res. Appl. Sci. Eng. Technol.*, 10, 4, 306–322, 2022, doi:10.22214/ijraset.2022.41190.
3. Ibrahim, N.M.A., Gabr, D.G., Emara, A.H.M., A New Deep Learning System for Wild Plants Classification and Species Identification: Using Leaves and Fruits, in: *Advances in Intelligent Informatics and Computing*, vol. 127, Lecture Notes on Data Engineering and Communications Technologies, F. Saeed, F. Mohammed, F. Ghaleb (Eds.), pp. 26–37, Springer International Publishing, 2022, doi:10.1007/978-3-030-98741-1_3.
4. Arceusz, A., Radecka, I., Wesolowski, M., Identification of diversity in elements content in medicinal plants belonging to different plant families. *Food Chem.*, 120, 1, 52–58, 2010, doi:10.1016/j.foodchem.2009.09.068.

5. *Proceedings of the International Conference on Trends in Electronics and Informatics (ICOEI 2019)*, 23–25, April 2019, IEEE, 2019.
6. Chen, G., Weng, Q., Hay, G.J., He, Y., Geographic object-based image analysis (GEOBIA): emerging trends and future opportunities. *GISci. Remote Sens.*, 55, 2, 159–182, 2018, doi:10.1080/15481603.2018.1426092.
7. Mehdipour Ghazi, M., Yanikoglu, B., Aptoula, E., Plant identification using deep neural networks *via* optimization of transfer learning parameters. *Neurocomputing*, 235, 228–235, 2017, doi:10.1016/j.neucom.2017.01.018.
8. Santos, S.G., Melo, J.C., Constantino, R.G., Brito, A.V., A Solution for Vegetation Analysis, Separation, and Geolocation of Management Zones using Aerial Images by UAVs, in: *2019 IX Brazilian Symposium on Computing Systems Engineering (SBESC)*, IEEE, p. 1, 2019, doi:10.1109/SBESC49506.2019.9046079.
9. Iqbal, Z., Khan, M.A., Sharif, M., Shah, J.H., Ur Rehman, M.H., Javed, K., An automated detection and classification of citrus plant diseases using image processing techniques: A review. *Comput. Electron. Agric.*, 153, 12–32, 2018, doi:10.1016/j.compag.2018.07.032.
10. Abdullahi, H.S., Sheriff, R.E., Mahieddine, F., Convolution neural network in precision agriculture for plant image recognition and classification, in: *2017 Seventh International Conference on Innovative Computing Technology (INTECH)*, IEEE, pp. 1–3, 2017, doi:10.1109/INTECH.2017.8102436.
11. Yigit, E., Sabanci, K., Toktas, A., Kayabasi, A., A study on visual features of leaves in plant identification using artificial intelligence techniques. *Comput. Electron. Agric.*, 156, 369–377, 2019, doi:10.1016/j.compag.2018.11.036.
12. Koch, A., Tamez, P., Pezzuto, J., Soejarto, D., Evaluation of plants used for antimalarial treatment by the Maasai of Kenya. *J. Ethnopharmacol.*, 101, 1–3, 95–99, 2005, doi:10.1016/j.jep.2005.03.011.
13. Moshi, M., Van Den Beukel, C., Hamza, O., *et al.*, Brine Shrimp Toxicity Evaluation Of Some Tanzanian Plants Used Traditionally For The Treatment Of Fungal Infections. *Afr. J. Tradit. Complement. Altern. Med.*, 4, 2, 219–225, 2008, doi:10.4314/ajtcam.v4i2.31211.
14. Kho, S.J., Manickam, S., Malek, S., Mosleh, M., Dhillon, S.K., Automated plant identification using artificial neural network and support vector machine. *Front. Life Sci.*, 10, 1, 98–107, 2017, doi:10.1080/21553769.2017.1412361.
15. Panchal, A.V., Patel, S.C., Bagyalakshmi, K., Kumar, P., Khan, I.R., Soni, M., Image-based Plant Diseases Detection using Deep Learning. *Mater. Today Proc.*, 80, 3500–3506, 2023, doi:10.1016/j.matpr.2021.07.281.
16. Saleem, M.H., Potgieter, J., Arif, K.M., Plant Disease Detection and Classification by Deep Learning. *Plants*, 8, 11, 468, 2019, doi:10.3390/plants8110468.

6

AI and Machine Learning in Healthcare: Transforming Treatment, Ethics, and Resource Optimization

Aakansha Khanna[1*], Inderdeep Kaur[2], Inzimam Ul Hassan[2] and Pratyansh Singh[1]

[1]*Department of Information Technology, Chandigarh University, Mohali, Punjab, India*
[2]*Department of Computer Science and Engineering, Chandigarh University, Mohali, Punjab, India*

Abstract

Diagnosis, treatment planning, ethics, and resource allocation have improved with AI and ML day by day. These technologies enhance drug accuracy, hospital efficiency, and data-driven treatment. ML algorithms can analyze vast data sets to find illness trends, predict health issues, and assist clinicians in making better decisions. DeepMind's AlphaFold and IBM Watson for Oncology exhibit healthcare AI. AI can improve drug formulation, diagnostics, and error reduction. AI improves healthcare diagnosis, treatment, and resource optimization. AI-powered predictive analytics is used in hospitals to decide how many patients to admit, how to use medical resources, tour arrangements, and staffing. This lowers costs and improves service, ensuring crucial resources are available. AI automates administrative work, helping doctors spend more time with patients. Despite these changes, ethical, open, industry-wide healthcare AI applications are still hard to create. AI healthcare decisions present data privacy, algorithmic bias, and regulatory compliance concerns. Underrepresented or biased AI models could undermine minority healthcare. To ensure fair access to AI-driven healthcare solutions, study AI algorithms, accuracy, and biases. AI needs private medical records, increasing privacy and security concerns. HIPAA and GDPR undermine patient trust and data security.

**Corresponding author*: aakanshakhanna575@gmail.com

Rajdeep Chakraborty, Aleem Ali, Amit Paul, Nawaf R. Alharbe and S. Balamurugan (eds.) Causal Artificial Intelligence: Fundamentals and Applications, (123–140) © 2026 Scrivener Publishing LLC

***Keywords*:** Treatment planning, privacy of data, algorithmic bias, ethical AI, resource optimization

6.1 Introduction

The one important concern is how health care innovates to keep communities healthy. ML and AI replaced knowledge and hard work with data-driven healthcare. These technologies simplify drug research, medical care, regulatory compliance, and insurance administration and improve diagnosis and treatment.

Rising AI research and data-driven decision support systems are common. These systems train algorithms to make healthcare decisions, forecasts, and suggestions utilizing enormous data sets [1]. Healthcare AI is back thanks to machine learning, deep learning, powerful processors, and big datasets. While model-based methods use field expertise to construct rules and equations, data-driven methods constantly examine data to find new solutions. Data is needed for algorithm training and diagnosis. Data supports algorithm creation by measuring potential, changing parameters, and choosing machine learning approaches. Final validation and testing assess the algorithms' unknown data performance. Knowledge creation and clinical model deployment require data [2]. Also, the thing is that healthcare benefits from data-driven systems.

Basically, the data is required for improving algorithms, learning algorithms, and understanding healthcare challenges. It is very important to ensure that the patient data, medical images, and electronic health records are accurate. The data analysis that is already in process boosts algorithm performance very accurately and nicely. Data testing is needed for algorithm development. Optimizing algorithm settings and selecting the best machine learning methods [3]. Avoid training data specificity by testing algorithms on new data. This stage is critical for potential assessment. Final testing evaluates the model in real life using data not used in training or development [4]. With ML, stakeholder satisfaction and data analysis and validation may improve healthcare systems' decision-making, patient care, and operational efficiency.

6.1.1 Decision Support System in Healthcare Industry

The system of healthcare decision support is quite an old one. It's been almost 50 years since researchers have examined how computer-based solutions can help healthcare workers. It has several prototypes and products for the same [5]. Computer software helps in making many decision-making tasks. Other decision-making duties include assessing risks like disease progression or adverse effects, predicting hospital resource needs, evaluating treatment efficacy, assisting in intervention planning (including surgical or treatment strategies), and monitoring patient progress. Modeling has produced several research papers. Highlights include deep research of prediction and statistical modeling, medicinal applications, and recent and prospective improvements, including AI breakthroughs.

There are so many techniques that are used in data science decision support tool processing [6]. Figure 6.1: indicates the Patient Management Decision Tool. It basically highlights the evaluation of defects, missing or inaccurate data, input data correctness, signal clarity, and also the critical feature extraction and selection are early methods [7]. This chapter examines objectively assessing system performance, particularly output quality.

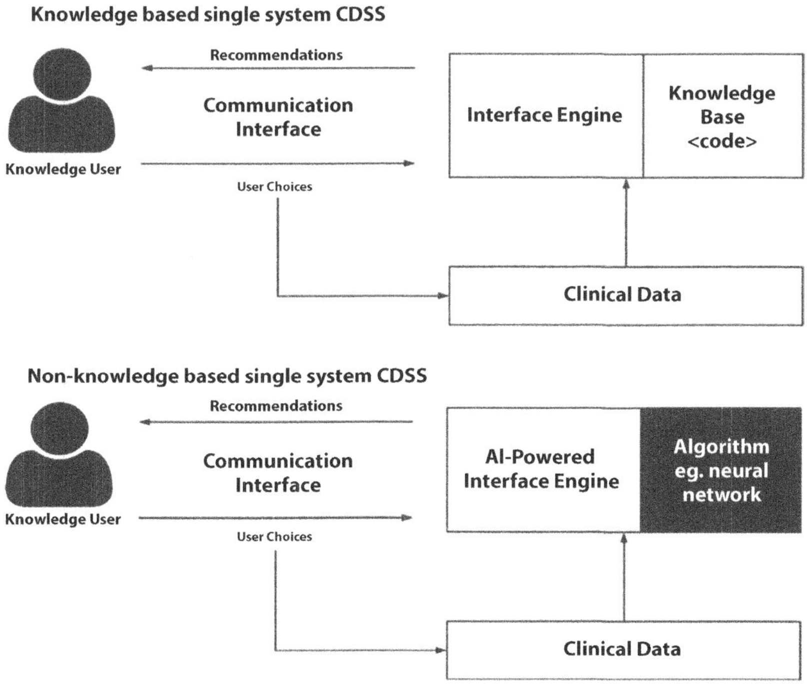

Figure 6.1 Patient management decision tool.

6.2 What is Machine Learning?

Machine learning acts as a teacher to teach AI machines to predict or work without instructions independently. It helps in improving disease identification, treatment, and prevention.

Machine learning improves software performance in task class T using output quality P and past occurrences E. Like AI, it uses math to detect patterns in complex datasets. Better data analysis approaches are employed in machine learning. Learning from data rather than algorithms helps computers find hidden insights [2]. Analytical methods enable computers to assess data without scripting. The method improves various tasks over time. In 1959, Arthur Samuel coined the term "machine learning".

Performance measures include sensitivity, specificity, and accuracy.

Health data must withstand errors and low quality.

6.2.1 Data Quality Quandaries

Machine learning in healthcare offers innovative choices but also hazards, barriers, and mistrust. Prophecy errors, system security and privacy vulnerabilities, and a lack of data for correct results are the main dangers discussed in this talk. Ethics, denial of healthcare, and finding clear and appropriate therapeutic therapies are difficulties. Professionals must explore the various challenges of applying machine learning algorithms to healthcare.

Healthcare ML models demand comprehensive data management. User-friendly goods data processing and machine learning pipelines are needed. These pipelines train machine learning models with raw data. Using bogus data by key parties requires strong data governance.

Decision tree models simplify ML predictions, making them sensible. A comprehensive legal and other permissions must be obtained before using machine learning to do this. A skilled healthcare worker can monitor and participate in surgery to prevent depression or breast cancer. These initiatives may inspire other healthcare workers, easing fears about job prospects and a diminishing workforce. Accurate and recurrent forecasts also require correct data. Data is essential for deep learning and machine learning.

The model of Singapore's 2019 AI governance framework helps in the private enterprises. The US government issued an executive order to monitor AI progress and preserve leadership. Lack of transparency has slowed the adoption of machine learning-based solutions in healthcare, but it may not in other industries. Early detection using machine learning may enhance primary care patient behavior. Finally, 5% of physicians had shorter patient appointments than 9 minutes, and 57% had 16 minutes [13]. Doctors may spend more time with patients in person by using AI to analyze and monitor symptoms, lowering stress and enhancing results and satisfaction.

6.3 Categories of Machine Learning

Figure 6.2 shows the four primary machine learning categories—Supervised, Unsupervised, Semi-Supervised, and Reinforcement—based on data input and learning aim.

6.3.1 Supervised Learning

Using supervised machine learning models requires a specified target output and labeled data. Diabetes and hypertension may arise. The suggested model will be less effective and relevant to a wider population than the training dataset if findings are misrepresented. Supervised ML model development is exact and advanced due to its frequent application.

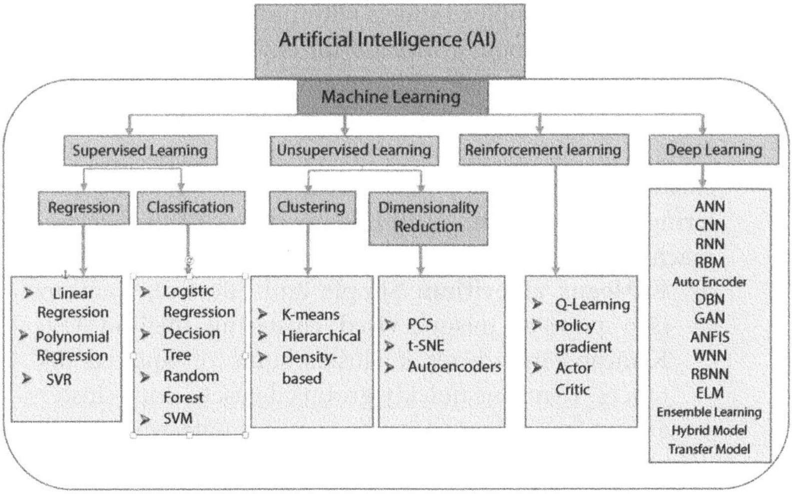

Figure 6.2 Major categories of machine learning.

Input data setup affects classification algorithms' predictions. Supervised machine learning is used for voice recognition, heart attack prediction, and medical imaging analysis.

Continuous variables are predicted using linear regression. Variables are presumed linearly connected. It examines independent variables. Healthcare workers comprehend linear regression better than other machine learning methods since it's so ubiquitous.

SVM Regression: This method finds non-linear correlations between quantitative dependent variables and predictors. SVM can generalize, predict accurately, and ignore outliers [11]. When handling plenty of data, this method may not work. We know that if the main sample size is smaller and there are many variables, this model may fail badly. Decision Tree Regression: This method predicts a numerical variable using yes/no questions [13]. This method does not prove outcome variable distribution theories. LASSO regression is used in selection and minimal shrinkage.

6.3.2 Unsupervised Learning

The outcome and data labels are not set in unsupervised machine learning. Multiple unsupervised learning methods exist. Clustering organizes data using an algorithm. Cluster analysis tends to overstate group similarities, caution is advised when drawing results.

A. **Algorithms for Unsupervised Learning:** Unsupervised machine learning analyzes unlabeled data using nonlinear learning and complex models with millions of parameters. Clustering is a popular method for exploratory data analysis, categorization, and pattern identification. Unsupervised machine learning draws conclusions from unlabeled data [15]. Main tactics include soft and hard clustering. Hard clustering places data points in one cluster, while soft clustering places them in several. Many popular unsupervised machine learning algorithms will be discussed.

   a) **K-Means algorithm:** Simple and effective, K-means is a popular unsupervised clustering method [12]. K-means minimizes k cluster sums of squared distances. K-means quickly groups datasets since clusters are set up. This strategy reorganizes data when unsupervised learning fails. K-means is affected by dataset size and form, calculates cluster number ahead of time, and does not maintain convex cluster size and density. This can lead to conflicting results when starting conditions differ.

b) **K-Medoids:** The K-Medoids cluster like K-Means. It concentrates clusters around real objects, not mean values. This is K-Medoids. It helps in keeping the closest object in the cluster [14]. With different starting centroids, K-medoids algorithms yield inconsistent outcomes. More resistant to outliers, they can change cluster membership.

c) **Hierarchical Clustering:** Clustering with hierarchical cluster analysis (HCA) is common in data mining. Create a hierarchy from cluster similarities and differences. Hierarchical clustering layers dendrogram clusters to form collections. Hierarchical cluster analysis includes agglomerative and divisive approaches. An agglomerative cluster tree "bottom up" mixes lower- and higher-level nodes. However, divided clustering starts at "the root" and descends to "the leaves." The first cluster of observations splits into smaller groupings as one descends the hierarchy. Hierarchical clustering identifies dataset sizes and types. Dendrograms can be made without cluster counts. Hierarchical clustering predicts mental health 90% precisely.

6.3.3 Reinforcement Learning

Early reinforcement learning research included statistics, cybernetics, neurology, psychology, and computer science. New research focuses on AI and machine learning [13]. Mesmerize, which teaches agents incentives and consequences, is my favorite without aid. Ten years of incremental reinforcement learning in customized medicine have paid off. Dynamic Treatment Regimes (DTRs), complex, multi-phase treatment decision-making processes, were created first. HIV, cancer, high blood pressure, and anemia patients had the highest chance of recovery at traditional clinics. This technique may change medication dosage, treatment, and other measures.

6.4 Challenges and Architecture of the I-Healthcare System

6.4.1 I-Health System Challenges

Remote healthcare systems have improved; however, many major issues remain to improve healthcare services. Because e-health technology is growing so quickly, it is now possible to collect, store, and analyze vast volumes of data from many different places and sources (such as hospitals, clinics, etc.) in order to give people good health care. Edge nodes, such as cellphones with cameras, fast computers, sensors, and storage space, let patients and users collect a lot of data from anywhere at any time. Experiential learning methods are typically essential in dynamic environments.

a) **Significant user base:** Due to the rising number of elderly and chronically ill persons, most hospitals see many patients daily. This statistic is easily repeatable during a pandemic like the COVID-19 pandemic, which strains numerous healthcare institutions. Due to its large patient/user base, the I-Health system struggles to provide precise and tailored clinical judgments in a set order.
b) **Distribution and imbalance of data:** Due to the I-Health system variability, patient data distribution and quantity vary greatly. I-Health systems distribute data unequally across cameras, sensors, hospitals, and cellphones. Unbalanced data can bias and mispredict many machine learning systems, compromising their quality and fairness.
c) **Architecture of Health System:** The suggested framework has three layers: perception, edge intelligence, and smart core network. Figure 6.3 shows the healthcare operational framework. This structure runs from data generation and collection to control and administration. The main components are as follows:
    i. **Perception layer:** It basically employs various data sources in real time to locate and monitor. Placement of modern sensors and IoMT equipment is done in hospitals, clinics, and patient rooms. Body, environment, wearables, and imaging sensors exist.

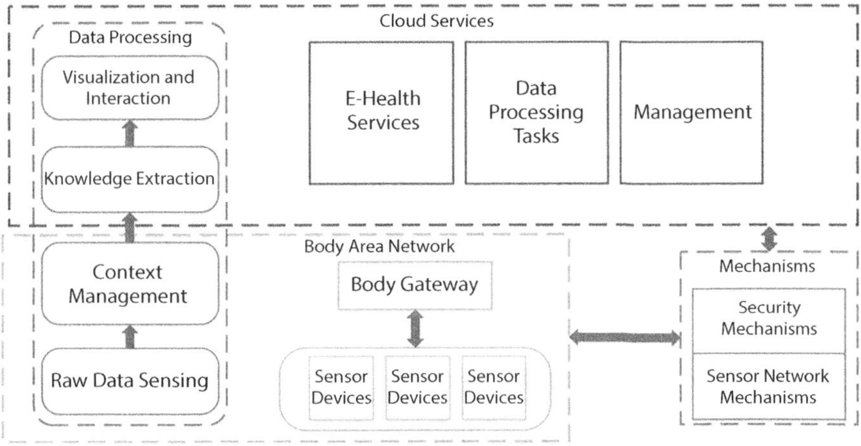

Figure 6.3 Healthcare operational framework.

ii. **Intelligence edge layer:** It connects many data sources to the primary network for transport, storage, and analysis [14]. Smart edge nodes take medical and non-medical data from numerous sources. It may then filter and extract important data. HetNet can transfer processed or extracted data to the core network. Second-group networks include cellular, WLAN, D2D, and sensor. This diversified network simplifies switching technology platforms for medical data delivery. Tell them smart edge nodes work with other health apps.

iii. **Smart Core Network Layer:** Smart core network layer in healthcare system design. Controlling, managing, and merging data improves healthcare. This layer simplifies healthcare by managing network traffic, resource allocation, and medical data protection. Sharing data for integrated care and strong analytics for decision-making simplifies healthcare platform growth and cooperation. Data-driven insights from the smart core network layer let doctors provide patient-specific care, modernizing healthcare.

6.5 Deep Learning

Deep learning is the representation of raw data differently, rather than machine learning. Deep learning helps neural networks and computers with varying processing levels understand complex data concepts. Most artificial neural networks have three layers and are taught to produce supervised representations with low generality. In contrast, each layer in a deep learning system uses knowledge from the previous layer to improve a local unsupervised criterion to represent observed patterns.

6.5.1 Neural Networks Reform the Deep Learning Architecture

a) **CNN:** The translation-invariant descriptors are created by CNNs using feature pooling, local connections, and connected units with shared weights. CNNs have one convolutional and pooling layer. A fully connected layer may be used for supervised forecasting. Most CNNs use convolutional and pooling layers. Computer vision benefits most from CNNs. CNN training normally requires many tagged papers.
b) **RNN:** RNNs help track constantly-incoming data. To overcome this problem, LSTM and GRU networks created cells that use the input value, current memory, and prior state to store and discard data. These versions capture long-term connections and Natural Language Processing jobs well.
c) **RBM:** Restricted Boltzmann machines (RBMs) learn and construct input space probability distributions. Restricted Boltzmann Machines (RBMs) form bipartite graphs with neurons. RBMs excel in collaborative filtering and dimension reduction. The usage of stacked Restricted Boltzmann Machines makes these systems "Deep Belief Networks".
d) **AE:** Autoencoders are self-learning machine learning models that use the same input as output. The encoder converts the input into a latent form, and the decoder rebuilds it. And AEs must minimize reconstruction errors.

6.6 Case Study and Applications

i. **Google DeepMind's AlphaFold:** DeepMind developed AlphaFold, a cutting-edge AI system that predicts protein three-dimensional structures [17]. AlphaFold employed deep learning and a new neural network design to predict protein structure based on amino acid order. This resolved protein folding, biology's toughest issue. AlphaFold achieved scientific aims by defeating computer algorithms in the Critical Assessment of Structure Prediction (CASP) competition in 2020 and 2021. It has accelerated medication development, helped scientists understand diseases at the molecular level, and allowed them to study protein structures from the human genome and other sources.

ii. **IBM:** IBM Watson for Cancer Watson for Oncology helps doctors diagnose and treat cancer. Memorial Sloan Kettering Cancer Center enabled it to access medical literature, patient data, and clinical trial data to recommend tailored cancer treatments [18]. Since it may modify cancer treatment, the system was popular, but it was criticized for uneven guidance and lack of real-world testing. IBM reduced Watson Health initiatives, closing many Watson for Oncology facilities before 2020. Watson for Oncology wasn't perfect, but it illustrated the possibilities and challenges of utilizing AI in complex medical decisions.

iii. **PathAI:** PathAI saves pathologists' time and improves cancer detection [19]. Deep learning algorithms let PathAI find things in pathology slides and tissue samples that humans miss. The diagnosis is more reliable.

iv. **Aidoc:** Radiology-focused AI Aidoc. CT scans identify brain hemorrhages, pulmonary embolisms, and fractures in real time [20]. It warns radiologists of life-threatening situations straight from hospital PACS systems for speedier response. Many FDA approvals make Aidoc useful in emergency and radiology departments globally. Improved productivity, diagnostic delays, and patient outcomes.

v. **Babylon Health:** Babylon Health uses AI and telemedicine to monitor and assess your health and call you. Users can write symptoms for a preliminary diagnosis or advice from the AI-powered chatbot. Docs can view medical data remotely. Babylon aims to improve low-income healthcare.

vi. **Butterfly iQ:** AI-powered handheld ultrasound device makes imaging affordable and accessible in many healthcare settings [24]. One semiconductor chip-equipped probe performs AI-based whole-body scanning. All the applications are illustrated in Table 6.1 and the use-cases are shown in Table 6.2.

Table 6.1 Application of machine learning [23].

Application	Description	Key features	Benefits	Challenges
Improved diagnostics with predictions of disease	AI-enabled diagnostic tools use advanced algorithms to scan large data sets, like medical images and clinical information, to improve diagnostics.	Enhanced capacity to diagnose diseases, early detection of tumors, precision matching or surpassing human expertise.	Improved diagnostic accuracy, early intervention, enhanced treatment planning.	Data quality, integration issues, need for continuous updates.
Detection of diabetes	Save lives by early detection of diabetes with machine learning.	Early identification, prevention of secondary complications, better resource allocation.	Timely diabetes detection, reduced risk of complications, improved patient outcomes.	Accuracy of data, compliance of the patient, existing system integration.
Accurately predicting patient's history	It majorly helps in the gathering of the patient's medical history and data efficiently so that they can choose the most relevant inquiries.	Efficient data gathering, accurate risk assessment, tailored inquiries.	Better medical decision-making, and also good personalized care.	Data privacy, need for comprehensive datasets, integration with clinical workflows.

(Continued)

Table 6.1 Application of machine learning [23]. *(Continued)*

Application	Description	Key features	Benefits	Challenges
Better processes for the treatment	ML helps in better research and clinical trials, which helping in the better choosing of the candidates.	Optimized candidate selection, real-time data analysis, error reduction.	More effective clinical trials, reduced errors, accelerated research.	Better and organized data management.
Operations involving robots also other such therapies which are guided by images	Many ML tools help surgeons to improve their perspectives by providing required precise information for the surgeries.	Enhanced surgeon's perspective, precise information, flexible AI-powered solutions.	Improved surgical outcomes, enhanced precision, better utilization of data.	Integration with existing systems, ensuring data accuracy, maintaining AI model performance.
Clinical trials	Machine learning predicts appropriate candidates for clinical trials, providing real- time data on participants' medical history, therapies, and health status.	Prediction of candidates, real-time data provision, informed decision-making.	Comprehensive patient history, improved clinical decision-making, personalized care.	Data privacy, patient recruitment, ensuring data accuracy.

6.6.1 Use Cases

Table 6.2 Use cases: applications, key features, benefits and challenges [23].

Application	Description	Key features	Benefits	Challenges
ProMED posting online reports of illness outbreaks	ProMED provides real-time analysis and reporting of infectious disease outbreaks worldwide, integrating data into a HealthMap for global display.	Real-time reporting, expert-reviewed reports, HealthMap integration.	Timely outbreak detection, comprehensive data integration, improved global health monitoring.	Data accuracy, integration of diverse data sources, maintaining real-time updates.
Altering smoking habits with SmokeBeat	SmokeBeat helps individuals quit smoking by gathering data on smoking patterns and providing instant rewards for engaging in cognitive behavior therapy.	Detection of hand-to-mouth movements, instant rewards, supportive community.	Support for quitting smoking, behavior therapy reinforcement, community support.	User compliance, accuracy of movement detection, effectiveness of rewards.

(Continued)

Table 6.2 Use cases: applications, key features, benefits and challenges [23]. (*Continued*)

Application	Description	Key features	Benefits	Challenges
Utilizing molly to streamline remote care	Molly, a virtual nurse, remotely monitors medical issues by gathering data from patients' Bluetooth-connected monitoring devices and providing speech and chatbot interactions.	Remote monitoring, speech comprehension, chatbot for discreet conversations.	Continuous patient monitoring, improved patient engagement, discreet communication.	Data privacy, reliability of remote monitoring devices, natural language comprehension.
Enhancing picture quality using subtle mr	Subtle MR, a machine learning-based software, improves MRI scan quality by reducing noise and increasing resolution.	Noise reduction, resolution enhancement, accelerated processes.	Enhanced MRI scan quality, faster imaging processes, better diagnostic accuracy.	Ensuring image accuracy, integration with existing MRI systems, maintaining process speed.
Enhance surgical system	Surgeons use the multi-armed enhanced surgical system, which utilizes deep learning and machine learning models for remote operations and simulations.	Remote operation, ML-powered simulations, eye-tracking camera adjustments.	Improved surgical outcomes, enhanced precision, advanced pre-surgery simulations.	System integration, maintaining ML model performance, ensuring data accuracy in simulations.

6.7 Conclusion

This chapter illustrated how machine learning and AI affect healthcare in various fields such as operations, ethics, treatment planning, and diagnostics. The findings could improve healthcare resource use and personalized treatment accuracy. AlphaFold from Google DeepMind and IBM Watson for oncology effectively predicts protein folding and provides excellent cancer treatment to people. Imagining a future where new technologies improve healthcare and speed recovery is crucial. To meet healthcare business objectives with the use of ML and AI applications, transformation must be a major focus because technology and healthcare are continually changing. Their accuracy, algorithms, and suitability for diverse patient groups need more research. The tightest patient privacy and transparency standards for AI applications are constantly researched, especially as laws and policies change. Improving apps and finding new uses requires substantial research and development commitment. This will inspire new healthcare operations and treatment planning solutions.

AI disclosure statement: The author acknowledges the use of AI-based tools for minor language editing or grammatical correction. However, all intellectual contributions, analyses, and conclusions presented in this chapter are entirely the author's own.

Bibliography

1. Aggarwal, A., Tam, C.C., Wu, D., Li, X., Qiao, S., Artificial Intelligence–based Chatbots for Promoting Health Behavioral Changes: Systematic Review. *J. Med. Internet Res.*, 25, 2023, https://doi.org/10.2196/40789.
2. Alanazi, A., Using machine learning for healthcare challenges and opportunities. *Inf. Med. Unlocked*, 30, 100924, 2022, https://doi.org/10.1016/j.imu.2022.100924.
3. An, Q., Rahman, S., Zhou, J., Kang, J.J., A comprehensive review on machine learning in healthcare industry: Classification, restrictions, opportunities and challenges. *Sensors*, 23, 9, 4178, 2023, https://doi.org/10.3390/s23094178.
4. Javaid, M., Haleem, A., Pratap Singh, R., Suman, R., Rab, S., Significance of machine learning in healthcare: Features, pillars and applications. *Int. J. Intell. Networks*, 3, 58–73, 2022, ISSN 2666-6030, https://doi.org/10.1016/j.ijin.2022.05.002. https://www.sciencedirect.com/science/article/pii/S2666603022000069
5. Habehh, H. and Gohel, S., Machine learning in Healthcare. *Curr. Genomics*, 22, 4, 291–300, 2021, https://doi.org/10.2174/1389202922666210705124359.

6. itransition, Machine Learning in Healthcare: 10 Use Cases, Examples & Benefits, 2023, https://www.itransition.com/machinelearning/healthcare.
7. Kaur, I. and Ali, A., An in-depth exploration of machine learning algorithms and performance evaluation approaches for personalized diabetes prediction, in: *2024 International Conference on Emerging Innovations and Advanced Computing (INNOCOMP)*, Sonipat, India, IEEE, pp. 532–538, 2024, https://doi.org/10.1109/INNOCOMP63224.2024.00093.
8. Kaur, I. and Ali, A., A complete study on machine learning algorithms for medical data analysis. In *Fog computing for intelligent cloud IoT systems*, S. Banerjee, A. Ghosh, R. Chakraborty, A. A. Elngar (Eds.), pp. [chapter pages], Wiley, Hoboken, NJ, USA, 2024, https://doi.org/10.1002/9781394175345.ch7.
9. Kaur, I. and Ali, A., Unveiling the power of prediction: A comprehensive guide to learning techniques, from data preparation to model interpretability for early prediction of diabetes and effective management, Taylor & Francis, 2025, Available at: https://www.taylorfrancis.com/chapters/edit/10.1201/9781003592969-1/unveiling-power-prediction-inderdeep-kaur-aleem-ali.
10. Sehgal, D., Kaur, I., Sharma, V., Gautam, B., Singh, A., Kumar, N., AI-Driven Early Diabetes Prediction, in: *2024 IEEE 3rd World Conference on Applied Intelligence and Computing (AIC)*, Gwalior, India, pp. 40–48, 2024, doi: 10.1109/AIC61668.2024.10730970.
11. Khanna, A., Singh, P., Inzimam-Ul-Hassan, Kaur, I., Predictive Analytics for Cardiovascular Health: A Machine Learning Approach, in: *2024 International Conference on Advances in Modern Age Technologies for Health and Engineering Science (AMATHE)*, Shivamogga, India, pp. 1–6, 2024, doi: 10.1109/AMATHE61652.2024.10582101.
12. Sharma, M., Kaur, I., Saini, G., Thakur, V., Mishra, A., Predictive Modeling for Stroke Risk Assessment Using Machine Learning, in: *2024 International Conference on Intelligent Systems for Cybersecurity (ISCS)*, Gurugram, India, pp. 1–6, 2024, doi: 10.1109/ISCS61804.2024.10581155.
13. Khanna, A., Khanna, A., Kaur, I., Hassan, I. U., Healthcare AI: Optimizing diagnosis & treatment plans: AI-driven precision medicine & personalized healthcare. In *Book title* (pp. chapter pages). Taylor & Francis, 2024, https://doi.org/10.1201/9781003674542-11.
14. Brown, S., Machine Learning, explained. MIT Sloan, 2021, April 21, https://mitsloan.mit.edu/ideas-made-to-matter/machine-learning-explained.
15. Javaid, M., Haleem, A., Pratap Singh, R., Suman, R., Rab, S., Significance of machine learning in Healthcare: Features, pillars and applications. *Int. J. Intell. Networks*, 3, 58–73, 2022, https://doi.org/10.1016/j.ijin.2022.05.002.
16. Jumper, J., *et al.*, Highly accurate protein structure prediction with AlphaFold. *Nature*, 596, 7873, 583–589, 2021, doi: 10.1038/s41586-021-03819-2.

17. Strickland, M., IBM Watson, heal thyself: How IBM overpromised and underdelivered on AI health care. *IEEE Spectr.*, 56, 4, 24–31, Apr. 2019, doi: 10.1109/MSPEC.2019.8675870.
18. Steiner, A., *et al.*, Impact of a deep learning assistant on the histopathologic classification of liver cancer. *npj Digital Med.*, 4, 1, 1–8, 2021, doi: 10.1038/s41746-021-00452-9.
19. Aidoc, Aidoc Medical Imaging AI Solutions, 2023, https://www.aidoc.com/.
20. Babylon Health, Our Technology, 2023, https://www.babylonhealth.com/.
21. Tempus, About Tempus: Enabling Precision Medicine Through Data and AI, 2023, https://www.tempus.com/.
22. Butterfly Network, Butterfly iQ+ - Whole-body imaging. One probe, 2023, https://www.butterflynetwork.com/.
23. Sarker, I.H., Machine Learning: Algorithms, Real-World Applications and Research Directions. *SN Comput. Sci.*, 2, 3, 160, 2021. doi: 10.1007/s42979-021-00592-x. Epub 2021 Mar 22. PMID: 33778771; PMCID: PMC7983091.
24. Khanna, A., Singh, P., Kaur, I., Khanna, A., Unraveling Causal Pathways in Heart Failure: A LiNGAM Approach to Understanding Clinical Factors Influencing Patient Outcomes, in: *2025 IEEE International Conference on Advances in Computing Research On Science Engineering and Technology (ACROSET)*, Indore, India, pp. 1–4, 2025, doi: 10.1109/ACROSET66531.2025.11281224. keywords: {Computational modeling;Mortality;Medical treatment;Machine learning;Predictive models;Blood pressure;Cardiovascular diseases;Optimization;Blood;Guidelines;Causal Inference;heart failure;LiNGAM;clinical factors;mortality risk;causal graph}

7

Real-Time Driver Fatigue Monitoring Using AI: An Ethical and Non-Intrusive Approach to Road Safety

Sumanta Chatterjee* **and Amit Majumder**

Dept. of CSE, NIT - Jamshedpur, Jharkhand, India

Abstract

The fatigue of drivers is the cause of astounding road accidents worldwide. These victims are human beings and finances. The chapter will offer a proposal for an in-cab, non-intrusive, and real-time driver fatigue detection system based on AI and ML technologies, with the aim of enhancing its final objective, which is that of road safety. The method that this system employs is the combination of digital image analysis solutions, including the eye aspect ratio (EAR) analysis, and also including the facial landmark tracking and monitoring of the physiological signals, including heart rates, and also the skin conductance measurement. Hi-tech AI algorithms guarantee exhaustion detection and on-time notification through an auditory, visual, or touch alert. It is designed to fit smoothly into vehicles and offers to cover all extremes in environmental and individual behavioral differences in drivers. The design puts emphasis on the ethical concerns regarding data privacy issues and algorithmic fairness in order to aid responsible deployment.

***Keywords*:** Driver fatigue detection, road safety, AI and ML technologies, real-time fatigue detection, eye aspect ratio (EAR), multimodal data fusion

7.1 Introduction

Drowsy driving is currently one of the most pressing considerations when it comes to road safety, as it is known to contribute significantly to many accidents, injuries, and losses at the global scale. For example, studies

**Corresponding author*: sumanta.prof@gmail.com

Rajdeep Chakraborty, Aleem Ali, Amit Paul, Nawaf R. Alharbe and S. Balamurugan (eds.) Causal Artificial Intelligence: Fundamentals and Applications, (141–174) © 2026 Scrivener Publishing LLC

mention that huge numbers of crashes are due to drowsy driving when the driver literally falls asleep at the wheel or loses alertness, slowly heading into a road accident [1, 4]. These accidents normally include loss and sorrow, but also a massive financial burden on an individual, organization, and government. Numerous innovative technologies have been developed in the struggle against this sort of overwhelming issue, typically driver fatigue detection and multifunctional systems to reduce road accidents [6, 7].

In that way, AI and ML have been highly integrated into the transportation systems to come up with a newer and improved concept that will eliminate drowsy driving. The majority of existing drowsy driver monitoring systems, including in-vehicle and periodic visual checkups, are incomplete and fail to capture the uniqueness and highly dynamic characteristics of fatigue-related behavior [10]. The objective of this study is to develop a non-invasive and real-time drowsy driving detector based on the latest AI and ML algorithms with the purpose of enhancing road safety as well as reducing the risk of road accidents resulting from fatigue among drivers [4, 10].

The point of all such systems is the ideal blend of a number of advanced computer vision methods and, at the same time, physical signal surveillance. Most of the techniques developed are used in computer vision, including EAR analysis and tracking facial landmarks to literally locate physical indicators of drowsiness, including either eye closure or head movements [6, 10]. The visual phenomena analysis, with reference to the real-time connection to the functional dynamism, is a valuable source of alertness information to the driver. In addition, it entails the observation of physiological indicators such as heart rate and skin conductance to document such distinctive physiological responses that accompany sleep deprivation in the driver [1, 13, 14]. These two develop a system of examination of visual and physiological data with the expectation of achieving the most comprehensive method in evaluating the condition of the driver with regard to the instance of drowsiness.

The answer that is to be received is a more faithful detection and is more timely than any other wake-detection system. Among the largest advantages this system can be attributed to is the fact that the system operates in real time, and the driver can be provided with instant feedback by use of audio or alarm, and even the sense of sight [10]. The particularity of these alarms to draw good attention without forgetting too little good attention in a driver is tact in the tactic of not inducing more distraction with the alerts. AI algorithms will maintain the system's adaptability to the slightest individual difference in how drivers react as a result of aspects such as their driving habits, road conditions, and changes in the environment [4, 7].

This is very crucial to the effectiveness of this system in the continually increasing realms of traffic since it is dynamically able to adjust to the changes that enter the driving space, and as such, it can provide more personalized feedback. Moreover, other than real-time detection, the system suggested can be integrated into several different automobile categories, starting from personal cars to public transportation and logistics fleets [11]. It is also scalable, thus making it versatile in being deployed in different sectors of the transportation industry, a very low-budget answer to fill up the likely gap of sleep-caused road mishaps [10]. In any personal vehicle, public transport, or cargo delivery mode, this system will significantly increase the security of all of them by alerting drivers before drowsy occurrences hinder road safety.

Ethics plays a major role in the development and application of any AI-based system, especially when delicate data such as physiological and driver behavior is concerned [12, 17]. The privacy of the data and equity issues in designing and implementing a driver drowsiness detection system are also of concern to this system. The protocol dictates that a privacy policy must dictate that any form of personal information obtained must be stored in a more secure and anonymous form to ensure that it cannot be accessed or abused by anyone. Besides, the AI algorithms are transparent and impartial regarding erroneous information on the basis of facts such as age, sex, or race, none of which would be determinants of any bias that it would inevitably have acquired [17, 18]. Discipline of these ethical guarantees is an advantage to the system installation, and simultaneously, it gains a little trust of trade partners and users.

In addition, a range of advancements will occur in the driver drowsiness-detection systems. These include research and development activities in developing its outputs to perfection, such as an emphasis on improvement in the performance and reliability levels of the system [4, 10]. Adaptive thresholding is one of the changes that will be integrated in this, and it can adjust system dynamics, depending on various kinds of factors, including the time of day, the road conditions, and driver-specific patterns, in order to enhance accuracy [7, 12]. These proposals would result in studies being done on multimodal data fusion, in which various types of sensors and other data sources will be examined to substantiate a far more all-inclusive view of a potential cumulative evaluation of driver fatigue [8, 13]. In addition, integration of the system with autonomous vehicles exhibits high prospects in advancing the overall safety of self-driving cars in order to allow seamless mixing of human and automated modes of driving and ensure that drivers are awake when needed [9, 17].

Such development would lead to its exponential sophistication and thus more capabilities. It would be perceptible only in the context of this variant opportunity, as we predicted as early as its inception, which corresponds to one of the most demanding tasks concerning road safety. With AI and ML set in place through highly informative monitoring of both kinds of real-time feedback, this has the potential to minimize accidents and death for the previously highly likely class of driver fatigue accidents in transportation. With a scalable and adaptable design, the serious ethical considerations invested in it necessarily make the integration of the system in a great variety of transport. It promises to make safer, more efficient movements of all those who use roads, and also to enhance road safety for pedestrians in an environment, the architecture of which is still to evolve for the safest travel lessons.

In Section 7.2, the relationship between AI-based real-time monitoring of fatigue and road safety is examined, wherein fatality-preventing detection of drowsiness takes place while still in the drowsy phase. Section 7.3 highlights the technologies of AI and machine learning for drowsiness detection, such as facial recognition and eye tracking, as well as physiological signal analysis. Section 7.4 discusses some of the major challenges affecting the implementation of these systems: data variability, sensor limitations, and privacy concerns. Section 7.5 highlights future directions and developments, such as personalized AI and multimodal sensing, whereas Section 7.6 concludes by summarizing what is currently underway and stresses the need for ethical and scalable solutions.

7.2 Leveraging Artificial Intelligence for Safer Roads through Real-Time Fatigue Monitoring

While drowsy driving is one of the fundamental ways of road traffic accidents being caused, other causes are quite important, including driver attentiveness problems, distractions, driver sight disturbances, drunkenness, drugged driving, and injuries, which have the potential to lead to a collision. It has been estimated that every year, some 2,000 to 2,500 persons are killed, and around a million or so people lose their lives or are either seriously or lightly injured because of driving-related drowsiness. While enforcement and public awareness campaigns have significantly helped in addressing the problem, present technologies can still not provide 100%

foolproof measures to prevent the perils linked with a drowsy driver. Real-time driver drowsiness monitoring techniques are potentially promising because advances in this field include AI and machine learning technologies. Being able to spot drowsy drivers, such systems also need close monitoring for real-time precision sensing, which means that they can alert drivers immediately. Long-term solutions are needed to address drowsiness crashes.

In summary, this chapter attempts to stress the utility that real-time fatigue monitoring systems paired with advanced artificial intelligence systems can bring about safer roads, alert drivers to the condition at hand, and save lives in the long term with the mitigation of conditions that could lead to drowsy or fatigued driving-related collisions.

7.2.1 The Impact of Driver Fatigue on Road Safety

What happens to a driver when they become really exhausted from a long road trip? One of the repercussions of being overworked is in the information, which usually accounts for approximately 20% of global road accidents, often with tragic outcomes. That is why, no longer able to drive, it takes longer to respond, which causes unusually slow decision-making, loss of judgment, and reduced situational awareness. It is a silent killer, and it is stated that just when one is already present, "it is too late for detection." Many fatigued drivers believe that they can continue on while already tired, but if the body and mind gradually become exhausted, cognitive and motor functions degrade gradually.

Fatigue comes about in many ways; for the motorist, often, incomplete micro-sleeps—brief moments where their brain, like, dozes off for a few seconds—of course, lead to a loss of focus. Also, in other cases, drivers just don't realize that they're way too exhausted to keep driving. The routine, traditional remedies to defeat drowsy driving, such as government regulations or manual monitoring by passengers, are proven to be inadequate to reduce driver fatigue accidents. Thus, real-time systems in which driver fatigue is detected and combated without any invasive approaches are not only needed but also urgently needed to improve the security levels on the road.

7.2.2 The Role of AI in Driver Fatigue Detection

Artificial Intelligence (AI) and specifically the Machine Learning (ML) technology are used to develop real-time systems and detect fatigue in drivers. The huge data sets and sophisticated algorithms, as well as pattern recognition, are subsequently leading to improved prediction of drowsiness prior to any form of accident. The AI-based systems may also enable active and proactive responses to the driving behavior of the individuals, the street conditions, or the conditions of the road linked to the environment, unlike traditional warnings. Therefore, they are equipped to offer more precise and tailored solutions. A system like this would take into consideration the data collected from the sensors in the vehicle, plus specific input physiologically, as pertinent to the real-time monitoring of fatigue by AI in the driver.

AI algorithms are best suited to pattern recognition, making them excellent at distinguishing the most subtle changes in behavior or physiological signs representing fatigue. For example, AI using computer vision would allow the car to understand the eye movement, the face, and the angle of users' heads to decide the alertness of the driver. Simultaneously, AI could examine other techniques, such as heart rate and skin analysis, that could indicate the level of fatigue of the driver at the time. There must be programs to send an alert, either visually, audibly, or tactfully in some robotic manner, motivating the drivers to rest or stop the car as they should.

7.2.3 Real-Time Fatigue Monitoring: The Key Issues

The real-time fatigue monitoring systems employ a combination of technologies to collect and analyze data. The accuracy, timely response, and non-intrusive recognition of the fatigue features in such systems must have several components.

1. Computer Vision for Eye and Face Identification:
AI-based systems using computer vision techniques can see through a driver's face to locate the eyes and head movements. One of the frequently used techniques is the eye aspect ratio (EAR) analysis, which measures the opening of the eye based on the distances between eyelids. The prominent decrease in the EAR value can lead to the inference of misrepresentation of drowsiness or even sleep that a motorist may experience. Likewise, we can determine the extent of alertness of a driver by monitoring the facial landmarks since the face can be less or more rigid or droopy, indicators of strain.
2. Physiological Signal Monitoring:
The number of such features that may be tracked online may be high. Physiological parameters such as pulse, skin conductance, and body temperature are also monitored by AI monitoring systems. As an example, the alteration in heart rate has been typically determined to be the cause of

fatigue problems; exhaustion may cause the pulse to become irregular. An indication that the driver is perspiring more than normal, such as skin conductance, is not a physiological phenomenon that can identify any such variation in the driver, particularly when combined with other data points. These signals will allow the system to continuously judge the welfare of the drivers when monitored online.

3. Machine Learning Algorithms for Pattern Recognition:

Machine-learning algorithms that process and interpret the data collected by various sensors are the most fundamental units of any AI system for fatigue detection. Based on the vast volumes of human behavior and physiological alterations, these algorithms are able to detect the indicators that the driver is exhibiting, which may be a symptom of fatigue. Over time, these systems are able to learn which early signs of fatigue to identify more accurately by specializing in various types of driver behavioral and environmental patterns. For instance, a deep-learning model could be trained for passive tracking of the driver's sleep pattern and daily life routine, and will trigger an alarm as soon as he/she becomes tired.

4. The Real-Time Alert and Feedback System:

Timely alerts are required as soon as a drowsiness event is detected to prevent major accidents. These alerts can only be made using sound, a vibration in the driver's seat, or even handy visual cues on the dashboard. Such an AI system, while figuring out strategies of adjustment to the driver's behavior, has mechanisms in order not to result in so many alarms repeatedly. Personalized notifications have proven capable of getting attention from the driver without further distractions being produced.

7.2.4 Challenges and Opportunities in Fatigue Detection

The AI technologies show the ability to recognize exhaustion, which is promising, but a number of challenges have to be solved to make recognition reliable and effective.

1. Environmental Variability:

There are lighting conditions, road noise, and traffic noise in real-time weariness monitoring systems. For example, poor lighting makes it nearly impossible for algorithms to find relevant facial features, or blackouts in adverse weather conditions do not show physiological signals. AI systems should provide the proper robustness to accept and overcome these continuously changing variables in the driving environment to ensure their accuracy.

2. Individual Differences:
Each of the drivers is personal, and fatigue will vary from one person to another. While some drivers could fall into unusual sleepiness after their eyes close for a long time, some can, with no signs showing at all. Therefore, it is essential to customize AI systems to interpret and accommodate every single pattern in order to make them more efficient.
3. Privacy and Data Security:
Any form of real-time surveillance is a nightmare for privacy and security of the data, particularly when they are collecting very sensitive physiological information. Therefore, among the main responsibilities, it is important to give the top priority to this information on the way data should be anonymized and safely and ethically managed.
4. Integration with Autonomous Vehicles:
The most unbelievable aspect of the future could be the possibility of connecting fatigue tracking devices to autonomous cars. Systems grounded on artificial intelligence make drivers safer, but the future autonomous cars are essentially going to be highly in need of unremitting monitoring to make the operator vigilant and prepared to take over in case of necessity. The same will, however, be required of the artificial intelligence in concomitant maintenance of both the autonomous system and the driver vigilance towards advancing highway safety.

The innovation in the application of Artificial Intelligence on real-time fatigue tracking is symbolized by fatigueness in the road safety improvement domain. Given the ability of AI to detect driver behaviors and conduct complicated analysis of physiological signals, and the ability to deliver feedback without latency, we are exploring the possibilities of AI to mitigate the impacts of drowsy driving accidents. These systems are promising in significantly lowering accidents caused by fatigue and, in the future, will replace them as a large portion of transport in personal as well as commercial automobiles. They will keep evolving to be more efficient in dealing with the problems associated with this objective, in that, as artificial intelligence, sensor technology, and machine learning increase, they will become a very strong system of fatigue monitoring, which will be more precise and responsive in providing safer roads overall. This AI possibility of road safety improvement *via* real-time fatigue recognition is a potentially thrilling and revolutionary step towards becoming useful in a global sector of smarter, safer, and more accountable motoring.

7.3 AI and ML Technologies for Drowsiness Detection

The increase in the drowsiness of drivers on the road has become the greatest concern in terms of road safety, as it has been reported to cause most road accidents and deaths worldwide. Drowsy driving causes loss of capacity to respond to threats, delay in decision-making, and loss of attention span, making it especially dangerous in cases of critical driving. The causes of huge work done to minimize drowsiness-related accidents were rather tangible; one of the most promising, at the moment, however, is the real-time and non-invasive creation of the technologies that would detect and prevent drowsiness causes. Following the massive progress in artificial intelligence (AI) and machine learning (ML), breakthroughs in the creation of innovative solutions were made, which allow tracking and detecting drowsiness by examining various behavioral and physiological parameters.

7.3.1 Understanding Drowsiness Detection

The major technique in drowsiness warning is tracking of the typical signs of fatigue, which could indicate something that the driver is not attentive to, and reacts promptly to reduce the risk of driving dangers. The conventional method of identifying the drowsiness condition of the driver would most frequently take the form of subjective reports or, in other instances, the real occupants conducting physical inspections of the facial skin and eyes of the subject. However, these measures are not that dependable, with the exception that most are simply too late to prevent accidents. Data can be monitored by various means, and identifying the main indicators of drowsiness in the earlier stage before reaching the threshold, the banner buzzword in the sphere of AI and ML is already playing its role.

7.3.2 AI and ML Approaches to Drowsiness Detection

Applications of artificial intelligence and machine learning are developed with a plethora of options to continually monitor the physical and behavioral cues of the driver around the clock. These applications can be broadly categorized into three categories: computer vision, monitoring using sensors, and data fusion and prediction algorithms. Each category uses different methods of AI and ML to judge the tiredness of the driver (Figure 7.1).

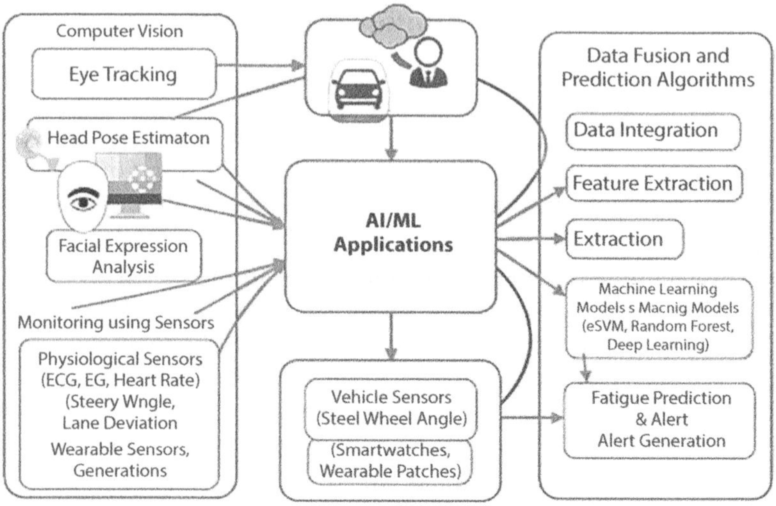

Figure 7.1 Multi-modal AI/ML framework for real-time driver fatigue monitoring.

7.3.2.1 Computer Vision Techniques

The accident rate on highways also shows that over a million people get killed in accidents each year; many more hundred thousand people get hurt, and billions' worth is lost. The prevalent cause of such accidents on freeways with two lanes in each direction, it turns out, would be motorists' fatigue. Detection of drowsy drivers would be vital as an advanced measure to minimize accidents. Among various computer vision techniques, monitoring a driver's alertness must be effectively achieved, and probably face monitoring is the most pragmatic approach that does not affect the driver in real-time. Typically, it involves using computer vision for monitoring visual signs or symptoms, including eye movement, facial expression, and head posture in real-time with the view to recognizing drowsiness. Such computer vision systems provide a more accurate identification and subsequent warning using cameras (image capturing) and sophisticated image processing algorithms. Consequently, the preventative capacity accelerates with fatigue symptoms and continues.

➢ **The Role of Computer Vision in Drowsiness Detection**

Computer vision refers to a collection of algorithms and technologies that enable a computer to understand visual data captured from a camera or other image-taking devices. Computer vision, when dealing with drowsiness detection, involves recognizing signs of weariness through tracking of various face and eye features. This may include:

- **Eye behavior:** eye closure and blinking speed, which are reflective symptoms of drowsiness.
- **Facial expressions:** yawning, eyelid drooping, or other signs of drowsiness provide the most promising characteristics to analyze under such circumstances.
- **Head posture:** nodding, tilting, and other motions of the head are features that can be interpreted to indicate sleepiness.

Tracking these visual signs continuously, computer vision systems have the power to inform or cause safety measures to prevent fatigue without dramatic consequences. One additional benefit these other methods offer is that they could be passive and require no intrusive intervention by the person at the wheel.

➢ **Blinking Pattern Analysis:**

Other important cues to the presence of sleepiness, other than EAR, are the verification of the blinking patterns. No wonder when one becomes tired, they will sluggishly close their eyes, or they will probably take long blinks. The rate of blinking and the length of the blink are easily analysed by using computer vision methods. The EAR analysis will be more precise with the addition of blink frequency to form a better fatigue detection system. In fact, it is possible to notice that when the blink duration or frequency of blinking is growing, the system is becoming aware that the driver is getting tired. Such a combination of measures of drowsiness detection, in fact, makes it quite robust since such a slight alteration of minor eye behavior may be interpreted as an indicator.

➢ **Facial Landmark Detection and Expression Analysis:**

Facial landmark detection method is commonly applied in drowsiness detection in the interesting world of computer vision. It includes an analysis of several key points on a face: eyes, eyebrows, nose, and, yes, the mouth. The movements of these facial landmarks can be tracked over time and watched for any changes that would indicate the facial expressions of the driver to accurately indicate whether that person was starting to get fatigued: a drooping eyelid, a yawn, or a slow look across the face.

➢ **Facial Landmark Detection Algorithms:**

One of the most frequently employed facial landmark detection models, based on a 68-point facial landmark model, identifies 68 unique points on the face, followed by eyes, eyebrows, mouth, and so on. The system recognizes the changes in facial expression from this given point, which can be a good indicator of drowsiness. For example, when focusing on the tracing of the positions of the eyelids vertically over time, any droop on the eyelids can be detected. As a driver becomes drowsy, the eyelids tend to droop over time, giving clues that the driver is experiencing the symptoms of fatigue. Yawning is another important indicator of sleepiness, as the mouth opens while yawning, one of the primary signs that a person is tired. The system is capable of detecting yawning by watching the width of the mouth opening, where the mouth opens more widely when a person yawns. Whenever these expressions are included, the system thus notifies or alerts the driver.

➢ **Head Pose Estimation and Head Nodding Detection:**
Moreover, head pose estimation finds its application in estimating drowsiness through head tracking of the driver. This gives a clear indication of the level of alertness of the driver by declaring whether the head nodding behavior indicates drowsiness or not. The presence of head nodding, which may indicate drowsiness, is detected by keeping eyes on the movement of angles while the head moves.

➢ **Head Pose Estimation Algorithms:**
Estimation of the head's pose is generally made by examining how the head addresses the three-dimensional orientation of faces according to the significant points where the facial landmarks come into view. Head pitch, yaw, and roll can be formed relatively simply by a system utilizing something as widely known as Euler angles or any form of rotation matrices. A sudden downward motion or jerky movement could easily reveal that the head is actually "falling forward"—the last perceptible act before a driver falls asleep or goes into a micro-sleep state. The usefulness of head pose tracking lies in the detection of micro-sleeps: brief moments where attention is lost by the driver that are often not perceived by him. This type of loss is usually not detectable using eye-tracking alone, but the pose estimation of the head enables the detection of all subtle movements that appear very early and are indicative of sleepiness onset.

➢ **Integration with AI and Machine Learning:**
In relation to AI influence, the above-mentioned findings lend support to Artificial Intelligence (AI) and Machine Learning (ML) model integration with more benefit than those developed by early methods of computer vision work. The system is expected to classify more complex patterns of fatigue due to the use of AI models, taking into account isolated facial cues as well as the temporal dynamic patterns of drowsiness.

➢ **Deep Learning Models:**
It is therefore referred to that deep learning mechanisms that can operate on raw images or video streams can be implemented by the convolutional neural networks (CNNs) for uncovering features regarding facial expressions, eye behavior, and motions of the head. If allowed to learn big datasets on driver behavior data, these models are able to detect patterns indicating drowsiness automatically.

Another use of using Recurrent Neural Networks (RNNs) and Long Short Term Memory (LSTM) networks would include them in monitoring the temporal dynamics of a particular function of the driver. It can be noted that the models are in such a position to analyze sequences of images or video frames captured over time. They are capable of detecting when the subject is about to doze, even when visual cues are quite subtle or occur intermittently.

Computer vision in integration with AI and ML models makes predictive modeling for drowsiness detection systems more accurate and flexible, for instance, in order to differentiate between the standard variation of facial expressions and genuine signs of fatigue, thereby decreasing false positives and increasing overall reliability.

7.3.2.2 Challenges in Computer Vision for Drowsiness Detection

Despite the advancements in computer vision for drowsiness detection, several challenges remain:

1. Lighting Conditions
In conditions like driving during the night and when facing the intense sunlight, cameras are to be out of good visibility to capture even the driver's face well, which causes inaccuracy in the detection of facial landmarks, among other visual cues.

2. Driver Variability
Images taken by automatic number plate recognition (ANPR) cameras can be used to match number plates with lists of plates and identify the wanted vehicle among them.

3. Real-Time Processing
The requirement is for high processing power as well as capturing images and video frames around the clock to produce real-time recognition drowsiness systems; it is difficult in environments with limited resources, e.g., embedded systems in vehicles.

4. Environmental Factors

One of the primary applications of the computer vision technologies is driver drowsiness detection, which involves monitoring based on the visual indicators such as eye movement, head nodding, and so on. This analysis can be a real-time application running on top of the eye aspect ratio (EAR) analyses, facial landmark detections, and head pose estimations to monitor the attentiveness of the driver, which can be subsequently input into AI and ML models to become more accurate and adaptable. Although the dilemma is contemplated in the light scenario, driver-to-driver differences and real-time processing, the approach can still quantify large to prevent road accidents caused by drowsiness in drivers. According to technological development, subsequent generations of the computer vision-based drowsiness recognition systems would become more believable and more personalized, and would still have a daily role to play in combating drowsiness.

7.3.2.3 Sensor-Based Monitoring Systems

In fact, the drowsiness of drivers is one of the most significant safety concerns that explains the large number of road traffic crashes and deaths worldwide. The earliest stage at which drowsy driving can be sensed, and before it, has been the focus of incorporating advanced safety features. Current technologies in the sphere are based on computer vision–based means of identifying drowsiness based on facial characteristics and eye-tracking; however, the sensor-based monitoring system can serve as an alternative or a complement. Such systems employ advanced physiological sensors that measure different signals that provide evidence of fatigue or drowsiness among drivers (Figure 7.2).

This is non-intrusive and reliable and can be said to be sensor-based because it records physiological information that cannot easily be manipulated or even concealed. The independence of the functioning of these systems, particularly in the reality ride conditions, will not require the input of the driver, as the constant monitoring will be attainable. The section explores the sensor technology that is offered by various researchers aimed at the detection of driver drowsiness, its mechanisms, and their applicability to driver safety.

➤ **Types of Sensors Used for Drowsiness Detection**

A variety of sensors are used in modern systems to detect drowsiness by monitoring physical signals that correlate well with fatigue. Numerous parameters can be observed by these sensors, for example, heart rate,

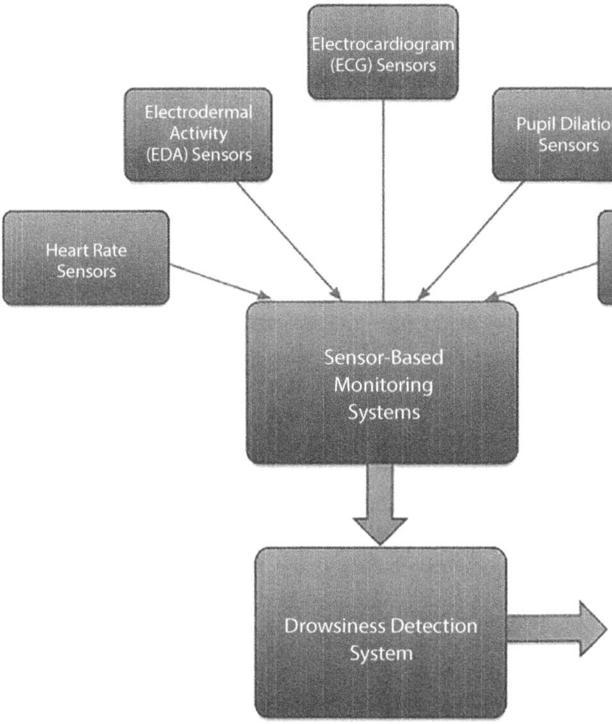

Figure 7.2 Multi-sensor driver drowsiness detection system.

skin-conductance level, and brain activity. Here is a summary of some of the most important sensor types:

1. Electrocardiogram (ECG) Sensors

ECG sensors tend to be used to discern alterations in the electrical activity of the human heart. HRV can characterize how ECG sensor-derived rhythms are altered by the fatigue or drowsiness of people, which is critical from a physiological standpoint: Fatigue depresses HRV, implying that the heart becomes less responsive to stress and that the variability increases between heartbeats. By monitoring HRV in real time, the ECG-based system may alert drivers when fatigue symptoms are already manifesting, long before physical fatigue indicators such as yawning or eye closure start to appear.

2. Electrodermal Activity (EDA) Sensors

Skin conductance is also known as electrodermal activity, which measures the electrical conductance of the skin and varies with the degree of sweat gland activity. EDA transducers are predicated upon the supposition that stress or fatigue will increase the activity of the sympathetic nervous system, which activates sweat glands. The fluctuations in the conductance of the skin are most often experienced as increased levels of physiological stress, or refracted by the body into related drowsiness or mental fatigue states.

3. Heart Rate Sensors

The heart rate sensor calculates the heartbeats per minute, which can indicate a good mode of biological analysis of a driver's state of awareness. With bodily fatigue, the heartbeats usually become stable or decrease as a reaction to reduced physical and cognitive exertion. Continuous monitoring of the heart rate can thus give an early warning of drowsiness and this trend.

4. Pupil Dilation Sensors

By means of Pupil Dilation, an insight into the physiological signals that can be obtained when someone happens to doze off can be easily detected. As a rule of thumb, the pupils are more constricted when the person is alert than when fatigue or sleep-related events must be clarified. To the obvious signs of cognitive load or sleepiness, you can add yet another device, which is changes in pupil size.

5. Sleep Monitoring Sensors (EEG)

EEG sensors monitor brain wave activity to determine one's consciousness to some extent. It is commonly used in the medical world and will probably one day be adapted to control and improve driver functions. Specific types of brain wave activity—like theta—become more dramatic during the onset of drowsiness or falling asleep. Thus, EEG sensors can detect them as a micro-sleep episode, meaning a driver would have taken a short nap without noticing anything.

7.3.2.4 Advantages of Sensor-Based Drowsiness Detection Systems

Sensor-based systems offer several advantages in the detection of drowsiness when compared to traditional methods such as visual or behavioral monitoring. These advantages include:

1. Non-Intrusive Monitoring

Systems composed of sensors (Table 7.1) to collect data do not require the active involvement of the driver, like stepping up to a camera or entering the system. Biomeasures, such as physiological activities, regulate the information passively, interrupting the safety-critical information input access to the driver.

Table 7.1 Comparative analysis of sensor types used for drowsiness detection.

Sensor type	Parameter monitored	Working principle	Drowsiness indicators	Advantages
1. Electrocardiogram (ECG)	Heart rate variability (HRV)	Measures the electrical activity of the heart.	Decrease in HRV indicates fatigue; the heart becomes less responsive to stress.	Early detection of fatigue before visible symptoms like yawning appear.
2. Electrodermal activity (EDA)	Skin conductance (sweat gland activity)	Measures changes in the skin's electrical conductance based on sweat gland activity.	Increase in conductance indicates sympathetic nervous system activation due to fatigue or stress.	Reflects physiological stress and mental fatigue effectively.
3. Heart rate sensors	Heartbeats per minute	Calculates BPM to assess alertness levels.	Stabilization of heart rate suggests reduced physical/ cognitive exertion.	Quite simple, continual monitoring; very useful for early fatigue warnings.
4. Pupil-dilation sensors	changes in pupil size	Detects changes in pupil size.	Dilated pupils suggest drowsiness; constricted pupils indicate alertness.	Non-invasive and can provide real-time feedback.
5. EEG (sleep monitoring sensors)	Brain wave activity (theta waves)	Compute the electrical activity of the brain.	Increase in theta wave activity indicates the onset of drowsiness or micro-sleep episodes.	High accuracy; detects even short, unnoticed sleep episodes.

2. Early Detection of Fatigue

Due to the sensor technology invented, any form of fatigue in the driver is already detected even prior to the behavioral symptoms being manifested. They are of any closed-eye features or yawning, for example. The characteristics of the material, including heart rate variability and skin conductance response, result in a level that can be used to identify symptoms at a high security margin before the symptoms appear. This initial detection can be used to issue a warning in time and force the driver to take preventive actions before unsafe conditions kick in.

3. Continuous Monitoring

The sensor-based system can offer far greater continuous real-time information regarding the physiological state of the driver compared to a periodic eye blink state monitoring system or a facial recognition-based monitoring system. As an example, long-term monitoring of commercial vehicle drivers or long-distance drivers is a more genuine and more relevant kind of monitoring of the elevation of drowsiness.

4. Adaptability to Individual Differences

The fact that it is possible to learn about the systems, to learn the peculiarities of their physiologic patterns, makes it adaptable to the individual driver. In simple words, he says, it customizes the system. The advantage is that it will enhance the accuracy of fatigue detection and reduce false positives. Such parameters as measurement of heart rate variability and skin conductance patterns already vary among different people. This leads to technology that learns and adapts to the individual-based measurements.

5. Extension to Other Detection Approaches

The combinations of conglomeration are possible, such as sensor-based systems in conjunction with other fatigue detection methods, such as the integration of computer vision systems to form multimodal solutions. This one-line combinatory intervention leads to better sensitivity and more precise diagnosis of fatigue as a result of incorporating physiological and behavioral data. As an illustration, the system may provide a dependable alarm of such kind in instances where large variations in HRV were identified concomitantly with a sudden increase in the number of eye close-ups.

7.3.2.5 Data Fusion and Predictive Algorithms

When used together, AI and ML may amalgamate the data from different sources to provide more precise forecasts on fatigue. It is referred to as the synergy of data fusion. It involves the integration of information from both visual and sensor inputs in order to offer a more generalized view of the state of the driver (Figure 7.3).

- **Multimodal Fusion:** The fusion of data would relate to various types of data input, such as eye-tracking, face recognition, body-sensor monitoring, physiology, and data of driving behavior to models owned by AI, which would give a more reliable and robust drowsiness detection.

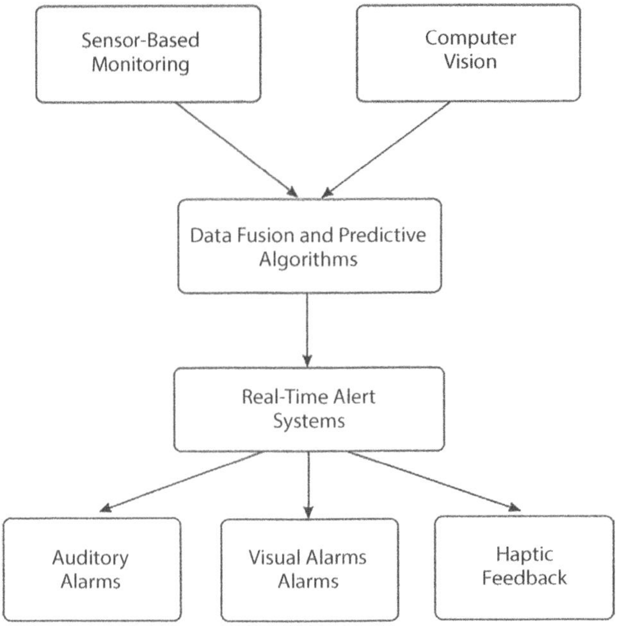

Figure 7.3 Multi-source data fusion model for driver fatigue alerts.

Multimodal systems consider smaller individual differences in fatigue expression, thereby adding to increased accuracy in prediction.

- **Predictive Modelling:** It would be accurate to state that an AI can predict whether fatigue has already set in, based on support vector machines and decision trees, all of which fall under the supervised learning approach, and RNN is the type that is confirmed to be the best. Such models are trainable using large datasets that depict the drowsiness of drivers at different phases throughout the temporal process. This kind of foresight, investigating early indications of fatigue, —a combination of factors, would allow AI systems to issue a warning to the driver before it is too late.
- **Adaptability:** ML models are able to follow the particular fatigue trend of a driver at a dramatically higher level of precision in recognizing drowsiness. This implies that a system might be in a position to cross correlate their thresholds and predictions with some information regarding how the behavior of some drivers may be when they are fatigued, like their eye movement or physiological norms.

7.3.2.6 Real-Time Alert Systems

An AI-based drowsiness detector system can assist in making sure that no accidents take place during the middle of the night in many ways. In case of fatigue in the driver, the alarms may vary depending on the severity of the issue and the type of user interface of the system.

Alarm Types:

- **Auditory Alarms:** The AI systems may create an alarm through the production of sounds, like a beep, and even talk to the driver.
- **Visual Alarms:** maybe, the warnings should appear on the driver panel or screen by incandescent lights or messages informing the driver to rest.
- **Haptic Feedback:** Haptics are also used by other people to warn drivers with haptic feedback, like a rumbling seat or rotating wheel, without interfering too much in those immediate instances.

In this manner, these AI alerts are able to keep a motorist informed because they provide an early warning to a driver who is abnormally fatigued in a dangerous state.

7.4 Challenges in Driver Drowsiness Detection

The most prominent cause of road traffic accidents is driver fatigue; the detection and mitigation of driver fatigue is relevant to enhancing road safety in the world. Fatigue may significantly lower the supply of mental processes like attention, decision-making, and reaction time that are important in safe driving. However, detecting drowsiness in drivers at the time it is occurring still remains a rather tricky challenge despite the overall improvement in technology. The assessment of the fatigue state of a driver within a short time, as well as accurate assessment thereof, has become essential in today's world. There have been numerous systems designed to supervise drowsiness; however, most of the systems developed present a number of limitations, aside from poor periodicity and sensitivity. There are also varied legal challenges, starting from environmental to technological, and even substantial ethical limitations. This project explores the main challenges facing the issue of drowsiness-driving detection and proposes some solutions.

7.4.1 Variation in Fatigue Signs

One problem is the recognition of fatigue among drivers: it is a very variable factor, different in every person, not really something to measure or quantify. Threadbare fatigue signs differ from one person to another. One driver might show obvious symptoms of fatigue, such as yawning, drooping eyelids, or nodding off while driving, while another may show less apparent signs, such as slower reaction times or minor lapses in attention resulting from fatigue, nearly invisible through conventional monitoring techniques.

7.4.1.1 Individual Difference

Drivers experience tiredness in various ways because they are caused by different factors, such as irregular sleep patterns, the physical condition or health care of the individual, the stress level, and even the habits of a driver. As an example, two drivers equally tired might manifest it in very different manifested behavior—all yawning, facial expressions, or something that shows something that is peculiar to controlling the eyeballs. Another man, maybe. Maybe he has a larger capacitance and more frequent and longer eyelid closures, and the other minor head tilts. Hence, machine-learning models for drowsiness detection should also consider these individual differences. Systems trained on relatively broad datasets that also take into account a wider age and gender spectrum, as well as various driving conditions, can optimize this detection but face hurdles when it comes to personal tailoring.

7.4.1.2 Adapting to Changing Fatiguing States

Fatigue is a dynamic process that changes in the course of driving. A driver may be awake to some extent, but later some drivers exhibit severe alertness followed by a brief outburst arising from an event sequence similar to this. However, identifying these changes and predicting when a driver is reaching severe fatigue are problems that are very difficult to predict accurately. This nature of adaptivity, thereby changing properties and predictable dangerous sleep levels in real time, is a necessary part of systems in order to prevent accidents. But these are efforts that demand continuous learning models, as they step into applications facing tremendous obstacles.

7.4.2 Environmental Factors

Situations of surroundings can sometimes easily affect efficiency in drowsiness detection systems. This will pertain to the type of light, weather, road surfaces, and vehicle interiors, so that there is a possibility of sensors and cameras not viewing fatigue indicators at all.

7.4.2.1 Conditions of Light

For example, in-camera-based monitoring of eye movements or facial expressions, a clearly lit room is needed to get good images. Low light conditions, such as nighttime driving or during very early hours of the morning, have a technological effect on output degradation from these systems. Also, low-light environments become a problem in tracking eye movements, facial landmarks, or head positions, leading to incorrect positives or missed detections. Alternatively, while most issues can almost be addressed by infrared cameras and other low-light technologies, extreme lighting conditions, for example, those caused by glare from headlights or direct sunlight, remain difficult to cope with.

7.4.2.2 Adverse Weather and Road Conditions

Bad weather can cause damaged cameras to be obstructed by images resulting from rainfall, snowfall, or fog, hence making visibility poor; thus, one can find that a close view of a driver's face is difficult, along with cases of eye gaze tracking. In addition, worse road conditions like bumps or sharp bends might cause shaking of the vehicle, hence not focusing so well for the cameras or sensors. Such events could make the detection of drowsiness prone to errors, especially when relying heavily on computer vision methods.

7.4.2.3 Interference of Passenger

For some vehicles, the drowsiness detection system is intended to observe the driver through cameras or sensors, and when there are passengers in the vehicle, these passengers' movements or facial expressions can interfere, dividing the system's attention between the driver and the passengers. To avoid misclassification of the driver's state, the system must be very specific concerning detecting the driver and, conversely, passengers, especially when the vehicle is occupied by multiple passengers.

7.4.3 Sensor Limitations

Devices like cameras, heart rate monitors, and skin-resistance sensors that are commonly employed in drowsiness detection, in fact, have their own limitations, which make them capable of creating discrepancies with their accuracy and reliability.

7.4.3.1 Problems of Cameras and Visual Tracking

In the case of camera-based eye-tracking or facial expression analysis, it is necessary to recognize that any object may come across the driver's way while the camera should have a clear view of the driver's face. Changes in the driver's head position, angle, or face structure can make dirty tracking. At the same time, the suppression of such sensors under lenses or some other kind of accessory object can also result in the obscuration of the face or eyes of certain drivers, making it difficult to monitor the fatigue signs from the accumulation of the necessary data. For example, when a combination of conditions includes the driver who just put his or her sunglasses on or during eye obscuration due to sunlight reflecting off the window glare, the system shall miss the drowsiness onset.

7.4.3.2 Limitations on Physiological Monitoring

Typically, the visual system, the eye-tracking, or visual facial expression recognition devices mentioned earlier, will be less intrusive than physiological measurements, like heart rate or skin conductance measurements. For instance, it will be uncomfortable for the driver to wear a wristband or chest strap to measure heart rate variability (HRV), which can end the person's resistance to the use of the system. Also, sensors such as the electrodermal activity (EDA) sensors are sensitive to environmental conditions, including temperature and humidity, which may lead to imprecise measurements.

7.4.3.3 Invasive

Though less commonly used systems are non-invasive, like cameras and heart-rate monitors, invasive techniques such as recording EEG (electroencephalographic) waves of the brain or even using wearable devices to measure brainwave activity may be implemented in some drowsiness detection systems. These facilities are very accurate but always rely on equipping or some additional procedure that is expensive in terms of real-life drive scenarios. Many of these technologies are actually so invasive that they are not scalable for real-world implementations.

7.4.4 Data Privacy and Ethical Issues

It is imperative for any drowsiness detection system to be tuned into handling sensitive data like video input of the driver and physiological response parameters; hence, a roadblock has arisen as to how this will be operationalized in intrusions on privacy and ethical dimensions.

7.4.4.1 Privacy Concerns

Since the capturing of a video image in real time poses some privacy issues, it can probably discompose the driver or make them apprehensive since someone can monitor their face continuously. Therefore, to some extent, the same holds true for physiological signal monitoring. Underneath that, there is a fear of wrongful misappropriation, such as if data falls into the wrong hands, or there is a case of unauthorized access or data loss. Hence, anonymizing data, zipping it, and ensuring that it is used for the detection of drowsiness is the only alternative to gaining public trust in these systems.

7.4.4.2 Consent and Control

Another important issue is the written consent required from the driver, a protection protocol in place before anything else is done with the critically important data. But the point is, while all other in-cab technologies require drivers' consent before their operation on their behalf, some of them seem to breach privacy by the use of data even without the driver's knowledge. Proper communication for the purpose, objectives, and duration of data recording, along with the opportunity for drivers to acclimatize to the system or choose not to use it at all, seems necessary.

7.4.4.3 Equal Opportunities in AI

A reality check in AI/ML-based systems for drowsiness detection could be the perpetuation of the bias of the data on which the model was trained. For example, a facial recognition system could be handicapped with racial differentiation in its trained population that may result in false identification of fatigue among people with dark facial tones. Similarly, if it is mostly formed of training data of a specific demographic, for example, young male drivers, it may deliver unfairly biased results for other collectivities. Hence, these systems have to reach equal opportunities, which include non-discrimination/safe drowsing detection.

7.4.5 Drive Behavior and Human Factor

Human behavior and the consequent fatigue nature could pose a significant problem. Tiredness does not make itself evident easily, nor does once-evident tiredness point to the danger it presages. A driver is worn out and yet appears Tory. Nonetheless, she may still be on the verge of falling asleep with cognitive fatigue. Also, it may happen that a driver with a dull appearance can drive the vehicle for a while in extreme safety.

7.4.5.1 Cognitive Fatigue

Though the most common methods used for identifying drowsiness are visual and physiological measures like eye movements and heart rate, they do not invariably indicate whether the person is asleep or not. It may not even indicate whether the person is really feeling such awakeness as can normally be expected or whether the person is impressed (or worrying) about something. There is always that risk of this not being the case, and by the time everything has become real, one is well into it.

7.4.5.2 Arousing Response of Drivers to Being Alerted

There will be cases wherein the car's management system would exhibit an alert, but the driver cannot respond appropriately. They often dismiss or do not acknowledge alerts since they consider that they could go on with their drive, or if they are very short of time. Such practice will compromise the system's efficiency. Other drivers experience an 'alert fatigue' stage, where the alert warnings remain desensitized so that they are less inclined to react to them.

Driver drowsiness detection is important to road safety, but it is complicated by the fact that there are significant challenges in this field. Other challenges to be overcome include the variability in how fatigue manifests, the influence of environmental elements, the current limitations that are already manifest in the technologies of sensors, and, of course, and this is just as important, the ethical considerations surrounding all this. But as AI and machine learning continue to develop along with sensor technologies and approaches to meeting the challenges presented by emerging data privacy issues, these can really be surmounted. These systems will, by far, evolve and become reliable, hence safer, in preventing the occurrence of cases of accidents caused by a drowsy driver, hence the prevention of loss of one's life.

7.5 Future Directions and Innovations

Road accidents due to drivers being sleepy are among the most prevalent causes of accidents on earth. It has been proven that a big part of accidents have a high probability of occurring because of drowsy driving. Work is still ongoing towards checking out whether driving fatigue can be detected with precision in real time, and this has been difficult in the recent past. However, with the availability of innovation in automotive technology, there are emerging newer and better approaches that take advantage of current knowledge in artificial intelligence (AI) and machine learning (ML) sensor-based systems that, when combined, are innovative ways to detect face drowsiness. The current chapter highlights future developments and advancements in drowsiness detection that come along with newer sensor technologies and accompany AI, machine learning, ethical considerations, and the integration of these systems with other emerging technologies in the field as it pertains to autonomous vehicles.

7.5.1 Advancements in Sensor Technology

7.5.1.1 Multi-Modal Sensors for Enhanced Detection

The traditional methods of drowsiness detection depend upon visual clues like eye tracking or facial expressions; however, with the advancement in the technology of sensors, we should now be talking about a more focused shift towards multilevel sensory integration towards fatigue detection in the driver. It is clear that current sleuth systems must not just incorporate sensors into vehicle functions in the context of the fusion of the multi-source information to reduce the opportunity cost of the false positives and consequently increase the skillfulness in sensitivity. Reflectometric wafer probe observes core health features of fabrication equipment and attempts to provide high-quality communication between wafer probing, test, and manufacturing.

- **Physiological Sensors:** The heart rate variability, galvanic skin response, and body temperature could offer a scientist important physiological indicators of drowsiness in a conductor. Put together with these behavioral clues, such as eye movement, a complete picture of their condition can be gained.

- **Environmental Sensors:** These sensors may incorporate future modes of road condition, vehicle speed, ambient lighting, and even air quality so as to come up with a more holistic model vis-a-vis drowsiness. Consequently, the predetermined drowsiness detection threshold can be modified according to the environmental conditions (i.e., weather or road conditions).
- **Wearable Devices:** Wearables, the systems of the future, could also have included the integration of wearable sensors such as smartwatches or biosignal monitoring devices. These kinds of wearables would constantly monitor the heart rate, skin conductance, and real-time variations in sleep mechanisms to continuously give the driver and systems feedback. It would also make personalized designs of drowsiness detection available because of a physiological baseline of individual drivers.

7.5.1.2 Non-Intrusive Detection via Advanced Cameras

The future of drowsiness detection is likely to rely on the creation of superior camera systems with greater resolution, infrared, and depth sensing that can be used alongside other advanced camera functions. The areas of improvement are to include:

- **Infrared and Night Vision:** The current cameras pretty much fail even in the infrared seeing or the night driving scenario. This can be corrected by incorporating IR sensors so that the camera system can track the eye movement and gaze on either side of the face using an extra enhanced dual beam source that would not disturb working with ambient light.
- **3D Sensing:** The current cameras are exploiting the third dimension of vision; movement is still more promising for specific head and body movement, other than all. The tracking of slight variations in head position, or that is, in microsleep instances that most of the camera system's current technology cannot detect, is another service of the future to elevate systems.

- **Adaptive Vision Algorithms:** AI-based computer vision will not only be able to recognize and interpret small sets of facial expressions, eye movement patterns, and minute head position changes but also perform much more automated routines. Other improvements that are usually realized in vision algorithms include higher system trust, resulting in real-time reading of facial landmarks irrespective of lighting in the environment or whether they are deteriorated.

7.5.2 The Role of Artificial Intelligence and Machine Learning

7.5.2.1 Deep Learning for Real-Time Drowsiness Detection

The emergence of deep learning algorithms has transformed the manner in which we process and analyze data. They are especially effective in drowsiness detection models, which are able to handle huge volumes of multi-dimensional information (e.g., video, physiological signals, driving behavior) in order to identify subtle trends that are suggestive of fatigue.

- **Convolutional Neural Networks (CNNs):** Their performance can be more readily applied to tasks in computer vision and, to a large degree, result in one point that enhances the quality of eye and facial recognition, particularly drowsiness detection. This entails a change in terms of structural adaptation to sense fatigue patterns that also involve micro-expressions or the very early onset of eye closure, which could avoid detection in the traditional approach.
- **Recurrent Neural Networks (RNNs) and Long Short-Term Memory (LSTM):** Specifically, RNNs and even more so LSTMs are great for tracking and analysis of time-related data. This implies long-time time-domain tracking of driver behavior and identifies changes in driving patterns, which, when they had been learning from past behaviors, may be seen to indicate drowsiness, such as erratic steering or slower response times.
- **Reinforcement Learning:** Adaptive, self-improving systems can eventually be established with the evolution of AI models, which may use reinforcement learning. Intelligent adjusting of fatigue thresholds or timing and types of fatigue alerts can be realized by learning reinforcement from previous drivers' demonstrations and states.

7.5.2.2 Personalization of Drowsiness Detection

Personalized adaptive training-based healthcare monitoring is the future in fatigue monitoring systems. Recently, existing systems have suffered from drowsiness detection due to using generic techniques. The future systems will have personalized algorithms. Individual sacrosanctity can be proven relative to other existing techniques because modifying the system may mean the need for an individual driver's assessment for drowsiness, aiming to give total accuracy and keeping the overall efficiency of detection intact.

- **Personalized Baselines:** AI will be able to acquire each physiology and behavior baseline of a driver on a real-time basis. This implies that the system will be in a position to change the alert levels in response to the age, sleeping patterns, or even experience in driving to identify an individual who is falling asleep on the road early. A personalized driver would rather sound like receiving a notification, even in such minimal variations in his alertness since it would do so before he becomes fatigued enough to cause harm.
- **Driver Adaptation:** With increased post-experience data gathered by the systems, the systems will be used to differentiate normal and abnormal behavior with time. To illustrate, these early warning systems would be vital and specific to long-haul drivers who develop tolerance to some of the symptoms of fatigue, such that the system would have reported the same even when the other drivers would have had a different salience.

7.5.2.3 Predictive Analytics for Proactive Fatigue Management

Fatigue can be predicted using AI models. These models can also warn of possible drowsiness, in addition to predicting fatal fatigue. Various data will be combined, e.g., the real-time driving behavior, sleeping habits, or climate conditions. As an example, the system in the future would have the capability to forecast fatigue in a driver based on data from multiple sources, and then store warnings to drivers or a recommendation to rest long before it is too late, not just the indicators of drowsiness.

- **Fusion of Data and Predictive Modeling:** The system can predict the sleep episodes using the data provided by an external source, such as a calendar (consequently, the schedules of travel) and the driving history of a particular driver. These predictive models may involve individual driver behaviors, i.e., time of day drivers, and the past level of sleepiness of the driver. They provide a warning at an early time before it is too late to get to the risky level of fatigue.

7.5.3 Integration with Autonomous Vehicles

7.5.3.1 Bridging Human and Autonomous Systems

The further development of self-driving technology will lead to a change in the type of driver monitoring demanded. At least partially, the car will be driven automatically, but the driver will have to be able to override the situation in particular circumstances. Even in such a case, the fatigue detection technologies will still be needed to provide the driver with the capacity to assume control should it be needed. The autonomous system of the vehicle can be incorporated into future systems in a workflow-friendly way to accomplish the following tasks:

- **Monitor Driver Readiness:** This will be available in vehicles, even those that are partially automated, to measure the alertness of the driver so that he can take action when needed. These systems will instruct the driver on alertness with real-time AI feedback or remind them of what they can do to always keep them alert.
- **Alert System Coordination:** New systems will work directly with the car's autonomous capabilities for monitoring the fatigue detection system. For example, if the systems discover high drowsiness, the car's automated functions, within the bandwidth of the vehicle control systems, may take the wheel or activate safety features, such as stopping the car in a safe spot or finding its way to a rest area.

7.5.3.2 Full Integration into Fully Autonomous Vehicles

In autonomous vehicles, fully autonomous driving systems can make humans obsolete, which would shift the application of drowsiness detection to monitoring the status of passengers within the vehicle. The extent of well-being monitoring will vary if such vehicles become a place where passengers can sleep while traveling on a particular journey. Then, the passengers will be monitored for critical physiological parameters to detect any possible life-threatening situations. Only this would be beyond the driver: an alarm system to be looked into, besides drowsiness detection.

7.5.4 Ethical Considerations and Data Privacy

7.5.4.1 Data Privacy and Data Security

As the driver's drowsiness detection system continuously checks the user data comprising personal data, e.g., physiological signals, and observation of the face and behavior while driving, concern about personal data security is most evident. Future drowsiness detection systems should be designed in such a way that they are compatible with data protection regulations while ensuring user data is well protected. It is suggested that the design has very strong security measures and end-to-end encryption standards, as well as a data retention policy and anonymization measures, just to secure consumer confidence.

7.5.4.2 Transparency and Consent

Drivers should know exactly what data is being collected, the purpose for which it is being used, and who has access to it. Then, they should be able to decide the issue of collection and use on a case-by-case basis. Systems should be designed to allow drivers to learn precisely how the provided personal data contributes to system functionality. To end this side, the consent of the driver may well be a crucial factor, fundamentally related to the design of the system.

7.5.4.3 Fairness and Avoiding Bias in AI Models

It is in drowsy detection where diversity is primarily capable of finalizing the bias that AI Systems can implement. An example of this bias is when a face recognition system could examine the skin of a person's face, indicating sleepiness from the person with different skin tones. Different age groups and genders could also exhibit other visible signs of tiredness. The message to developers is thus: have reps across the globe so as to dump the bias before it grows.

As a matter of fact, the future of drowsy driver detection is projected to be bright, especially with the advancements in sensor development, AI, ML, and self-driving vehicles, which will deliver highly precise and highly reliable, as well as personal systems. Nonetheless, even after the accidents caused by drowsy driving, the ideas of these technologies may also be combined and lead to the seamless integration of road safety with safety in general. Advance the driving with sleep detection technologies, as the technologies become advanced enough to make their tailoring processes smarter and more adaptive in the future, in terms of ensuring the safety of a driver and passengers, but would definitely take into account important issues of ethics and privacy. There is only one thing that one can expect: innovation because it will take place in the future, an ongoing evolution to further the fields of automotive engineering, data science, and the policy processes, which would allow making the roads worldwide safer.

7.6 Conclusion

Thousands of injuries, deaths, and economic losses are the result of road accidents, with drowsiness being one of the greatest risks. Besides the evident benefits of safety hardware, which are promised by intelligent AI and machine learning-enabled drowsiness detection systems, the transformative benefits of an immediate intervention can be assumed to be delivered by non-invasive monitoring of driver drowsiness, which can be achieved with the help of facial cues, eye movements, heart rate, and other physiological indicators. The systems are capable of changing and adjusting to many different drivers and environmental conditions using advanced algorithms and multimodal data fusion, which provides reliable and accurate results. However, it could be significantly overcome, though there are a number of challenges, such as data privacy, sensor constraints, and fluctuation of fatigue manifestations, with additional innovations to be done, especially in adaptive thresholding and ethical system design. In this regard, the implementation of such smart, scalable, and equitable technologies in various vehicle categories will be very applicable in proactive road safety, particularly at a time when most of the situations are transitioning into semi-autonomous and shared mobility. Lastly, these systems serve to strengthen the safeguarding of drivers and passengers and the long-term goal of a safer and more responsive transportation ecosystem.

AI disclosure statement: The author confirms that no artificial intelligence (AI)-generated content or AI-assisted writing tools were used in the preparation of this chapter (including summaries and the abstract). All text, analysis, and conclusions are the result of the author's original work.

Bibliography

1. Stancin, I., Cifrek, M., Jović, A., A Review of EEG Signal Features and Their Application in Driver Drowsiness Detection Systems. *Sensors*, 21, 3786, 2021.
2. Pandey, P. and Seeja, K., Subject independent emotion recognition from EEG using VMD and deep learning. *J. King Saud Univ.-Comput. Inf. Sci.*, 34, 1730–1738, 2022.
3. Blalock, D.W., Ortiz, J.J.G., Frankle, J., Guttag, J.V., What is the State of Neural Network Pruning. *Proc. Mach. Learn. Syst.*, 2, 129–146, 2020.
4. Ojha, D., Pawar, A., Kasliwal, G., Raut, R., Devkar, A., Driver Drowsiness Detection Using Deep Learning, in: *2023 4th International Conference for Emerging Technology (INCET)*, Belgaum, India, pp. 1–4, 2023, doi: 10.1109/INCET57972.2023.10169941.
5. Zeng, J., Qian, Y., Yin, F., Zhu, L., Xu, D., A multi-value cellular automata model for multi-lane traffic flow under lagrange coordinate. *Comput. Math. Organ. Theory*, 28, 178–192, 2022.
6. Dewi, C., Chen, R.-C., Chang, C.-W., Wu, S.-H., Jiang, X., Yu, H., Eye Aspect Ratio for Real-Time Drowsiness Detection to Improve Driver Safety. *Electronics*, 11, 3183, 2022.
7. Chand, H.V. and Karthikeyan, J., Cnn based driver drowsiness detection system using emotion analysis. *Intell. Autom. Soft Comput.*, 31, 717–728, 2022.
8. Mamieva, D., Abdusalomov, A.B., Kutlimuratov, A., Muminov, B., Whangbo, T.K., Multimodal Emotion Detection *via* Attention-Based Fusion of Extracted Facial and Speech Features. *Sensors*, 23, 5475, 2023.
9. Mamieva, D., Abdusalomov, A.B., Mukhiddinov, M., Whangbo, T.K., Improved Face Detection Method *via* Learning Small Faces on Hard Images Based on a Deep Learning Approach. *Sensors*, 23, 502, 2023.
10. Albadawi, Y., AlRedhaei, A., Takruri, M., Real-Time Machine Learning-Based Driver Drowsiness Detection Using Visual Features. *J. Imaging*, 9, 91, 2023.
11. Kavitha, K.R., Lakshmi, S.V., Reddy, P.B.K., Reddy, N.S., Chandrasekhar, P., Driver Drowsiness Detection Using Face Expression Recognition. *Ann. Rom. Soc. Cell Biol.*, 25, 2785–2789, 2021.
12. Sharifuzzaman Sagar, A.S.M., Tajken, S., Abdur, R., Drowsiness detection using combined neuroimaging: Overview and Challenges, arXiv, 2022, arXiv:2202.13344.
13. Estrany, B. and Fuster-Parra, P., Human Eye Tracking Through Electro-Oculography (EOG): A Review, in: *Cooperative Design, Visualization, and Engineering*, CDVE 2022, Lecture Notes in Computer Science, vol. 13492, Y. Luo (Ed.), Springer, Cham, Switzerland, 2022.
14. ieira, R., Näf, F., Martins, R., Horta, N., Lourenço, N., Póvoa, R., A Tunable Gain and Bandwidth Low-Noise Amplifier with 1.44 NEF for EMG and EOG Biopotential Signal. *Electronics*, 2023.

15. Abdusalomov, A.B., Islam, B.M.S., Nasimov, R., Mukhiddinov, M., Whangbo, T.K., An Improved Forest Fire Detection Method Based on the Detectron2 Model and a Deep Learning Approach. *Sensors*, 23, 1512, 2023.
16. Abdusalomov, A.B., Nasimov, R., Nasimova, N., Muminov, B., Whangbo, T.K., Evaluating Synthetic Medical Images Using Artificial Intelligence with the GAN Algorithm. *Sensors*, 23, 3440, 2023.
17. Khang, A., Rath, K.C., Satapathy, S.K., Kumar, A., Das, S.R., Panda, M.R., Enabling the future of manufacturing: integration of robotics and IoT to smart factory infrastructure in industry 4.0, in: *Handbook of research on AI-based technologies and applications in the era of the metaverse*, A. Khang, V. Shah, S. Rani (Eds.), pp. 25–50, IGI Global, Hershey, PA, USA, 2023.
18. Khang, A., Rath, K.C., Anh, P.T., Rath, S.K., Bhattacharya, S., Quantum-based robotics in the high-tech healthcare industry: innovations and applications, in: *Medical robotics and AI-assisted diagnostics for a high-tech healthcare industry*, A. Khang (Ed.), pp. 1–27, IGI Global, Hershey, PA, United States, 2024, https://doi.org/10.4018/979-8-3693-2105-8.ch001.

8

AI-Powered Collision Detection: A Neural Network System for Automotive Safety

Sumanta Chatterjee* **and Amit Majumder**

Dept. of CSE, NIT - Jamshedpur, Jharkhand, India

Abstract
The higher level of road traffic accidents creates a need for innovative solutions that can be implemented in car safety. In many cases, the traditional methods of collision detection incorporate rule-based algorithms, which can barely cope with the real-life situations, particularly in some of the diverse conditions, such as poor weather or traffic jams. The neural networks would bring about a revolution since they are capable of providing the possibility to handle a huge quantity of data in high dimensions and identify complex patterns. The chapter elaborates on the conceptualization, design, and practical applications of an artificial neural network–based collision detection system integrated with advanced sensor technologies such as LiDAR, radar, and cameras. It will also mention possible gains of adaptation and accurate real-time decision-making, such as neural networks, for their downsides, like dependency on data and high computational intensity. This chapter will contribute to intelligent overhauls to improve safety while minimizing accidents by associating recent advancements with novel solutions.

Keywords: AI in vehicle safety, AI-powered sensor fusion, collision detection, advanced driver assistance systems, autonomous vehicles

8.1 Introduction

The rapid increase in road traffic accidents globally requires the attention of people to come up with developments in safety technology for vehicles. The world over, millions of accidents happen yearly, with many resulting

**Corresponding author*: sumanta.prof@gmail.com

Rajdeep Chakraborty, Aleem Ali, Amit Paul, Nawaf R. Alharbe and S. Balamurugan (eds.) Causal Artificial Intelligence: Fundamentals and Applications, (175–216) © 2026 Scrivener Publishing LLC

in injuries or death, and it is, therefore, necessary to prescribe and adopt new solutions that can prove effective in significantly reducing the occurrence of accidents [1]. It is pertinent that collision detection systems be put in place in every vehicle; however, these systems commonly lack enough capacity to cope with the complexities and dynamic nature of the real-world driving environment [1, 8]. Conventional systems depend on rule-based algorithms, which fail frequently during adverse weather and with a high density of traffic or unpredictable driver behavior [1, 6]. It is due to this that these deficiencies in those systems are currently a case to shift to those more sophisticated, user-dependent, and more precise methods of collision detection.

One of the branches of machine learning is neural networks, which have gained strength as an alternative to a traditional rule-based architecture [1, 2]. Neural networks are powerful beyond the capacity to handle massive data and hence identify extremely complicated patterns and to continually evolve these patterns or learning algorithms in response to changing environments [5]. Therefore, the neural networks are able to learn using the input they generate using the acquired data as opposed to making use of predestined rules, thus facilitating generalization and more precise predictions even in cases they have not been specifically programmed to address [2]. This property renders the neural networks an excellent candidate for improvement in the collision detection system of modern cars [1].

In this chapter, the theoretical and practical elements of the design of collision detectors are revealed, including the neural networks working on the novel sensor technologies. Such sensors, including LiDAR, radar, and cameras, will inherently possess supplementary data concerning the surroundings of the vehicle, which will allow taking actions that will assist the most in viewing and comprehending the possible obstacles, road conditions, and hazards [6, 8, 11].

Neural-network-based automotive systems will be able to better internalize the environment with the help of sensor technology and make more real-time decisions [1, 5]. Enormous accuracy is built because the convergence between neural networks and sophisticated sensor systems supplants conventional systems. One of the greatest advantages here would be the improved accuracy since it would now be able to extend neural networks to consume very large-dimensional sensor inputs to improve in detecting objects, distances, and collision situations [2, 5]. This type of accuracy is necessary when the tolerance is typically very small, such as at high speed or in low visibility [11].

Among the strengths of neural networks, there is adaptability, in addition to accuracy. Most collision-detection systems are generally conventional, which means that they rely on strict algorithms that cannot be readily adjusted to unique differences based on environmental factors [1]. As an example, when it is raining, foggy, or snowing, sensor performance will be vastly different, and so will the manner in which they perceive objects or obstacles. Neural networks that learn with massive quantities of nonhomogeneous conditions cause them to be flexible and adaptive to constantly evolving conditions and provide trustworthy collision detection even in the most rugged conditions [1, 6, 11].

Real-time decision-making is another characteristic of the modern collision detection systems. It entails a move that ought to be undertaken instantly by the vehicles upon risks that possibly can be hazardous; spontaneity is required to prevent accidents. This can be easily handled with neural networks since they have a reputation for handling big data within a shorter time in order to conduct successful prediction of possible collision, and at the same time activate emergency braking or similar evasive steering without the need for much time in human interaction [2, 5].

Notwithstanding, the virtues of the neural networks in collision detection are immense—but they are not flawless. This is possibly the most grave drawback since networks require sufficient high-quality data to be trained [1]. Such systems require very large amounts of labeled data in order to develop regularities indicating evidence of potential collisions. The process of gathering such data is tedious and costly, more so in diverse environmental conditions [1, 11].

Additionally, since noisy or inaccurate data would lead to poor predictions, the performance of the system is highly dependent on the quality of such data [1]. The other issue is that the neural net models running in runtime do not even have the capability to run on their own real-time computational complexity in the vehicle. The neural network sensor data, particularly that of deep learning, requires highly intensive computational resources, and thus, the use of neural networks further complicates the prediction [1]. These are only a few of the key challenges associated with the attempts to install such systems in cars, which must work effectively and consume a minimum load on the onboard processing resources [11].

Researchers and engineers are still working on how to improve those models, to make them more efficient, and on the best way to make sure that they can be used in real time without jeopardizing safety [1]. By taking advantage of recent developments in deep learning, reinforcement learning, and transfer learning, more and more complicated models have been developed that are capable of dealing with increasingly complicated driving situations [1, 2, 11]. The new systems were more precise and flexible, but efficient with regard to calculating resources.

New opportunities in collision detection systems could be provided by the current developments in neural networks and state-of-the-art sensor modalities like LiDAR, radar, cameras, etc. [6, 8, 11]. LiDAR creates extremely detailed 3D maps of the surrounding environment that have high spatial density and can be used to better identify objects and measure distance [6]. Radar is the most appropriate in terms of low visibility because of the fog or rain, and may supplement the system of target detection with other sensors [6, 11]. Cameras are ideal for high-definition imagery in regard to object recognition and scene comprehension [5, 12]. The combination of such sensors with neural networks is projected to offer more enriched, correct, and holistic automotive units in understanding their surroundings in order to make their system safer [1, 6].

Collision detection systems based on neural networks have the potential to have far-reaching impacts on road safety. These systems may help in the mitigation of accidents, and even death, and surely injury severity [1, 8]. They not only make driving safer but also make driving in general more enjoyable, which makes the process of automated driving and situational awareness a higher priority to a driver [1].

This chapter will be all about a comprehensive exploration of collision detection systems based on the use of neural networks. In essence, the chapter will discuss various concepts of neural networks, design aspects of how such systems would be utilized in real-life scenarios, and how they might be used with advanced sensor devices incorporated. In addition, it would talk of the advantages and some of the challenges attached to them, as well as how they can be further enhanced to perform better and operate more efficiently. Based on the recent advancements in the region, the chapter would come up with solutions to the current issues, and in the process, they would help in coming up with a smart automotive safety system that would have the potential of overhauling the region in which vehicles would identify and respond to a collision, among other attributes.

This will form a critical element of the safety case that neural networks will undertake as we continue into the future, where such vehicles are ubiquitous among their occupants. Very complex systems today would be needed to understand the driving conditions, adjust to extremely different conditions, and make real-time decisions. In that connection, intelligent solutions could be achieved by exercising the power of both advanced sensor technologies and neural networks. Thus, roads would become smarter and safer, minimizing the potential of accidents and protecting lives.

A quick look at the chapter is provided. The chapter starts with the Introduction, followed by the Background and Literature Review, which set the grounds. Next, the Proposed Framework and Neural Network–Based Collision Detection Architecture are discussed in more detail, describing the finer points of the core component and training processes. Following this will be the discussion on the Collision Prediction Framework, including its architecture, models, and training methodologies. The chapter then addresses the System Integration Framework, performing the deployment of the neural network, real-time inference, and control-feedback loops. Subsequent sections include Testing and Validation, Practical Applications and Benefits, and finally, a chapter summary highlighting the significant acquired knowledge and proposed future work.

8.2 Background and Literature Review

The alarming increase in the number of accidents occurring on roads in different parts of the world is compelling the need for new and effective automotive safety solutions. Traditional collision avoidance mechanisms have been based on rule-based algorithms, and these methods have been the primary solution to the problem of collision avoidance. However, such systems have been found ineffective under dynamic conditions, e.g., adverse weather and high traffic congestion [8]. Over the last several years, AI technologies, especially NNs, have been given much attention because they are able to process complex, high-dimensional data and can effectively find complicated patterns as well as generalize to new driving environments [1]. This paper presents a survey of such works that have advanced neural network–based collision detection systems in the last five years, as integrated with highly advanced sensor technologies such as LiDAR, radar, and cameras. It is concerned with the major innovations, possible advantages, and ongoing challenges in using neural network–based techniques.

8.2.1 Conventional Collision Detection and Its Limitations

Initially, before the emergence of AI-based systems, collision detection in automobiles depended solely upon rule-based systems that worked by bringing them up against the preset threshold for determining the detection of objects and predicting possible collisions. Common sensors used in such systems are ultrasound, infrared, and radar-based sensors. The restrictions of existing systems emerge prominently in more complicated driving scenarios, even when these systems may have satisfactory results in simpler and static environments. Such systems operate under predefined conditions and still fail in real-time adaptation against various factors in the environment: changeable weather such as fog, rain, and snow; increased density of traffic; and complicated geometry of roads [8].

Talaat, F.M. and Hamza, A.A. reported that, as often found, a rule-based system would have the problems of false positives (not detecting a nonexistent obstacle) or false negatives (not detecting any obstacle), particularly in congested and/or unpredictable driving conditions [1]. All these make the systems lose much of their reliability because they cannot process the high-dimensional data available in real-world environments. For example, being dependent heavily upon sensor signals from one or two types of sensors, rule-based systems do not allow much flexibility in fusing data from different sources and, as a result, can be less accurate in their responses to occluded objects or ambiguous scenarios.

8.2.2 Neural Networks for Collision Detection

Neural networks, especially deep learning systems, are now being offered as superior alternatives to traditional collision detection methods with respect to strength and flexibility (Table 8.1). This ability of neural networks to automatically process large amounts of data without programming much of what is understood about complex patterns has been a boon in the detection and avoidance of contact between objects [1].

8.2.3 Convolutional Neural Networks (CNNs)

Convolutional Neural Networks (CNNs) have taken a very dominant role in detecting objects, particularly within vision-based collision detection systems. Artificial CNNs permit hierarchical automatic extraction of features using multiple layers of filters of raw images and sensor data, so that a system can be capable of identifying the presence and positioning of objects in a high-accuracy way. CNNs have been modified to deal with visual information from cameras and LiDAR sensors and are highly efficient in performing pedestrian identification, vehicle identification or detection, and identification of obstacles [2, 5].

Talaat, F.M. and Hamza, A.A. [1] examined the specific time of monitoring the collisions that are achieved using CNN models in multiple-camera systems that envelop car setups. According to the study, CNNs can be trained to be able to identify the presence of a pedestrian, a bicycle, or some other vehicle and anticipate potential collisions in various traffic settings [1]. In addition, CNN-based modeling is superior to all the

Table 8.1 Comparison of detection methods, associated technologies, benefits, and drawbacks.

Approach	Technologies	Key advantages	Key limitations
Rule-based systems	Infrared, radar	Simple, effective in static conditions	Poor adaptability in dynamic/ weather conditions
CNNs	Cameras, LiDAR	Accurate object detection, handles occlusion	Sensitive to lighting also needs large datasets
RNNs/LSTMs	Radar, Cameras	Models temporal movement; predicts collisions	Complex training, needs time-series data
LiDAR + neural nets	LiDAR + CNN	Precise 3D detection, and it works in low visibility	Expensive; affected by severe weather
Radar + neural nets	Radar + DNN	Reliable in bad weather and measures speed/ distance	Lower resolution; needs fusion for detail
Camera + neural nets	Cameras + CNN	High-res visuals and effective urban detection	Limited by glare/ darkness; needs sensor fusion

traditional ones, as far as the detection speed and accuracy are concerned. What is more interesting is that CNNs are more effective than rule-based algorithms at overcoming the problem of occlusion and changing environmental conditions; therefore, they can be well-suited to a dynamic road environment.

8.2.4 Recurrent Neural Networks (RNNs) and Long Short-Term Memory Networks (LSTMs)

The CNNs are more suitable for spatial data, whereas the RNN and LSTM networks have been increasingly applied to the modeling and analysis of sequence-based data, such as time series sensor signals. The time parameters are dynamic parameters in time, i.e., the movement of other vehicles and objects in collision detection, depending on the forecasted detections. RNNs and LSTM networks have been widely used for studying time-dependent data and predicting collisions from the movement behavior of the objects over time.

Zhang *et al.* [15] had a good experience studying the application of an LSTM in the prediction of vehicle-to-vehicle collisions. In this scheme, data from multiple sensors, including radar and cameras, would be transmitted to an LSTM network and trained in such a way that it predicts collision risk based on vehicle trajectories and speeds. With that, they proved that LSTMs substantially increased the accuracy for predictions of collision because they could take into account temporal evolution in the movement of the vehicle, which was missing in classical rule-based systems [11].

8.2.5 Integration of Neural Networks with Advanced Sensor Technologies

The success of neural network–based collision detection systems depends very much on the integration of the sensors, such as LiDAR, radar, and cameras, which provide complementary coverage and can therefore be fused to produce a better input model to the environment. All sensor types have an advantage, but at the same time, some of their limitations can be overcome by the others [1].

8.2.6 LiDAR and Neural Networks

LiDAR stands for Light Detection and Ranging. It provides 3D maps with considerable detail of the environment and favors distance filings and object detection. Along with a neural network, it may therefore optimize the detection of collisions in instances where the use of cameras alone or radar fusion does not suffice. Liu and others therefore demonstrated the combination of LiDAR and CNN for the detection of both cars and pedestrians in recent studies conducted in 2021 [1]. The resultant model was trained with a large LiDAR dataset that taught the network the ability to identify an object in a 3D space at high precision. This has proven useful in low-visibility scenarios, such as during night driving or foggy conditions. Since LiDAR operates in dynamic behavior, this sensor is critical when it comes to real-time collision detection from an autonomous vehicle.

Again, LiDAR systems have a number of limitations, chief among them being costs and vulnerability to environmental interference such as heavy rain or snow. To mitigate such odds, many researchers have come up with sensor fusion models that integrate LiDAR data with other sensor inputs, such as those from radars or cameras.

8.2.7 Radar and Neural Networks

Radar sensors are among the most popular techniques for ensuring safety in automobiles because of their dependability in bad weather. Radar always helps in determining the speed and relative position of surrounding vehicles, making it an effective aid for estimating rear-end collisions. Progress in radar-neural network blending is showing improvement for effective collision detection in high-speed or high-traffic scenarios.

Chen *et al.* [13] searched for the combination of radar data with deep learning applied to collision avoidance. The team thought of building a methodology where the radar will measure the velocity and distance of objects in the surroundings, while a deep neural network will analyze the data and predict if a collision scenario will arise. The research concluded that the system outperformed conventional radar-based systems because the system was able to detect objects as well as predict movements, leading to better decision-making in real-time.

Also, it is very common that applications of radars are integrated with various other sensors in order to increase the robustness of the system. For example, the combination of LiDAR and radars is a force that works as a supplement to each other in the characterization of stationary and moving objects under various weather conditions. Moving object detection is identified by radar at larger ranges, while LiDAR provides better results with shape and distance measures of objects close by. Radar helps in the detection of the speed and position with respect to other vehicles and hence is useful for estimating the case of a rear-end collision. Further progress in using neural networks with radar has already shown improvement in collision detection in high-speed or high-traffic environments.

The study by Chen *et al.* [6] examined the combined use of radar data and deep learning models for collision avoidance. The idea behind this was that information from the radar would include the velocity and distance of surrounding objects, while a deep neural network would process the information, predicting collision scenarios. The system was applicable beyond normal radar systems because it did not just detect the objects but also looked into their movement, hence better decision-making in real time [6].

In addition, the use of radar is usually supplemented with other sensors to improve robustness. The fusion of LiDAR and radar actually complements the common advantages of detecting stationary and moving objects in various environments. While radar is a very good detection for longer distances of moving objects, LiDAR gives detailed information required for the shape as well as the distance of nearby objects.

8.2.8 Cameras and Neural Networks

Varying the type of cameras has made them an indispensable part of collision detection systems. The cameras capture a very high resolution of images that is necessary for understanding and classifying the different obstacles on the roadway. This combination of neural network and camera technology has significantly improved vehicle safety systems [1].

According to Zhang *et al.* [14], CNNs are effective at detecting pedestrians and vehicles in urban camera footage. The model was developed on a very large dataset comprising images taken in different snowy weather and at different times of the day. The results indicated that CNN-based systems were very effective at detecting pedestrians and other vehicles in challenging light. This shows that much useful information can be drawn from camera data employing neural networks, which lets the system predict and avoid future accidents. Camera addition is also challenged by glare, darkness, and adverse weather conditions. This creates various problems in visualizing whatever is available. To resolve such situations, research has gone into sensor combination, for example, radar and LiDAR with cameras—multisensor.

8.3 Proposed Framework

With the increasing incidence of road traffic accidents across the globe, automotive researchers and engineers have started to strive for more innovative mechanisms in improving vehicle safety. Neural networks may be put to use for collision detection, which could have the potential to be a more accurate or more flexible solution than systems based on rules. Learning complex patterns from high-dimensional data makes neural networks capable of real-time detection of possible collisions under different driving conditions, such as inclement weather or heavy traffic. This framework highlights conceptualization and the practical implementation of a neural network–based collision detection system comprising data acquisition, preprocessing, architecture of the neural network, collision prediction, and system integration.

8.3.1 Data Acquisition

Initially, data acquisition is completed for setting up a collision detection framework based on neural networks. The successful establishment of the framework depends primarily on data collection that is diverse and of high quality, which is used to train a neural network regarding the detection of collisions in a dynamic environment.

a. Sensor Data Acquisition

For the various applications of collision detection in real scenarios using different sensors to collect data, all those sensors measure the environmental scene, the objects, and the agent's position. These sensors generally have:

- LiDAR (light detection and ranging): It takes very accurate distances from the objects that can be used to build a 3D map of the environment.
- Cameras (RGB or Depth): Offer visual information for detecting collisions using techniques of image processing and segmentation.
- Ultrasonic sensors: Generally closer to detecting distance, they are also very effective in short-distance environments with lesser complexity.
- IMUs (Inertial measurement units): Help track the movement and orientation of an object, thus providing useful data for dynamic collision detection.

The temporal structure of their data is usually timestamped and grouped into sequences through these sensors; hence, they would be able to detect time changes, which is very important in dynamic environments where the obstacles are not static.

b. Data Augmentation

Upgrading of over-collision detection may need apprehension into different conditions of the environmental states (lighting, weather, sensor noise, etc.); therefore, the expansion in data augmentations is intended to boost the model robustness. Among several techniques for data augmentation are the following:

- Rotation and Scaling: By rotation and scaling, different views can be attained through transformations in images or point cloud data.
- Noise Injection: Noisy environments can be posed for good generalization in model performance through random noise addition into the sensor data, mimicking real-world flaws.
- Synthetic Data Generation: Synthetic data generation, largely using simulation software such as Unity, CARLA, or Gazebo, is very helpful when real-world data collection is expensive or simply lacks value in terms of costs. C: Labeling and Annotation.

In supervised learning, where labeled data is needed to train a neural network to learn collision, it can include application-specific labels, such as:

- Collision Events: An event is equal to the collision of an object with another, usually marked with binary identifiers (collide/no-collision).
- Collision Severity: The type of collision or impact is annotated (like minor, major, or critical) so that the network can be trained to predict severity.
- Bounding Boxes: In image-based systems, bounding boxes or segmentation masks can be used to annotate objects that need to be avoided or detected in order to prevent collisions.

Manual labeling can be tedious; one can adopt semi-automatic techniques as one of the means to reduce efforts. Using both labeled real-world matched data and synthetic data can also improve the model's generalization ability over various conditions.

c. Data Preprocessing

After collecting the data, it needs to be preprocessed before being taken as input into the neural network. Some of the very basic preprocessing could be:

Normalization: Some sensor measurements (say, of distance or speed) can be normalized so as to make the model more stable during the training phase.

Feature Engineering: Sometimes it may be necessary to convert raw sensor signals to more appropriate features. Take relative velocity or angular displacement, for instance; they can be very useful when determining a collision.

d. Real-Time Data Streaming

The best way to avoid having any collision is by eliminating actions that are delayed or even having a critical process done by humans. Collisions are avoided when immediate actions are taken to treat the situation. In the robotic or autonomous vehicle, the most correct setup would be to utilize an appropriate real-time data streaming pipeline to handle the incoming data, apply necessary preprocessing, and feed such data into the neural network for inference. This is how data collection continues. The other part of it includes real-time processing completion, which would give information that is part of the system.

In a nutshell, data acquisition underpins the development of a collision detection framework that leverages neural networks. When data from various sensors is collected, augmented, and preprocessed, it will be used to train the model in cognizing and anticipating probable collisions in a complicated, dynamic environment. Next, the neural network will be designed and trained on the data, where it will learn to identify the patterns for collisions.

8.3.2 Preprocessing

Collision detection models utilize a very high-quality input data set for their prediction, especially when based on neural networks (NN). Raw sensor data, such as LiDAR, radar, cameras, etc., usually suffer from noise, discontinuities, and high dimensionality. Not to mention that poor-quality data input may lead to unsatisfactory performance during model training. Preprocessing will include cleaning the data, feature extraction, and appropriately formatting the data set for feeding into a neural network for collision prediction.

Key Steps in Preprocessing

8.3.2.1 Data Cleaning

The first step of preprocessing is data cleansing, which guarantees that the dataset has no errors, inconsistencies, noise, etc. It is, indeed, the quality of data that directly affects the functioning of the neural network.

- Handling Missing Data: Sensors sometimes go out of range to collect data and record it incompletely. Thus, the ways of handling missing values include:

- Imputation: Fill in the missing values with the mean, median, or mode from the neighboring data points. In the case of time-series data, there can be interpolation.
- Deletion: This affects the rows or instances of data that do not have some necessary data points. The scattered condition makes it incapable of recovering that data.
- Noise Reduction: Raw sensor data (LiDAR, cameras, etc.) is usually noisy (because of environmental factors, e.g., weather, interference). Noise could be reduced using:

  Filtering: Gaussian smoothing or a median filter is a favorite method of smoothing irregularities in data, not to mention noise.
- Detecting outliers in the dataset: Removing the outliers allows for avoiding distortion of the model learning process. The Z-score measure or IQR (interquartile range) is considered a common method of detecting outliers in numerical data.
- Data Validation: First of all, the following thing would be to ensure that the data format is the same across all sources of input. GPS coordinates are to be typed in the correct format; sensor time is expected to match; and sensor data size is to be the correct size for the expected input.

8.3.2.2 Feature Engineering

The concept of feature engineering consists of selecting, altering, or creating novel features that transform raw data such that a neural network can learn significant patterns. In the case of collision detection, feature engineering is important to the model's performance.

- Trajectory Features: Important characteristics of objects in motion in space, such as velocity, acceleration, and direction of movement, must be calculated. Among such features, there are:
- Speed: The change in position during a given time interval.
- Acceleration: The speed at which speed changes take place. It may indicate the likelihood of sudden movements.
- Relative distance: Distance between an interested object and other nearby objects.

- Geometric Features: Besides trajectory features, there are also features that describe, geometrically, the size, shape, and orientation of an object with respect to other objects that might be important in predicting a collision.
- Object coordinates: Sensor detections of objects having 3D coordinates in the LiDAR point cloud are required for predictions of spatial relationships. Sensor-specific features: There are some other features available with other types of sensors:
- Radar: Signal strength and angular velocity of objects detected by radar sensors.
- Temporal Features: Indeed, time features are imperative for the prediction of collisions. Giving more information about the evolution of the behavior of a competitor in terms of velocity, trajectory, or proximity to other competitors in time may indeed give us insight into future collision scenarios.

8.3.2.3 Data Transformation

- Once the raw features have been engineered, the data transformation methods are applied so that the data are put in an appropriate format for the neural network. Transformation helps in making the features easier for interpretation by the model and improves the accuracy of predicting results.
- The reshaping of data files: It is all done to meet the required data shape by the architecture of the neural network. For example, a convolutional neural network requires image data as a 3D tensor, which includes height, width, and channels, while for RNNs and LSTMs, it needs data in the sequential format of a time series.
- About sensor data, like LiDAR point clouds, the issue that arises is that the 3D point cloud needs to be converted into 2D grid data or voxel grid for CNN-based architectures.
- In the case of time-series representations, such as the trajectories of objects, it can be reshaped into time sequences that capture the temporal nature of the problem.
- One-hot encoding: This approach is typically applied to the classification of categorical types of data into categories, i.e., the type of objects in the case of vehicles or pedestrians. One-hot encoding transforms these categories into binary vectors that could be processed by the neural network.

- Data augmentation is used to better generalize a model or to reduce overfitting effects, particularly for all kinds of data, working for image data. It artificially increases a dataset by transformations such as:
- Rotation: It rotates images or sensor readings to create several different viewing angles for real-world objects.
- Translation: It shifts images or sensor readings in the x and y directions at the same time.
- Flipping: Images are flipped either horizontally or vertically.

8.3.2.4 *Normalization and Scaling*

Normalizing or scaling ensures that each feature equally contributes to the learning of the neural network itself. The reason for this is that neural networks are affected by the input data scale. Large-scale features can be the most dominant feature if scaling is not done.

- Min-Max Scaling: In this type of scaling, values are scaled between the specified values, which are generally [0, 1] or [min, max]. For example, if the distances of objects in the dataset ranged between 10 and 100 meters, all the values would now be between 0 and 1 after applying the min-max scaling.
- Z-Score Normalization: In this method, the data is centered at zero by subtracting the mean and dividing by the standard deviation. This works when features have a Gaussian distribution and neural networks can converge quickly.
- Log Transformation: In such heavy skew or exponential growth features, such as distance between objects, log transformations would stabilize the variance and de-emphasize extreme values.
- Sensor-Specific Scaling: Different sensors have different resolutions while giving their output. Camera image pixel values might be on a different scale than those of LiDAR data. So, one should scale such sensor data individually.

8.3.2.5 *Data Balancing*

In the case of collision detection experiments that apply supervised learning, most of the time, the dataset used is imbalanced. Indeed, collisions happen very rarely compared to other events, which causes a class imbalance that might bias the neural network towards predicting the larger class (non-collision).

- Oversampling- Duplicate instances from the minority class (collision) to balance the dataset.
- Undersampling- Reduce the number of examples from the larger class (non-collision) to balance the dataset.
- Generation of Synthetic Data- Apply a technique like SMOTE (Synthetic Minority Over-sampling Technique) for the generation of synthetic collision examples, whereby class balance may be achieved.

Preprocessing is a vital step in the development of a collision detection system using a neural network. Clearing the data, engineering informative features, transforming it into the correct format, and scaling all work in concert properly to improve the chances of learning. Moreover, some other issues, such as data imbalance, improve the reliability and accuracy of the collision model. Real-time and accurate collision detections in dynamic environments depend upon this preprocessing stage and ensure that they will receive the best quality data possible after training a neural network.

8.4 Neural Network–Based Collision Detection: Architecture Framework

Neural networks have naturally become a component of collision detection systems, where the sensor data are learned to form complicated representations of these data. Neural network architecture is the most important aspect of the neural network because it determines the performance and accuracy of the model. A well-constructed neural network can forecast the likelihood of a collision based on various types of sensor data (LiDAR, cameras, radars, ultrasonic devices, etc.). It explores the design factors, layers, and methodologies of training a neural network using an intelligent collision detection system model.

8.4.1 Introduction to Neural Network Architecture for Collision Detection

The definition of the architecture of the neural network is the arrangement of the neurons and the layers that constitute the neural network.

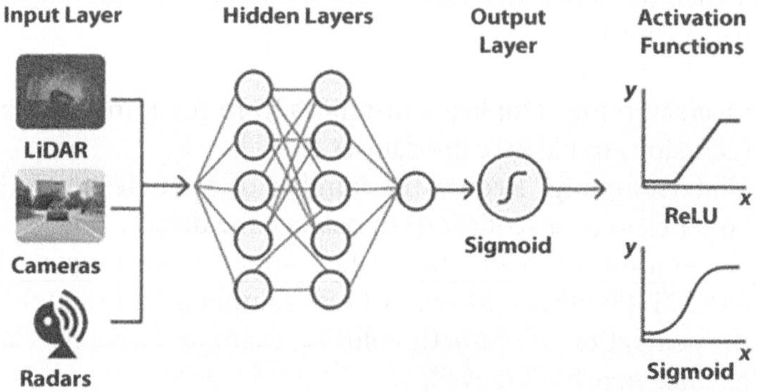

Figure 8.1 Neural network–based collision detection architecture framework.

It determines the ways in which the data may flow across the network and the manner in which the model can learn the input data. To accomplish collision detection, the neural network should be trained on the various types of data, which are images, time series, and scanned 3D point clouds, to learn spatiotemporal patterns that can represent a possible collision possibility. To this end, we observe a procedure for constructing the concrete structure of the neural network that is aimed at predicting the collision events (Figure 8.1).

8.4.2 Design Considerations for Neural Network Architecture

8.4.2.1 Input Data Types

The entire architecture has to be configured depending on the data type the system is utilizing. For example, in collision detection, different sets of input data may be :

- Image Data: Cameras provide large volumes of visual information that can be processed using CNN-based algorithms.
- Time Series Data: These consist of typical sensor data that rely on GPS or accelerometers that capture temporal dependency for some model to be implemented, that is, RNNs or LSTMs.
- Point Cloud Data: Systems that transform 3D point clouds given by LiDAR or radar sensors through their specific

networks (PointNet or voxel-based architectures). The neural network very much depends on the type of input provided.

8.4.2.2 *Problem Type*

Collision detection can also be posed as a binary classification problem (collision vs. no collision) or a regression problem (predicting the probability or severity of a collision). Binary classification would, however, require output in the form of a single neuron with a sigmoid activation function, whereas regression may require multiple neurons or continuous output.

8.4.2.3 *Model Complexity and Overfitting*

The neural network should be complex enough to learn intricate patterns, avoiding overfitting when constructed in a very complex manner with a very limited training set. Regularization techniques, like dropout, L2 regularization, or data augmentation, aid in making the model generalize well.

The neural network should be complex enough to learn difficult patterns, yet not overfit, as may happen in a very complex model with very limited training data. Dropout, L2 regularization, or data augmentation are important regularization techniques that help the model generalize well.

The neural network should be sufficiently complex in itself so that intricate patterns can be captured: it should not be overfit in the way that it becomes a very complex model based on a very small training set. Regularization techniques such as, but not limited to, dropout, L2 regularization, or data augmentation are helpful in ensuring good generalization by the model.

8.5 Components of Neural Network Architecture

8.5.1 Input Layer

Here is where raw data is fed into the neural networks. Depending on the sensory data, it performs as follows:

- For image data: the input layer can accept fixed-size 2D arrays (images), for example, 224x224x3, where the first two dimensions refer to the spatial resolution of an image, while the third dimension refers to the color channels (RGB).

- For time-series data, the input layer may accept sequences with an observation represented in each timestep (such as position and velocity). The input shape may be a 2D array so that rows represent time steps and columns represent the features.
- For point clouds: The input could be a 3D grid or a point cloud, where every point is assigned to an object or is a reading from a sensor; then, there are networks such as PointNet that are developed to process raw 3D point clouds directly.

Its input layer normally resembles the shape of the data to ensure proper alignment with the following layers of the network.

8.5.2 Hidden Layers

The information is processed by several hidden layers as it learns what might appear to be collision features. The type and number of hidden layers are dependent on the complexity of the task.

- Convolutional Layers (CNNs): For spatial data like images or 2D spaces from a sensor, they work great. They convolve filters across the input, capturing the spatial features, such as edges, textures, and object boundaries. They help detect objects and determine where they could collide.
  Example: In the case of images, additional vehicles, pedestrians, or objects can be identified in a camera image.
- Recurrent Layers (RNNs/LSTMs): When the issue revolves around time-variant data, such as with predicting collisions based on an object's movement over time, then RNNs or LSTMs are mostly used. These layers capture dependencies that are sequenced, by which patterns shown over time are learned to denote the possibility of a collision.
  Example: LSTMs in this scenario would support modeling of the succession of time by tracking an object's current position and how fast it would go in successive time intervals.
- Fully Connected (Dense) Layers: After all the previous layers, within which some may be CNNs or RNNs, in such a scenario, these layers constitute the final configuration and bring those extracted features together. These layers make

up the decisive part of the network; as such, they take in the high-level features from earlier layers and convert them to the final output.

8.5.3 Output Layer

The prediction made by a model is made from the output layer. The nature of the task determines the configuration of the output layer:

- Binary Classification: In case the classification task is whether or not a collision should happen, a single neuron will be present with a sigmoid activation function. The range of the output value will be between 0 and 1, giving the probability of a collision occurring.
- Multi-Class Classification: If different kinds of collision types have to be classified by the model (for instance, minor, moderate, or severe collision), an output layer would have multiple neurons with softmax activation.
- Regression: For those cases where the model currently predicts a continuous value like the time before collision or severity, the output will come with one or more neurons without any activation function (linear activation).

8.5.4 Activation Functions

Activation functions are nonlinear functions that make the model learn some complex relations:

- The ReLU (Rectified Linear Unit) is the most commonly used activation function in hidden layers because it breaks linearity and prevents the vanishing gradient problem.
- Sigmoid: Typically used in the output layer of binary classification tasks, where output is squashed into a 0-1 range.
- Softmax: It is used in multi-class classification problems to normalize the output into a probability distribution over multiple classes.

8.5.5 Loss Function

The purpose of the loss function is to measure how far away the predictions are from the model to the label, so that the network learns:

- Binary Cross-Entropy: For binary classification, say, collision and no collision.
- Categorical Cross-Entropy: For multi-class classification, such as collision by some other means.
- MSE: For regression, i.e., outputs such as time before collision are predicted by the model.

8.5.6 Optimizers

During training, the optimizer works on the adjustments of the weights of the network to reach the minimum possible value of the loss function at the end. Among the most well-known ones, the following can be highlighted:

- Adam (Adaptive Moment Estimation): Perhaps the most well-known optimizer, it modifies its learning rate depending on gradients.
- SGD (Stochastic Gradient Descent): A simpler optimizer that updates weights based only on the gradient of the loss function.
- RMSProp: It's usually selected for RNN and LSTM training, especially when learning rates need to be adapted for various parameters.

8.6 Training the Neural Network

Once the architecture was defined, the model went for training, which allowed it to predict collisions with the help of labeled data. Some important steps are:

- Training and Validation: The dataset is split into training and validation sets so that the generalization ability of the model can be interpreted. If one wants to ensure that overfitting does not take place during training, an early stop can be signaled.
- Batch Size and Epochs: Determining the batch size—the number of samples taken under consideration before the model is updated—and then defining the epochs, which are the number of complete passes through the training dataset, for optimum learning.

- Regularization: Dropout (randomly setting to zero a fraction of the neurons during training) helps prevent overfitting by forcing the network to generalize.

It can be said that this architecture for neural network designs is essentially meant for addressing and dealing with intricate, key-data modeling and mapping functions, besides ideal prediction of the same, so that the process is ensured to be safe. The choice of layers, activation functions, and loss functions will be affected by the type of data (e.g., images, time series, or point clouds) as well as the nature of the task, such as binary classification or regression. Convolutional, recurrent, and fully connected layers allow the network to predict possible collisions in dynamic environments very well. Coordinated training techniques joined with careful model evaluation will allow neural networks to become a mainstay in real-time collision detection systems.

8.7 Neural Network–Based Collision Detection: Collision Prediction Framework

Collisions do predict future events based on current sensors' output within the constraints of collision detection systems, where it stands within models. Since neural networks have been shown to learn effectively with even raw data sets and apply them to make current predictions, they become very attractive for such tasks. This makes collision detection a central component for many autonomous systems, especially self-driving cars, drones, and industrial robots, trying to improve the safety and prevention of accidents.

This framework deals with every aspect concerning collision prediction by neural networks, from input data and network processing to prediction models and performance evaluation.

8.7.1 Understanding Collision Prediction in Neural Networks

It involves the analysis of data derived from sensors, generated from streams of data obtained from attached accelerometers, including object velocity, trajectory, and proximity, for the purposes of predicting a collision at a specific point in time. This detection task can be defined in two different ways: as a binary classification problem (collision versus no collision) or as

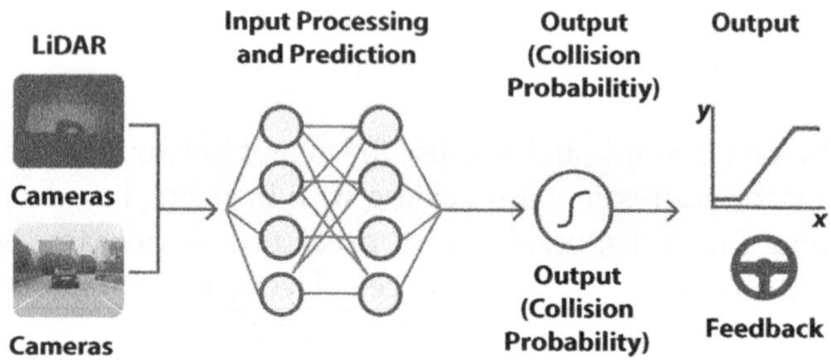

Figure 8.2 Neural network–based collision detection: collision prediction framework.

a regression problem (predicting the time-to-collision or impact severity) associated with an impending collision.

However, the trick is to develop a neural network model, which can take input data from an array of sources such as images, point clouds, time series, or radar signals and predict the occurrences of collisions with great accuracy but minimum time latency (Figure 8.2).

8.7.2 Input Data for Collision Prediction

The collision prediction data can be derived from various sensors that provide different aspects of the environment. Each sensor provides different kinds of data that must be appropriately processed by the neural network.

8.7.3 Visual Data (Camera Images)

The cameras placed in the autonomous vehicles can detect any object that falls in the way of the vehicle. The data from these images are processed through CNNs (Convolutional Neural Networks). The network can then be given images, and it has convolutional layers that perform the identification of objects (like vehicles, pedestrians, and road signs) and their positions, as well as other details that help predict collisions.

- Data Representation: Single raw images or fully processed data, such as bounding boxes and object segmentation maps.

- Use Case: Object detection and classification, which will be used in the incorporation of the dynamic objects, for which collisions can occur.

8.7.4 LiDAR and Radar Data (Point Clouds)

LiDAR and radar sensors are quite appropriate to give three-dimensional space details. LiDAR makes 3D point clouds and, therefore, the 3D location of the objects; radar, in its turn, measures the relative speed and the distance of the objects.

- Data Representation: Point cloud data for LiDAR or reflection maps for radar, which essentially provide measurements of distances, velocities, and relative positions.
- Use Case: For finding out the distances between objects in a three-dimensional world, as well as how they move in relation to others, in order to evaluate how likely a collision might be.

8.7.5 Time-Series Data (Velocity, Acceleration, and Position)

The continuous sensor readings must be available to understand the motion of the car and surrounding objects, such as the velocity, position, and acceleration of an object at any given time under varying cases, to predict future trajectories and infer collision risks.

- Data Representation: Motion can be depicted by the sequential data of position, velocity, and acceleration of an object in time.
- Use case: Trajectory prediction of an object and interaction of distance relation with the vehicle.

8.8 Neural Network Architecture for Collision Prediction

In terms of input data type and complexity of the task, different neural network architectures should possibly be applied for collision prediction. Here are some frequently used architectural components in collision prediction systems:

8.8.1 Convolutional Neural Networks (CNNs)

Convolutional neural networks are really great processes designed to cope with image data. The most interesting part is that with the help of CNNs, processing image data is made easy because they automatically internalize hierarchical features present in the images, such as edges, textures, and object shapes. Collision prediction as well is possible to be done with a CNN detecting items and how they are arranged in the filing space in the environment.

- Feature learning: Convolutional layers extract features from images (edges, corners, and contours of an object).
- Object Detection: Provides localizations and classifies instances in images from object detection models like YOLO (You Only Look Once) and Faster R-CNN to give the neural network a glimpse of expected obstacles.

8.8.2 Recurrent Neural Networks (RNNs) and LSTMs

RNNs and LSTMs are used for working with time-series data because they are very capable of dealing with sequential data and thus allow the network to learn and predict the future positions of objects as time goes on. These architectures are the finest when it comes to predicting the future likelihood of collision based on various parameters like velocity and acceleration.

Sequential data modeling - RNNs and LSTMs capture dependencies through time, so the network can also learn the patterns in sequences like movements of objects, and also sensor readings.
Prediction for time of collision- These models are capable of predicting the time when objects will collide with each other, potentially allowing collision forecasting.

By predicting the future position of the object based on various parameters in the future, there come times when these architectures become the best at predicting how the future is going to save itself from collision based on velocity, acceleration, and position data.

- Sequential Data Modeling- Airlines and other business sectors can effectively capture what type of availabilities exist in an industry: RNNs and LSTMs capture dependencies throughout, parameters from the object moving, and also readings from different sensor points.

- Prediction of time of collision: It is also possible for predictive modeling by these prototypes to tell the time when the two objects will eventually impact.

8.8.3 PointNet for Point Cloud Data

PointNet is a specific kind of neural network used in the processing of 3D point clouds of LiDAR. In contrast to most models, which suppose that the input is ordered or a manifold topological input, with PointNet, one can simply use unordered point sets and learn on them. This renders it extremely thrilling to locate point cloud characteristics and detect obstacles, as well as gauge the chance of collisions in a 3D area.

- Spatial Feature Extraction: Raw 3D data processing is applied to the learning object and relative positioning to take into consideration collision prediction in a complex environment.
- Dynamic Object Tracking: In addition, it is time-dependent because the PointNet can track objects dynamically, and the network can predict collisions concerning object paths.

8.8.4 Fusion Networks

In practice, multiple complementary sensors usually provide such data as camera images, radar data, and LiDAR point clouds in real-life situations. The neural networks can be designed to integrate data from different sources, considering any factor that is taken into account. This is the reason why this can make the model gain information from each sensor. Fusion usually uses a feature map of several networks (i.e., CNN on images and PointNet on point clouds) and combines them in a later stage of the network.

- Multimodal Input: It is a fusion network that is employed to obtain sensor data streams, and this makes it more robust and more accurate than the models.

Hybrid Accuracy of Prediction: The fusion network, when combined with the visual, spatial, and temporal data, would give much more accurate predictions in relation to potential collisions.

8.9 Collision Prediction Models

Hence, on the basis of the neural network architecture, the next thing is designing the model to output predictions with respect to possible collisions. Task-dependent can be the different prediction models:

8.9.1 Binary Classification

Basically, the model predicts whether a collision will happen with very few time lapses. The output usually gives a value between 0 and 1, which indicates the possibility of the crash occurring, instead of outputting a direct string of "yes or no." Such tasks are typically simple yes/no-type cases.

- Output Layer: A unique neuron with a sigmoid activation function gives a probability score beyond the output.
- Thresholdization: The output is thresholded, for example, at 0.5 to determine if the event is classified as a collision or no collision.

8.9.2 Regression Model (Time-to-Collision)

In time-to-collision (TTC), it can be predicted in quite advanced tasks. So it will be a collision prediction task in which the model is expected to output the time index as to when the collision is likely to take place. The output of the model will hence be represented as a continuous real number for the second before the predicted collision actually takes place—a regression problem.

- Output Layer: A single neuron with a linear activation function predicts the time-to-collision.
- Prediction in Real Time: It provides mechanisms whereby potential collisions will not only be detected, but the time before the actual collision might also be estimated, allowing appropriate actions by the systems.

8.10 Training the Collision Prediction Model

This involves optimizing weights in the neural network to minimize the difference in prediction error. Training methods typically used for the model are:

8.10.1 Loss Functions

- Binary Cross-Entropy: Theoretically, all parts of the system are made of binary concepts, such as collision versus no-collision.
- Mean Square Error (MSE): Used in cases of continuous prediction by a model, like time to collision, so, in general words, it is used in regression tasks.

8.10.2 Optimization

- Adam Optimizer: It is noted for its adaptive learning rate, enabling faster convergence of the model.
- Stochastic Gradient Descent (SGD): It is a conventional optimizer for many of the deep learning tasks, but tuning might be needed more compared with others.

8.10.3 Evaluation Metrics

- Accuracy: In binary classification, accuracy is used to measure the frequency with which the model is correct in its prediction of collisions.
- Mean Absolute Error: MAE has been employed in the regression problem to establish the proximity between the time the computer guesses a collision and the actual time of collision.

Neural networks have turned into a key instrument of the autonomous systems of the present time, enabling the systems to predict potential collisions in real-time and prevent them. Various sensors, such as cameras, LiDAR point clouds, and time-series data, could be used to train neural networks, therefore predicting future collisions with a great deal of precision. The inherent architecture of the neural network, i.e., any CNN, RNN, LSTM, or fusion model, is the one that shows the explicit scope in which both raw sensor and time-state data can be included in a single model to be applied to the task. The right model, training mode, and evaluation indicator will ensure that the neural networks predict collisions prior to the incidence and are thus safe under the changing environments.

8.11 Neural Network–Based Collision Detection with System Integration Framework

The actual implementation of collision detection using a neural network is a complex task that requires extensive attention to hardware, software, sensor, and integration considerations. Such a system can potentially achieve seamless communication to complement the operation of the neural network model, sensors, vehicle control systems, and decision-making modules, while providing real-time output in predicting and avoiding collisions. System integration entails the combination of different subsystems and their concurrent functioning toward accurate, timely collision prediction.

This framework outlines key aspects of introducing a neural network–based collision detection system, such as hardware components, data processing, telecommunications, real-time inference, and feedback mechanisms (Figure 8.3).

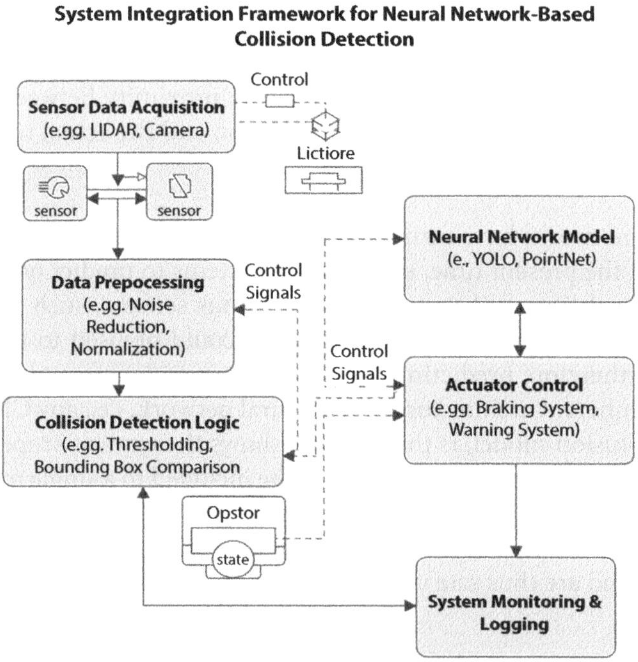

Figure 8.3 System integration framework for neural network–based collision detection.

8.11.1 Overview of System Integration

Neural network–based collision detection involves system integration for such a system where a trained neural network model can be deployed on a platform to interact with sensor data in real-time. This platform should possess the capabilities of processing larger amounts of data from sensors like cameras, LiDAR, radar, and ultrasonic devices, which must pass through the neural network for inference, and be ready to give feedback to the control or decision-making system of the vehicle.

The following would include some components of the system integration:

- Fusion of sensor data and preprocessing
- Deployment of a neural network
- Real-time inference
- Control and feedback loop

8.11.2 Sensor Fusion and Data Preprocessing

The sensors are usable in forms of different outputs like images, point clouds, velocity data, etc. For collision detection, they should give high-quality synchronized inputs. Therefore, the sensor output fusion is able to combine different outputs into one known environment representation, which must then act for collision prediction.

8.11.3 Data Fusion

Multimodal Inputs: With all such sensors as cameras and LiDAR, images from cameras can be merged (using CNNs) with the LiDAR point cloud (using PointNet or other 3D models) to get a comprehensive picture of all static and dynamic obstacles.
Fusion Techniques: Early fusion and late fusion are the two methods. Early fusion means bringing data into the network in its raw state, while late fusion merges the decisions of different models.
Neural Network Uses: A neural network should take inputs from multiple different sensors. For example, the camera images (using a CNN) can be fused this way with the LiDAR point cloud data (using PointNet or other 3D models) to get not only a complete picture of the static but also to introduce the dynamic areas of obstacles.
Fusion techniques: These kinds of fusion techniques include early fusion (raw input channel for the network) and late fusion (takes output from different models). The latter's usage is based on the requirement specifications

of the system, as it improves robust collision predictions for the neural network.

8.11.4 Data Preprocessing

Normalized and Scaled: Sensor data, including images and LiDAR, would become normalized and scaled so it could be usable for a neural network model. For example, an image would need resizing and normalizing pixel values, while point LiDAR data may require the alignment of a point cloud along the transformation to a grid-based or voxel-based representation.
Synchronizing time: That is critical in a real-time system because it has to be synchronized to talk about the same time sensor data from different sources, including the camera, radar, and LiDAR. In this way, you'll guarantee that everything given to the neural network is accurate and time-correlated when it has to make predictions.

8.12 Neural Network Deployment

When trained, the neural network model will need to be deployed on a computational platform capable of ingesting input data and generating predictions in real time. The deployment system must cope with the computational demands posed by the neural network, but should keep the latency very low to make timely predictions regarding possible collisions.

8.12.1 Edge Computing vs. Cloud Computing

- **Edge Computing:** The neural network models are installed on edge nodes such as onboard computers in cars, drones, or robots so that they can be used in real-time applications. GPUs or, alternatively, specialized accelerators like TPUs or FPGAs, are widely available on such high-performance devices to carry out the calculations locally without the support of remote servers. This would minimize the latency and make the collision predictions instant.
- **Cloud Computing:** On the other hand, there are other circumstances where cloud computing is used to offload processing tasks, and specifically, in instances when the edge device lacks the capacity to process a given piece of data. Given the fact that collision detection cannot wait because it

has to do with real-time decisions, cloud-based solutions are not very suitable for the detection of such collisions.

8.12.2 Model Optimization

For real-time deployment of the neural network, most reliance is placed on techniques such as model pruning (getting rid of redundant weights), quantization (reducing precision), and knowledge distillation (transmitting giant model knowledge to smaller models). All of these methods serve to downsize the model and make it less computationally demanding, allowing for expeditious inference.

Last but not least, the model should also be optimized to run in real-time while incorporating model pruning, which is getting rid of unnecessary weights; quantization, reducing precision; and knowledge distillation, which refers to the knowledge transfer of large models to smaller models, that minimizes the size of the model and its computational requirements so that faster inference can be performed.

8.13 Real-Time Inference

Live inference is the mode by which the system continuously feeds sensor data into trained neural networks, which define the opportunity for collision. All that must be done in this step is to ensure that the system can come up with reactive measures in ways that are more dynamic and faster to ever-changing environments.

8.13.1 Data Flow

The routine of real-time inference pipelines usually runs such that:

1. Sensor Data Acquisition: Raw data is continuously collected from the sensors (e.g., cameras, LiDAR, radar).
2. Preprocessing: The data is preprocessed into a format that the neural network can process. Normalizing images, transforming point clouds of LiDAR, and adjusting the time synchronization of the inputs are all included.
3. Model inference: Under this phase, the model feeds forward the ingested preprocessed data; through this operation, the prediction can be generated per the essence of the problem.

It may be the collision probability (binary classification) or the time-to-collision value (regression).

4. Actionable Prediction: With the inference produced, it can be decided whether a collision will take place. Such an inference happens almost in the blink of an eye—that is, between a few milliseconds to nearly 1 second—after which, the appropriate action must be taken.

8.13.2 Latency Considerations

Inference time is one of the critical aspects regarding real-time performance. If a network takes too long to process an input to generate predictions, it can lose its chance to avoid an accident. Thus, optimizing the inference speed requires efficient hardware and optimized models. Low-latency inferencing becomes important where speed is high, such as in autonomous driving.

8.14 Control and Feedback Loop

After making a prediction, the consequent action has to be taken to prevent an eventual collision. For this purpose, a solid feedback loop needs to be established where the collision prediction is joined with control mechanisms to take corrective measures.

Once the prediction is done, necessary action must be taken to prevent a collision from occurring. A strong feedback loop will be the system integrating collision prediction and control mechanisms to bring about corrective action.

8.14.1 Decision-Making

For example, in an autonomous vehicle, the prediction made by the collision detection system will be sent to the vehicle's decision-making module. Depending on the collision probability or time-to-collision, the system will choose one or more of the following:

- Braking: The vehicle will apply brakes if it is very likely to collide.
- Steering: The vehicle will steer away from a possible collision.
- Speed Adjustment: The vehicle may reduce speed or stop to incur no further danger.

8.14.2 Actuators

Following that, once the decision-making system has found out what actions are necessary, it transfers these commands down to the vehicle actuators (the brake system, steering mechanism, and throttle control).

It then decides the necessary actions for this vehicle. These are given as commands to this vehicle's actuators, such as the brake system, steering mechanism, and throttle control; thereby, they would perform required actions to mitigate collision or avoid collision.

8.14.3 Feedback for Continuous Improvement

The feedback system should also have an ongoing learning mechanism. Anything that happens in a collision will be registered in the system for future analytical reference, as will any untoward or wrong responses by the system. Such pieces of information can retrain the neural network to improve accuracy over time in prediction. Other methods, such as reinforcement learning and online learning, can be used to adapt the model to any real-time occurrence regarding new scenarios.

8.15 Testing and Validation

The complete integrated system testing and validation would be done in full measure to ensure that the integrated system operates reliably in various conditions. The process of testing includes the following:

- Simulation Testing: To test the performance of the system under different conditions, the system is executed under simulated settings.
- Field Testing: This is the one that involves the use of the actual site to determine whether the system will operate correctly in the actual operating conditions.

The enhanced prediction competence and inhibition with complete precision remain intact even in the circumstances of the dynamic and unpredictable conditions.

Integration of a neural network–based collision detection system includes hardware, sensor data processing, model deployment, and the subsequent real-time decision-making within its premise. This smooth assimilation into the system is due to its well-thought-out and well-optimized nature, which would be required to process all the massive real-time inference demands, and which is, at the same time, low on latency and high in consumer accuracy. Good feedback mechanisms that facilitate such processes presuppose the ongoing enhancements of models that are aimed at providing a model to react to changes in the nature of the environment in which such neural network–driven collision detection can be deemed of paramount importance in terms of the safety of the autonomous systems.

8.16 Applications and Benefits of Neural Network–Based Collision Detection Systems

Sadly, they can no longer afford to sustain traditional rule-based methods. This is due to the growing number of road traffic accidents. The current methods are now progressively failing to reflect the realities of the real world in different conditions, including bad weather, heavy traffic, or dynamic conditions on the road. Innovations in neural network applications in fresh collision detection systems have the potential to revolutionize the realm of safety in car movement through the use of modern high-technological devices like LiDAR, radar, and cameras. The following are some of the primary uses and advantages of this system.

8.16.1 Applications in Automotive Safety

One of the most advanced uses of collision detection using neural networks has been in autonomous vehicles. These cars are not operated manually and are instead driven by sophisticated algorithm systems based on navigation. The combination of neural network models with sensors such as LiDAR, radars, and cameras enables autonomous vehicles to learn everything in their surroundings, in every dimension. Neural networks can process that sensor data to anticipate possible collisions and activate preventive actions such as emergency automatic braking or steering adjustments. This feature can, thus, greatly reduce the chances of accidents and make them quite safe to drive in complex and unpredictable traffic situations.

An advanced driver assistance system neural network–based collision detection system that helps a human driver operate advanced driver assistance systems, or ADAS. Other things that can be installed in ADAS include collision warning, automatic emergency braking, lane-keeping assistance, and adaptive cruise control. Using neural networks, ADAS can interpret the real-time sensor data to better detect obstacles, pedestrians, and vehicles compared with manual driving. It also leads to huge safety levels for both the human drivers and pedestrians, decreasing the chances of accidents due to human errors and delayed reflexes.

Commercial vehicles experiencing accidents have their own set of internal complications. Collision avoidance generally involves using front cameras, side sensors, and radar from multiple angles and processing this information with a neural network–based model. Neural networks can be trained, making them even capable of object identification, risk assessment, and issuing warnings, or in the case of gross errors, braking or steering, thereby securing the vehicle operators and all other road users significantly.

Collision avoidance in commercial vehicles like trucks and buses usually has its own internal differences regarding collision detection, owing to their different sizes and the areas they cover with minimal visibility. The present neural network–based system improves safety for a commercial vehicle operator against accidents by accumulating data from different sensor bearings, like front—even at angles from side sensors and radar—that could be utilized to predict risky events. The models of the neural networks will then be able to identify the objects and calculate their risks. It can also give necessary warnings or trigger autonomously guided actions, such as braking or steering when needed. Thus, highly enhanced safety for both vehicle operators and other road users is assured.

8.17 Benefits of Neural Network–Based Collision Detection

8.17.1 Improved Accuracy

Given their massive capability of dealing with huge collections of high-dimensional data, neural networks are convenient tools for obtaining collision detection in time-varying environments. Neural networks can detect extremely complex patterns and can fit new circumstances, unlike the traditional rule-based systems, which use set algorithms or rules, and thus, their prediction capabilities are higher in very complex environments, such as poor weather, traffic congestion, and various highway conditions, than their traditional counterparts. Training on the massive data of actual driving conditions with time enhances the performance of these systems and reduces the false positive and false negative rates of collision detection significantly.

8.17.2 Adaptability to Changing Environments

The thing is, the world is diverse; sometimes it even results in the low efficiency of traditional collision detection systems, such as in the downpour, fog, or direct sunlight. Neural networks are capable of learning how to fit properly to these atmospheric conditions. The ongoing training on various datasets, such as illumination, weather, and road status variations, makes the neural networks behave strongly and learn as well. It will certainly be in a position to make an accurate prediction of a collision when it comes to these very highly variable contexts. This renders it a good precaution under non-static conditions, which are dynamic and unpredictable.

8.17.3 Real-Time Decision-Making

Neural network collision detection systems are real-time systems, enabling quick decisions to be made based on sensor data. For instance, in case of the autonomous vehicles, the system must, in a very short span of time, take sensor inputs, predict hazardous events, and then actuate corrective measures at a very short time frame, in the order of milliseconds. This is an important aspect of safety for autonomous and semi-autonomous vehicles since it can eliminate delays and slow human responses to accidents. Real-time also allows the system to provide instant feedback to convey information to the driver in ADAS-equipped vehicles, such as issuing a warning or activating braking systems before an accident event occurs.

8.17.4 Reduced Dependence on Rule-Based Algorithms

In conventional collision detection systems, there are sets of rules that the system uses to inform its action on differing objects and circumstances. This approach is only useful in a selection of conditions, while failing in most cases with respect to the level of complexity and unpredictability in the real world. A neural network, meanwhile, can learn from an enormous number of pieces of information, thus allowing it to generalize better to various objects, obstacles, and situations without having been explicitly programmed to do so. This would make the framework less dependent on such rules-based algorithms and provide neural network–based solutions greater flexibility in dealing with newly unforeseen situations.

8.17.5 Enhanced Safety and Reduced Road Accidents

Safety improvement and accident reduction have always been the common benefits of utilizing neural networks in collision detection systems. By having the ability to predict and avoid collisions, the system can save lives, help prevent injuries, and minimize property damage. Collision detection systems based on neural networks will further safeguard autonomous or semi-autonomous vehicles in a high-risk situation for accidents, where the cars are said to be driving themselves by colliding with other vehicles. Besides, these systems will help a great number of ADAS-equipped automobiles avoid accidents brought about by human errors that constitute one of the leading causes of traffic deaths in the world.

8.18 Conclusion

Accidents involving road traffic show increased rates of incidence. This fact indicates innovation and designing effective solutions in terms of automotive safety. Conventional techniques for collision detection, which are heavily rule-based, significantly lack the ability to cater to dynamically complex environments involving a high degree of noise, such as traffic density, poor weather conditions, or unpredictable road situations. Neural networks are a very promising option, as they have the capabilities of processing data into higher dimensions and identifying more sophisticated related patterns, which can ultimately increase the effectiveness of such systems to a tremendous degree in identifying collisions.

The concept of neural network–oriented systems in safety in vehicles presented in this chapter has taken into account their combination with sophisticated forms of sensors, including LiDAR, radar, and cameras. In addition to this, they also have an advantage in terms of performance, which includes greater accuracy, flexibility, robustness in the environment, and real-time decision-making. In addition, it is possible to train neural networks using various kinds of collections, such that within a short period of time, neural networks have learned about new driving situations and have increased safety in a broad spectrum of situations. Their real-time processing and consumption capabilities of large volumes of data are also viewed as the point of entry to the future of driver aids (ADAS) and autonomous driving, where decision-making speed and accuracy are of the essence. The issue, though, is that these systems are full of challenges in regard to neural network–based implementations of collision detection.

In fact, ultimatum neural networks may become part and parcel of the automotive safety system and save even more lives with efficient, versatile, and responsive road accident detectors. With time, these systems will be enhanced, more efficient, and above all, contribute to the functionality that is needed to realize the vision of safe, smart, and indeed highly autonomous transport. The automotive safety future is clearly the very progressive development of such intelligent systems that hold a future promise regarding the transformation of the paradigm in the manner in which we will look forward to safety at the global road level.

AI disclosure statement: The author confirms that no artificial intelligence (AI)-generated content or AI-assisted writing tools were used in the preparation of this chapter (including summaries and the abstract). All text, analysis, and conclusions are the result of the author's original work.

Bibliography

1. Talaat, F.M. and Hamza, A.A., Blockchain-enhanced artificial intelligence for advanced collision avoidance in the Internet of Vehicles (IoV). *Neural Comput. Appl.*, 37, 4915–4936, 2025, https://doi.org/10.1007/s00521-024-10842-7.
2. Ren, S., He, K., Girshick, R., Sun, J., Faster R-CNN: Towards Real-Time Object Detection with Region Proposal Networks, in: *Advances in Neural Information Processing Systems (NeurIPS)*, vol. 28, pp. 91–99, 2015.
3. Xu, G., Bai, H., Xing, J., Luo, T., Xiong, N.N., Cheng, X., Zheng, X., SG-PBFT: a secure and highly efficient distributed blockchain PBFT consensus algorithm for intelligent Internet of vehicles. *J. Parallel Distrib. Comput.*, 164, 1–11, 2022.
4. Sharma, S., Ghanshala, K.K., Mohan, S., Blockchain-based internet of vehicles (IoV): An efficient secure *ad hoc* vehicular networking architecture, in: *2019 IEEE 2nd 5G World Forum (5GWF)*, IEEE, pp. 452–457, 2019.
5. Bochkovskiy, A., Wang, C.Y., Liao, H.Y.M., YOLOv4: Optimal Speed and Accuracy of Object Detection, arXiv preprint arXiv:2004.10934, 2020.
6. Chen, C., Liu, L., Qiu, T., Jiang, J., Pei, Q., Song, H., Routing with traffic awareness and link preference in internet of vehicles. *IEEE Trans. Intell. Transp. Syst.*, 23, 1, 200–214, 2022. https://doi.org/10.1109/TITS.2021.3063627.
7. Gong, C., Xiong, L., He, X., Niu, X., Blockchain-based conditional privacy-preserving authentication scheme for vehicular *ad hoc* networks. *J. Ambient Intell. Hum. Comput.*, 14, 5, 6273–6286, 2023.
8. Elsagheer Mohamed, S.A., Alshalfan, K.A., Al-Hagery, M.A., Ben Othman, M.T., Safe driving distance and speed for collision avoidance in connected vehicles. *Sensors*, 22, 18, 7051, 2022.

9. Aman, M.N., Javaid, U., Sikdar, B., A privacy-preserving and scalable authentication protocol for the internet of vehicles. *IEEE Internet Things J.*, 8, 2, 1123–1139, 2020.
10. Aung, N., Kechadi, T., Zhu, T., Zerdoumi, S., Guerbouz, T., Dhelim, S., Blockchain application on the internet of vehicles (IoV), in: *2022 IEEE 7th international conference on intelligent transportation engineering (ICITE)*, IEEE, pp. 586–591, 2022.
11. Almutairi, M.S., Almutairi, K., Chiroma, H., Hybrid of deep recurrent network and long short term memory for rear-end collision detection in fog based internet of vehicles. *Expert Syst. Appl.*, 213, 119033, 2023, https://doi.org/10.1016/j.eswa.2022.119033.
12. Chaudhry, S.A., Designing an efficient and secure message exchange protocol for internet of vehicles. *Secur. Commun. Netw.*, 2021, 1–9, 2021.
13. Chen, L., Retracted Article: Road vehicle recognition algorithm in safety assistant driving based on artificial intelligence. *Soft. Comput.*, 27, 1153–1162, 2023, https://doi.org/10.1007/s00500-021-06011-w.
14. Zhang, H. and Lu, X., Vehicle communication network in intelligent transportation system based on Internet of Things. *Comput. Commun.*, 160, 799–806, 2020, https://doi.org/10.1016/j.comcom.2020.03.041.
15. Zhang, S. and Abdel-Aty, M., Real-time crash potential prediction on freeways using connected vehicle data. *Anal. Methods Accid. Res.*, 36, Art. no. 100239, Dec. 2022, doi: 10.1016/j.amar.2022.100239.

9

Facial Emotion Detection Using Causal AI

Esha Kundu and Arijit Ghosal*

Department of Information Technology, St. Thomas' College of Engineering and Technology, Kolkata, West Bengal, India

Abstract

The objective of the work is to propose a facial emotion detection algorithm that can detect the facial emotion of a person. Activities carried out based on the detected emotions fall under causal AI, which is a sub-domain of artificial intelligence (AI) that focuses on understanding and modelling cause-and-effect relationships within data, instead of just identifying patterns or correlations. This work helps determine the facial emotion, which can be utilized in healthcare domains like music therapy or even for the purpose of music recommendation and other modern AI-based automated tasks.

The facial emotion detection model has been trained and tested on the FER-2013 dataset collected from Kaggle. Emotion detected from the face is classified into seven common emotions: surprise, neutral, sad, fear, happy, angry, and disgust. First, data cleaning was done on the FER-2013 dataset using "Haar Cascade" to identify if a human face exists in each of the images of the dataset and remove images in which a human face was not detected. Facial features like region of interest (ROI), facial landmarks, and histogram of oriented gradients (HOG) magnitude and direction from the images were extracted. Several machine learning approaches were implemented to judge the performance of the approach. Due to the poor accuracy level in machine learning methods, deep learning was applied through CNN, which helps to implement causal AI efficiently. The deep learning approach consists of a sequential CNN model implemented on the face detection FER-2013 dataset obtained after data cleaning using "Haar Cascade". The model gives an accuracy of 60.88% for all 7 emotions and for 6 emotions (without disgust) an accuracy of 67.02%. Several "data augmentation" practices were also carried out to enhance generalization. The CNN model consists of three convolutional blocks with increasing filter size, followed by batch normalization, max pooling,

**Corresponding author*: arijitghosal.official@gmail.com

Rajdeep Chakraborty, Aleem Ali, Amit Paul, Nawaf R. Alharbe and S. Balamurugan (eds.) Causal Artificial Intelligence: Fundamentals and Applications, (217–240) © 2026 Scrivener Publishing LLC

and dropout layers to prevent overfitting. After completion of feature extraction, the network levels the output, and then it passes through a thick layer that is fully connected with dropout before the final softmax layer for the multi-class emotion categorization. This representation is also collated with the famous "Adam optimizer" and profound cross-entropy loss to optimize performance.

Keywords: CNN, ReLU, softmax, max pooling, dropout, batch normalization

9.1 Introduction

Facial emotion detection is a fast-growing area in causal AI, with applications across various industries like healthcare, marketing, education, security, and human-computer interaction. Deep learning techniques that focus on pattern recognition in visual data are the traditional emotion recognition models. Some of these models have achieved high accuracy, but they lack interpretability.

Inclusion of causal AI into facial sentiment identification implies a basic transition from correlation-based forecasting to causation-based approaches. Causal models intend to uncover different approaches that produce detected facial sentiments, which offer better generalizability, transparency, and robustness.

Using causal methods to detect facial emotion poses several challenges, such as data complexity. To get causally relevant facial features, high-quality, diverse datasets with annotated causal factors (e.g., lighting, pose, cultural variation) are needed. Also, emotions are not static; thus, the temporal causality in facial expressions over time makes it more complex.

Even though there are many challenges, combining causal reasoning with facial emotion analysis offers great potential in the development of intelligent systems that are not only accurate but also fair, easy to understand, and adaptable.

In the following sections, we have discussed our approach and the performance of the model. Section 9.2 provides a detailed literature survey of several similar papers. Section 9.3 contains the proposed approach, where Section 9.3.1 discusses the machine learning approach and Section 9.3.2 describes the deep learning approach using CNN in detail. Section 9.4 contains the experimental results with accuracies, classification report, and ROC curve with AUC values, followed by a conclusion in Section 9.5.

9.2 Literature Survey

For our paper, we have studied some research papers, which are mentioned below:

The FER-2013 dataset collected from Kaggle contains 48x48 pixel grayscale images of human faces of seven emotions [1].

S. Minaee *et al.* presented "Deep-Emotion", a CNN model that was augmented with a spatial attention methodology to emphasize the most informative areas of the face. They handled the issue of class imbalance in FER-2013 by loss reweighting and focused on areas like eyes and mouth. Their model achieved about 70% accuracy and performed well in detecting subtle emotions like sadness and surprise. The significance of integrating CNNs with attention processes to improve recognition accuracy is the main emphasis of this work [2].

The paper by Khaireddin and Chen used a single CNN model on the FER-2013 dataset without the usage of any external datasets or ensemble methods. A VGG-style architecture was fine-tuned by optimizing learning rates, dropout values, and filter sizes; it reached an accuracy of 73.28%. This work demonstrates that with careful tuning and augmentation, a network can yield excellent results on FER tasks [3].

Lonkar, by varying the depths, kernel sizes, filter counts, and activation functions of CNNs, and by evaluating them under different optimizers like Adam and SGD, examined how different CNN configurations impact performance on the FER-2013 dataset. The best-performing model reached a perfection of 70.10%. Thus, emphasizing that the architectural design and hyperparameter selection are as important as the dataset [4].

In another approach, by using a multi-task CNN model that simultaneously predicts emotion and gender, Lahariya and colleagues proposed a model architecture that included shared layers followed by two task-specific heads. About 68% accuracy was attained on the FER-2013 dataset, and the model was also tuned for real-time interference to function on mobile and embedded devices [5].

J. Luo *et al.* researched various machine learning–based models to identify different facial expressions through the FER2013 dataset. The performance of popular classifiers like SVM was compared with deep learning models such as ResNet, VGG16, and AlexNet. They also focused on the drawbacks of the dataset and proposed data augmentation methods to improve model performance. Experimental results indicate that VGG16 performs better than other models in accuracy on FER2013. The paper has placed more importance on choosing the correct model and carrying out data preprocessing for better recognition of facial expression [6].

Gaddam *et al.* in their deep-learning dependent method for detection of emotion of face by using the popular FER-2013 dataset containing squared dimensional gray-scale images having 48 pixels in each dimension, classified emotions using the ResNet50 architecture without a lot of preprocessing. On the same dataset, the model outperformed traditional CNN architectures like AlexNet and VGG16, achieving a test accuracy of 55.6% [7].

Oguine *et al.* suggested a hybrid real-time FER model that amalgamates "Haar Cascade" detection of faces with a deep CNN classifier. They trained their model exclusively on FER-2013 and improved its robustness using data augmentation. The method maintained quick inference times while achieving about 70% accuracy. Their research highlights the fact that mixing conventional computer vision approaches with deep learning approaches may create accurate real-time systems [8].

T. Podder *et al.* worked on a lightweight CNN model that has achieved 70.2% perfection on the FER-2013. They prioritized minimal preprocessing and model efficiency. For effective training, "data augmentation" methods, namely, cropping, flipping, and rotation, were registered. For enhancing spatial feature extraction, they also employed a feature-boosting layer [9].

For the sake of comprehending the trade-offs between accuracy, parameter efficiency, and computational complexity on FER 2013, Y. Liu carried out a thorough assessment of a number of traditional CNN architectures, including Visual Geometry Group (VGG), ResNet, MobileNet, and DenseNet. According to the study, small designs like MobileNet provide faster inference with respectable accuracy, while deeper models like ResNet and DenseNet perform better in accuracy but need more resources. This paper provides a roadmap for selecting suitable CNN backbones for high-accuracy research settings or lightweight edge deployments based on application limitations [10].

Kalsum and Mehmood published a study in Sensors that used a lightweight CNN architecture trained on FER-2013. The goal was to find a balance between accuracy and speed of computation. Their model was around 69% accurate, and they focused on making it work better on edge devices. The authors focused on energy efficiency and latency for targeting scenarios where emotion detection is required in wearable health devices and driver monitoring systems [11].

C. Mejia-Escobar *et al.* proposed a datacentric method for facial expression recognition to demonstrate that improving the dataset quality is as important as modifying the model architecture. A fixed CNN model was trained iteratively such that after each round, only the correctly classified images were used for the next training, gradually improving the dataset. After the final round, the model is used to reclassify the entire original dataset without deleting or augmenting images. Experimental results show 20.45% improvement in validation accuracy for FER2013 compared to training on the original datasets [12].

The research by Pham and colleagues focused on analyzing inter- and intra-class confusion in FER-2013 using CNNs. They examined a number of approaches, such as ResNet and MobileNet. They designed a latest loss function to manage inter-class along with intra-class imbalances. They reached a perfection of 61.05% on the FER2013 dataset [13].

D. Bhagat and team examined various pre-trained CNN architectures, such as EfficientNet, VGGNet, ResNet, and the Haar face classifier, which were fine-tuned on FER-2013 for real-time facial expression recognition applications. Among them, the proposed model of DCNN reached the maximum training perfection of 82.56% and validation perfection of 65.68% [14].

Y. El Boudouri and A. Bohi presented "EmoNeXt", which is an adaptation of the ConvNeXt architecture tuned for facial emotion recognition. In addition to "Squeeze-and-Excitation" or SE chunks that can retain channel-wise protectorates, their model incorporates a "Spatial Transformer Network" or STN to dynamically concentrate on informative areas of faces. In order to promote compact feature representations, they also added a self-attention regularization term. "EmoNeXt" balanced spatial localization and channel attention to achieve state-of-the-art accuracies during training and evaluation on FER 2013 [15].

S. Roy *et al.* used a CNN-dependent approach for the identification of facial expressions through the FER-2013 dataset. To categorize facial images into fundamental emotion categories like happy, fear, angry, etc., a convolutional neural network was designed and trained. By improving the architecture and applying preprocessing methods, they increase accuracy. The model performs well in the identification of facial emotion when tested on the popular FER-2013 dataset. This demonstrates how well CNNs perform automated emotion recognition tasks [16].

9.3 Proposed Approach

In our proposed approach for facial emotion detection, dataset selection and dataset cleaning were performed on the FER-2013 dataset. Then, a machine learning approach was implemented first, followed by deep

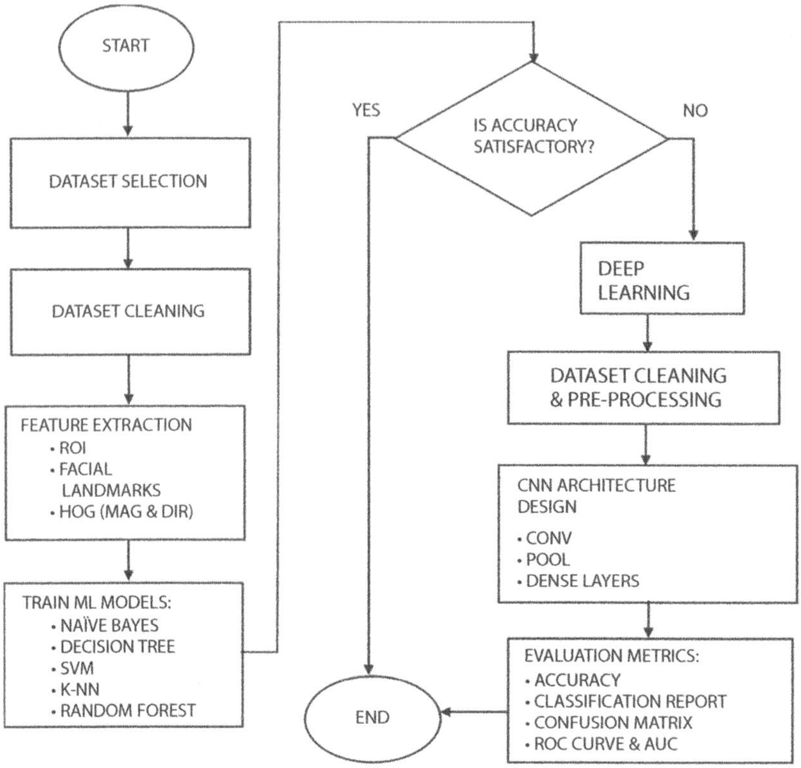

Figure 9.1 Schema chart of suggested procedure.

learning, as satisfactory accuracy was not achieved by the machine learning approach. Figure 9.1 provides a detailed schema chart for the suggested procedure.

Section 9.3.1 discusses the machine learning approach, including the dataset used, feature extraction methods used, and the models implemented. Section 9.3.2 describes the deep learning approach using CNN, where it describes the dataset selected, dataset cleaning, and preprocessing, followed by the CNN architecture implemented in the model.

9.3.1 Machine Learning Methods

The machine learning approach involves extracting features from facial images and then applying different machine learning models for classification. The following subsections contain details of the machine learning approach implementation: Section 9.3.1.1 covers the dataset, Section

9.3.1.2 describes dataset cleaning, and Section 9.3.1.3 is about the different facial feature extraction techniques, which are further covered in separate sub-subsections.

9.3.1.1 Dataset

The facial emotion detection model has been trained and tested on the FER-2013 dataset collected from Kaggle. 48x48 pixel-dimensional gray-scale figures of human faces are present in that dataset. The faces have been impulsively inscribed such that they occupy approximately the same amount of area and are positioned roughly in the center of each image. Emotion detected from the face is classified into seven facial emotions: surprise, neutral, sad, fear, happy, angry, and disgust [1].

9.3.1.2 Dataset Cleaning

First, data cleaning was done on the FER-2013 dataset to remove images in which a human face was not detected. This was mainly due to the face being half visible or covered by hands. Data cleaning was performed using "Haar Cascade" to detect if a human face exists in each of the images of the dataset. Then, all the images in which a face was detected were stored in separate folders classified as testing and training folders and based on emotion labelling as present in the original dataset.

9.3.1.3 Extraction of Facial Feature

Facial facets like region of interest (ROI), facial landmarks, along with histogram of oriented gradients (HOG) magnitude and direction from the images were extracted and stored in csv files separately for the training and testing datasets, containing each image filename and emotion labelled.

The different facial feature extraction methods are discussed in the following sections, where Section 9.3.1.3.1 is for the extraction of facial features using region of interest (ROI), Section 9.3.1.3.2 is for the extraction of facial features using facial landmarks, and Section 9.3.1.3.3 is for the extraction of facial features using histogram of oriented gradients or HOG magnitude as well as direction.

9.3.1.3.1 Facial Feature Extraction Using Region of Interest (ROI)

Region of interest or ROI focuses on analyzing facial areas like eyes, nose, and mouth, ignoring the irrelevant background. It helps reduce noise and improve accuracy by isolating meaningful areas. Also, emotions are primarily expressed in specific facial regions. People smile when they are happy. Eyes are widened when surprised, squinted when angry. Eyebrows are raised when surprised and furrowed when confused or angry, and so on.

For detecting faces, a Haar-like cascade classifier is initialized, which returns the bounding boxes for all detected faces. For each region of interest, specific detectors are used: 'EyePairBig' for eyes, 'Nose' detector for the nose, and 'Mouth' detector for the mouth.

9.3.1.3.2 Extraction of Facial Feature Using Facial Landmarks

Facial landmarks are the key points or corners around the eyes, nose, mouth, etc. It helps in the analysis of distance and angles for emotion classification, like a smile curvature indicates happiness, eyebrow raising or lowering can indicate surprise or anger, and so on.

9.3.1.3.3 Facial Feature Extraction Using Histogram of Oriented Gradients (HOG) Magnitude and Direction

HOG describes local border orientation and gradients. It captures subtle shape deformations in the face. It is useful for detecting smiles, frowns, or tension in facial muscles. It is robust to lighting changes and captures facial structure details critical for emotion cues.

Several machine learning approaches, like naïve Bayes, SVM, decision tree, random forest, and k-NN, were registered to judge the performance of the approach.

Facial emotion detection from face using machine learning methods produced very low accuracies, with the maximum accuracy produced by the random forest method among the implemented methods of naïve Bayes, decision tree, SVM, k-NN, and random forest. Due to the poor accuracy level in machine learning methods, deep learning was applied through CNN, which is discussed in Section 9.3.2.

9.3.2 Deep Learning Methods Convolutional Neural Network (CNN)

The following subsections contain details of the deep learning approach implementation, where Section 9.3.2.1 covers the dataset, Section 9.3.2.2 describes the dataset cleaning and preprocessing, and Section 9.3.2.3 is about the CNN architecture of the model in detail.

9.3.2.1 *Dataset*

A Convolutional Neural Network (CNN) was developed to conduct multi-class facial sentiment detection on the FER-2013 dataset. The dataset contained training and testing directories, with grayscale facial images resized to 48×48 pixels and normalized for input ranging across 7 emotional classes: surprise, neutral, sad, fear, happy, angry, and disgust [1].

9.3.2.2 *Dataset Cleaning and Preprocessing*

The Haar cascade face detector was used to clean the dataset and use only those images for training and testing in which a face is detected. The face detection dataset, the FER-2013 dataset, thus formed, includes 7 types of sentiments: sad, surprise, neutral, fear, happy, angry, and disgust. Class weights were computed and applied during training to manage class imbalance.

"Data augmentation" methodologies like rotation, translation, zoom, and horizontal flipping were registered using ImageDataGenerator to enhance generalization.

9.3.2.3 *CNN Architecture*

The suggested CNN design contains three convolutional blocks with filter sizes that go bigger (64, 128, and 256). Each block is followed by normalization of batches as well as dropout layers to arrest overfitting of the model. After that, they were linked to a fully linked layer with 256 units and a softmax output covering that matched the number of emotion classes.

The model starts with an input layer and then has three convolutional blocks. The first block comprises two convolutional layers, having 64 filters, that use 3x3 kernels and ReLU activation, which is succeeded by batch normalization layers to ensure training consistency. A max pooling layer reduces spatial dimensions, while a 25% dropout layer prevents overfitting.

The second block has a similar structure, with two convolutional layers, 128 filters, batch normalization, and a max pooling layer, but accompanied by a higher dropout rate of 35% due to increased model complexity. The third block includes a mono convolutional covering with 256 filters, succeeded by batch normalization, max pooling, and an even higher dropout rate of 40%.

Succeeding the convolutional coverings, the output is leveled and sent to a dense fully connected covering having 256 neurons with ReLU as activation. This is succeeded by batch normalization and a 50% dropout covering to achieve strong regularization. Finally, the model includes a softmax

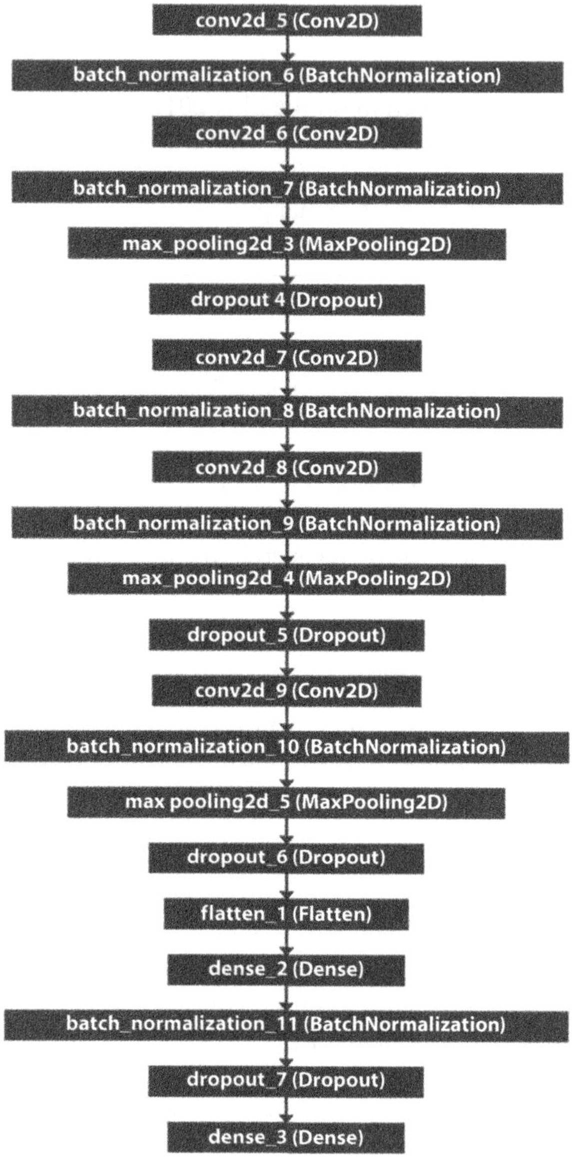

Figure 9.2 Simplified CNN layout showing layer names only for a clean high-level overview.

output layer, where the counts of units represent the number of classes considered in the classification task. The model contains the popular Adam optimizer and the explicit cross-entropy as the loss function because it is pertinent for categorization involving multiple classes, and accuracy as the evaluation metric.

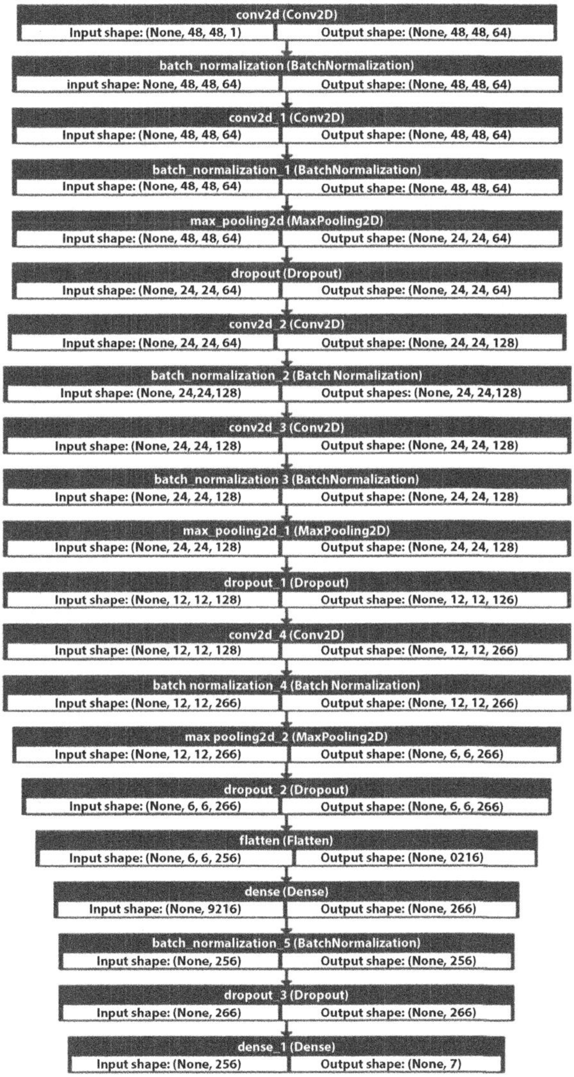

Figure 9.3 Detailed CNN architecture with layer names and tensor shapes for full model visibility.

To track validation loss, the model was trained with the popular Adam optimizer, ReduceLROnPlateau's rate of learning scheduler, and early stopping. Model checkpoints were utilized to retain the best-performing weights.

The Adam optimizer was used in training because of its flexible learning rate capabilities, which combine the benefits of momentum and RMSProp optimization approaches. The ReduceLROnPlateau callback was also used to further improve training efficiency and prevent stagnation during optimization. This technique will be able to dynamically reduce the rate of learning whenever the validation loss stops improving for a particular number of epochs, thus it will help the model to make excellent adaptations to the weights as it converges. Also, by using EarlyStopping, training can be halted when no improvement in validation loss is observed over a certain period, which helps to avoid overfitting while also reducing unnecessary training time.

Overall, the model is designed for high accuracy and generalizability, employing a mix of feature extraction, normalization, and regularization. An overview of the CNN architecture layout is displayed in Figure 9.2. Figure 9.3 shows different CNN layer names along with tensor shapes for detailed comprehension.

In Section 9.4, experimental results using CNN have been discussed in detail.

9.4 Experimental Results: Deep Learning Methods

The same CNN model was implemented on the FER-2013 dataset, with 7-emotion and 6-emotion datasets, by excluding disgust to improve accuracy. Accuracies of the two proposed approaches are tabulated in Table 9.1, given below.

Table 9.1 Accuracies of deep learning methods for facial emotion detection.

Model name	Number of emotions	Accuracy
Proposed CNN-based model	7 emotions: surprise, sad, neutral, happy, fear, disgust, angry	60.88%
Proposed CNN-based model	6 emotions: surprise, sad, neutral, happy, fear, angry	67.02%

Section 9.4.1 explains the size of the dataset, the classification report, the confusion matrix, the class-wise accuracy, the ROC curve with AUC values, the model accuracy, and the model loss graph for facial emotion detection using the FER-2013 dataset on 7 emotions.

9.4.1 Facial Emotion Detection on 7 Emotions

Dataset:
After applying the Haar cascade face detector on the FER-2013 dataset, the count of figures under each category is curtailed to:
Count of figures under each category in the training dataset:
Angry: 925
Fear: 740
Happy: 2182
Neutral: 1544
Sad: 734
Surprise: 708
Disgust: 129
Count of figures under each category in the testing dataset:
Angry: 241
Fear: 196
Happy: 523
Neutral: 383
Sad: 190
Surprise: 174
Disgust: 34
Accuracy:
The model produced an accuracy of **60.88%,** as mentioned in Table 9.1.
Classification Report:

Table 9.2 shows the categorization exposition, indicating the precision, f1-score, recall, and support of every category, along with the overall performance metrics, including the macro average and weighted average.

The corresponding confusion matrix depicted in Figure 9.4 gives a visualization of the categorization accomplishment of the model by showing the distribution of predicted versus original emotion markers. Every row represents the original emotion category, and each column represents the forecast category. Elements on the diagonal indicate the count of correctly predicted samples for each emotion, and the elements off the diagonal represent the wrongly classified elements.

Table 9.2 Categorization exposition of CNN implemented on 7 emotions.

	Precision	Recall	f1-score	Support
Angry	0.52	0.38	0.44	241
Disgust	0.22	0.76	0.35	34
Fear	0.41	0.26	0.32	196
Happy	0.90	0.83	0.86	523
Neutral	0.64	0.63	0.64	383
Sad	0.32	0.38	0.35	190
Surprise	0.60	0.83	0.69	174
Accuracy			0.61	1741
Macro average	0.52	0.58	0.52	1741
Weighted average	0.63	0.61	0.61	1741

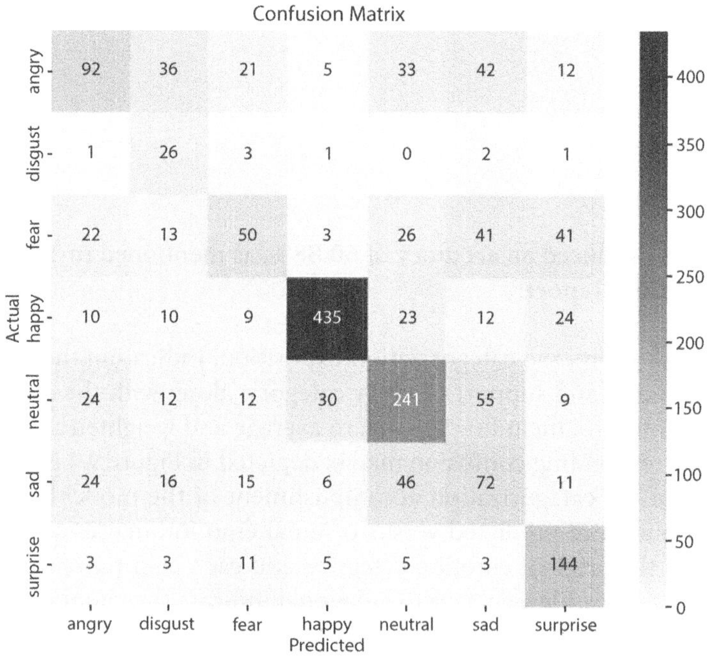

Figure 9.4 Confusion matrix of CNN implemented on the face detection FER-2013 dataset containing all 7 emotions.

This matrix helps to identify that the happy emotion is classified correctly the majority of the time, and neutral is frequently confused with sad. Also, the amount of correctly classified disgust samples is low due to a smaller number of disgust samples in the dataset.

Class-wise Accuracy:
For 'Angry', the accuracy is 38.17%; for 'Disgust', it is 76.47%. Whereas for 'Fear', it is 25.51%; in the case of 'Happy', the obtained accuracy jumps to 83.17%. For 'Neutral', the accuracy is 62.92%. But in the case of 'Sad', the accuracy obtained is 37.89%, and for 'Surprise', the accuracy jumps to 82.76%. All these accuracies are achieved using the proposed CNN model.

ROC Curve and AUC (Area Under the Curve) values:
The ROC curve, in addition to the values of AUC, is displayed in Figure 9.5 below. This describes the performance of the classification model by providing the true positive rate versus the false positive rate. The curve shows the capability of the model to differentiate among classes, having AUC values of 0.95 for surprise, 0.96 for happy, 0.82 for sad, 0.88 for neutral, 0.95 for disgust, 0.85 for angry, and 0.81 for fear, highlighting great capability to differentiate among the various emotional states. A model with an AUC close to 1.0 means high sensitivity and specificity, while an AUC around 0.5 represents a lower ability to differentiate among classes. All AUC values

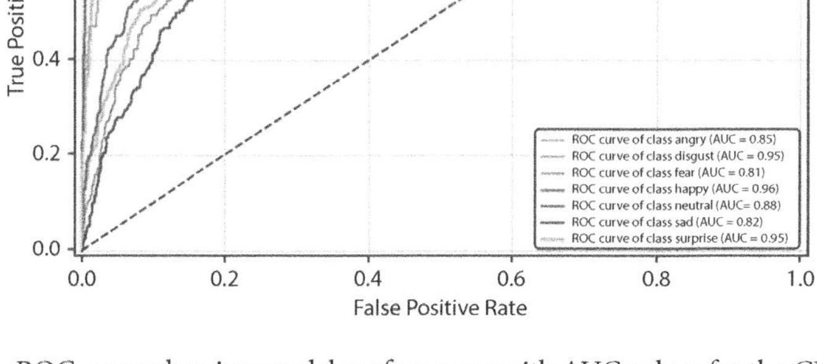

Figure 9.5 ROC curve showing model performance with AUC values for the CNN model on 7 emotions.

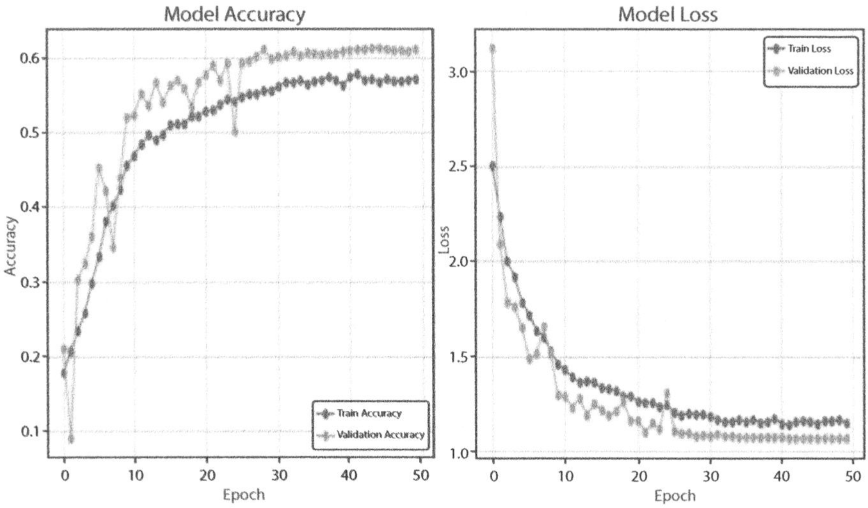

Figure 9.6 Model accuracy and model loss graph for the CNN model on 7 emotions.

are greater than 0.80, thus ensuring the model's robust and reliable performance in recognizing a wide range of facial emotional expressions.

Model Accuracy and Model Loss Graph Description:
The accuracy graph in Figure 9.6 depicts the performance of the model over every epoch, both for the training and validation sets. As the validation accuracy closely aligns with the training accuracy, it suggests effective generalization.

The loss graph in Figure 9.6 represents the reduction in error during training. A decreasing trend in training and validation loss over time as each epoch progresses indicates effective learning.

Section 9.4.2 explains the size of the dataset, the classification report, the confusion matrix, the class-wise accuracy, the ROC curve with AUC values, the model accuracy, and the model loss graph for facial emotion detection using the FER-2013 dataset on 6 emotions.

9.4.2 Facial Emotion Detection on 6 Emotions

After applying the Haar cascade face detector on the FER-2013 dataset, the count of figures under each category is diminished to:

Dataset:
Count of figures under every category in the training dataset:
Angry: 925

Fear: 740
Happy: 2182
Neutral: 1544
Sad: 734
Surprise: 708
Count of figures under every category in the testing dataset:
Angry: 241
Fear: 196
Happy: 523
Neutral: 383
Sad: 190
Surprise: 174
Accuracy:
The model produced an accuracy of **67.02%,** as mentioned in Table 9.1.
Classification Report:

Table 9.3 shows the categorization exposition indicating precision, f1-score, recall, and support of every category, along with accuracy, macro average, and weighted average.

The corresponding confusion matrix depicted in Figure 9.7 gives a visualization of the categorization accomplishment of the model by showing the distribution of predicted versus original emotion tags. Every row

Table 9.3 Categorization report of CNN implemented on 6 emotions.

	Precision	**Recall**	**F1-score**	**Support**
Angry	0.54	0.65	0.59	241
Fear	0.53	0.35	0.42	196
Happy	0.91	0.84	0.87	523
Neutral	0.64	0.68	0.66	383
Sad	0.42	0.41	0.41	190
Surprise	0.67	0.82	0.74	174
Accuracy			0.67	1707
Macro average	0.62	0.62	0.62	1707
Weighted average	0.67	0.67	0.67	1707

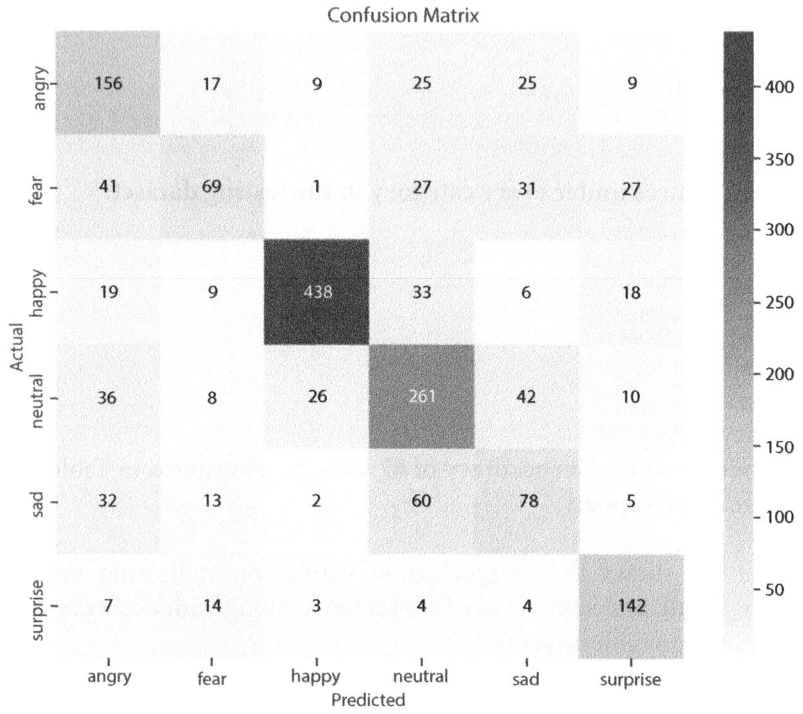

Figure 9.7 Confusion matrix of CNN implemented on the face detection FER-2013 dataset containing 6 emotions.

represents the original emotion category, and each column represents the forecast category. Elements on the diagonal indicate the count of correctly predicted samples for each emotion, and the elements off the diagonal represent the wrongly classified elements.

This matrix helps to identify that the happy emotion is mostly classified correctly, while neutral is often confused with sad, and fear is sometimes misclassified as angry.

Class-wise Accuracy:

The accuracy for every class, as obtained by the CNN model, is given below:

Angry: 64.73%

Fear: 35.20%

Happy: 83.75%

Neutral: 68.15%

Sad: 41.05%

Surprise: 81.61%

ROC curve and AUC values:
ROC curve, along with AUC (area under the curve) values shown in Figure 9.8, illustrates the accomplishment of the classification model by framing the true positive rate against the false positive rate. The curve demonstrates the model's capability to classify between categories, with an AUC of 0.97 for happy, 0.96 for surprise, 0.89 for angry, 0.89 for neutral, 0.87 for fear, and 0.85 for sad, indicating excellent capability to distinguish between different emotional states. A model having an AUC close to 1.0 means high sensitivity and specificity, while an AUC around 0.5 represents a lower capability to differentiate between classes. All AUC values are equal to or greater than 0.85, thus reflecting the model's robust and reliable performance in recognizing a wide range of emotional expressions.

Model Accuracy and Model Loss Graph Description:
The accuracy graph in Figure 9.9 depicts the performance of the model over every epoch, both for the training and validation sets. The success of the proposed model is clearly understood from the overlapping nature of the validation accuracy and training accuracy in the graph.

The loss graph shown in Figure 9.9 represents the reduction in error during training. Effective learning is reflected through the decreasing nature of training and validation loss with the increase in epochs.

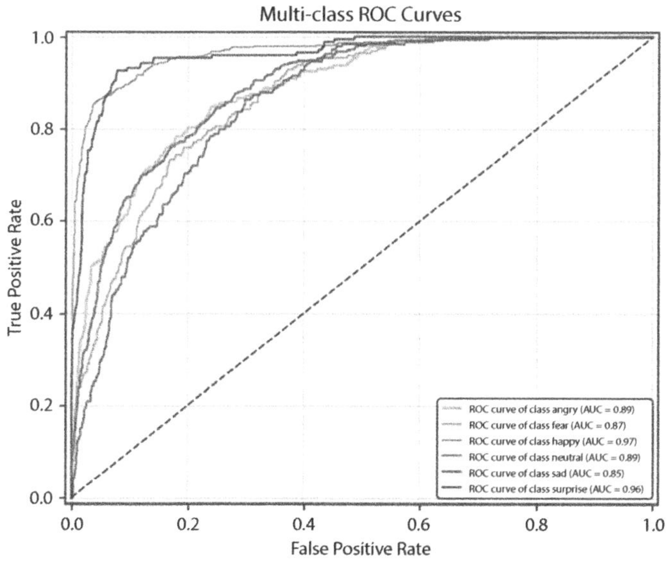

Figure 9.8 ROC curve showing model performance with AUC values on 6 emotions.

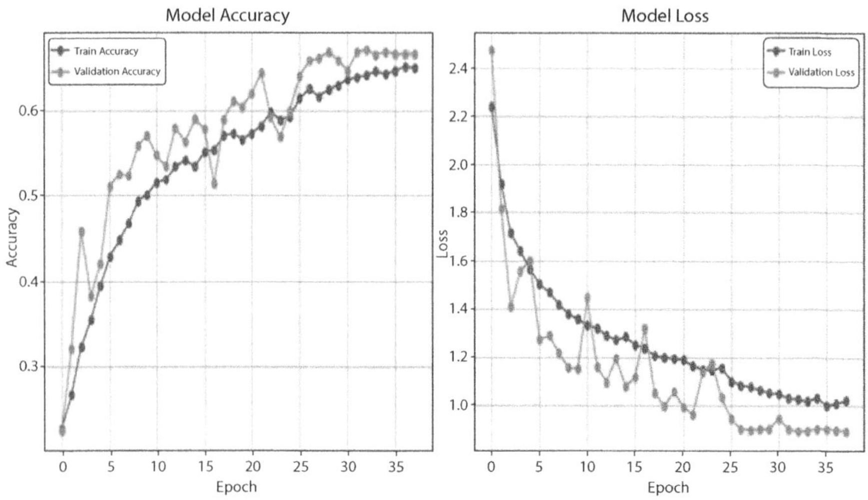

Figure 9.9 Model accuracy and model loss graph for the CNN model on 6 emotions.

Section 9.4.3 contains a comparative research paper analysis of our CNN model with Gaddam *et al.* in their paper "Human Facial Emotion Detection Using Deep Learning" [7] for detecting facial sentiment using the popular FER-2013 dataset.

9.4.3 Comparative Research Paper Analysis

A deep learning-based approach proposed by Gaddam *et al.* [7] recognizes different facial expressions from various static images. They used the FER-2013 dataset containing 48×48 grayscale photos to classify seven emotions: anger, fear, disgust, sad, happy, surprise, and neutral. They improved

Table 9.4 Relative assessment of the deep learning methods for facial emotion identification.

Model name	Number of emotions	Accuracy
Comparative paper CNN model	7 emotions: surprise, sad, neutral, happy, fear, disgust, angry	55.6%
Proposed CNN-based model	7 emotions: surprise, sad, neutral, happy, fear, disgust, angry	60.88%
Proposed CNN-based model	6 emotions: surprise, sad, neutral, happy, fear, angry	67.02%

ResNet-50 by fine-tuning it to classify the seven emotions. Their model achieved a maximum accuracy of 55.6% on the FER-2013 dataset.

Table 9.4 provides a comparison between the accuracy achieved by our CNN model and the accuracy achieved by Gaddam *et al.* [7].

9.5 Conclusion

The test accuracy, classification exposition, and corresponding confusion matrix all show that the proposed model performed well in terms of generalization. In addition, multi-class ROC curves and AUC scores were calculated to evaluate class-wise discrimination capability. Training history graphs showed convergence tendencies over epochs, with perfection and loss metrics plotted for training as well as validation sets. Overall, the CNN performed well in emotion categorization, as validated by the cleaned sample of the FER-2013 dataset.

Facial emotion identification using causal AI is a transformative technique to better understand human emotions in a more advanced but interpretable manner. By moving beyond the surface-level correlations and incorporating causally grounded methodologies, this method has the ability to significantly enhance the reliability by focusing on causally relevant features; the model is less likely to be misled by irrelevant correlations or noise. As the field is still in its early stages, it faces several open research questions in terms of identifying and modelling causal relationships in high-dimensional visual data. Further improved data collection by causally annotated datasets with diverse demographics and contexts are carried out. Also, making hybrid models by combining causal reasoning with deep learning to harness both performance and interpretability. Advancing causal models will significantly help to develop real-time facial emotion detection applications. Integration of cross-discipline by leveraging insights from psychology, neuro-science, and social science to inform causal structures are carried out. As research continues, facial emotion detection powered by causal AI could redefine how machines perceive and respond to human emotions, which can lead to more trustworthy, human-centric AI systems.

AI disclosure statement: The author confirms that no artificial intelligence (AI)-generated content or AI-assisted writing tools were used in the preparation of this chapter (including summaries and the abstract). All text, analysis, and conclusions are the result of the author's original work.

References

1. FER-2013 Dataset, Kaggle, provided by msambare.
2. Minaee, S., Minaei, M., Abdolrashidi, A., Deep-Emotion: Facial Expression Recognition Using Attentional Convolutional Network. *Sensors*, 21, 9, 3046, April 2021, doi: 10.3390/s21093046.
3. Khaireddin, Y. and Chen, Z., Facial Emotion Recognition: State of the Art Performance on FER2013, arXiv preprint arXiv:2105.03588, May 2021, doi: 10.48550/arXiv.2105.03588.
4. Lonkar, S., Facial Expressions Recognition with Convolutional Neural Networks, arXiv preprint arXiv:2107.08640, Jul. 2021, doi: 10.48550/arXiv.2107.08640.
5. Lahariya, A., Singh, V., Tiwary, U.S., Real-time Emotion and Gender Classification using Ensemble CNN, arXiv preprint arXiv:2111.07746, Nov. 2021, doi: 10.48550/arXiv.2111.07746.
6. Luo, J., Xie, Z., Zhu, F., Zhu, X., Facial expression recognition using machine learning models in fer2013, in: *2021 IEEE 3rd International Conference on Frontiers Technology of Information and Computer (ICFTIC)*, pp. 231–235, IEEE, November 2021.
7. Gaddam, D.K.R., Ansari, M.D., Vuppala, S., Gunjan, V.K., Sati, M.M., Human facial emotion detection using deep learning, in: *ICDSMLA 2020: Proceedings of the 2nd International Conference on Data Science, Machine Learning and Applications*, pp. 1417–1427, Springer Singapore, Singapore, November 2021.
8. Oguine, O.C., Oguine, K.J., Bisallah, H.I., Ofuani, D., Hybrid Facial Expression Recognition (FER2013) Model for Real-Time Emotion Classification and Prediction, arXiv preprint arXiv:2206.09509, Aug. 2022, doi: 10.48550/arXiv.2206.09509.
9. Podder, T., Bhattacharya, D., Majumder, P., Balas, V.E., A feature boosted deep learning method for automatic facial expression recognition. *PeerJ Comput. Sci.*, 9, e1216, 2023.
10. Liu, Y., The Study of Performance Related to Classical Convolutional Neural Networks in the Field of Facial Emotion Recognition. *Appl. Comput. Eng.*, 8, 470–474, 2023.
11. Kalsum, T. and Mehmood, Z., A Novel Lightweight Deep Convolutional Neural Network Model for Human Emotions Recognition in Diverse Environments. *J. Sens.*, 2023, 6987708, 11, Aug. 2023, doi: 10.1155/2023/6987708.
12. Mejia-Escobar, C., Cazorla, M., Martínez-Martín, E., Towards a Better Performance in Facial Expression Recognition: A Data-Centric Approach. *Comput. Intell. Neurosci.*, 2023, 1394882, 22, Nov. 2023, doi:10.1155/2023/1394882.
13. Pham, T.D., Duong, M.T., Ho, Q.T., Lee, S., Hong, M.C., CNN-based facial expression recognition with simultaneous consideration of inter-class and intra-class variations. *Sensors*, 23, 24, 9658, 2023.

14. Bhagat, D., Vakil, A., Gupta, R.K., Kumar, A., Facial Emotion Recognition (FER) using Convolutional Neural Network (CNN). *Procedia Comput. Sci.*, 271, 135–142, May 2024, doi: 10.1016/j.procs.2024.04.197.
15. El Boudouri, Y. and Bohi, A., EmoNeXt: an Adapted ConvNeXt for Facial Emotion Recognition, arXiv preprint arXiv:2501.08199, Jan. 2025, doi: 10.48550/arXiv.2501.08199.
16. Roy, S., Dutta, M., Ghosh, A., Choudhury, T., Dutta, S., CNN-Based Model for Facial Expression Recognition Using FER 2013 Dataset, in: *Proc. Data Mining and Information Security (ICDMIS 2024),* Lecture Notes in Networks and Systems, vol. 1389, Springer, Singapore, 2025, doi:10.1007/978-981-96-6066-7_28.

10

Causal and Data-Driven Machine Learning Algorithm for Predicting Temperature Profiles in Friction Stir Additive Manufacturing of Aluminum Alloy A16061

MD Masud Rana

Computer Science, Lamar University, Beaumont, Texas, USA

Abstract

This article is an attempt to solve the problem of predicting the effective parameters of friction stir welding additive manufacturing without producing in real-time by proposing a machine learning algorithm. First, the friction stir welding process is experimentally modeled. Basically, the friction stir additive manufacturing process is a solid-state–based complex metal joining technique that has been significantly used in the modern manufacturing industry. The manufacturing quality is significantly affected by its design parameters, such as torques, force, and temperature. Real-time implementation of this process is very expensive, time-consuming, and labor-intensive. We have proposed an artificial neural networks based friction stir additive manufacturing effective parameters measurement method. To train the proposed network, the experimental data, such as torque profiles of alloy specimens, are used. The temperature and cooling rate are determined from the neural network–based machine learning output. The results show that the proposed algorithm can properly measure the additive manufacturing parameters, such as temperature, with high accuracy. When the microstructure and scientific quality of metal meet the required specifications, features, and demand, we will be able to manufacture the final product in a cost-effective way.

Keywords: Aluminum alloy, artificial neural networks, back propagation, friction stir additive manufacturing, temperature and torque

Email: mrana15@lamar.edu; rana03311998@gmail.com

Rajdeep Chakraborty, Aleem Ali, Amit Paul, Nawaf R. Alharbe and S. Balamurugan (eds.) Causal Artificial Intelligence: Fundamentals and Applications, (241–254) © 2026 Scrivener Publishing LLC

10.1 Introduction

Additive manufacturing has gained significant interest in the manufacturing sectors, such as automotive, transportation, aerospace, sporting equipment, and medical. In this technique, the physical items with complex shapes have been designed and implemented based on a layer-by-layer metallic joining process [1]. For example, the friction stir additive manufacturing (FSAM) process can produce variable microstructures with excellent metallurgical properties in the joint zone for particular applications [1]. In order to have faster production rates, less material wastage, and guaranteed quality, the solid-state–based friction stir additive manufacturing is the best choice. Figure 10.1 shows the friction stir additive manufacturing process. In this process, stacks of weld plates are lap-welded and then friction stir–welded to form an item layer by layer. The joints are made in the solid state, and there is no need for melting.

The significant technical challenges arise for designing specifications and guaranteeing the quality of the products. Sometimes, it will need the trial-and-error principles to achieve the desired scientific qualities and a cost-effective metallic solution. In other words, the input and output

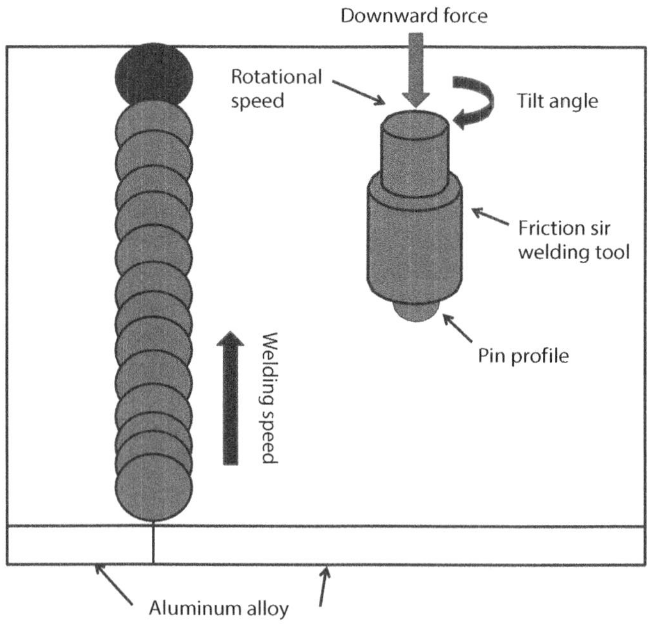

Figure 10.1 Simple diagram of friction stir additive manufacturing process.

relationships of the design parameters are the key to developing a state-based friction stir additive manufacturing product. For doing this, recently, the machine learning algorithm can play an important role in developing the relationship. Figure 10.2 shows the typical input and output relationship of metal from a machine learning point of view. It is observed that the machine algorithm can create a virtual relationship with the microstructures. The input of the machine learning algorithm can be rotational speeds, thrust force, and tool geometry. The output of the machine learning process can be temperature, cooling rate, and strengths. When there is a good match between specifications and the final product through the machine learning algorithm process, the desired items can be fabricated.

The traditional additive manufacturing system is being modernized using a machine learning algorithm. This is due to the fact that it takes a significant amount of time and cost to implement the product. Sometimes the design quality is not properly guaranteed after manufacturing. In order to solve this problem, machine learning algorithms can be adopted to develop the virtual relationship between the input and output

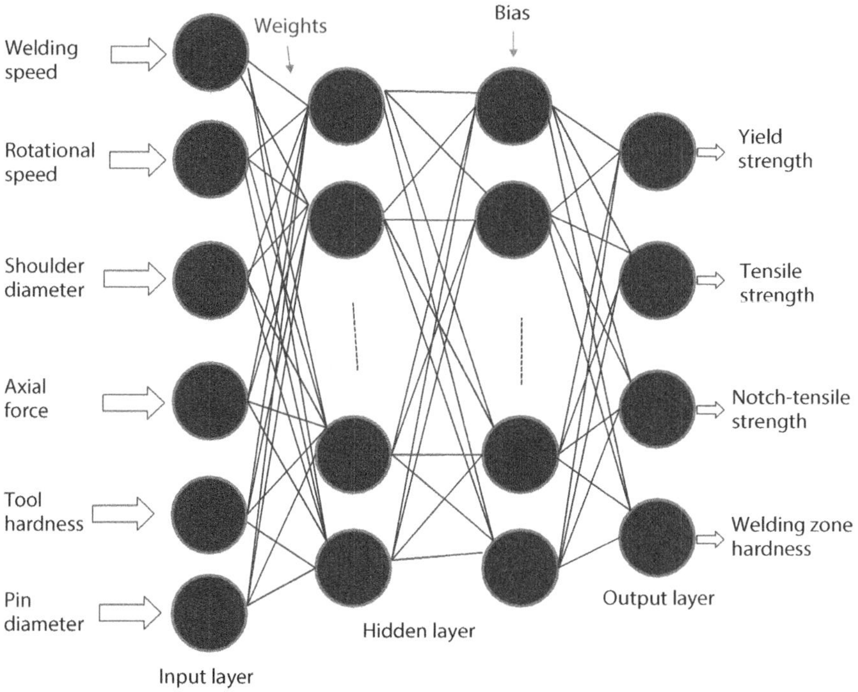

Figure 10.2 Machine learning–based friction stir additive manufacturing process: Metallic input and output relationship.

characteristics of metals. This paper proposes an innovative and fast neural network–based friction stir additive manufacturing parameters measurement technique.

Numerical results illustrate that the proposed algorithm can properly predict the friction stir additive manufacturing parameters. In this way, we will be able to design and implement cost-effective products.

10.1.1 Literature Review: FSAM and Machine Learning

There have been significant works related to friction stir additive manufacturing process and machine learning. To begin with, temperature evolution and heat generation during additive friction stir deposition process are described in [2].

The state-of-art survey shows that data-driven–based machine learning algorithm to predict temperature evaluation of FSAM is very important, and only a few publication has been published. To the best of author's knowledge, the machine learning–based temperature prediction in FSAM is barley recorded and requires detailed analysis in both numerical and experimentally. This paper proposes a data-driven–based machine learning algorithm to forecast temperature profile of FSAM. Considering several input parameters such as velocity, speed, and force, the train model is designed so that better predictions are accomplished. The numerical simulation and experimental results are reasonable agreement.

10.1.2 Main Contributions

- For friction stir additive manufacturing, the experimental data have been collected for investigation. Using an aluminum alloy, the real-time data, such as torques and temperature profiles, have been collected. The thermocouples are used for this process to gather temperature data.
- A neural network–based machine learning algorithm is proposed to measure the temperature of this process. The temperature is the key indicator of the scientific quality of the metal.
- Simulation results show that the proposed algorithm can perfectly measure the friction stir additive manufacturing parameters, such as temperature.

The aforementioned contributions and innovations are significant to developing a friction stir additive manufacturing process. In other words, without physically producing the items, we can establish the input and output relationship of the friction stir additive manufacturing parameters such as torques, rotational speeds, and temperatures. As a result, the labor cost, time, and powder can be saved in the virtual manufacturing process. The friction stir additive manufacturing process moves forward to an advanced level based on the automated machine learning–based quality prediction process.

10.1.3 Outline

The paper is organized in the following manner. The friction stir additive manufacturing process is described in Section 10.2. The problem statement is illustrated in Section 10.3. The proposed neural network–based machine learning algorithm is developed in Section 10.4. The simulation result and discussion are provided in Section 10.5. We conclude in Section 10.6 with a few final remarks.

10.2 Friction Stir Additive Manufacturing Process

The FSAM is the latest class of metal additive manufacturing process for enhanced mechanical and microstructural properties [3]. The microhardness, refined and equiaxed grains, lightweight alloys, and enhanced tensile strength are the key features of this method [3]. In FSAM, a rotating non-consumable tool with a pin and shoulder is injected into the overlapping/abutting surfaces of plates to be joined and eventually traversed along the joint line without melting [1]. To illustrate, Figure 10.3 illustrates a self-explanatory friction stir additive manufacturing process. The heat required to weld the aluminum material is given by the frictional contact between the shoulder and workpiece, coupled with intense plastic deformation accomplished by the motion of the pin. Development of the weld nugget is promoted by the continuous movement of aluminum material from the front end to behind the pin, and the macro structure is dependent on the geometrical characteristics of the pin. In this way, the joints are formed in a solid state and do not melt. Consequently, the resultant build height depends on the layer thickness, assembly stages, and layers [1]. During the welding process, the macroscopic shape and size of the build can be controlled by changing the design geometry.

Overall, the FSAM is a multi-layer additive manufacturing process, and it can help to design as well as implement complex geometry. To gain accurate structural performance and mechanical properties through the

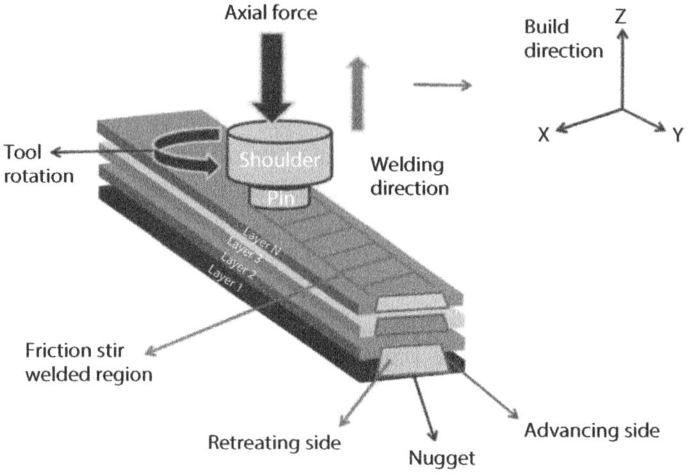

Figure 10.3 Friction stir additive manufacturing process [1].

grain refining process, this method is widely used in automotive, marine, and other sectors. In this FSAM process, melting temperature is negligible due to nonmelting fabrication, and the peak temperature ranges up to 60% to 90% of the melting temperature [1]. Therefore, FSAM can fabricate the required products with minor formation of porosity, particle segregation, inclusions, and internal cavities. These unique features can make it handy compared with the existing beam-based methods, which are high-temperature and high-energy processes [4, 5]. The interactions of the powders and high-energy beam can destroy powder microstructures during melting [4].

10.3 Problem Statement Related to Friction Stir Additive Manufacturing

It is a challenging task to produce high-quality items such as ventilators based on the design specifications in a cost-efficient and effective way. The modeling of metal-based physical items is very difficult due to correlated physical parameters and thermodynamic profiles. Fortunately, the machine learning algorithm can effectively play an important role in designing the items virtually. Considering this impending problem and requirement, the problem statement of this paper is described as follows.

With the given friction stir additive manufacturing input parameters, such as torque, find the temperature profile of the multi-layer welding process. The measured temperature must be aligned and comparable with the real-time experiential data. This paper solves the problem after proposing a neural network–based machine learning algorithm. Results show that the developed scheme can accurately measure the process parameters, such as temperature, which is the key indicator to develop a solid-state–based modern additive manufacturing industry. When the microstructure and scientific quality of metal meet the required specifications, features, and demand, we will be able to manufacture the final product. Consequently, we will be able to save time, powder, and money on the friction stir additive manufacturing process. In this way, hopefully, the additive manufacturing process will move forward to a sustainable, innovative, and more profitable industry.

10.4 Proposed Machine Learning Algorithm for Parameter Predictions of the FSAM Process

The artificial neural network is a machine learning process, and the information processing principle is similar to that of the human brain [6]. Specifically, the connected neurons are gathered to process information from the multiple input nodes. Figure 10.4 shows the artificial neural

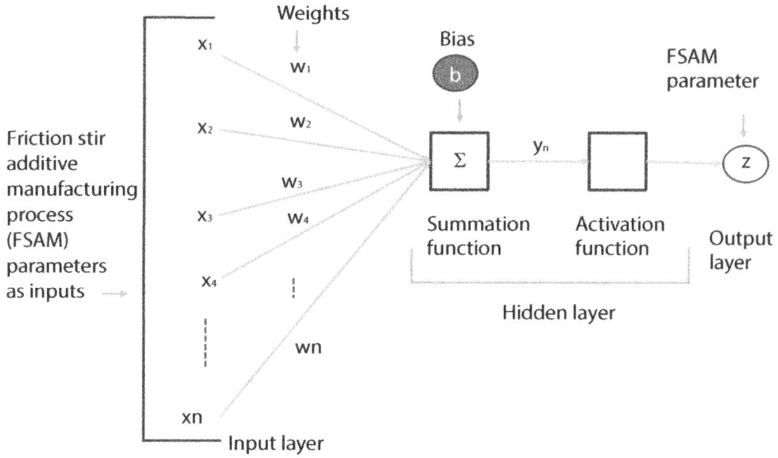

Figure 10.4 Multi-input neural network for the FSAM process.

network–based friction stir welding parameter prediction process. The input information of the FSAM process parameters is linearly combined after multiplying them with weight parameters. The bias parameters are enforced to add them. The combined term is moved forward to the activation function, which can represent the nonlinear relationship between input FSAM parameters and output. After processing them internally, the output of this neural network is obtained.

10.5 Results and Discussions

Figure 10.5 provides a step-by-step process of the proposed algorithm. After giving the initial parameters, the forward and backward processes are run. In each iteration, the algorithm can minimize the FSAM error, leading to a true predicted parameter.

With the given welding parameters and specifications, the additive manufacturing process is run in the laboratory. We have collected experimental

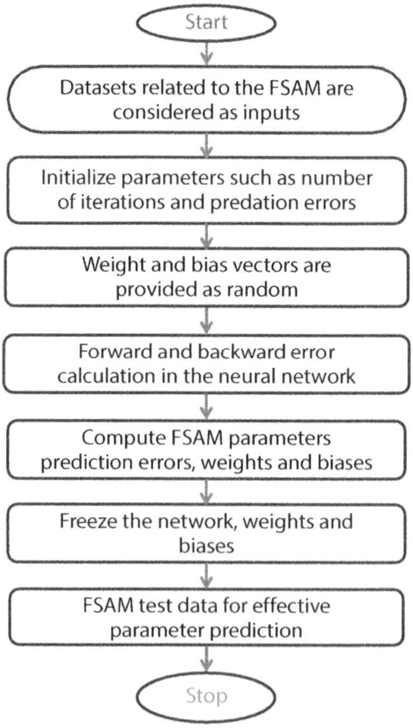

Figure 10.5 Flow diagram of the proposed FSAM parameter prediction process.

data using an aluminum alloy. Figure 10.6 shows the considered geometry for item production in the laboratory. The thermocouple 1 is used to collect temperature. The input of the machine learning algorithm is torque, and the output is the temperature.

From the simulation results in Figures 10.7–10.12, it can be seen that the machine learning algorithm can effectively predict the FSAM parameters, such as temperature. When the number of layers in the neural network is increased, the performance is significantly improved. Specifically, Figure 10.7 shows the absolute error between the true and predicted temperatures. There are four peaks and valleys in this diagram. When the solid-state joining process is started, the temperature fluctuates between 250 and 450 seconds. The maximum temperature is 377°C which is significantly lower than the meting temperature.

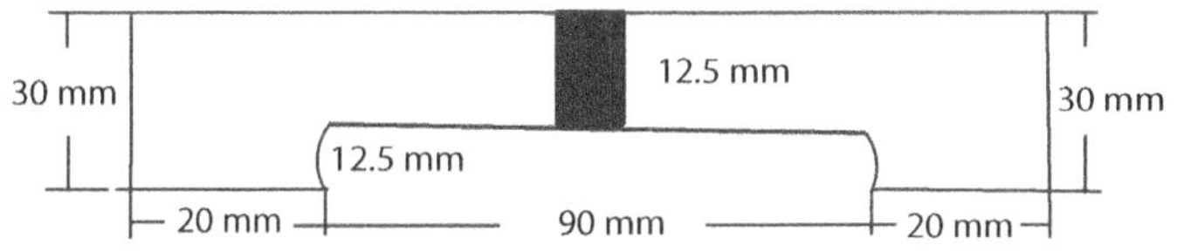

Figure 10.6 Considered geometry for item production.

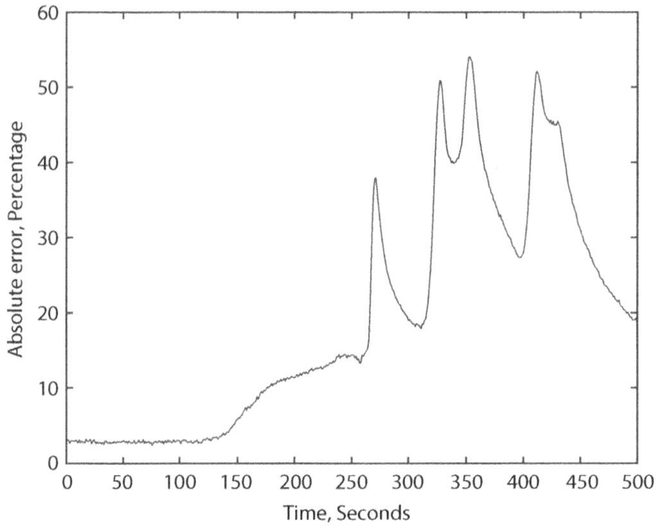

Figure 10.7 Absolute error between true and predicted FSAM data with 3,4 hidden nodes in two hidden layers.

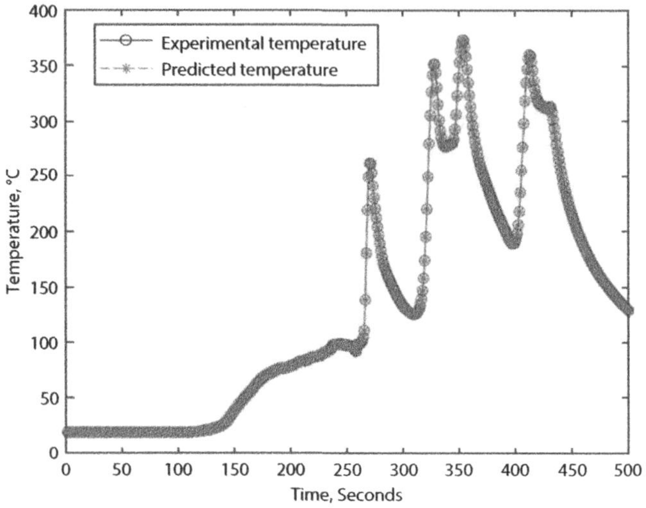

Figure 10.8 Experimental and predicted FSAM temperatures with 3,4 hidden nodes in two hidden layers.

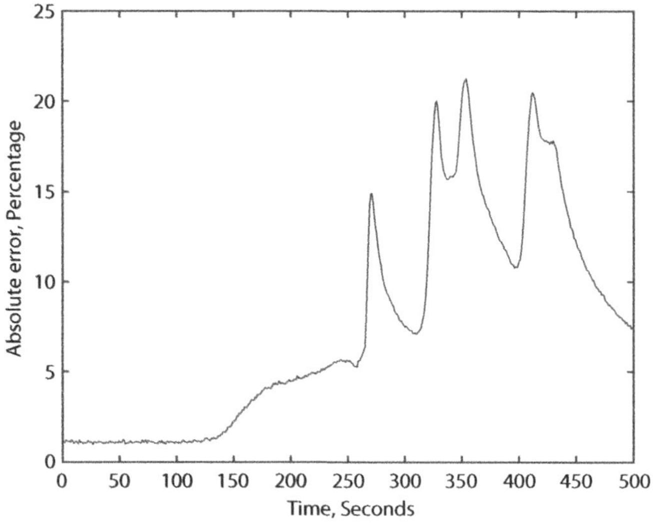

Figure 10.9 Absolute error between true and predicted FSAM data with 5,15 hidden nodes in two hidden layers.

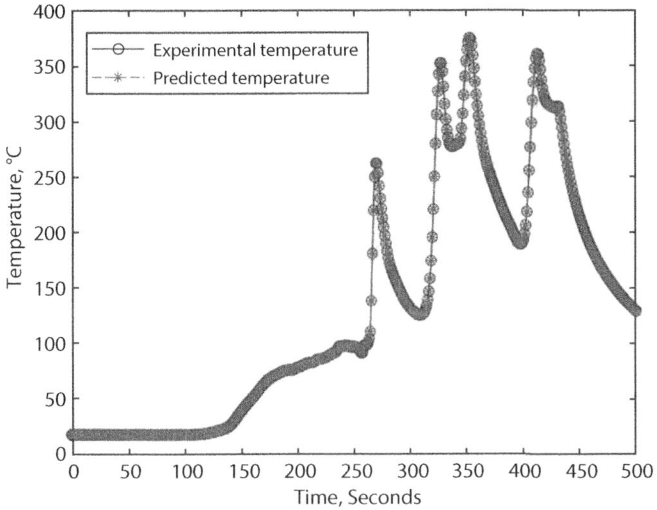

Figure 10.10 Experimental and predicted FSAM temperatures with 5,15 hidden nodes in two hidden layers.

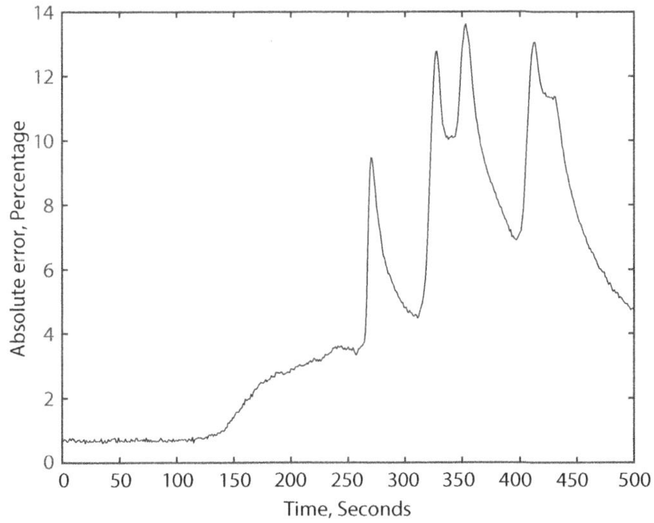

Figure 10.11 Absolute error between true and predicted FSAM data with 10,25 hidden nodes in two hidden layers.

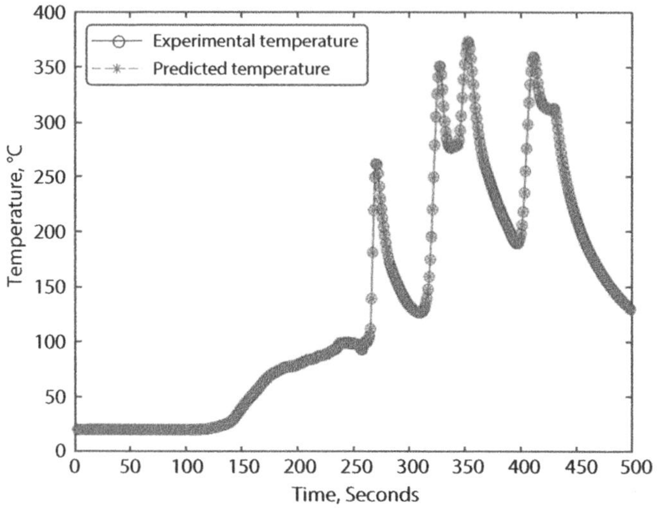

Figure 10.12 Experimental and predicted FSAM temperatures with 10,25 hidden nodes in two hidden layers.

10.6 Conclusion

The FSAM is a solid-state–based, fast, and scalable dynamic process. In order to save time, powder, and money, this paper proposes an innovative approach for the prediction of friction stir additive manufacturing parameters, such as temperature. Specifically, we want to establish an input and output relationship of the friction stir additive manufacturing process. We have proposed a neural network–based machine learning scheme to predict temperature evolution using experimentally generated data as input. Simulation results show that the proposed algorithm provided high accuracy for the prediction of the friction stir additive manufacturing parameter. Therefore, this work is valuable to design a smart friction stir additive manufacturing system so that we can maintain the scientific quality of metal without producing the item.

AI disclosure statement: The author confirms that no artificial intelligence (AI)-generated content or AI-assisted writing tools were used in the preparation of this chapter (including summaries and the abstract). All text, analysis, and conclusions are the result of the author's original work.

References

1. Palanivel, S., Nelaturu, P., Glass, B., Mishra, R., Friction stir additive manufacturing for high structural performance through microstructural control in an Mg based WE43 alloy. *Mater. Des.*, 65, 934–952, 2015.
2. Garcia, D., Hartley, W.D., Rauch, H.A., Griffiths, R.J., Wang, R., Kong, Z.J., Zhu, Y., Hang, Z.Y., *In situ* investigation into temperature evolution and heat generation during additive friction stir deposition: A comparative study of Cu and Al–Mg–Si. *Addit. Manuf.*, 34, 101386, 2020.
3. Srivastava, A.K., Kumar, N., Dixit, A.R., Friction stir additive manufacturing-An innovative tool to enhance mechanical and microstructural properties. *Mater. Sci. Eng. B*, 263, 114832, 2021.
4. Hang, Z.Y., Jones, M.E., Brady, G.W., Griffiths, R.J., Garcia, D., Rauch, H.A., Cox, C.D., Hardwick, N., Non-beam-based metal additive manufacturing enabled by additive friction stir deposition. *Scr. Mater.*, 153, 122–130, 2018.
5. Srivastava, M., Rathee, S., Maheshwari, S., Siddiquee, A.N., Kundra, T., A review on recent progress in solid state friction based metal additive manufacturing: friction stir additive techniques. *Crit. Rev. Solid State Mater. Sci.*, 44, 5, 345–377, 2019.
6. Gao, Y., Fang, Y., Dong, H., Kong, Y., A multifactorial framework for short-term load forecasting system as well as the jinan's case study. *IEEE Access*, 8, 203 086–203 096, 2020.

11

Enhancing Cybersecurity in EVs: Causal and Resilient ML-Based Detection of False Data Injection and Denial of Service Attacks

MD Masud Rana[1]*, Amir Shahirinia[2], Amer Dawoud[3] and Ahad Ali[4]

[1]Computer Science, Lamar University, Beaumont, Texas, USA
[2]Dept. of ECE, University of the District of Columbia, Washington, DC, USA
[3]School of CSCE, The University of Southern Mississippi, Hattiesburg, MS, USA
[4]Mechanical Robotics and Industrial Engineering, Lawrence Technological University, Southfield, MI, USA

Abstract

Electric vehicles (EVs) have been widely used and produced for public purposes, such as creating an eco-friendly and resource-efficient environment. Unfortunately, the vulnerability and safety of the EV framework have been growing at an alarming rate. In particular, vehicle communication protocols such as CAN bus are prone to cyberattacks, including false data injection (FDI) and DoS attacks. These attacks can create some upcoming problems, such as (1) manipulating sensor readings, such as car speed, battery voltage, and brake pressure, (2) overloaded CAN bus latency to reduce environmental awareness, and (3) a lack of a robust machine learning (ML) model in a real-time EV environment. To solve these key problems at an acceptable level, this study introduces, investigates, and analyzes ML models such as random forest, XGBoost, and LightGBM in the EV framework under the FDI and DoS attacks. We have developed a framework that can generate real-time EV data, which includes key interconnected features such as car speed, battery voltage, motor temperature, brake pressure, CAN latency, packet size, and signal-to-noise ratios. The results have shown, based on simulations, that the XGBoost algorithm earned more than 96% accuracy under cyberattacks, while in normal circumstances, it provides more than 98% accuracy. Based on this process, the FDI

**Corresponding author*: mrana15@lamar.edu; rana03311998@gmail.com

Rajdeep Chakraborty, Aleem Ali, Amit Paul, Nawaf R. Alharbe and S. Balamurugan (eds.) Causal Artificial Intelligence: Fundamentals and Applications, (255–272) © 2026 Scrivener Publishing LLC

attacks score CVSS is 8 by spoofing critical sensors, while the DoS attacks score is 7.5 by flooding CAN buses, both of which trigger real-time EV ECU isolation. Hopefully, this work with new datasets, frameworks, and ML algorithms can be helpful for education and training as well as research development. In the future, the integration of edge computing in EV controllers can significantly improve driver safety, resilience, and confidence.

Keywords: Common vulnerability scoring system, denial-of-service (DoS) attacks, electric vehicles, false data injection attack, random forest, XGBoost, LightGBM

11.1 Introduction

The development of EVs has revolutionized the automotive industry but has introduced unique cybersecurity threats that breach confidentiality, integrity, and availability (CIA) [1]. Figure 11.1 shows the EV cyberattack properties and impact matrix. It can be observed that the EV cyberattack impact matrix maps FDI, DoS, and Replay attacks against the core CIA triad to visualize critical car vulnerabilities. Any violation of any property leads to a breach of cybersecurity properties.

Indeed, the modern EVs rely on CAN bus protocols for critical operations and run [2]. Compromising this EV framework can lead to catastrophic failures in real-time, from inaccurate car braking to battery overheating [3]. Figure 11.2 shows the self-explanation–based cyberattack profile on EV ecosystems [4]. To illustrate, the attack can happen in EV CAN bus across the globe [5]. Therefore, there is a pressing demand for machine solutions to detect and investigate such cyberattacks on EV networks.

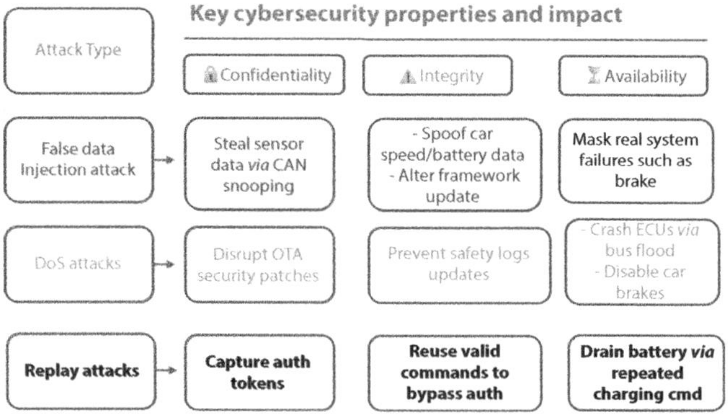

Figure 11.1 EV cyberattack properties and impact matrix.

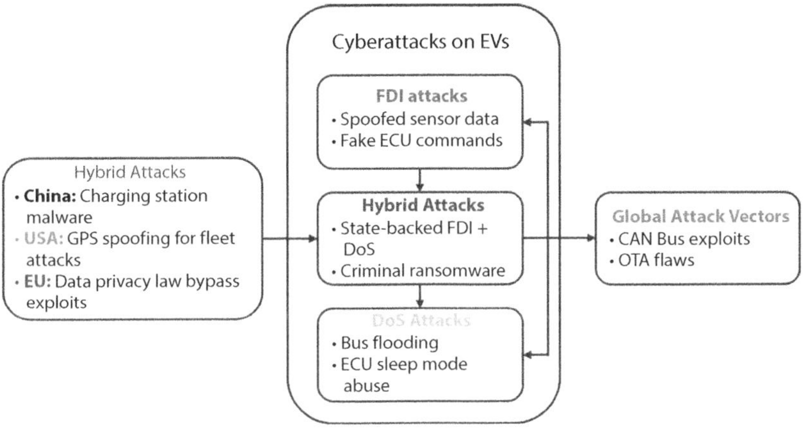

Figure 11.2 Cyberattack profile on EV ecosystems.

For instance, in Figure 11.3, cyberattacks such as FDI sensor spoofing cascade through the CIA, and they can compromise Integrity (false speed data), threatening Availability (CAN bus floods), and risking Confidentiality (data leaks) [1]. Therefore, it can ultimately enable physical EV threats and risks.

There has been an existing vehicle digital twin platform, a practical EV framework, ML models, and a threat detection process. Table 11.1 shows the summary of previous work. It can be seen that the previous studies described from the Random forest (RF) and XGBoost on CAN data to LSTM, CNN, and Bayesian models for EV intrusion detection [17–19]. Unfortunately, most of the work focused on single-feature anomalies, no common vulnerability scoring system (CVSS) assessment, clean datasets, and required heavy computation. Additionally, there is limited work on multi-class attacks like FDI and DoS under noisy conditions. This proposed

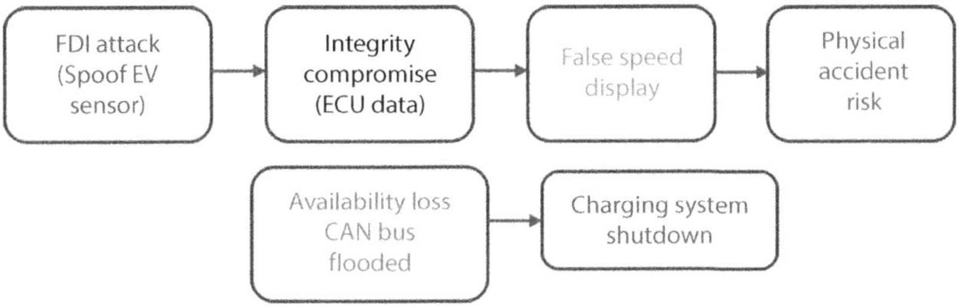

Figure 11.3 EV cyberattack on the CIA flow.

Table 11.1 Literature review: EV cybersecurity.

Technique	Considered problem	Shortcoming
RF on CAN [6]	CAN message anomaly detection	Consider single-feature deviations
LSTM autoencoders [7]	Time-series attack detection	Needs large data sequences, drift sensitive
Isolation forest [8]	DoS detection	Misses subtle FDI with multi-characteristic patterns
CNN on packets [9]	Sequence anomalies in CAN	High computational complexity
SVM [10]	Traffic entropy shifts	Fails for FDI
Bayesian networks [11]	CAN intrusion probability systems	Limited scalability
XGBoost for VANETs [12]	VANET intrusion detection	Not fine-tuned for EV telemetry cyber attacks
Rule thresholding [13]	Abrupt change detection	Limited for realistic FDI
KNN+ANN [14, 15]	Mixed EV anomaly detection	High tuning cost for noisy environments
LightGBM [16]	Multi-class EV anomalies	Tested mainly on clean EV data
Proposed	DoS and FDI detection in noisy EV environment	Robust multi-class under noise and cyberattacks

approach fills this gap by leveraging a robust ML approach to detect EV attacks with high resilience, even amid label noise.

To know the cyberattack profiles and impact on the EV system, ML can play an important role. Table 11.2 shows the cyberattack profiles and impact on the EV systems. It can be observed that FDI and DoS can impact the EV safety and resilience. The attack can increase unexpected speed and reduce battery voltage, for example.

Table 11.2 Considered cyberattack profiles on EV systems and impacts.

Attack profile	Affected EV features & patterns	EV impact
FDI	↑ Car speed, ↑ motor temp, ↓ battery voltage, ↓ brake pressure, realistic SNR, and packet sizes	Wrong safety actions, hard to detect due to plausible ranges [20]. Safety and reliability issues.
DoS [21]	↑ CAN bus latency, ↓ SNR, and ↓ packet size	Delays safety-critical car commands, and risk of collision.

Inspired by aforementioned reasons, this study introduces, investigates, and analyzes ML models such as RF, XGBoost, and LightGBM in the EV framework under the FDI and DoS attacks. We have developed a framework that can generate real-time EV data, including key correlated features such as car speed, battery voltage, motor temperature, brake pressure, CAN latency, packet size, and signal-to-noise ratios. Simulation results demonstrate that the XGBoost algorithm earned more than 96% accuracy under cyberattacks, while in normal cases, it provides more than 98 % accuracy.

11.2 Problem Statement

In order to define the problem of interest, Figure 11.4 shows the system-level diagram of the EV systems. This article addresses the following business problems:

1. How can we effectively detect FDI attacks that subtly manipulate EV telemetry data?

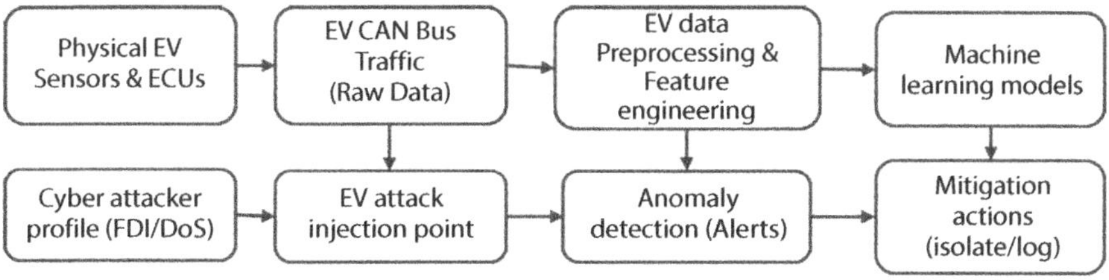

Figure 11.4 System-level diagram of the EV system.

2. What ML models can robustly learn from a complex, noisy, and potentially mislabeled EV telemetry dataset to classify multi-class attacks (Normal vs. FDI vs. DoS) with high reliability?
3. What are the CVSS (Common Vulnerability Scoring System) scores to quantify the severity of EV cyberattacks?

To solve these, this study introduces, investigates, and analyzes RF, XGBoost, and LightGBM in the EV framework under the FDI and DoS attacks. We have developed a framework that can generate real-time EV data, including key features such as car speed, battery voltage, motor temperature, brake pressure, CAN latency, packet size, and signal-to-noise ratios. The calculated CVSS score is very high. Hopefully, this work advances automotive cybersecurity through RF, XGBoost, and LightGBM that detect FDI and DoS attacks on EV CAN buses, as shown in Figure 11.5.

The EV dataset is shown in Table 11.3. This simulates EV data under normal and attack conditions, such as FDI and DoS, applies preprocessing and label noise, and evaluates multiple MLs on their anomaly detection accuracy. Results based on simulations demonstrate that the XGBoost algorithm earned more than 96% accuracy under cyberattacks, while in normal cases, it provides more than 98% accuracy.

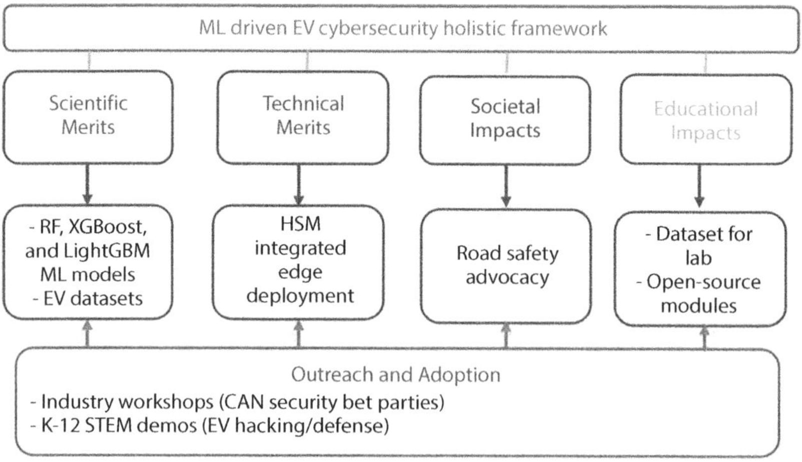

Figure 11.5 Scientific, technical, societal merits and broader impacts.

Table 11.3 EV dataset.

Speed (km/h)	Voltage (V)	Motor temp (°C)	Brake pressure	CAN latency (ms)	Packet size (kb)	SNR	Irrel. 1	Irrel. 2	Attack
54.96	400.48	93.09	25.03	3.22	1.59	19.01	-2.07	1.62	0
63.84	378.93	71.65	25.42	0.81	1.49	38.12	2.71	0.21	0
61.64	405.98	67.66	20.14	3.72	1.12	40.90	0.16	-1.50	0
68.69	179.28	112.00	15.88	4.57	2.31	6.90	0.17	0.14	1
56.69	411.77	83.87	16.63	0.27	1.19	38.09	-0.86	-0.38	1
85.72	287.56	117.41	17.68	3.10	2.09	20.24	-1.36	-1.91	0
65.74	401.86	63.32	16.28	1.79	0.14	21.49	-0.40	-0.29	0
56.45	405.58	74.34	24.76	1.28	0.95	18.03	1.56	-2.05	0
63.90	390.22	95.57	11.68	1.92	1.11	30.20	-1.49	1.01	0
44.94	419.06	90.63	40.36	2.88	0.65	18.48	0.64	-0.49	0
52.81	415.43	83.51	33.17	3.12	1.05	30.49	1.54	0.11	0
50.66	356.94	89.22	27.12	2.91	1.66	26.85	-0.02	-1.91	0
92.16	383.93	62.89	17.20	-0.34	1.35	27.78	-0.63	1.06	0

(Continued)

Table 11.3 EV dataset. *(Continued)*

Speed (km/h)	Voltage (V)	Motor temp (°C)	Brake pressure	CAN latency (ms)	Packet size (kb)	SNR	Irrel. 1	Irrel. 2	Attack
117.56	197.40	115.85	13.87	4.01	1.61	15.88	-1.41	-0.97	1
61.30	398.00	59.14	24.69	4.09	0.71	29.84	0.34	-1.33	0
31.99	406.20	68.52	37.57	3.27	1.21	29.68	-2.27	0.97	0
63.86	387.52	71.71	34.51	1.70	0.66	35.34	-2.37	1.11	0
56.40	390.71	79.69	54.85	0.81	1.83	24.84	-0.50	-1.12	0
56.42	368.32	57.24	35.14	-0.39	1.27	28.73	-0.56	-2.01	0
56.39	385.66	80.49	47.12	1.12	1.52	22.38	0.22	0.24	0
-	-	-	-	-	-	-	-	-	-

11.3 Proposed Methodology

In this work, we have generated 250 sample EV data, including attacks using Python, then preprocessed and fed it to RF, XGBoost, and LightGBM for real-time intrusion detection. Algorithm 11.1 demonstrates the proposed method. To begin with, the RF processes CAN bus features such as car speed, voltage, and latency through decision trees, leveraging majority voting to deliver robust cyberattack classification [22, 23]. Moreover, XGBoost uses gradient boosting with regularization to sequentially minimize prediction errors [24, 25]. Finally, LightGBM explores histogram-based approximation and leaf-wise tree growth to enable ultra-low latency inference and decision [26, 27].

Algorithm 11.1 RF, XGBoost, and LightGBM-based Detection of EV Cyberttacks.

Require:

Raw EV telemetry data $\mathbf{D} = \{\mathbf{x}_i, y_i\}^{N\,i=1}$

Cyberattack profiles: $y \in \{0 : \text{Normal}, 1 : \text{FDI}, 2 : \text{DoS}\}$

Ensure:

Trained ensemble ML models M, performance metrics **P**

1: **EV Data Generation:** $D_{norm} \leftarrow$ GenerateNormalData(), $D_{F\ DI} \leftarrow$ GenerateFDIAttack(), $D_{DoS} \leftarrow$ GenerateDoSAttack()

2: $\mathbf{D} \leftarrow Dnorm \cup DFDI \cup DDoS$

3: **Label Noise Injection:** Flip 5% of labels randomly to simulate sensor uncertainty.

4: **Preprocessing:** $X, y \leftarrow$ SplitFeaturesLabels(**D**), $X_{scaled} \leftarrow$ StandardScaler(X) $(X_{train}, X_{test}, y_{train}, y_{test}) \leftarrow$ TrainTestSplit(X_{scaled}, y)

5: **ML Model Initialization:**

6: M ← {RF, XGBoost, LightGBM}

7: **ML Model Training and Performance Evaluation:**

8: **for** m in M **do**

9: $\quad m \leftarrow m.\text{fit}(X_{train}, y_{train})$

10: $\quad \hat{y} \leftarrow m.\text{predict}(X_{test})$

11: $\quad$ Compute metrics: Accuracy, Precision, Recall, F1, MSE

12: $\quad \mathbf{P}[m] \leftarrow$ {Accuracy, Precision, Recall, F1, MSE}

13: **end for**

14: **return** M, **P**

11.4 Simulation Results and Discussions

The simulation flow diagram is shown in Figure 11.6. Tables 11.4–11.6 show the simulation results. Figures 11.7–11.10 show the simulation results. It can be observed that the EV CAN bus data flows through pre-processing, gets analyzed by adopted algorithms, and triggers cyber threats when attacks are detected. Based on the framework, the simulation results

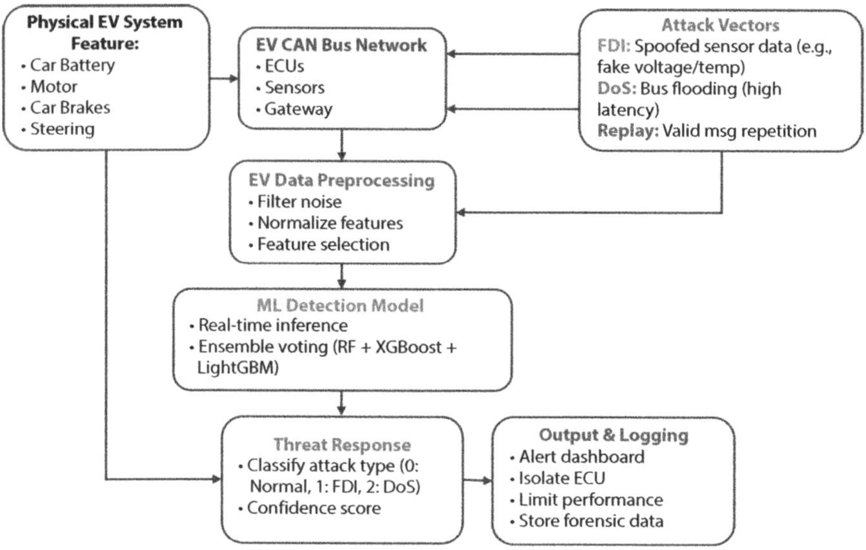

Figure 11.6 Flow diagram of the proposed method.

Table 11.4 RF classification performance report for EV.

Class	Precision	Recall	F1-score	Support
Normal	0.97	0.99	0.98	192
FDI	0.93	0.85	0.89	33
DoS	0.96	0.88	0.92	25
Accuracy: 0.964 (MSE: 0.060)				
Macro Avg	0.95	0.91	0.93	250
Weighted Avg	0.96	0.96	0.96	250

Table 11.5 XGBoost classification performance report for EV.

Class	Precision	Recall	F1-score	Support
Normal	0.97	0.99	0.98	192
FDI	0.93	0.85	0.89	33
DoS	0.96	0.88	0.92	25
Accuracy: 0.964 (MSE: 0.060)				
Macro avg	0.95	0.91	0.93	250
Weighted avg	0.96	0.96	0.96	250

Table 11.6 LightGBM classification performance report for EV.

Class	Precision	Recall	F1-score	Support
Normal	0.96	0.99	0.98	192
FDI	0.93	0.82	0.87	33
DoS	0.96	0.88	0.92	25
Accuracy: 0.96 (MSE: 0.064)				
Macro avg	0.95	0.90	0.92	250
Weighted avg	0.96	0.96	0.96	250

are presented below. It is clear that RF, XGBoost, and LightGBM—the classification performance remains consistently strong, with high precision and recall for detecting both normal and cyberattack patterns. Each model achieved an overall accuracy of 96%, demonstrating robust detection capabilities across DoS and FDI threats. The confusion matrix and mean squared error (MSE) are demonstrated. For example, in Figure 11.7, the confusion matrix depicts that the RF can be accurately classified as most Normal, FDI, and DoS instances, with only a limited set of misclassifications (e.g., 4 FDI as Normal, 1 DoS as FDI), showing a strong overall performance.

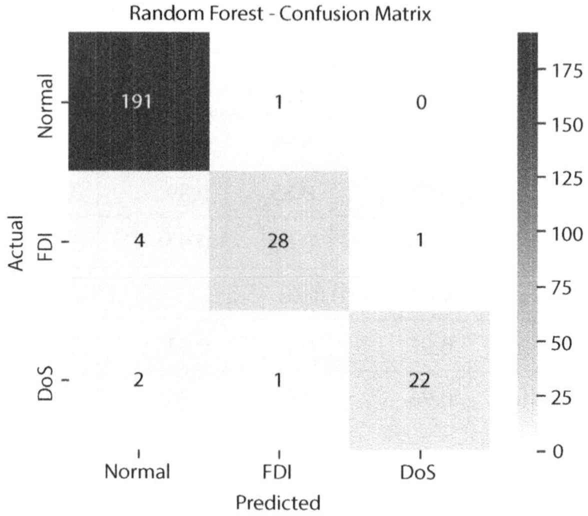

Figure 11.7 Confusion matrix based on RF.

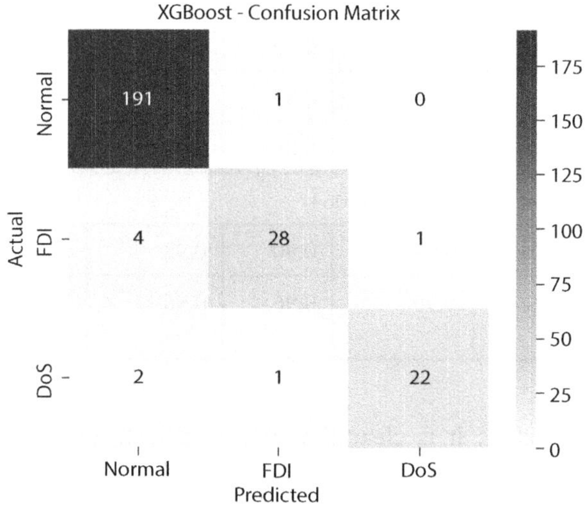

Figure 11.8 Confusion matrix based on XGBoost.

11.5 EV Cyberattack CVSS Assessment

Both these cyberattacks exceed standard IT vulnerability thresholds because they bridge cyber-physical boundaries, such as changing the scope. and trigger critical mitigation requirements for high risks [28–30].

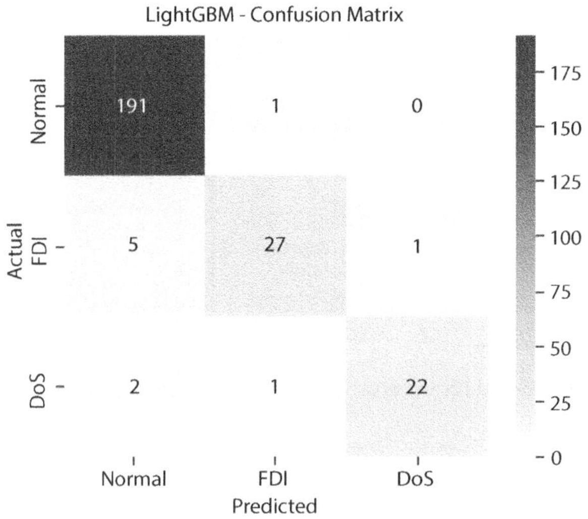

Figure 11.9 Confusion matrix based on LightGBM.

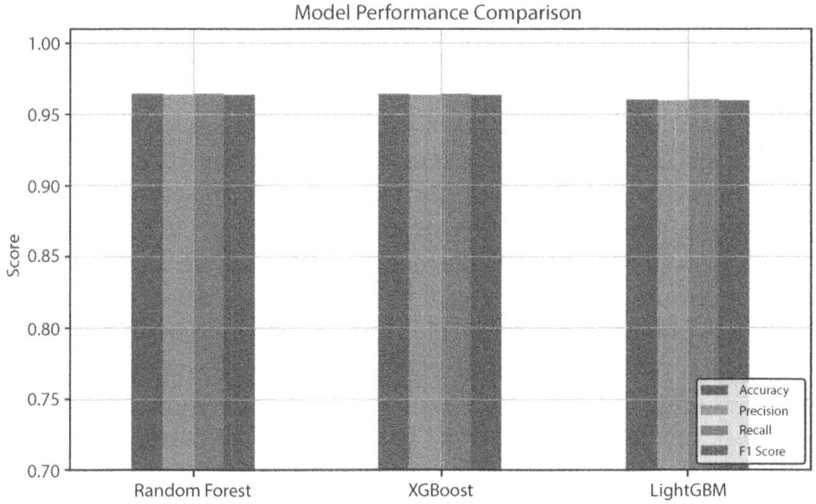

Figure 11.10 ML model performance.

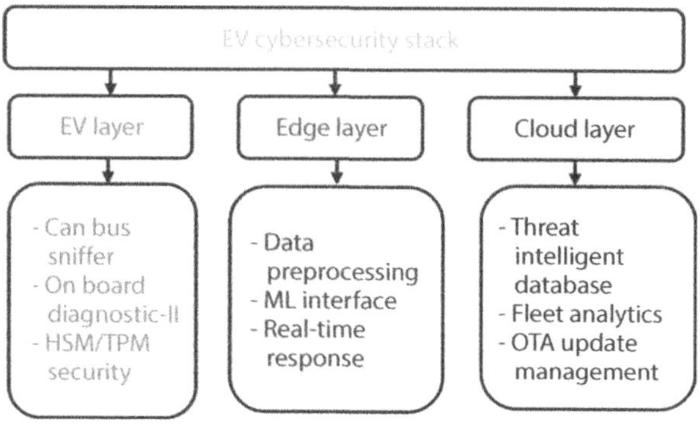

Figure 11.11 End-to-end EV cybersecurity software development.

11.6 Conclusion and Future Work

This article introduces, investigates, and analyzes the RF, XGBoost, and LightGBM in the EV framework under the FDI and DoS attacks. Developing a framework that generates real-time EV data, which includes important components. The simulation indicates the XGBoost algorithm has earned more than 96% accuracy under cyberattacks, while in normal cases, it provides more than 98% accuracy. The confusion matrix illustrates that the ML model correctly classified 250 samples, correctly classifying most Normal, FDI, and DoS attacks, with only a limited and acceptable mix-up between the categories. The calculated CVSS score is very high. In the future, the integration of edge computing in EV controllers can improve drivers' safety, resilience, and confidence. We aim to combine both deep learning and deploy a solution on EV edge devices for real-time response, as shown in Figure 11.11. This process combines CAN/OBD-II data capture, hardware-secured preprocessing, and ensemble ML (RF/XGBoost/LightGBM) detection to identify cyberattacks in real-time. The framework can be on edge devices (Jetson/RPi) with central cloud backup for fleet monitoring. Moreover, validating with real EV datasets remains a critical next step.

AI disclosure statement: The author acknowledges the use of AI-based tools for minor language editing or grammatical correction. However, all intellectual contributions, analyses, and conclusions presented in this chapter are entirely the author's own.

References

1. Muhammad, Z., Anwar, Z., Saleem, B., Shahid, J., Emerging cybersecurity and privacy threats to electric vehicles and their impact on human and environmental sustainability. *Energies*, 16, 3, 1113, 2023.
2. Fakhfakh, F., Tounsi, M., Mosbah, M., Cybersecurity attacks on CAN bus based vehicles: A review and open challenges. *Lib. Hi Tech*, 40, 5, 1179–1203, 2022.
3. Abbas, E.K., Ashraf, S., Muqadas, B., Talani, R.A., Haq, M.A.U., Rafique, M., Ali, M.S., Qadeer, A., Ahmad, B., Smart battery management solution for electric vehicles: Enhancing performance with advanced algorithms and real-time monitoring. *Spectr. Eng. Sci.*, 3, 4, 138–153, 2025.
4. Mousavian, S., Erol-Kantarci, M., Ortmeyer, T., Cyber attack protection for a resilient electric vehicle infrastructure, in: *IEEE Globecom Workshops*, IEEE, pp. 1–6, 2015.
5. Morrison, G.S., Threats and mitigation of DDoS cyberattacks against the US power grid *via* EV charging, Master's thesis, Wright State University, 2018.
6. Purohit, S. and Govindarasu, M., ML-based anomaly detection for intravehicular CAN-bus network, in: *International Conference on Cyber Security and Resilience*, IEEE, pp. 233–238, 2022.
7. Elsayed, M.S., Le-Khac, N.-A., Dev, S., Jurcut, A.D., Network anomaly detection using LSTM based autoencoder, in: *Proceedings of the 16th ACM Symposium on QoS and Security for Wireless and Mobile Networks*, pp. 37–45, 2020.
8. Duan, X., Yan, H., Tian, D., Zhou, J., Su, J., Hao, W., In-vehicle CAN bus tampering attacks detection for connected and autonomous vehicles using an improved isolation forest method. *IEEE Trans. Intell. Transp. Syst.*, 24, 2, 2122–2134, 2021.
9. Javed, A.R., Usman, M., Rehman, S.U., Khan, M.U., Haghighi, M.S., Anomaly detection in automated vehicles using multistage attention-based convolutional neural network. *IEEE Trans. Intell. Transp. Syst.*, 22, 7, 4291–4300, 2020.
10. Muter, M. and Asaj, N., Entropy-based anomaly detection for in-vehicle networks, in: *IEEE Intelligent Vehicles Symposium*, pp. 1110–1115, 2011.
11. Dong, K., Vehicle CAN bus intrusion detection model based on Bayesian network, in: *International Conference on Computer Network Security and Software Engineering*, vol. 13175, SPIE, pp. 7–12, 2024.
12. Zeng, Y., Qiu, M., Zhu, D., Xue, Z., Xiong, J., Liu, M., DeepVCM: A deep learning based intrusion detection method in VANET, in: *IEEE Intl Conference on Big Data Security on Cloud, IEEE Intl Conference on High Performance and Smart Computing, and IEEE Intl Conference on Intelligent Data and Security*, IEEE, pp. 288–293, 2019.
13. Hoppe, T., Kiltz, S., Dittmann, J., Security threats to automotive CAN networks–practical examples and selected short-term countermeasures, in:

International Conference on Computer Safety, Reliability, and Security, Springer, pp. 235–248, 2008.

14. Guerreiro, M.T., Guerreiro, E.M.A., Barchi, T.M., Biluca, J., Alves, T.A., de Souza Tadano, Y., Trojan, F., Siqueira, H.V., Anomaly detection in automotive industry using clustering methods—a case study. *Appl. Sci.*, 11, 21, 9868, 2021.
15. Lo, W., Alqahtani, H., Thakur, K., Almadhor, A., Chander, S., Kumar, G., A hybrid deep learning based intrusion detection system using spatial-temporal representation of in-vehicle network traffic. *Veh. Commun.*, 35, 100471, 2022.
16. Liu, J., Gao, Y., Hu, F., A fast network intrusion detection system using adaptive synthetic oversampling and LightGBM. *Comput. Secur.*, 106, 102289, 2021.
17. Bari, B.S., Yelamarthi, K., Ghafoor, S., Intrusion detection in vehicle controller area network (CAN) bus using machine learning: A comparative performance study. *Sensors*, 23, 7, 3610, 2023.
18. Al Isawi, O.A.M., Electric vehicles CAN bus cyber-attacks detection using machine learning and deep learning techniques, Ph.D. dissertation, Khalifa University of Science, 2023.
19. Lee, H., Jeong, S.H., Kim, H.K., OTIDS: A novel intrusion detection system for in-vehicle network by using remote frame, in: *2017 15th Annual Conference on Privacy, Security and Trust*. IEEE, pp. 57–5709, 2017.
20. Mavikumbure, H.S., Cobilean, V., Wickramasinghe, C.S., Varghese, B.J., Carlson, R.B., Rieger, C., Pennington, T., Manic, M., Cy-Phy ADS: Cyber-physical anomaly detection framework for EV charging systems. *IEEE Trans. Transp. Electrif.*, 10, 4, 9904–9915, Dec 2024.
21. Tadepalli, P.S., Pullaguram, D., Alam, M.N., Cyber-resilient strategy for DC microgrids against concurrent FDI and DoS attacks. *IEEE Trans. Ind. Inf.*, 21, 6, 4756–4767, June 2025.
22. Avatefipour, O., Al-Sumaiti, A.S., El-Sherbeeny, A.M., Awwad, E.M., Elmeligy, M.A., Mohamed, M.A., Malik, H., An intelligent secured framework for cyberattack detection in electric vehicles CAN bus using machine learning. *IEEE Access*, 7, 127580–127592, 2019.
23. Alsumaidaie, M.S.I., Alheeti, K.M.A., Alaloosy, A.K., An assessment of ensemble voting approaches, random forest, and decision tree techniques in detecting distributed denial of service (DDoS) attacks. *Iraqi J. Electr. Electron. Eng.*, 20, 1, 16–24, 2023.
24. Zhang, X., Yan, C., Gao, C., Malin, B.A., Chen, Y., Predicting missing values in medical data *via* XGBoost regression. *J. Healthcare Inf. Res.*, 4, 4, 383–394, 2020.
25. Cortes, C., Mohri, M., Storcheus, D., Regularized gradient boosting, in: *Advances in Neural Information Processing Systems*, vol. 32, 2019.

26. Zhang, D. and Gong, Y., The comparison of LightGBM and XGBoost coupling factor analysis and prediagnosis of acute liver failure. *IEEE Access*, 8, 220 990–221 003, 2020.
27. Jafari, S. and Byun, Y.-C., Xgboost-based remaining useful life estimation model with extended Kalman particle filter for lithium-ion batteries. *Sensors*, 22, 23, 9522, 2022.
28. Wang, Y., Yu, B., Yu, H., Xiao, L., Ji, H., Zhao, Y., Automotive cybersecurity vulnerability assessment using the common vulnerability scoring system and Bayesian network model. *IEEE Syst. J.*, 17, 2, 2880–2891, 2022.
29. Riggs, H., Tufail, S., Parvez, I., Tariq, M., Khan, M.A., Amir, A., Vuda, K.V., Sarwat, A.I., Impact, vulnerabilities, and mitigation strategies for cyber-secure critical infrastructure. *Sensors*, 23, 8, 4060, 2023.
30. Kure, H.I., Islam, S., Razzaque, M.A., An integrated cyber security risk management approach for a cyber- physical system. *Appl. Sci.*, 8, 6, 898, 2018.

12

Cyber Resilience in Industry 4.0: Causal and Ethical ML-Based Detection of Cyberattacks in Smart Manufacturing Systems

MD Masud Rana

Computer Science, Lamar University, Beaumont, Texas, USA

Abstract

With the rapid development of Industry 4.0 and IoT technologies, manufacturing systems have been modernized after improving operational efficiency and reducing production costs. The integration of OT and IT core components and infrastructures into the autonomous manufacturing process can increase vulnerabilities and risks. The core business issues identified in this study are (1) limited manufacturing-labeled and key features–based data for cyberattack detection, (2) the need for a fast and reliable, real-time anomaly detection technique, (3) the need to consider, investigate and analyze multiple attack types in the manufacturing process, and (4) choosing appropriate and trustworthy ML methods for this. These problems are important because they protect the manufacturing process from cyber threats, drive fast ML holistic solutions, and assist secure factories that power worldwide production progress.

This study proposes a digital twin simulation platform that analyzes and investigates anomaly detection through different machine learning (ML) models, such as isolation forest, local outlier factor, k-means, random forest, one-class SVM, and autoencoder. Considering different manufacturing features, such as resource usage, computer network traffic, and packet drop rate, and threats like malware, DoS, and replay attacks, the simulation has been conducted and synthesized. Ethical ML is adopted here to ensure the frameworks are safe, reliable, and practical for real-world manufacturing industries. Other simulations considered factors such as temperature, vibration, voltage, packet integrity, malware, data exfiltration,

Email: mrana15@lamar.edu; rana03311998@gmail.com

Rajdeep Chakraborty, Aleem Ali, Amit Paul, Nawaf R. Alharbe and S. Balamurugan (eds.) Causal Artificial Intelligence: Fundamentals and Applications, (273–292) © 2026 Scrivener Publishing LLC

and man-in-the-middle attacks. These types of cyberattacks are important in smart manufacturing because they target the key to automated production processes, where any disruption can lead to quality degradation, downtime, privacy, security, or safety hazards. Finally, the ML performance is assessed in terms of accuracy, precision, recall, F1-score, confusion matrix, and ROC AUC. The isolation forest achieves better performance compared with the other methods. Finally, the complete end-to-end software development process, along with practical recommendations and broader impact, has been discussed from an implementation and usability perspective. Hopefully, these scientific and technical merits will lay the foundation for real-time anomaly detection, databases, results, and scalability that are core parts of Industry 4.0's resilience against cyberattacks.

Keywords: Cybersecurity, smart manufacturing, Industry 4.0, causal AI, machine learning, ethical AI, cyber resilience

12.1 Introduction

In the era of Industry 4.0, automated manufacturing systems integrate cyber-physical systems, IoT technologies, and smart sensors to optimize and effectively produce [1–3]. It can integrate AI, ML, and cyber-physical systems, cybersecurity, digital twins, smart manufacturing, IoT, data analytics, and cloud computing. Smart manufacturing is key in Industry 4.0, as it integrates IoT, sensors, connected devices, and automation to streamline production processes and enhance product quality and efficiency, paving the way for a competitive industrial landscape [4]. It leverages these core technologies to transform traditional centralized manufacturing into highly interconnected, smart, and distributed manufacturing systems.

Unfortunately, this digital transformation has also created a manufacturing ecosystem highly vulnerable to cyberattacks, such as malware, DoS, replay, exfiltration, and MitM attacks [5, 6]. These types of threats can cause manufacturing equipment damage, production downtime, and safety violations [7, 8]. As labeled cyberattack production data is scarce in real industrial environments, there is a growing demand for ethical, lightweight machine learning (ML) methods that reliably detect these types of attacks using operational data [9, 10]. Basically, ethical ML approaches—those that are reliable, transparent, interpretable, and data-efficient—are urgently needed to detect such attacks in real-time using sensor-level operational data [11]. This work proposes a holistic framework using supervised and unsupervised.

ML models to detect cyberattacks in smart manufacturing ecosystems while promoting transparency and trustworthiness. Additionally, the full software development cycle, along with practical tips and its wider impact, has been examined from both an implementation and usability viewpoint.

12.1.1 Research Gap

There has been existing work related to digital twin design, manufacturing data generation, smart manufacturing processes, and industrial and networked control systems [10, 21, 22]. To begin with, Umer *et al.* [23] reviewed ML-based cyber detection in industrial control systems (ICS), while Chevtchenko *et al.* [13] gave a systematic mapping of cyberattack detection in ICS. Liu *et al.* [12] proposed an AMCNN-LSTM model for IIoT cyberattack detection, although such models are resource-intensive. Table 12.1 shows a summary of the literature review. It can be seen that limited work compares unsupervised and supervised ML models across distinct cyberattack types (malware, DoS, replay, exfiltration, and MitM attacks) in smart manufacturing. This paper addresses that gap.

12.1.2 Contributions and Goals

This work proposes a digital twin simulation platform that analyzes and investigates anomaly detection through different machine learning (ML) models, such as isolation forest, local outlier factor, k-means, random forest, one-class SVM, and autoencoder. Considering different manufacturing features such as resource usage, computer network traffic, and packet drop rate, and threats like malware, DoS, and replay attacks, the simulation has been conducted and synthesized. Ethical ML is adopted here to ensure the frameworks are safe, reliable, and practical for real-world manufacturing industries. Other simulations considered factors such as temperature, vibration, voltage, packet integrity, malware, data exfiltration, and man-in-the-middle attacks. These types of cyberattacks are important in smart manufacturing because they target the key to automated production processes, where any disruption can lead to quality degradation, downtime, privacy, security, or safety hazards. The ML performance is assessed in terms of accuracy, precision, recall, F1-score, confusion matrix, and ROC AUC. The isolation forest achieves better performance compared with the other methods. Moreover, the full software development lifecycle has been explored with practical tips, focusing on how it's built and how easy it is to use, along with its broader impact.

Table 12.1 Literature review: Ethical ML-based detection of cyberattacks in smart manufacturing systems.

ML model	Attack type	Findings
AMCNN-LSTM [12]	Outliers	Effective without labeled data
One-Class SVM [13]	Unknown patterns	Kernel-dependent anomaly detection
Autoencoder [14]	Sensor faults	Flags subtle deviations *via* reconstruction error
Random Forest [15]	Malware	High accuracy with labeled network data
Hybrid (RF + SVM) [16]	DoS	Improved detection performance *via* ensemble
LOF, RF, K-Means [17, 18]	DoS, MitM	Supervised baseline outperforms unsupervised
Deep Ensemble [19, 20]	Malware	Combines AE + RF for robustness
Hybrid ML	Malware, DoS, Replay, MitM, Exfiltration	Multi-model ML using manufacturing sensor data

12.2 Proposed Methodology and Algorithm

The dataset is generated to represent real-time sensor data from manufacturing machines, including production features like temperature, pressure, and vibration. There are 651 sample data points. The simulation flow diagram is described as follows. After collecting data, ML-based classification (supervised and unsupervised) is applied. Based on the threshold value, the attack identification, such as malware, replay, and DoS, is determined, and the ethical decision logging with performance is reported. Figure 12.1 shows the proposed algorithm.

Algorithm 12.1 shows the proposal algorithm. Each ML model then predicts anomalies, and their outputs are evaluated using metrics such as accuracy, precision, recall, and ROC AUC to measure how effectively each can detect different cyberattack types.

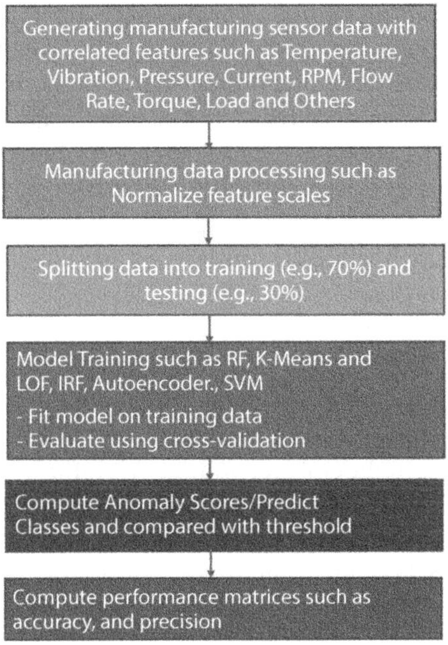

Figure 12.1 Flow diagram of the proposed method.

Algorithm 12.1 Ethical ML-based detection of cyberattacks in smart manufacturing systems.

1: Generate manufacturing sensor data with injected attacks such as malware, DoS, replay, exfiltration, and MitM attacks.
2: Apply standard scaling to selected features.
3: Train isolation forest, local outlier factor, k-means, random forest, one-class SVM, and autoencoder models
4: Predict anomalies using each model
5: Compute predicted error for autoencoder and threshold for attack detection.
6: Evaluate performance matrices such as accuracy, precision, recall, F1, and ROC AUC.

12.3 Simulation Results and Discussions

The dataset in Table 12.2 is generated to represent real-time sensor data from manufacturing machines, including production features like temperature, pressure, and vibration. There are 651 sample data points, and some of them are mentioned here. The malware, replay, and DoS are simulated by injecting anomalies, time delays, and abnormalities.

The performance in Table 12.3 demonstrates random forest as the strongest model, achieving perfect recall (1.000) and high ROC AUC (0.917) across all cyberattacks, showing reliable detection when labeled data is available. LOF, while unsupervised and label-free, performs poorly on malware (precision: 0.000), emphasizing the trade-off between detection power and deployment feasibility in ethically sensitive environments.

The ROC curve is described in Figure 12.2.

It can be seen that RF provides better results compared with K-means and LOF.

For the second simulation, the dataset in Table 12.4 is generated to represent real-time sensor data from manufacturing machines, including production features like temperature, voltage, vibration, latency, and packet integrity. There are 651 sample datapoints, and some of them are mentioned here. The malware, exfiltration, and MitM are simulated by injecting specific abnormal patterns into these sensor streams.

The simulation results are in Tables 12.5 and 12.6. It can be seen that IF provides better performance in terms of precision, recall, and F1-score compared with the SVM and AE.

The IF earned the highest accuracy of 0.991 and perfect recall (1.00) for MitM cyberattacks, making it the best dependable option for situations where missing an intrusion carries severe operational or ethical risks. Although AE underperformed in precision for malware (0.103), its higher recall in MitM (0.82) suggests it excels in detecting complex temporal anomalies—critical for safeguarding vulnerable manufacturing ecosystems.

The IF model earned perfect recall (100%) and high precision (92.6%) in detecting MitM attacks, as described by 50 true positives and zero false negatives, indicating strong sensitivity to anomalies in network latency and packet integrity. In contrast, the malware detection performance shows low recall (26%) and precision (76.5%) due to 37 missed attacks and only 13 correct detections, exhibiting challenges in identifying subtle temperature and voltage shifts amidst normal manufacturing variability. Additionally, the autoencoder took 6.74 seconds due to deep neural network training, while IF completed in 0.19 seconds and one-class SVM in 0.01 seconds, showing major differences in computational complexity.

Table 12.2 Manufacturing samples across malware, replay, and DoS.

Temperature	Pressure	Vibration	Network traffic	CPU usage	Packet drop rate	Attack type
60.993	5.463	0.370	107.784	26.624	1.114	Normal
59.723	5.955	0.346	94.488	29.277	1.194	Normal
61.295	4.301	0.303	91.818	26.038	0.934	Normal
63.046	5.281	0.268	99.966	28.460	0.878	Normal
59.532	4.675	0.335	98.298	20.532	0.783	Normal
59.532	4.756	0.320	95.468	31.066	0.835	Normal
63.158	4.704	0.345	106.964	30.006	1.590	Normal
61.535	4.568	0.332	109.553	25.915	1.249	Normal
59.061	5.024	0.352	100.884	33.296	0.730	Normal
61.085	4.585	0.273	114.775	34.688	0.736	Normal
–						
59.277	4.314	0.315	166.840	80.926	2.302	Malware
62.419	4.645	0.393	142.616	82.127	2.149	Malware
63.759	4.856	0.432	91.860	81.111	2.319	Malware

(Continued)

Table 12.2 Manufacturing samples across malware, replay, and DoS. (*Continued*)

Temperature	Pressure	Vibration	Network traffic	CPU usage	Packet drop rate	Attack type
70.663	4.608	0.404	142.504	86.394	2.529	Malware
66.670	5.867	0.314	129.229	75.238	2.184	Malware
60.994	4.572	0.368	117.374	76.615	2.074	Malware
66.458	4.722	0.285	125.251	76.137	1.559	Malware
60.358	5.102	0.379	152.188	84.151	1.644	Malware
68.248	4.399	0.373	176.573	84.502	2.593	Malware
63.587	4.802	0.257	156.264	82.256	2.718	Malware
–						
60.677	4.740	0.325	105.224	35.903	8.937	Replay
58.124	4.830	0.328	97.449	26.863	6.864	Replay
60.433	5.214	0.310	108.723	30.226	10.693	Replay
57.948	5.039	0.295	104.394	30.256	15.023	Replay
62.202	4.703	0.322	80.706	27.491	6.320	Replay
62.123	4.917	0.173	130.530	23.138	9.935	Replay

(*Continued*)

Table 12.2 Manufacturing samples across malware, replay, and DoS. (*Continued*)

Temperature	Pressure	Vibration	Network traffic	CPU usage	Packet drop rate	Attack type
61.064	5.039	0.334	120.888	31.615	11.281	Replay
60.723	3.936	0.306	106.237	29.695	10.246	Replay
63.522	5.229	0.289	110.188	32.501	9.774	Replay
59.999	4.510	0.402	98.283	27.332	7.402	Replay
–						
65.880	4.663	0.507	270.704	85.834	17.377	DoS
66.404	4.720	0.545	316.455	85.199	22.468	DoS
80.249	4.678	0.308	362.642	86.348	26.480	DoS
70.003	4.170	0.316	277.589	90.478	14.464	DoS
73.911	4.560	0.386	265.387	87.322	18.172	DoS
66.046	4.646	0.431	201.554	91.541	19.244	DoS
66.101	4.503	0.348	305.172	90.104	13.021	DoS
75.410	3.665	0.535	402.104	84.094	22.957	DoS
63.252	4.564	0.442	313.868	91.965	16.380	DoS
67.924	5.385	0.404	298.886	92.432	19.023	DoS

Table 12.3 Performance comparison on malware, replay, and DoS detection.

ML model	Attack	Accuracy	Precision	Recall	F1-score	ROC AUC
LOF	Malware	0.697	0.000	0.000	0.000	0.378
	Replay	0.790	0.205	0.600	0.305	0.703
	DoS	0.738	0.091	0.267	0.136	0.522
K-means	Malware	0.856	0.333	0.867	0.481	0.861
	Replay	0.826	0.256	0.667	0.370	0.753
	DoS	0.836	0.282	0.733	0.407	0.789
Random forest	Malware	0.846	0.333	1.000	0.500	0.917
	Replay	0.846	0.333	1.000	0.500	0.917
	DoS	0.846	0.333	1.000	0.500	0.917

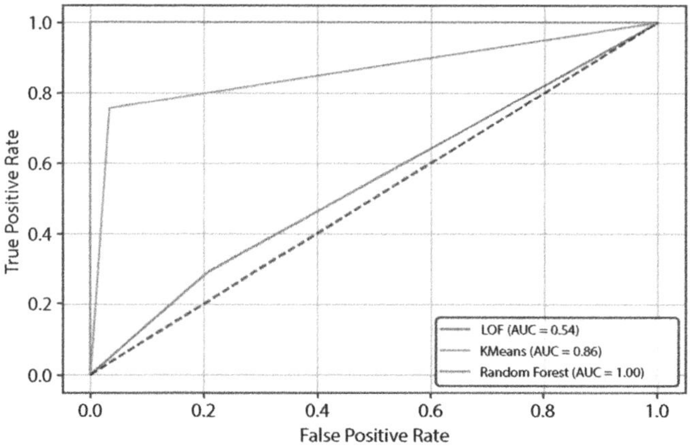

Figure 12.2 ROC curves for cyber attack detection.

Table 12.4 Manufacturing sensor data for isolation forest (IF), one-class SVM, and autoencoder (AE).

machine_id	robot_temp	Voltage	Vibration	Latency	Integrity	attack_type	enc_label	Binary	IF	SVM	AE
M2	69.99	460.51	0.0306	2.17	0.9932	normal	0	0	0	0	0
M3	77.34	507.20	0.0242	1.67	0.9726	normal	0	0	0	0	0
M2	81.78	469.80	0.0157	1.94	1.0013	normal	0	0	0	0	0
M3	82.17	484.47	0.0377	2.63	0.9934	normal	0	0	0	0	0
M2	78.09	460.58	0.0372	2.00	0.9841	normal	0	0	0	0	0
M3	73.26	465.93	0.0131	2.06	0.9850	normal	0	0	0	0	0
M2	68.28	470.50	0.0302	2.16	0.9579	normal	0	0	0	0	0
M1	68.19	517.61	0.0147	3.35	0.9798	normal	0	0	0	0	1
M3	77.54	466.46	0.0205	1.80	0.9645	normal	0	0	0	0	0
M2	80.68	503.80	0.0113	1.48	0.9576	normal	0	0	0	0	0
M1	75.87	477.75	0.0200	0.96	1.0016	normal	0	0	0	0	0
M2	79.98	474.21	-0.0031	1.48	1.0010	normal	0	0	0	0	0
M1	74.40	503.88	0.0166	2.17	0.9863	normal	0	0	0	0	0

(Continued)

Table 12.4 Manufacturing sensor data for isolation forest (IF), one-class SVM, and autoencoder (AE). *(Continued)*

machine_id	robot_temp	Voltage	Vibration	Latency	Integrity	attack_type	enc_label	Binary	IF	SVM	AE
M3	69.48	478.97	0.0369	1.14	0.9708	normal	0	0	0	0	1
M1	70.54	471.08	0.0276	2.36	0.9961	normal	0	0	0	0	0
M3	73.90	472.32	0.0211	2.51	0.9710	normal	0	0	0	0	0
M3	65.48	499.62	0.0116	2.00	1.0274	normal	0	0	0	0	1
M1	65.93	474.22	0.0370	2.43	0.9977	normal	0	0	0	0	0
M3	72.93	462.20	0.0153	2.02	0.9498	normal	0	0	0	0	0
M1	72.53	495.18	0.0279	2.47	1.0125	normal	0	0	0	0	0
M3	81.83	477.12	0.0357	2.41	0.9496	normal	0	0	0	0	1
M1	75.50	458.94	0.0168	2.44	0.9670	normal	0	0	0	0	0
M3	82.76	512.30	-0.0019	2.52	0.9755	normal	0	0	0	0	0
M2	85.34	462.23	0.0148	2.22	0.9900	normal	0	0	0	0	0
M2	73.59	484.02	0.0225	2.32	0.9687	normal	0	0	0	0	0
M3	75.94	503.21	-0.0102	2.53	0.9978	normal	0	0	0	1	0

(Continued)

Table 12.4 Manufacturing sensor data for isolation forest (IF), one-class SVM, and autoencoder (AE). (*Continued*)

machine_id	robot_temp	Voltage	Vibration	Latency	Integrity	attack_type	enc_label	Binary	IF	SVM	AE
M2	77.87	469.29	0.0329	2.59	0.9666	normal	0	0	0	0	1
M2	78.11	512.22	0.0223	2.19	0.9652	normal	0	0	0	0	0
M1	76.03	475.69	0.0249	1.81	0.9924	normal	0	0	0	0	0
M3	78.75	453.85	0.0127	2.65	0.9853	normal	0	0	0	0	0
M2	71.59	489.43	0.0223	1.56	0.9539	normal	0	0	0	0	0
M1	79.28	483.62	0.0366	2.70	0.9790	normal	0	0	0	0	0
M2	73.69	494.35	0.0110	1.79	0.9695	normal	0	0	0	0	0
M2	79.14	469.82	0.0392	2.07	1.0070	normal	0	0	0	0	0
M2	72.15	477.96	0.0236	3.20	0.9968	normal	0	0	0	0	0
M1	79.04	501.84	0.0233	2.54	0.9717	normal	0	0	0	0	0
M2	74.68	466.05	0.0290	1.94	0.9922	normal	0	0	0	0	0

Table 12.5 MIF, SVM, and AE performance across malware, exfiltration, and MitM.

Model	Attack	Accuracy	Precision	Recall	F1-score	ROC AUC
Isolation forest	Malware	0.918	0.667	0.20	0.308	0.595
One-class svm	Malware	0.904	0.444	0.24	0.312	0.605
Autoencoder	Malware	0.867	0.103	0.06	0.076	0.504
Isolation forest	Exfiltration	0.960	0.868	0.66	0.750	0.825
One-class svm	Exfiltration	0.905	0.464	0.26	0.333	0.615
Autoencoder	Exfiltration	0.913	0.519	0.56	0.538	0.754
Isolation forest	MitM	0.991	0.909	1.00	0.952	0.995
One-class svm	MitM	0.924	0.605	0.46	0.523	0.715
Autoencoder	MitM	0.936	0.612	0.82	0.701	0.884

Table 12.6 Confusion matrices for isolation forest across attack types.

Attack type	TN	FP	FN	TP
Malware	496	4	37	13
Exfiltration	496	4	19	31
MitM	496	4	0	50

12.4 End-to-End Software Development Life Cycle

The software development process starts with defining the problems and requirements for detecting cyberattacks in smart manufacturing [24, 25]. It focuses on cyber threats such as malware, DoS, and MitM attacks [26].

We generate and preprocess industrial sensor data to mirror real-world distributions and interactions. This supports strong ML model training without supervision using Isolation Forest, one-class SVM, and autoencoders. For model evaluation, we use key detailed metrics and confusion matrix analysis. After that, we deploy the framework as a modular pipeline that is ready for real-time integration. Continuous monitoring, ethical compliance, and retraining help maintain long-term resilience, adaptability, and reliable ML deployment in industrial settings. In summary, the flow is Problem Definition → Data Generation/Collection → ML Model Training → ML Model Evaluation → Deployment → Monitoring → Ethical Compliance —all tailored to smart manufacturing.

12.5 Action Recommendations

There are some recommendations so that the manufacturing system can be smart.

1. Test models in pilot industrial setups and improve them based on actual data.
2. Use rule-based firewalls or IDS for added security [27].
3. Implement SHAP (SHapley Additive exPlanations) or LIME (Local Interpretable Model-agnostic Explanations) to clarify model decisions [28].
4. Adjust models for embedded devices in factory and automation settings.
5. Model aggregation and verification through distributed ML.

12.6 Intellectual Merit and Broader Impacts

This research focuses on combining cybersecurity-aware ML models with digital manufacturing environments, one such malware comparisons is given in Figure 12.3. It aims at detecting anomalies using unsupervised and semi-supervised ML on simulated industrial sensor data. By addressing real-world attack scenarios such as malware injection, data exfiltration, and MitM attacks, the proposed framework provides adaptable, smart, and scalable protection mechanisms. These support safe collaboration and connectivity across the value chain.

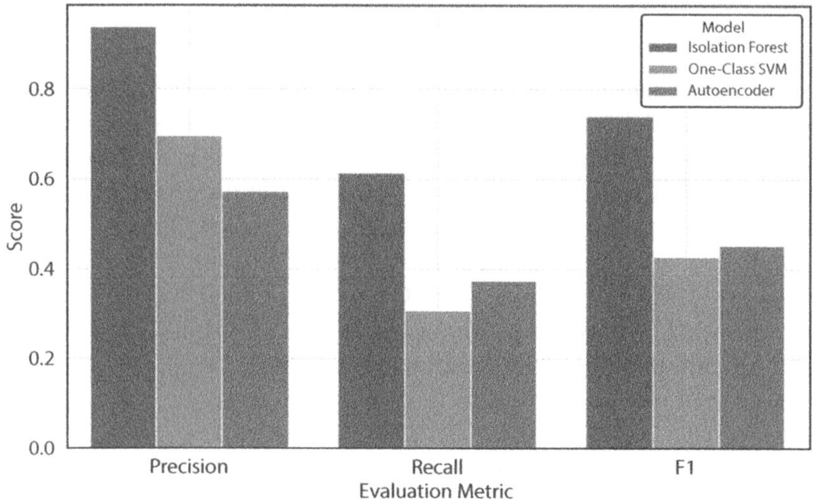

Figure 12.3 Performance comparison for malware, exfiltration, and MitM attacks.

The framework encourages reproducibility, modular integration, and future extensions for distributed edge learning and secure federated analytics. This aligns with the industry's mission to support the integration of scalable, ethical, and secure manufacturing systems.

12.7 Conclusions

This study proposes a digital twin simulation platform that analyzes and investigates anomaly detection through different ML frameworks such as isolation forest, local outlier factor, k-means, random forest, and one-class SVM, and Autoencoder. The ML performance is assessed in terms of accuracy, precision, recall, F1-score, confusion matrix, and ROC AUC. The isolation forest achieves better performance compared with the other methods. Hopefully, these scientific and technical merits will lay the foundation for real-time anomaly detection, databases, results, and scalability that are core parts of resilience Industry 4.0 against cyberattacks. The entire software development framework, along with practical tips and its wider impact, has been examined from the viewpoints of implementation and usability. Scaling these ML models for real-time manufacturing deployment in resource-constrained industrial IoT settings will also be a priority to ensure practical usability.

AI disclosure statement: The author acknowledges the use of AI-based tools for minor language editing or grammatical correction. However, all intellectual contributions, analyses, and conclusions presented in this chapter are entirely the author's own.

References

1. Andronie, M., Lăzăroiu, G., Stefănescu, R., Ută, C., Dijmărescu, I., Sustainable, smart, and sensing technologies for cyber-physical manufacturing systems: A systematic literature review. *Sustainability*, 13, 10, 5495, 2021.
2. Ryalat, M., ElMoaqet, H., AlFaouri, M., Design of a smart factory based on cyber-physical systems and internet of things towards industry 4.0. *Appl. Sci.*, 13, 4, 2156, 2023.
3. Xu, H., Yu, W., Griffith, D., Golmie, N., A survey on industrial internet of things: A cyber-physical systems perspective. *IEEE Access*, 6, 78 238–78 259, 2018.
4. Hammad, M., Jillani, R.M., Ullah, S., Namoun, A., Tufail, A., Kim, K.-H., Shah, H., Security framework for network-based manufacturing systems with personalized customization: An industry 4.0 approach. *Sensors*, 23, 17, 7555, 2023.
5. Tsiknas, K., Taketzis, D., Demertzis, K., Skianis, C., Cyber threats to industrial IoT: A survey on attacks and countermeasures. *IoT*, 2, 1, 163–186, 2021.
6. Stellios, I., Kotzanikolaou, P., Psarakis, M., Alcaraz, C., Lopez, J., A survey of IoT-enabled cyberattacks: Assessing attack paths to critical infrastructures and services. *IEEE Commun. Surv. Tutorials*, 20, 4, 3453–3495, 2018.
7. Bourassa, D., Gauthier, F., Abdul-Nour, G., Equipment failures and their contribution to industrial incidents and accidents in the manufacturing industry. *Int. J. Occup. Saf. Ergon.*, 22, 1, 131–141, 2016.
8. Ani, U.P.D., He, H., Tiwari, A., Review of cybersecurity issues in industrial critical infrastructure: Manufacturing in perspective. *J. Cyber Secur. Technol.*, 1, 1, 32–74, 2017.
9. Ajala, O.A., Okoye, C.C., Ofodile, O.C., Arinze, C.A., Daraojimba, O.D., *et al.*, Review of AI and machine learning applications to predict and thwart cyber-attacks in real-time. *Magna Sci. Adv. Res. Rev.*, 10, 1, 312–320, 2024.
10. Yu, J., Shvetsov, A.V., Alsamhi, S.H., Leveraging machine learning for cybersecurity resilience in industry 4.0: Challenges and future directions. *IEEE Access*, 2024.
11. Rasheed, K., Qayyum, A., Ghaly, M., Al-Fuqaha, A., Razi, A., Qadir, J., Explainable, trustworthy, and ethical machine learning for healthcare: A survey. *Comput. Biol. Med.*, 149, 106043, 2022.

12. Liu, Y., Garg, S., Nie, J., Zhang, Y., Xiong, Z., Kang, J., Hossain, M.S., Deep anomaly detection for time-series data in industrial IoT: A communication-efficient on-device federated learning approach. *IEEE Internet Things J.*, 8, 8, 6348–6358, 2020.
13. Chevtchenko, S.F., Rocha, E.D.S., Dos Santos, M.C.M., Mota, R.L., Vieira, D.M., De Andrade, E.C., De Araújo, D.R.B., Anomaly detection in industrial machinery using IoT devices and machine learning: A systematic mapping. *IEEE Access*, 11, 128 288–128 305, 2023.
14. Littek, A.R.G., Explainable anomaly detection in surveillance videos: Autoencoder-based reconstruction and error map visualization, 2024.
15. Shaukat, S.U., Optimum parameter machine learning classification and prediction of internet of things (IoT) malwares using static malware analysis techniques, Master's thesis, University of Salford (United Kingdom), 2018.
16. Hossain, M.A. and Islam, M.S., Enhancing DDoS attack detection with hybrid feature selection and ensemble- based classifier: A promising solution for robust cybersecurity. *Meas.: Sens.*, 32, 101037, 2024.
17. Al-Abadi, A.A.J., Mohamed, M.B., Fakhfakh, A., Enhanced random forest classifier with K-means clustering (ERF-KMC) for detecting and preventing distributed-denial-of-service and man-in-the-middle attacks in internet-of-medical-things networks. *Computers*, 12, 12, 262, 2023.
18. Sun, Z., Yang, H., Liu, K., Yin, Z., Li, Z., Xu, W., Recent advances in LoRa: A comprehensive survey. *ACM Trans. Sens. Netw.*, 18, 4, 1–44, 2022.
19. Hossain, M.A., Haque, M.A., Ahmad, S., Abdeljaber, H.A., Eljialy, A., Alanazi, A., Sonal, D., Chaudhary, K., Nazeer, J., AI-enabled approach for enhancing obfuscated malware detection: A hybrid ensemble learning with combined feature selection techniques. *Int. J. Syst. Assur. Eng. Manag.*, 1–19, 2024.
20. Alsharif, E. and Alharby, M., An ensemble machine learning approach for detecting and classifying malware attacks on mobile devices. *Arab. J. Sci. Eng.*, 1–17, 2025.
21. Liu, Q., Leng, J., Yan, D., Zhang, D., Wei, L., Yu, A., Zhao, R., Zhang, H., Chen, X., Digital twin-based designing of the configuration, motion, control, and optimization model of a flow-type smart manufacturing system. *J. Manuf. Syst.*, 58, 52–64, 2021.
22. Tao, F., Qi, Q., Wang, L., Nee, A., Digital twins and cyber-physical systems toward smart manufacturing and industry 4.0: Correlation and comparison. *Engineering*, 5, 4, 653–661, 2019.
23. Umer, M.A., Junejo, K.N., Jilani, M.T., Mathur, A.P., Machine learning for intrusion detection in industrial control systems: Applications, challenges, and recommendations. *Int. J. Crit. Infrastruct. Prot.*, 38, 100516, 2022.
24. Lorenzoni, G., Alencar, P., Nascimento, N., Cowan, D., Machine learning model development from a software engineering perspective: A systematic literature review, arXiv preprint arXiv:2102.07574, 2021.

25. Assres, G., Bhandari, G., Shalaginov, A., Gronli, T.-M., Ghinea, G., State-of-the-art and challenges of engineering ML-enabled software systems in the deep learning era. *ACM Comput. Surv.*, 57, 10, 1–35, 2025.
26. Ghoshal, A., Intrusion detection in industrial OT environment by combination of different machine learning techniques, Ph.D. dissertation, Dublin, National College of Ireland, 2022.
27. Nalepa, G.J. and Ligeza, A., Designing reliable web security systems using rule-based systems approach, in: *International Atlantic Web Intelligence Conference*, Springer, pp. 124–133, 2003.
28. Kalusivalingam, A.K., Sharma, A., Patel, N., Singh, V., Leveraging SHAP and LIME for enhanced explainability in AI-driven diagnostic systems. *Int. J. AI ML*, 2, 3, 2021.

13

Explainable Privacy-Preserving Federated LLM Fine-Tuning on Distributed Edge Healthcare Infrastructure

Amit Chakraborty[1*], Chirantana Mallick[1], Saptarshi Das[1], Madhvi Chakraborty[2] and Abhijnan Chakraborty[3]

[1]JISIASR, Kolkata, West Bengal, India
[2]MS Program, BITS, Pilani, Rajasthan, India
[3]MAKAUT, Kolkata, West Bengal, India

Abstract
Increasing the use of large language models (LLMs) in healthcare has presented not only large opportunities but also severe challenges, such as data privacy, high infrastructure requirements, and the complexity of model training. The conventional centralized training methods involve the accumulation of large clinical data in a centralized server, which would expose sensitive patient data, and this is against data protection laws. Also, training LLMs requires the computational resources that are prohibitively expensive, which are not accessible to many healthcare organizations. Federated learning is a promising technology since it allows training a model jointly on distributed healthcare devices and institutions without transferring raw patient information. This paradigm enables the local updates of the local LLMs in individual machines or hospital systems, and then the aggregate improvements are made centrally, and this is done without compromising patient confidentiality. Through a combination of federated learning and TinyML techniques, which train models in a resource-constrained environment like edge medical devices, it is possible to fine-tune LLMs in a distributed, privacy-preserving way. This will minimize the use of a centralized infrastructure, allow parallel training on many nodes, and reduce the computational load, thus providing advanced LLMs to healthcare organizations that were previously unable to afford them. In this chapter, we examine how federated learning and TinyML can be used technically to fine-tune LLMs on healthcare applications. We present

**Corresponding author*: Amit13.ons@gmail.com

Rajdeep Chakraborty, Aleem Ali, Amit Paul, Nawaf R. Alharbe and S. Balamurugan (eds.) Causal Artificial Intelligence: Fundamentals and Applications, (293–322) © 2026 Scrivener Publishing LLC

major considerations such as model partitioning, communication optimization, and the heterogeneity of devices, practical examples, and experimental findings, which prove feasibility and performance advantages. We find that a framework like that would make it possible to build privacy-preserving, contextually aware LLMs optimized for distributed healthcare systems and handle the issues of scalability, data security, and computational constraints.

Keywords: Federated learning, data minimization, HIPAA-compliant, instruction tuning, stochastic gradient descent, centralized machine learning

13.1 Introduction

Large language models, or LLMs, have emerged as a highly effective and versatile means of multiple natural language processing activities such as generation, summarization, and translation. These models are trained on millions of documents found on the World Wide Web and therefore can achieve a wide variety of learning. Nonetheless, concerns arise when applying the pre-trained LLMs to applications that deal with sensitive and private information, including health data, financial data, or some sensitive business data. One limitation of the traditional machine learning techniques is that data is normally pooled in one place for use in model training. While this approach may be helpful when developing models, the general centralization of large amounts of data can be highly dangerous in terms of data privacy and protection. Confidential information that patients or clients provide can at times be at risk of hacking, break-ins, and other misuses. In addition, compliance regulations like those of HIPAA in health sciences & GDPR in the EU impose severe limitations on the use of individual information. These regulations add more layers of challenges when using basic kinds of machine learning algorithms due to the need to protect data.

In response to these challenges, federated learning provides the best solution. Different from centralized learning, where the data is transferred to the model, in federated learning, the model is transferred to the data. This decentralized regime allows shared training model acquisition across the devices or centers while protecting data privacy. In a federated learning environment, the different participants, like different hospitals or financial institutions, build a local model on their data. The new local parameters are then sent securely to a central server, and the integrated global parameters are sent back to all participants. This process enables shared learning as a group while still maintaining the preventive security of a disparate set of information. It also concerns data minimization principles, as federated learning does not require data sharing, and the raw data can be kept within a specific organization. It also reduces the associated risks of data leakage and unauthorized access and keeps the data owner firmly in charge of their data, regardless of the method of access used. Also, federated learning is useful to maintain the requirements of data privacy regulations by protecting and processing data appropriately. The distributed approach could be used in the healthcare domain to fine-tune LLMs for such tasks as diagnosis, drug recommendations, and searching for information about a certain patient. For example, a hospital may have a large collection of clinical notes, research papers, and patients' records. In this way, by seemingly adapting an LLM on this private data by means of federated learning, the hospital can develop a strong assistant for knowledge acquisition and decision-making. The model is capable of ramping up basic medical knowledge, recognizing informative parts, and formulating brief, effective syntheses of intricate cases. This can greatly enhance the effectiveness of considering human resources in health care solutions. In addition, federated learning enables healthcare organizations to be HIPAA compliant. The disclosure of patients' records is also limited by confining access to the data to the hospital's Local Area Network. Moreover, federated learning can foster multiple hospitals cooperating in learning without infringing on patients' privacy. This study shows that instead of exchanging large datasets that may contain sensitive patient information and hence may violate patient data protection laws, hospitals have everyone update their models to improve the performance of their AI models.

13.2 Literature Review and Gap Identification

The study conducted by Thirunavukarasu *et al.* [1] brings up the applicability of today's popular LLMs like ChatGPT in the healthcare context. It stresses the potential of the systems to cope with free-text queries and the effectiveness and potential usefulness of employing such systems in clinical, educational, and research practices. However, it may also address the weaknesses of LLMs and the importance of the appropriate use of such tools. There can be a space when federated fine-tuning of LLMs can help fill the lack of data and privacy considerations. Therefore, in the proposed approach, we use federated learning to train or update LLMs with local and private healthcare data from private hospitals. This can be particularly useful in health facilities where the transfer of a patient's information from one institution to another is highly prohibited. A final weakness that has not been described but can be seen if L2 data is used extensively is potential bias in LLMs. Thus, federated learning that merges models trained on a variety of samples and with fair representation of the population can reduce bias and increase the objectivity of LLM-supported healthcare applications. This is done using data obtained from more than one healthcare institution because one can help in minimizing biases that might be present in the other.

The study conducted by Chen *et al.* [2] discusses the use of the federated learning method to update LLMs in healthcare while maintaining data privacy. This method helps avoid privacy issues since patients' data remain stored at individual hospital levels. However, several issues, such as communication overhead, data heterogeneity, and security issues, are still problems in WoT. Although there are leaps in addressing the data privacy and sharing issues by federated fine-tuning, there's more research that can be done to enhance the communication efficiency, data variability, and security solutions being implemented.

Zhang *et al.* [3] examine instruction tuning, a method used to improve LLM effectiveness due to the delivery of precise instructions. Although there are advantages of this method, such as increased precision and diverse data availability, there are disadvantages that include lowered generalizability measures and dependence upon closed APIs or data sharing. These issues can be resolved using federated learning, a privacy preservation technique. As one of the efficient strategies to achieve such goals, federated learning can provide perspectives on improving privacy, generalization, and breaking dependence on closed APIs when training on local data in the future of LLM development.

13.3 Prerequisites

13.3.1 Federated Learning

A one-of-its-kind concept in machine learning, federated learning can be seen as the answer to the perennial issue of training strong models with consideration of data constraints. Here, the training process is shifted to the data where the model needs to go and not the other way round. This profound approach helps many clients to train the joint model, but they do not share the raw data of each other [4]. The process starts by having the core server store the initial global model. This model is then communicated to the participating clients. Every client gets a copy of the global model and then updates it with a local dataset unique to that client.

The last local phase of training involves adjusting some values of the model, such as a process of stochastic gradient descent. The new model, which is specific to the data distribution of the client, is then stored back in the central server. After all the clients have sent the updated models to the server, the server then applies the aggregation algorithms to form a new superior global model. One of the basic techniques of aggregation is federated averaging, for which the server calculates a weighted mean of the received updates of the model [5]. This aggregated model is then broadcast to all the clients, therefore starting the next round of training. At a high level, federated learning makes it possible to develop strong models that harness the intelligence possessed by data sets that are spread out across various networks without compromising privacy. This approach is very important when dealing with areas such as health care and finance, as well as the IoT areas, due to security constraints that prevent the sharing of data [6].

The primary benefits of federated learning over additional conventional centralized machine learning are the following: First of all, competence considerably improves the data privacy by reducing the share of information with extraneous individuals. This advantage is due to the fact that any data that is processed and maintained within a client's own environment is much less likely to be exposed to breaches and other forms of unauthorized access. Secondly, federated learning can increase model accuracy due to a larger dataset with high variability of data partition among the clients. In this way, the information, with the help of different clients, can be collected, and the model acquires more stable and general patterns. Third, we see that federated learning can be implemented on resource-poor devices like mobile phones and IoT [7] sensors since it does not need much inter-device communication and processing. Nevertheless, there are some issues that federated learning has to solve to be implemented effectively. One of the important issues arises from the fact that communication needs to happen between the central server and numerous clients. To tackle this problem, some of the strategies that can be used include model compression and selective client participation [8]. The heterogeneity of client data is another limitation since the effect may compromise convergence and efficiency in federated learning. In order to prevent this, certain approaches such as personalized FL and adaptive aggregation can be implemented. Apparently, federated learning is a promising solution for training machine learning models in privacy-concerned scenarios. Therefore, federated learning allows collaboration in the learning process and reduces the risk while training the models. Thus, in the future, there is potential for developing new methods to address the problems and expand the concept of federated learning [9].

In federated learning, the convergence is when the global model remains static; it is beneficial to add no more basic updates at each site. This process can be generally measured by coefficients, such as a model's accuracy or loss function. If the convergence criteria, like a certain threshold or some maximum number of inter-company communication rounds, are achieved, the FL process is said to be complete. Otherwise, the process goes through the system; communication and local training are done again [10].

Federated learning is a distributed machine learning paradigm, formulated as a solution for the challenges of data privacy and regulations. It is atypical that in conventional machine learning methods, large datasets should be centralized; federated learning ensures that models may be trained on data distributed among several devices or servers without their data privacy being violated. Instead of moving such sensitive data to a central location for training, federated learning brings the model to the data. The key operations provide for running distributed jobs at the locations where the training data is located, whereby the model trains on local datasets without exposing the raw data to external parties. The process ensures very high data privacy and data use compliance with regulations like GDPR and HIPAA. Important steps in the federated learning process include the following: First, a global model is initialized and shared with all participating nodes. Then, each node trains a local model initialized using its data. Then, the trained models are sent back to a central server, where the contribution of each transmission is aggregated to improve the global model. Importantly, the central server cannot access the individual datasets; therefore, data privacy is maintained. The model is shared at the aggregated level across all the nodes, which then update their local models in the training loop for further iterations. This iterative approach empowers the global model to learn from the different data residing at various locations, which eventually leads to better performance and generalization of the model. In other words, federated learning paves the way forward for the training of machine learning models in privacy-sensitive environments. Therefore, with the decentralization of the training process and the confidentiality of data, federated learning unlocks the potential of big data while observing the same principles and provisions of the regulatory laws on data protection [11].

13.3.2 Fine-Tuning of LLMs

Parameter-efficient fine-tuning (PEFT) techniques are designed to reduce the number of trainable parameters for training Large Language Models (LLMs). It is essential for tackling the LLMs' large size and computational cost problem. PEFT methods allow the training time as well as computational resources needed to reach a high training accuracy to be greatly reduced by focusing on very specific layers or parameters in the network that are most relevant to the downstream task. Adapter tuning is one of the most popular PEFT techniques, where small trainable modules are inserted into the LLM's architecture. By being trained on specific tasks, these adapters can learn efficiently to fine-tune without reinventing the wheel with respect to the parameters of the original model. Another technique that is very effective is prompt tuning (optimizing LLM instructions or prompts). Through careful crafting of prompts, we can influence the LLM's behavior without the need for extensive fine-tuning. Prefix tuning is also a method where only a handful of parameters that we call prefixes are trained to be prepended to the input token [12]. They can be optimized naively to steer LLM's gaze to interesting parts of the input. We can meanwhile reduce the computational burden of fine-tuning LLMs while keeping high accuracy by leveraging PEFT techniques. This allows organizations to scale LLMs faster and for less cost, thereby enabling the rapid development of AI-powered applications [13].

13.4 Privacy Enhancement Technique

Consequently, federated learning is a powerful technique that aims at data privacy, given that very little data is actually shared. Traditional machine learning differs from federated learning in that, rather than taking the data to the model, the model is taken to the data. This means distributed data is secure because it only resides in the specific devices or organizations, not allowing any external transference, thus minimizing chances of data invasion and scams. Due to restricting information exposure to the local devices only, federated learning offers an optimal solution to numerous privacy-invasion attacks. A certain type of adversarial attack, known as a membership inference attack, which seeks to determine whether a particular record was used to train the model, is heavily constrained in federated learning. Since the model is trained locally, it becomes virtually impossible for an adversary to guess the existence of specific instances in the training set [14]. Likewise, when attacking attribute inference, where the objective is to use a trained model to infer sensitive information about individuals, the effectiveness is also low. However, federated learning with the incorporation of decentralized model training restricts the amount of data that can be derived by inspecting model parameters. Furthermore, from the point of view of the attacker, data reconstruction attacks that try to reconstruct the original datasets from the model's outputs are less effective in federated learning. This work shows that federated learning, which trains the model on distributed and diverse data sets, hinders an adversary from rebuilding the information contained in the model. Hence, federated learning minimizes the data shared to a significant extent, and it trains the models in a decentralized manner; therefore, the proposed model offers a perfect solution to protect the sensitive data in various applications against a set of different possible attacks [15].

13.4.1 Concerns of Centralized Training of Machine Learning Models in Private Data

The most significant limitation when training machine learning models using private data is preserving data privacy. Pooling data from different sources for the purpose of training and validation could involve centralization, which might compromise individuals' data privacy when unauthorized access is made or due to breaches. Furthermore, the sharing of such data with third parties might pose legal and ethical issues, especially in the most regulated industries, like healthcare and finance. Another challenge is the logistical complexity that involves data streams being actually collected from different sources and transferred to a central server. This not only has the potential to be a time-consuming, costly affair but also raises the margin of errors. Furthermore, large amounts of data that are generated in this age of technology have the potential to make the task of managing and storing data in one place very difficult [16].

13.4.2 Characteristics of Private Data and Related Compliances

Private data, particularly in the health sector, has features that require it to be highly secured. First of all, an S3 is by its nature private since it may store data that clients do not want to be shared. This ranges from detailed information like health history, family history, or recent records, including employment and financial history. Secondly, private data is very sensitive and is mostly regulated, especially in health. Many countries, such as the US, have adopted the HIPAA law, while in the EU, there is the GDPR to ensure that any type of data is not breached or misused. These regulations set high standards for storing, transmitting, and making data available. Thirdly, information that belongs to an individual is highly personal; the disclosure of which results in losses, fraud, and damage to character.

That is why the leakage of medical records containing personal information can lead to serious consequences for the health of the person. Finally, private data is usually confined to certain organizations or institutions and thus is very restricted [17]. This could limit partnerships, further studies, and inventions, because moving data between different legal entities is rather dangerous in terms of privacy. The approach of training a machine learning model, federated learning, is the solution to this challenge. Federated learning means that model learning can be done collaboratively while the raw data are not shown to other organizations, which helps organizations to embrace the use of AI without divulging their data. Alleviating privacy, regulatory, sensitivity, and isolation features of private data, federated learning enables organizations to utilize the AI potential without compromising on data confidentiality.

13.5 Dataset

We have used the medAlpaca dataset [4]. It provides a collection of pre-trained models and training data that is specifically tailored towards the healthcare domain and named MedAlpapa. The intent of the authors is to offer this open-source platform and enable the development of medical chatbots and other conversational AI applications to serve as an aid towards improved communication between patients and healthcare providers. The paper most likely talks about the challenges involved in training AI models on sensitive medical data, while at the same time, MedAlpaca is promoting privacy and security of data [18].

13.6 Proposed Architecture

13.6.1 Federated Fine-Tuning of LLMs

Federated LLM fine-tuning is a decentralized way to train large language models on private data. In this architecture, there is a central server that coordinates the whole training process. Various organizations or institutions have private datasets, and multiple trainees participate in the training and provide their own private datasets [19, 20].

Then, the central server creates a global model by initializing it. Next, the initial model is distributed to all the participating clients. A global model is sent to each client, who fine-tunes that model on their local dataset. Updating the parameters of the model to satisfy the specific characteristics of the client's data makes up this local fine-tuning process. After the local training is complete, we send back the updated model parameter to the central server. It aggregates the received model updates from all clients and does it in a weighted average way. And this aggregation process combines what we learned from different datasets into a more robust and generalizable global model. The final model is then redistributed to all clients to launch another round of training [21]. The model is trained in the local stage and aggregated to the global stage iteratively until it achieves a convergence criterion, which indicates that model performance has been sufficiently attained. This architecture benefits from being able to use federated learning. One thing it does for us is ensure data privacy by ensuring that sensitive data remains within the client boundaries. It prevents us from actually sharing raw data with the central server or other clients, thereby minimizing the risk of data leaks and unauthorized access. Second, we enable collaborative training on a range of datasets, which helps drive higher model performance and generalizability. The model can combine to learn more robust patterns and learns to adapt to other scenarios. Finally, it can be used in resource-constrained devices with minimal communication and computation overhead. But federated learning isn't without its challenges [22]. The communication bottleneck that is the server also has to communicate with many clients, and is part of a major challenge. In order

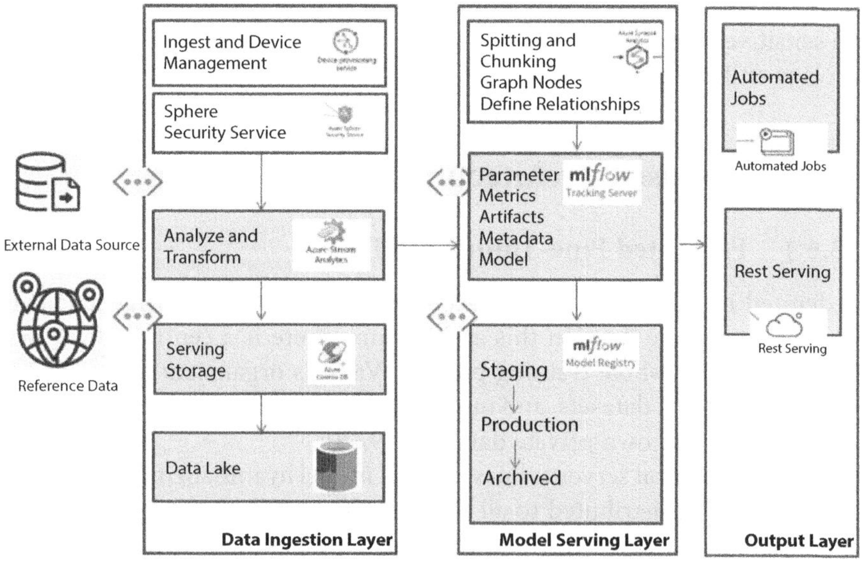

Figure 13.1 Architecture for distributed federated training of LLM.

to reduce this, model compression and selective client participation, as well as other techniques, can be used as shown in Figure 13.1. The heterogeneity of client data poses yet another challenge, as it affects convergence and process performance during federated learning. For this, personalized federated learning, for example, can be used along with adaptive aggregation. This proposed architecture offers solid grounds for federated LLM fine-tuning. Addressing these challenges of data privacy, communication overhead, and data heterogeneity, this approach allows the development of powerful language models adhering to data privacy and security [23].

LLM Used – EleutherAI/Pythia
LLM Model Description: The Pythia Scaling Suite consists of models developed for interpretability research. The article includes two sets of eight models with sizes of 70M, 160M, 410M, 1B, 1.4B, 2.8B, 6.9B, and 12B. For each size, there are two models: two, with one trained on the Pile and one trained on the Pile after the dataset has been globally reduplicated [19]. We train all 8 model sizes on the exact same data in the exact same order. Additionally, we host 154 intermediate checkpoints per model as branches on Hugging Face [20]. The reasons behind the deliberately designed Pythia model suite include the promotion of scientific research on large language models, especially interpretability research. Unlike downstream performance, we go without centering it as a design goal, and yet the models still match or exceed that of similar or same-sized models in the OPT and GPT-Neo suites [21].
Model Variant Selected – 6.9 Billion
We took 0.27% of the total number of parameters (70,623,232), i.e., 196,608, for our study. That is, we had modified the weight of 196,608 parameters using parameter efficient fine-tuning (PEFT).

13.6.2 Federation Architecture

Although federated fine-tuning is a powerful technique that discusses how large language model training can work across many decentralized clients without having direct access to the data to enhance the model, it has one critical disadvantage that is the same as with the first method. In this paradigm, the training process is centered on a server, which sends the global model to clients and receives their updates. In particular, clients, having their own private data, perform the received model updates on their data and send back updated parameters to the server. The server then combines these updates in order to construct a new global model and send it to the clients [22]. This iterative process is maintained until the solution is satisfactory and thus reaches the model's goal. Nevertheless, federated fine-tuning of LLMs raises several issues. First of all, the high volume of parameters existing within LLMs can create considerable communication overhead since the clients must transfer their new parameters to the server. Second, due to the variability of client data distribution, the global model may take time to update. The third merit is privacy, since clients can be uncomfortable providing information to a central server even when encrypted. Finally, the limitations of the clients' hardware often result in a decreased ability to contribute to the training process when dealing with complex LLMs. In response to these challenges, the following techniques have been put forward. The flexible model update techniques, like low-rank adaptation and prompt tuning, let the clients update only a portion of the parameters of the model, which minimizes the communication load and the computation costs. The application of federated learning can be combined with the subsequent compression methods, such as quantization and scarification, in order to decrease the size of transmitted model updates [23]. Frameworks such as techniques in differential privacy and secure aggregation can be applied to minimize privacy inaccuracy by either adding noise to the models' updates or transmitting them in encrypted forms. This way, it is shown that among hybrid approaches, it is possible to get more powerful and effective federated fine-tuning solutions. Multilingual and multilingual fine-tuning of large language models on horizontally scalable, general-purpose machines in a public cloud environment represents a useful architectural solution for achieving scalability and cost efficiency with a focus on the privacy of personal data. This architecture allows multiple participants to remotely come together and make fine-grained adjustments to LLMs without compromising their individual sovereignty and data protection. However, in this system, the information does not flow out of the source, which is a great way to consider privacy regulations and issues arising from sensitive information. Designing such an architecture involves the specification of a number of features, including computing, media, security, and structure. Combined, this makes for an architecture centered around the role of the federated coordinator—essentially serving as the conductor for the orchestration of fine-tuning. The federated coordinator works towards controlling the flow of communication and cooperation between individual compute nodes and the global model. It partitions tasks to the individual machines, monitors task execution, and gathers accumulated model updates from the nodes. This aggregation commonly uses methods such as federated averaging (FedAvg) in order to amalgamate different local models and produce a single global model.

The coordinator of the system also checks the amount of resources used in the system and regulates the system to its suitable capacity concerning the workload of the system resources. To improve reliability and availability, the coordinator is usually run as a container on top of Kubernetes; it has built-in capabilities for entity scaling, failure, and load balance. Security is always a concern in federated fine-tuning, more so in the context of the public cloud, where resources are shared across tenants. On the same note, the architecture applies the right measures of encryption to work towards the protection of information and correspondence. Information about each compute node is always encrypted, both when stored and when being transferred, so that no intruder can gain access to this information. Interactions between the federated coordinator and the compute nodes are protected through intelligent means such as the Transport Layer Security (TLS) to avoid interference [24]. Secondly, through federated learning, only the model parameters are transmitted between clients, and not the raw data. To provide privacy enhancement beyond the level described above, more sophisticated techniques known as differential privacy can be used before the model update is sent to the coordinator. This injects randomness into the updates, which prevents straightforward extraction of other points from this aggregated model. Another level of security that can be added to this architecture is through the use of secure enclaves or hardware-based trusted execution environments (TEEs). These enclaves afford micro-areas in the compute nodes, which means even if the system has been breached, data and model computations will still be safe. The federated coordinator can also work on a secure enclave to ensure that the global model and the aggregation part are secured from access. ALSO, to prevent unauthorized access to the cloud resources, the system has incorporated a role-based access control mechanism as well as identity verification mechanisms to confine the participants to the federated learning process. Many features come into play as far as the reliability and security of a cloud networking topology are concerned [25]. To maintain the resources of the federated system virtually separate from other cloud tenants, the concept of Virtual Private Clouds (VPCs) is adopted. In the context of the VPC, the subnets put constraints on the topology to partition the network for various parts of the system, which include the federated coordinator, compute nodes, and the monitoring systems. Security groups and firewalls are used to make strict policies for admitting traffic to and from the components as required. The nodes and the coordinator are connected by means of private endpoints and virtual network peering to reduce exposure to public IPs [26]. Moreover, effectively dedicated inter-region or inter-zone network links help the formation of low-latency connections between the nodes, even if the compute nodes are situated in different regions. Another benefit of hosting our system in a public cloud environment for federated fine-tuning is scalability. The architecture is itself flexible, which will allow for the dynamic distribution of computations for LLM training. In horizontal scaling, it is possible to add new compute nodes or remove some of them depending on the load demands. When more individuals are added to the federated system or when massive data has to be cleared, more ordinary machines are instantiated. On the other hand, when utilization of resources is low, what is not needed is removed to avoid high cost [27]. This flexibility is controlled by the federated coordinator, which is coordinated with the auto-scaling of the cloud provider. This helps to ensure that the system is running at its best while at the same time having an excellent value-for-money ratio as well. The architecture also has an incorporated monitoring and logging system that will allow for better tracking and monitoring of the performance and health of the federated system. The above systems provide efficiency indicators like resource consumption, network delays, and training rates, and have interfaces in the form of configurable dashboards. Specific alarms are to be set so that the administrators are informed of certain problems, which include node down status or any activity that is abnormal [28]. Logging systems record activities performed in an application, which is helpful in identifying problems, as well as in ensuring accountability, among other uses. The types of monitoring and logging mentioned here are built to work with cloud-native services while relying on the elastic nature and fault tolerance of the public cloud platform. Therefore, the architecture of general-purpose machines of LLMs for federated fine-tuning at the horizontal scale of a public cloud environment is complex but well-designed. It is designed to incorporate the advantages of general-purpose machines for edges together with the scalability and predictability of the cloud for information center services. The federated coordinator manages the process, and security for data and communication is also ensured. The physical topology specifically aims at minimizing latency and maximizing reliability, and the system architecture is elastic to accommodate changing needs. Being a pervasive system without specific details of the data to be taught, LLMs, this architecture offers a solid framework for efficient and accurate fine-tuning of the models while preserving the fault tolerance, monitoring, and compliance features of the corporate environment [29].

13.6.3 Distributed Computing Infrastructure for the Architecture

A large-scale machine learning in the space that does not require vertical scaling of single large machines in the public cloud, a horizontally scalable architecture for fine-tuning LLMs relying on many small machines addressing a grand challenge of distributed computing, remains cost-effective and privacy-preserving. General-purpose virtualized VMs, usually horizontal in form and small in terms of computational resources, are preferred in such architectures because of their flexibility, relatively low cost, and expandability. It still remains effective horizontally by organizing the systems in parallel across more machines rather than vertically in powerful but expensive machines. It also complements well larger federated learning paradigms in which data owner privacy and security are crucial, because the architecture proposed prevents the transmission of valuable data to other nodes in the system, while at the same time, the model can be trained cooperatively across several nodes in the distributed system. In a cost-optimized design using many small machines, horizontal scaling enables computational load to be divided between a number of nodes, which are created as required. This elasticity is characteristic of public cloud offerings, where virtual instances can be provisioned or un-provisioned on the spot [30]. Every small machine is used for a part of it; for example, it can be a shard of data, a local model, or some lightweight services. This distribution minimizes the per-instance (volume) load as the system gets the gas from the cost-effective petty machines rather than putting it into the gas-hungry instances. Another advantage is cost-efficient pricing, or rather cost-effective pricing; this is because most of the public cloud price structures come with a per-second billing structure [31]. Thus, the smaller machines pose fewer chances of underutilization, and at the same time, each of the instances runs more or less at its full capability since loads are distributed evenly. For using this strategy, you can apply spot instances or preemptible VMs provided by cloud providers to optimize the costs even more. While these instances are far cheaper than the on-demand instance, there is always the proviso of interruption. Interruptions are less hostile in the horizontally scaled architecture since the workloads are already divided across several nodes and can therefore work on the redistribution of tasks. It must be noted that the federated system provides some of the fault tolerance mechanisms to ensure that a task is always redirected to a working node, which makes the system always highly available at a low cost. In the same regard, through price zones and time bands, the system can leverage cheaper areas or periods to host and run the various workloads.

This full-proof privacy-wise makes the architecture efficient in protecting data confidentiality as well as meeting legal standards [32]. It is important to note that federated learning by design prevents data from being sent to cloud servers, as its processing remains on the device or local machine. In conventional federated learning, the raw data are not sent to the server for computation and updating; rather, only the model updates, such as gradients or weights, are sent back by each node in the federated system to the central coordinator for updating the federated model. These updates are then combined at the coordinator level to enhance the global model without compromising the participant's data. It minimizes the disadvantages of having a centralized unit with exclusive access to information, as it may be hacked, compromised, or have a single point of failure. Privacy-preserving techniques are also endemic in this architectural design. Differential privacy is one such technique; it adds controlled noise into the local model updates before they are shared with the central coordinator. This additionally protects individual statistical coordinates and cannot be deciphered from the composite model even if the updates are attained, unlikelihood notwithstanding. This approach can also be applied to encrypt the updates to the local model en route so that the central coordinator is able to perform computations on encrypted data. Secure Multi-Party Computation (SMPC) offers an extra level of privacy by partitioning the significant data into several shares such that no node gets a full view of the data [33]. Its network topographical layout is done in such a way that communication is optimized while privacy is achieved. This usually occurs in a hub-and-spoke system where the central coordinator is the hub, while small horizontal machines are spokes. One of the small-world network designs is reducing the number of connections greatly to limit the path by which an intruder can infiltrate a network. Encryption methods to safeguard the node-to-coordinator and the inter-node traffic have employed the transport layer security protocol. Moreover, virtual private networks (VPNs) or virtual private clouds (VPCs) are used to compartmentalize the federated learning system from other external networks to enhance security. But one of the architectural drawbacks of small horizontal machines is the overhead, which may appear due to communications and synchronization among the nodes. However, the advancement of federated learning approaches copes with this problem. For example, model updates can be compressed before transmission and hence save a lot of bandwidth. Methods such as scarification and quantization, together with clustering, assist in reducing the size of updates while still being useful. Strategies for periodic communication, where nodes concurrently synchronize only after multiple iterations of local training, alleviate the need for frequent network communication, which increases the costs of data exchange in the public cloud. This particular architecture is also fault-tolerant, meaning that regardless of what happens to the nodes throughout the system, the whole system continues to hold up [34]. Some features of checkpointing enable the federated learning system to periodically save the federated global model and the status of local computations. If one corrupts, the system may restore the most recent data saved, eliminating higher degrees of data loss and extra time. This is because redundancy of tasks with one or more critical tasks implemented across various nodes boosts reliability. This is especially true when working with such cheap pricing models as spot instances, which are much more prone to disruption. Supervision and optimization become the cornerstones for designing an affordable and least invasive structure. Primary cloud-native tools for monitoring are named Amazon CloudWatch, Google Cloud Monitoring, or Azure Monitor, which generate real-time insights regarding resource consumption, network performance, and system health state. These tools can find out which of the machines is idle or which part of the system is completely loaded, so the administrator can modify resource allocation in this system on the fly. The load distribution is fully optimized to guarantee that loads are balanced within the system so that resources can be quickly and efficiently scaled to the level of need and demand instead of over-provisioned to reduce idle time [35]. Ultimately, the architecture based on a large number of horizontally scalable, individual machines in the public cloud is cost-efficient and respects privacy when performing distributed computations, such as LLM fine-tuning. Due to flexibility and cost-effectiveness, characteristics of public cloud infrastructure, the architecture is capable of dealing with fluctuating loads without high additional costs. Modern federated learning methods ensure that the data is secure and will remain private, which conforms to the set regulatory measures and ethical considerations. Enhanced privacy-preserving techniques, additional tolerance to faults, and optimal network traffic patterns make the system more reliable. This architecture is a vision for the future of distributed machine learning that takes the best of traditional cloud computing, privacy concerns, and costs.

The diagram illustrates a distributed federated training system for a Large Language Model (LLM) that is divided into three interconnected stages. This paper aims to identify, analyze, and compare the subsequent three roles assigned to the federation, namely, federation tracking, centralized aggregation, and output serving. In the federation tracking stage, individual clients or edge devices feed data at the local level to the LLM through system apps, without compromising the raw data on the source

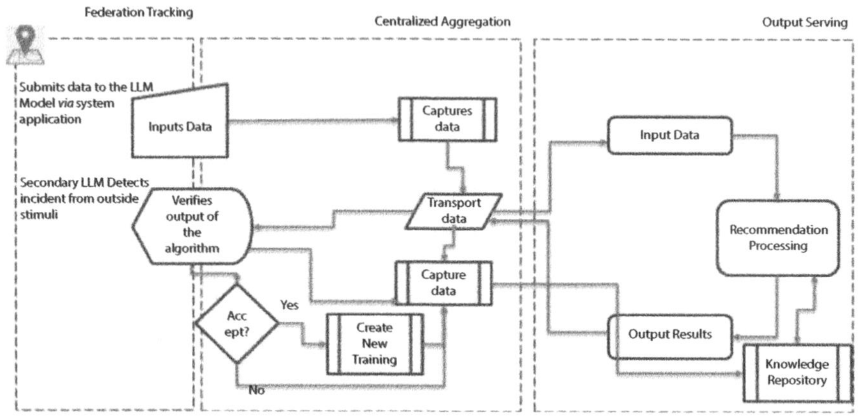

Figure 13.2 Distributed federated training of LLM in private data.

devices as shown in Figure 13.2. An additional LLM or a monitoring mechanism confirms the actual external stimulus or the accuracy of output discrepancies checked by the algorithm. If the results are acceptable, then the process continues; else, it forms more training cycles. During the centralized aggregation stage, not the data, but the updates to the model are gathered and sent securely to a central point for incorporation in the global model. This stage enables models to be in sync with one another regarding privacy. Lastly, at the output serving stage, the modified global model is used for producing the recommendation, prediction, or output that is further passed through a preprocessing stage to store it as knowledge in a knowledge base. In the same regard, this repository reciprocates into the system in order to rectify any defaults and guarantee that the distributed training process reflects the intended goals.

13.7 Architectural Telemetry

To implement the federated, distributed, privacy-measuring training of LLMs on low-capacity machines, an architecture needs to be developed, and therefore, it is crucial to have a good telemetry system to measure the performance and efficiency of the system as well as ensure compliance with privacy policies. In such architecture, telemetry includes factors relating to the usage of the system, communication costs, and convergence of models, security considerations, and methods of preserving the privacy of information being passed within a network. In low-capacity machines, including VMs or small edge devices, shared resources have to be used efficiently, as the compute and memory capacities are small, while the communication has to be secure and the data sensitive. Metrics of the telemetry system include CPU and memory utilization, specific network bandwidth, and training delay for these devices to avoid both overloading and underloading. It also has the privacy value that estimates differential privacy budgets, noise injection consistencies, and privacy threats to data transmission. Moreover, telemetry provides centrality on model performance using metrics such as accuracy, loss, and whether nodes contribute equally as a means to confirm how distributed training compares with global training. Another important function of the telemetry system is tracking such security aspects as encryption, for instance, the integrity of radio links, as well as the cases of their failures, and more, to maintain the compliance of the system with the high privacy-preserving standards [36]. This telemetry infrastructure does more than handle real-time monitoring and debugging; it also helps with auditing after the deployment and generation of compliance reports. Shown below is a tabular format that encompasses the general key measures for monitoring the architecture in question [37].

The table gives the machine learning and AI-centric metrics as well as their targets for the massive-scale federated learning system to be deployed for training the LLMs, noting that telemetry is critical to efficiency, scalability, privacy, and security in FL. Thus, to ensure that low-capacity machines are utilized effectively and not overloaded or underutilized, CPU usage (65%–85%), memory (4 GB out of 8 GB), and disk I/O (100 MB/s) are used. For instance, if a high average CPU value is depicted on the picture, then the system may require the dynamic workload migration or the addition of more nodes. The same applies to the network resource utilization, which is characterized by bandwidth utilization (20–50 Mbps), latency (100–200 ms), packet loss (<1%), and timely cost-effective synchronization between the nodes of the distributed infrastructure. Synchronization frequencies at every 10 rounds avoid a good balance between training effectiveness and communication overhead, which is important to prevent occasional lags or interruptions in very large FL systems. The final value of training loss is 0.03, accuracy reaches 92%, and the model's convergence rate is 2% for the 10th round to prove the efficiency of training at the node dispersion [38]. A currently stalling loss above zero point one would indicate changes of hyperparameters or fine-tuning local training algorithm processes. These metrics prove that the FL updates are useful for the global model, which converges without compromising on the model's accuracy. Privacy preservation is a fundamental aspect of federated learning with a differential noise level of $\pm$ 0.5 on gradients, privacy budget of $\varepsilon = 5$, and a leakage rate below 0.01%. To make it hard to recover individual data from the updates, the system uses noise injection and privacy budget tracking while offering very good performance as shown in Table 13.1. Encryption status: AES-256 enabled, Transport Integrity Check: 100%, Authentications Success Rate: 99.5% make the security of the system reliable against trespassers and ensuring the confidentiality of data transmissions. AES-256 encryption gives security, as it is a highly effective level of protection, while 99.5% authentication success rates give good identity management when implemented in a distributed environment. Another major factor is fault tolerance: node failure rates are controlled at 2% per round, task redistribution is at 98%, and checkpoint time is less than 10 seconds.

Table 13.1 Telemetric of proposed architecture.

Metric category	Specific metrics	Measurement purpose
Resource utilization	CPU utilization, memory usage, disk I/O, GPU usage (if applicable)	Tracks hardware resource consumption.
Network efficiency	Bandwidth consumption, latency, packet loss, synchronization frequency	Optimizes communication overhead.
Model performance	Training loss, model accuracy, convergence rate, local contribution consistency	Evaluates training quality.
Privacy monitoring	Differential privacy noise levels, privacy budget consumption, privacy leakage risks	Monitors privacy.
Security	Encryption status, secure transport integrity, authentication success rate	Tracks security.
Fault tolerance	Node failure rates, task redistribution success, checkpoint recovery time	Measures system resilience.
Training efficiency	Training time per iteration, energy consumption, task completion rate, idle node percentage	Optimizes process efficiency.
System scalability	Node provisioning rate, resource scaling efficiency, workload balancing metrics	Tracks system elasticity.

These metrics ensure that the system remains stable because the time it takes to redistribute a task and the time it takes to recover from a node failure are small, since node failures exist in a distributed system. There are training efficiency measures such as training time per iteration/round (5 min), energy consumption for each machine (100W), task success rates (95%), and idle node percentages (3%), which ensure resource utilization without compromising on energy consumption. For instance, training times over 10 minutes in each round or idle node percentages more than 3% may usually signify that some adaptations are needed. Last but not least, system scalability is evaluated in terms of node provision rates (10 nodes per minute), resource scaling performance (90% efficiency), and workload distribution deviation (less than 10%). All these metrics make sure that the system is malleable in case of workload change, adding the nodes instantly and ensuring that the load is evenly distributed to avoid a particular node being overloaded. All these telemetry metrics collectively help the federated learning system to strike a perfect balance of performance, scalability, and privacy while using distributed low-capacity machines efficiently and securely [39].

Some improvements can be made further towards the distributed, federated learning architecture that deals with LLM training on low-capacity machines. An important area that is not well developed is related to ADWM, which uses data from machine learning systems to predict resource bottlenecks and to manage the workload in a way that optimally operates underperforming nodes. For instance, incorporating prognostic algorithms that work on real-time log data, like CPU or memory usage patterns, enables automated nodal provisioning/de-provisioning to avoid unnecessary downtime and bring operational efficiencies that optimize cost. Network optimization can also be raised to another level through low communication overhead methods, including quantized or significantly reduced gradient updates. Further, high-level synchronization mechanisms, such as asynchronous updates or partial aggregation, can be used to minimize the synchronizations more frequently and cope with latency issues where setup is done at geographically diverse locations. To level up data privacy from the privacy perspective, it is possible to use federated learning frameworks that utilize hierarchical or hybrid aggregators, which perform computations on updates before their transfer to a main server, resulting in less network load. The efficiency of privacy-preserving mechanisms can be increased through the development of newer cryptographic techniques, including federated homomorphic encryption, or through enhancements in faster secure multi-party computation protocols that later involve lower computational requirements on the low-capacity devices. Furthermore, the improved monitoring techniques resulting from AI anomaly detection can define potential indicators of an upcoming node failure or a security breach, thus enabling preventive measures to be put in place. In terms of model performance, future versions might use personalized federated learning, where local nodes customize parts of a global model with their personal data distributions while contributing to the shared learning objective. This would render the model significantly more relevant and accurate for various use cases globally. On the other hand, training efficiency would benefit from hardware-aware optimizations, distributing computing tasks depending on every machine's capability, hence using heterogeneous resources within the network. For instance, simple computations can be handled by edge devices, whereas high-resource-consuming computations are allocated to more powerful devices. Security can be improved further through fine-grained identity and access management policies using advanced cryptographic authentication along with zero-trust architectures. By continuously validating the identity and integrity of the participating nodes, the system becomes resilient to harm inflicted by malicious actors during the learning process [40]. Finally, building solid observability platforms offering real telemetry is expected to help administrators make more rapid data-backed decisions against arising inefficiencies. Through such iterated refinement of these characteristics, the architecture may be even more resilient, efficient, and adaptable, paving the way to broader adoption of federated learning environments constrained by resources and privacy concerns.

13.8 Explainability

Explainability is a critical aspect of privacy-preserving federated LLM fine-tuning in healthcare. It helps bridge the gap between advanced machine learning optimization and the need for trust and transparency. This is especially important in healthcare, where decisions directly affect patient safety and outcomes.

In federated systems, large language models are fine-tuned across distributed healthcare edge nodes. These nodes can include hospital servers, diagnostic devices, and wearable health monitors. In this setup, raw patient data never leaves the local environment. This ensures privacy while still enabling collective intelligence.

However, this decentralized architecture introduces challenges in interpretability. The model's decision-making process can become opaque. This is due to heterogeneous and non-independent data distributions across sources.

Explainability mechanisms must go beyond traditional techniques. These include attention heatmaps, feature attribution, and counterfactual explanations. They must also address federated settings where local contributions remain private.

To achieve this, local attention-based visualization tools were implemented on edge nodes. These tools highlight important clinical features influencing predictions. Examples include abnormal blood pressure, irregular ECG signals, and key terms in physician notes.

At the global level, federated SHAP was used for interpretability. This method summarizes how updates from different institutions affect model behavior. It allows clinicians to understand cross-institution learning patterns.

For example, updates from rural clinics improved sensitivity for rare conditions. Meanwhile, urban hospital data improved accuracy for complex comorbidities.

In practice, this supports real-world diagnosis. If the model flags early-stage heart failure, clinicians can see the reasoning. It may prioritize NT-proBNP levels and echocardiogram anomalies.

Global summaries reinforce confidence in these signals. They show consistency across multiple healthcare sites. This creates a multi-layered explainability pipeline.

Explainability was also adapted to work with privacy-preserving techniques. These include differential privacy and secure aggregation. Instead of exposing raw gradients, interpretable summaries were used.

This approach maintains confidentiality while still providing insights. It helps clinicians trust predictions. It also allows regulators to audit fairness and robustness. This ensures no demographic group is systematically disadvantaged.

Lightweight explainability modules were also developed. These are optimized for edge devices with limited compute power. They enable real-time interpretability without sharing sensitive data.

Finally, these practices were aligned with regulations like GDPR and HIPAA. They were integrated into clinical decision support systems. This ensures the system delivers not just accuracy, but also transparency and ethical compliance.

13.9 Conclusion

In conclusion, the architecture for the federated training of LLMs using low-capacity, horizontal scaling in the distributed public cloud is a revolution in how large-scale machine learning can be performed in terms of cost, scale, and privacy. This architecture is designed based on distributed computing and federated learning to face the problems that appear in traditional centralized training, including high resource consumption, privacy leakage, and restrictions from data localization regulations. Low-capacity machines are employed and logically expanded in the horizontal dimension to meet various workloads and reduce operational costs. For example, small VMs or end devices can work on local data and perform simple computations; thus, the load on any node is not particularly high, and the system is highly scalable. The above cost efficiency is supported by dynamic resource allocation, the utilization of the spot or preemptible instances, and regional pricing models in cloud computing that help to draw the maximum utilization of cloud resources while still delivering excellent performance. This architecture, with privacy being the focal pillar of this design, is protected by secure federated learning models. Original data stays on its individual nodes, and only the encrypted update or gradient information is transmitted to the central aggregator. These updates cannot be reverse-engineered from the techniques, including differential privacy, homomorphic encryption, and secure multi-party computation. The architecture ensures that information shared through the constructed decentralized data systems is kept secure while allowing organizations to meet the required regulations in data protection laws, so as to ensure that users will continue to have trust in such a new paradigm shift in data systems. As is the case with most architecture, the telemetry system built into this architecture is very crucial in determining its reliability and effectiveness. As a result, the system stays informed on operational health indicators based on resource use, network performance, models, privacy, and security in real time. For example, the amount of completed CPU and/or memory work as successful restrictions counter low-capacity machines from being overloaded, and it is similar to bandwidth utilization and latency measurements that seek to reduce channel overhead. Differential privacy budgets and noise injection levels are used to measure how private a system is when collecting and releasing data, while recovery time and success rates of task redistribution provide evidence of how resilient the system will be if nodes fail. Besides keeping the stability of the system, what is important is that all these metrics can serve as the basis for further enhancements of the system, as well as for the periodicity of the compliance audit. This architecture's modularity and its ability to incorporate failure are key success factors. With the help of horizontal scaling, the system can increase the number of nodes in response to increased load and, on the other hand, reduce the number of nodes to save money when the load is low. Redundancy through replication of tasks and checkpointing guarantees that node failures on the global level are localized and do not affect the training process. This resilience is particularly important in cases where cost savings are sought through spot instances, which are prone to interruptions. On the other hand, the system works in a way that workloads are distributed appropriately and nodes are effectively used; thus, the training process continues as planned, especially when resources are scarce. Security is the other foundational aspect of the architecture, with safe transfer of data and data storage being encrypted. This is achieved through the integration of role-based access control (RBAC), identity and access management (IAM), and audit logging, which ensures the system possesses safe security policies against any unfavorable parading by other field exercises, apart from providing detailed records of all activities. Thus, the described approach maximizes protection and guarantees the reliable and uninterrupted execution of distributed training [41]. However, in the output serving stage, the knowledge repository and recommendation system present a strong way to leverage the trained global model. By incorporating new information into future practice, the architecture provides constant enhancement in the model's functioning and performance and, additionally, the ability to adapt to additional data or demand. In sum, the federated training architecture suggests the possibilities of decentralized machine learning to liberate the power of artificial intelligence for everyone and meet such essential challenges as costs and privacy. It enables organizations to train mega models with distributed data for cooperation, avoiding the need for a central data hub to compile the data in a compliant and efficient manner. This approach provides a roadmap for practical, accessible, and safe development of AI applications to meet increased demands as privacy rules evolve. Technological improvements to hardware, federated learning algorithms, and privacy protection measures will improve this architecture's prospects, definitively making it a resource applicable to more extensive forms of machine learning as they become a possibility. Because of such a telemetry-guided, privacy-preserving design, it is a strong solution to using LLMs in more extensive and various domains without compromising trust and hindering the realistic application.

13.10 Future Work

Future work in the development of distributed federated learning architectures for the training of large language models on low-capacity machines should be aimed at a few key areas to further improve performance, scalability, privacy, and security. One avenue is to explore and then implement more sophisticated optimization techniques for resource management. Techniques such as quantization, scarification of gradient updates, and adaptive aggregation methods could be integrated to reduce the volume of data exchanged between distributed nodes without impairing model accuracy and convergence rates. It would also decrease bandwidth usage, but latency would actually be reduced, making synchronization faster and the federated learning system more responsive overall. Privacy is still paramount, and studies on federated learning frameworks with higher differential privacy guarantees and more efficient cryptographic protocols will be important. Federated homomorphic encryption and secure multi-party computation can be optimized for reducing the computational overhead, so these techniques can be run efficiently even on low-capacity devices. Hybrid privacy mechanisms that combine edge and cloud-based processing might also offer more fine-grained control over data privacy while preserving confidentiality, thereby scaling up and flexing without compromise. A security upgrade of the system also requires a more complex anomaly detection system to be developed, which will detect possible security threats in real time. Machine learning models trained to recognize anomalies in node behavior, data transmissions, or access requests can potentially prevent or mitigate attacks by allowing for rapid intervention before they have an impact on the integrity of the system. Personalized federated learning approaches represent a very promising direction. This might help the model better handle diverse data distributions at different nodes by allowing individual nodes to fine-tune local parts of the model while contributing to global updates. This may yield a more realistic and personalized forecast method, and the system becomes more adaptable to applications that have varying real-world applications. The area of hardware-aware optimizations will become one of the key directions of development in terms of the efficiency of training. Take advantage of the special capabilities of edge devices, mobile phones, or cloud-based servers to delegate more computationally intensive work to nodes with higher capacities and retain more simplistic work for lower-capacity nodes. Finally, to ensure the federated learning systems are able to keep growing and flourishing, the user-friendly and resilient monitoring and observability tools are certainly on the future agenda. Such tools would provide administrators with more detailed real-time information on system performance, resource usage, security, and privacy indicators and enable them to identify issues and make more informed decisions. The federated learning framework can be even more efficient, scalable, and secure with these improvements, which will make it be adopted by an even greater number in privacy-sensitive and resource-limited settings, revolutionizing the training and deployment of LLMs in a variety of fields.

AI disclosure statement: The author confirms that no artificial intelligence (AI)-generated content or AI-assisted writing tools were used in the preparation of this chapter (including summaries and the abstract). All text, analysis, and conclusions are the result of the author's original work.

References

1. Thirunavukarasu, A.J., *et al.*, Large language models in medicine. *Nat. Med.*, 29, 8, 1930–1940, 2023.
2. Chen, Y., *et al.*, Longlora: Efficient fine-tuning of long-context large language models, arXiv preprint arXiv:2309.12307, 2023.
3. Zhang, S., *et al.*, Instruction tuning for large language models: A survey, arXiv preprint arXiv:2308.10792, 2023.
4. Han, T., *et al.*, MedAlpaca--an open-source collection of medical conversational AI models and training data, arXiv preprint arXiv:2304.08247, 2023.
5. Chakraborty, A., Shaw, A.K., Samanta, S., On a References Architecture to Build Deep-Q Learning-Based Intelligent IoT Edge Solutions, in: *Convergence of Deep Learning In Cyber-IoT Systems and Security*, pp. 123–146, Wiley Online library, 2022. https://onlinelibrary.wiley.com/doi/abs/10.1002/9781119857686.ch6.
6. Chakraborty, A., *et al.*, Exploring genetic algorithm to optimize hyper parameter for training of artificial neural network. *AIP Conf. Proc.*, 2878, 1, AIP Publishing, 2023.
7. Keshri, R., Chakraborty, A., Saptarshi Das, Mallick, C., Using Dilated CNN and MLOPS for PII Detection in Pharmaceutical Reporting. *Afr. J. of Biol. Sci.*, 6, 10, 4406, 2024.
8. Mohapatra, D., Chakraborty, A., Shaw, A.K., Exploring novel techniques to detect aberration from metal surfaces in automobile industries, in: *Proceedings of International Conference on Communication, Circuits, and Systems: IC3S 2020*, Springer Singapore, 2021.
9. Shaw, A.K., *et al.*, Scalable IoT solution using cloud services–An automobile industry use case, in: *2020 Fourth International Conference on I-SMAC (IoT in Social, Mobile, Analytics and Cloud) (I-SMAC)*, IEEE, 2020.
10. Oduro-Afriyie, J., Improving Personal Health Question Answering Through Knowledge Graph Enhancement, Diss. University of Idaho, 2024.
11. Jawahar, G., *et al.*, LLM Performance Predictors are good initializers for Architecture Search, arXiv preprint arXiv:2310.16712, 2023.
12. Jeong, C., A study on the implementation of generative ai services using an enterprise data-based LLM application architecture, arXiv preprint arXiv:2309.01105, 2023.
13. Wu, Y., *et al.*, SecGPT: An execution isolation architecture for LLM-based systems, arXiv preprint arXiv:2403.04960, 2024.

14. Rho, D., *et al.*, Encryption-friendly LLM architecture, arXiv preprint arXiv:2410.02486, 2024.
15. Kumar, V., *et al.*, Large-Language-Models (LLM)-Based AI Chatbots: Architecture, In-Depth Analysis and Their Performance Evaluation, in: *International Conference on Recent Trends in Image Processing and Pattern Recognition*, Springer Nature Switzerland, Cham, 2023.
16. Nasir, M.U., *et al.*, LLMatic: neural architecture search *via* large language models and quality diversity optimization, in: *Proceedings of the Genetic and Evolutionary Computation Conference*, 2024.
17. Ganesh, S. and Sahlqvist, R., Exploring Patterns in LLM Integration-A study on architectural considerations and design patterns in LLM dependent applications, 2024.
18. Dhar, R., Vaidhyanathan, K., Varma, V., Can LLMs Generate Architectural Design Decisions?-An Exploratory Empirical study, arXiv preprint arXiv:2403.01709, 2024.
19. Yin, J., *et al.*, Comparative Study of Large Language Model Architectures on Frontier, arXiv preprint arXiv:2402.00691, 2024.
20. Cho, J., *et al.*, LLMServingSim: A HW/SW Co-Simulation Infrastructure for LLM Inference Serving at Scale, in: *2024 IEEE International Symposium on Workload Characterization (IISWC)*, IEEE, 2024.
21. Zhang, H., *et al.*, A hardware evaluation framework for large language model inference, arXiv preprint arXiv:2312.03134, 2023.
22. Minaee, S., *et al.*, Large language models: A survey, arXiv preprint arXiv:2402.06196, 2024.
23. Nikolova-Stoupak, I., *et al.*, LLM-generated contexts to practice specialised vocabulary: Corpus presentation and comparison, in: *Actes de JEP-TALN-RECITAL 2024, 31ème Conférence sur le Traitement Automatique des Langues Naturelles, volume 1: articles longs et prises de position*, ATALA & AFPC, 2024.
24. Chen, Y., *et al.*, Netgpt: An ai-native network architecture for provisioning beyond personalized generative services. *IEEE Network*, 2024.
25. Korvala, A., Analysis of LLM-models in optimizing and designing vhdl code, 2023.
26. Weber, I., Large Language Models as Software Components: A Taxonomy for LLM-Integrated Applications, arXiv preprint arXiv:2406.10300, 2024.
27. Li, Y., *et al.*, Personal LLM agents: Insights and survey about the capability, efficiency and security, arXiv preprint arXiv:2401.05459, 2024.
28. Dvivedi, S.S., *et al.*, A comparative analysis of large language models for code documentation generation, in: *Proceedings of the 1st ACM International Conference on AI-Powered Software*, 2024.
29. Abbasiantaeb, Z., *et al.*, Let the LLMs talk: Simulating human-to-human conversational qa *via* zero-shot LLM-to-LLM interactions, in: *Proceedings of the 17th ACM International Conference on Web Search and Data Mining*, 2024.

30. Kim, B., *et al.*, The Breakthrough Memory Solutions for Improved Performance on LLM Inference. *IEEE Micro*, 2024.
31. Zhao, J., *et al.*, Galore: Memory-efficient LLM training by gradient low-rank projection, arXiv preprint arXiv:2403.03507, 2024.
32. Rubungo, A.N., *et al.*, LLM-prop: Predicting physical and electronic properties of crystalline solids from their text descriptions, arXiv preprint arXiv:2310.14029, 2023.
33. Zhang, R., *et al.*, {REMARK-LLM}: A robust and efficient watermarking framework for generative large language models, in: *33rd USENIX Security Symposium (USENIX Security 24)*, 2024.
34. Kuang, W., *et al.*, Federatedscope-LLM: A comprehensive package for fine-tuning large language models in federated learning, in: *Proceedings of the 30th ACM SIGKDD Conference on Knowledge Discovery and Data Mining*, 2024.
35. Wu, F., *et al.*, Fedbiot: LLM local fine-tuning in federated learning without full model, in: *Proceedings of the 30th ACM SIGKDD Conference on Knowledge Discovery and Data Mining*, 2024.
36. Jiang, J., *et al.*, Low-parameter federated learning with large language models, in: *International Conference on Web Information Systems and Applications*, Springer Nature Singapore, Singapore, 2024.
37. Ye, R., *et al.*, Openfedllm: Training large language models on decentralized private data *via* federated learning, in: *Proceedings of the 30th ACM SIGKDD Conference on Knowledge Discovery and Data Mining*, 2024.
38. Wu, F., *et al.*, On the Client Preference of LLM Fine-tuning in Federated Learning, arXiv preprint arXiv:2407.03038, 2024.
39. Zheng, J., *et al.*, Safely Learning with Private Data: A Federated Learning Framework for Large Language Model, arXiv preprint arXiv:2406.14898, 2024.
40. Ding, S. and Hu, C., eFedLLM: Efficient LLM Inference Based on Federated Learning, arXiv preprint arXiv:2411.16003, 2024.
41. Luo, W., *et al.*, When Fine-Tuning LLMs Meets Data Privacy: An Empirical Study of Federated Learning in LLM-Based Program Repair, arXiv preprint arXiv:2412.01072, 2024.

14

Enhancing the Robustness of Causal AI Systems against Adversarial Threats

Sakshi Thakur, Mohit Singh Bisht* and Dinesh Singh Dhakar

Department of Computer Science & Engineering, Chandigarh University, Mohali, Punjab, India

Abstract
Artificial intelligence (AI) has become a substantial catalyst for change in sectors such as healthcare, finance, cybersecurity, and autonomous systems. The recent advances of adversarial attacks pose a threat to the integrity and credibility of such systems because they have become increasingly sophisticated. Adversarial manipulations, including data poisoning, model evasion, and confounder exploitation, can undermine predictions, decision-making, and system performance, emphasizing the need for reliable, interpretable AI frameworks capable of uncovering authentic cause-and-effect relationships. This chapter emphasizes causal AI, which improves interpretability, fairness, and reliability by modeling underlying causal mechanisms. It talks about how AI systems are vulnerable to adversarial attacks in healthcare, finance, and self-driving cars, and how small perturbations can result in false diagnoses or fraudulent authorizations. Hybrid causal defense architecture: It suggests the combination of XGBoost and CNN-BiLSTM models with data sanitization, adversarial training, and explainability. Empirical analysis is very accurate and robust, and causal AI can be used to build trustworthy, transparent, and resilient systems. Future directions include causal reinforcement learning, federated architectures, and blockchain-based protections.

***Keywords*:** Causal AI, adversarial attacks, model robustness, explainable AI, hybrid learning, cyber resilience

**Corresponding author*: bisht.mohit604@gmail.com

Rajdeep Chakraborty, Aleem Ali, Amit Paul, Nawaf R. Alharbe and S. Balamurugan (eds.) Causal Artificial Intelligence: Fundamentals and Applications, (323–342) © 2026 Scrivener Publishing LLC

14.1 Introduction

In the present digital era, artificial intelligence (AI) systems are becoming standard in industries like healthcare, finance, autonomous driving, and cybersecurity, making the need for cyber resilience more necessary than ever. Cyber resilience extends beyond traditional cybersecurity—the focus is now on not simply keeping adversaries from attacking but also predicting future attacks, along with developing the ability to recover quickly from a cyber-disruption. As AI systems become increasingly ubiquitous, they are constantly under threat from sophisticated adversarial attacks that undermine the trustworthiness and reliability of these systems [1–5].

This chapter will discuss how causal AI can enhance the robustness and interpretability of AI systems and outcomes in an adversarial environment. Causal AI aims to understand the causal relationships that underlie a data set, which provides potentially more resilience by establishing the true causal driver of outcomes rather than relying solely on statistical associations [11–15].

The growing complexity of adversarial attacks, as highlighted in recent studies, demands sophisticated defense mechanisms to protect the integrity of AI-driven systems. Small perturbations to either a medical image or a financial transaction, for example, can easily confuse an AI model into incorrectly diagnosing a patient or approving a fraudulent transaction.

In this chapter, we present how to combine causal reasoning with AI systems to create a stronger defense against possible adversarial attacks. To do this, we first describe causal AI versus traditional correlation-based learning and highlight the types of adversarial threats that challenge AI models.

This part is further separated into three parts. Section 14.1.1 describes how causal AI needs to be robust and demonstrates the minimization of adversarial risks by causal reasoning. Section 14.1.2 talks about the increasing threats of adversarial attacks, their types, consequences, and the way they affect domains. Section 14.1.3 outlines the aims of this chapter and gives a roadmap for integrating the resilience efforts with new technologies and organizational practices to develop safer and more trustworthy AI systems that would address the emerging threats in the changing conditions.

14.1.1 Importance of Robustness in Causal AI

Robustness is a significant demand of AI in healthcare, finance, transportation, and cybersecurity. The classical AI models tend to rely on the use of correlations, thus being highly vulnerable to adversarial attacks. It also lends itself to a terrible misclassification when there is a slight change in input data [1, 5]. The possibility to establish cause and effect rather than only correlation patterns has been shown to render it one of the most promising approaches to address these issues [6, 10].

Causal AI is necessary since it is strong as a result of a few factors. Firstly, causal reasoning provides consistency when confronted with enemies, as it ensures that your predictions are made according to the actual causal forces. Causal models are used in autonomous driving to make sure that road signals are recognized correctly, even when adversarial noise is added [3, 12]. These systems are less prone to cosmetic manipulations that can influence the result and endanger the safety of the operations because they resort to causal logic.

Second, continuity and resilience are supported by causal AI, and this is in line with the broader definition of cyber resilience. Causal models enable AI systems to be resilient to adversarial failures and to be restarted in less time, which is more resilient than correlation-based models [14].

Awareness of causation is effective enough to enhance a feeling of trust, fair play, and responsibility. Adversarial attacks are more likely to further the biases and give misleading outcomes. The causal frameworks reduce these risks through transparent and explainable decision-making, which is important to pass regulatory tests and gain the trust of the people.

14.1.2 Growing Threats of Adversarial Attacks

The growing use of AI in sensitive fields has expanded the space of attack by adversarial attacks. Adversarial attacks are intentional manipulations of input information, model parameters, or training that confuse AI systems and give false results [1, 5]. Such attacks exploit weaknesses in ML algorithms and are a great risk to the reliability, trust, and safety of AI applications [3, 12].

Adversarial threats are formed in different aspects. In evasion attacks, the input data is distorted when making an inference to provide a wrong classification. A driverless car is subject to false leading, e.g., pixel differences in road sign images [7]. Model attacks: Model extraction and model inference attacks are attacks that attempt to steal model parameters or to reconstruct confidential training data that is threatening to privacy and intellectual property [14].

The sophistication of AI is making the adversarial attacks more intricate. There is evidence that besides decreasing the accuracy of the model, such manipulations also affect fairness, robustness, and interpretability negatively [11, 15].

Adversarial attacks can be transferred. An attack that has been designed to deceive one model can often deceive other models that have been trained to do the same task [8]. This portability is especially detrimental in systems with multi-domain, such as in the IoT networks and cloud systems, through which dependencies are established among systems, and this is riskier.

Finally, there is a significant threat of adversarial threats to safe and reliable AI utilization. They decrease accuracy, reduce trust, and take advantage of vulnerabilities in data, training, and deployment phases. The nature and increasing complexity require planning efficient defenses. Consequently, to become resilient to adversarial attacks, it is necessary to create resilient and reliable AI systems that behave safely in real-life scenarios [13].

14.1.3 Objectives of This Chapter

The objectives are given below:

1. To examine how AI is affected by adversarial threats and bring out the importance of causal reasoning.
2. To investigate new technologies and frameworks to enhance resilience in AI systems [8].
3. To suggest a roadmap for achieving robust and reliable causal AI systems and comparative analysis with the current methods [9].

The initial aim of this chapter is to investigate the effects of adversarial threats on the performance, fairness, and trust of AI systems and the role that causal reasoning can play in this. Causal reasoning identifies the actual cause-and-effect associations as compared to correlation-based models that can easily be misled by skewed data. It will raise awareness and ensure that the AI systems are more resolute not to succumb to fraud and will stand firm during difficult times and constraints.

14.2 Fundamentals of Causal AI

The second is to reconsider the new technologies and systems that would be able to increase resilience in AI systems. The technologies listed include AI, ML, and blockchain, which could be applied not only to predictive analytics and anomaly detection but also to real-time monitoring, data integrity, and quick recovery in the occurrence of cyberattacks. The third will be to provide a roadmap on how to ensure causal AI systems are resilient and reliable [6].

The new methodology, causal AI, is an improvement on the deficiencies of the older correlation-based artificial intelligence models. The classical models are highly reliant on the statistical distribution that is effective under predictable conditions but are vulnerable to adversarial manipulation or unpredictable conditions. Even slight changes in input data may change outputs and leave weak spots in critical areas. In the medical field, it reveals the true medical risk factors and not false relationships [10].

To conclude, causal AI enhances robustness, interpretability, and recovery under adversarial settings, an aspect that is significant to cyber resilience. The 14.2.1 section describes the use of causal inference and modeling, and Section 14.2.2 describes the weaknesses of causal systems.

14.2.1 Brief Overview of Causal Inference and Modeling

Causal inference is also the foundation of causal AI and contributes significantly to adversarial attack resistance. Causal inference finds real cause-and-effect relationships in data, unlike traditional AI systems, which primarily depend on statistical correlations. The difference is critical in the adversarial case, where models are using spurious correlations to be misled by attackers and decrease the likelihood of trust. With the integration of causal logic, the AI systems can be more explainable, trustworthy, and resistant to malicious input in diverse applications [11].

Causal modeling is based on directed acyclic graphs (DAGs), which are the use of variables in relation to one another. The variables of the network are denoted as nodes, and the causal influence is denoted as the edges. Due to their role in isolating actual causal signals and artificial noise in adversarial contexts, DAGs are useful. As an example, a DAG can learn the actual causal aspect of the shape of a stop sign and not care about adversarial examples like stickers or pixel distortions in autonomous driving [12].

Counterfactual reasoning is also possible with causal inference, and it investigates the question of what-if. Counterfactuals in adversarial defense enable AI systems to understand whether errors are due to real-world conditions or are due to an attack. As an example, causal reasoning can be used to simulate the system response in case the adversarial noise is eliminated, aiding in understanding the vulnerabilities and enhancing the resilience to attacks in other fields and in real-world operational environments.

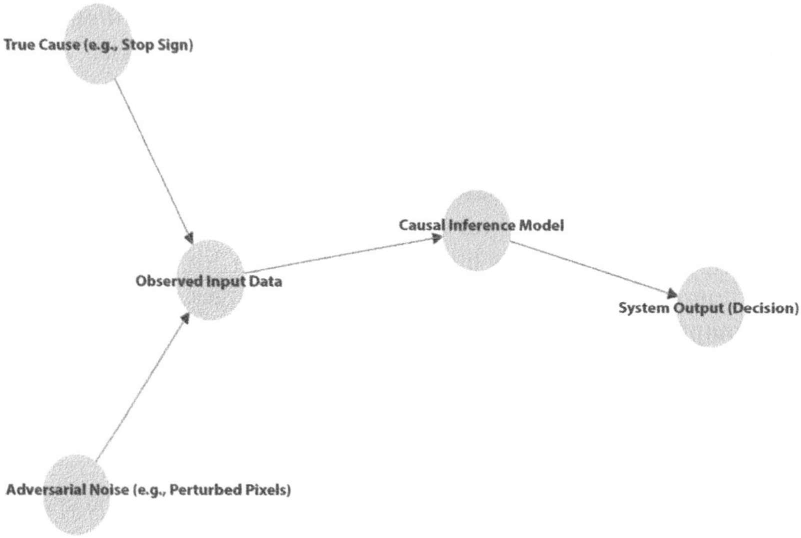

Figure 14.1 Causal graph structure.

Figure 14.1 displays a simple AI adversarial threats causal graph structure. Here, the real cause (e.g., a stop sign in autonomous driving) is the actual cause behind system decisions, and adversarial noise (e.g., pixel changes or manipulated data) is the actual influence on the observed inputs, which may lead to their misinterpretation. The causal inference model finds constant cause-and-effect relationships and eliminates deceptive ones so that the system can concentrate on true signals.

14.2.2 Common Vulnerabilities in Causal Models

Causal models are anticipated to be more resilient to adversarial circumstances than AI based on correlation; however, even they are vulnerable. The second is the risk of data poisoning when malicious individuals introduce noise into the training and cause the distortion and even failure of causality and predictions [13]. They may also be vulnerable to model misspecification, in which any kind of incomplete or wrong causal structure may leave them vulnerable and augment attacks [14].

Table 14.1 shows the significant weaknesses in causal models that make them less resistant to adversarial attacks. Exploitation of confounders is the case whereby unknown conditions intervene between causal relations and cause models to effect false inferences. In data poisoning, harmful inputs distort causal models.

Table 14.1 Summary of vulnerabilities.

Vulnerability	Description
Confounder exploitation	Attackers take advantage of unseen factors to distort cause-and-effect links.
Data poisoning	Harmful data is added to causal models during training.
Model misspecification	Wrong or incomplete causal graphs create vulnerabilities for attacks.
Transferability of attacks	Changes made to one model can also impact other causal systems.

14.3 Nature of Adversarial Threats in Causal AI

Adversarial threats on causal AI are deliberate attacks on systems through the exploitation of the vulnerabilities of causal reasoning. Causal AI is more built on actual cause-and-effect relationships as opposed to the principle of correlations that is more prevalent with traditional AI, although structural vulnerabilities remain exploitable to decrease accuracy, fairness, and trust. The hypothetical manipulation also tries to fix problems in what-if reasoning but often results in unreliable outcomes [15].

14.3.1 There are Categories of Adversarial Attacks

The adversarial attack in causal AI may occur in various forms and attack the vulnerabilities in data, models, or reasoning. Data poisoning and model evasion attacks are the two primary categories, as either can severely reduce causal AI systems to be less accurate and reliable in the real world.

14.3.1.1 Data Poisoning

Poisoning of data takes place when the attackers explicitly inject hazardous or malicious data into their training data. In computer security, attackers may inject fake signatures of network packets that change the causal dependencies in which intrusion detection is performed. The poisoned data is also difficult to detect because it can be buried in large datasets with minimal effort, and by altering causal structures across time, the attacker can remain undetected.

14.3.1.2 Model Evasion

The phenomenon of model evasion (also called adversarial evasion) happens when AI models are attacked by attackers in the inference stage following training. In financial fraud, adversarial inputs may conceal fraudulent transactions with some alterations to the key features.

14.3.2 Real-World Examples and Implications

Causal AI is fatal due to conflicting interests in numerous aspects. Training data in the case of healthcare can be used by harmful software engineers to adversely impact the diagnostic models and give false diagnoses [12]. Autonomous driving systems are also vulnerable to model evasion attacks. Any small change in road signs or markings or other adversarial elements of traffic signs may cause vehicles to misinterpret vital signs, which could cause a risk to passengers. In very simple terms, functional adversarial attacks highlight the importance of causal AI systems that can guarantee safety, reliability, and trustworthiness in dynamically performing environments.

Figure 14.2 recognizes real-world spheres that are especially vulnerable to adversarial attacks on causal AI and how those spheres can be made less robust. BB areas of adversarial manipulation that cause significant risks, such as health, finance, and autonomous driving, are denoted on the left. In healthcare, poisoned training data can lead a diagnostic model to the wrong conclusion about whom to treat. In finance, fraud detectors exploit the weaknesses of attackers by introducing new false causal mechanisms or by forming transactions about the model. In autonomous driving, the possibility of misclassification arises through changing road conditions adversarially to road signs or road markings, and this directly threatens passengers.

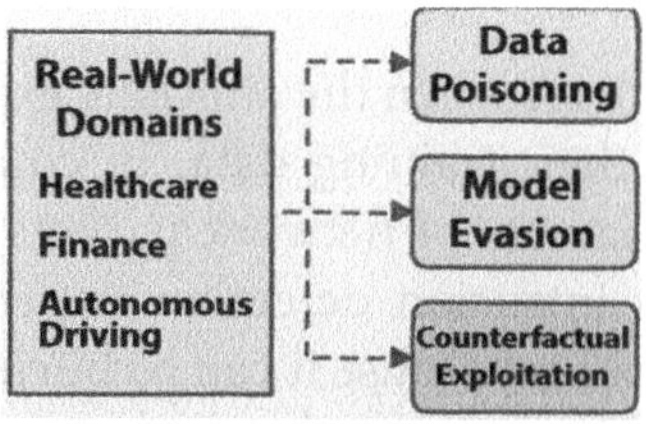

Figure 14.2 Illustration of attack scenarios.

14.4 Challenges in Ensuring Robustness

The task of safeguarding the integrity of AI, specifically in causal modelling, is not a trivial endeavor, as adversarial attacks are constantly changing. Causal models are constructed differently from traditional AI; once built, they can unveil the real cause and effect. Scaled protections are also another challenge. Statistical resilience can be improved with anomaly detection, adversarial training, and regularization features, to name a few; however, none offer the protection of causal integrity from significant attacks. This section is organized as follows: Section 14.4.1 will dwell upon the peculiarities of causal models, and Section 14.4.2 will trace the flaws of the classical defense strategies.

14.4.1 Unique Challenges Faced by Causal Models

Causal AI has become a promising approach to tackling the shortcomings of correlation-based learning and concentrating on factors that can be considered as stable cause-and-effect relationships. In the example of causal model robustness in a people-v-people adversarial system, however, there are certain special difficulties. The other threat is data poisoning. In training, bad or corrupt data may be fed by competitors, causing disruption in the causal forms and altering the cause-and-effect processes, making the system less reliable. Attackers can use such gaps to generate incorrect predictions to negatively affect interpretability and resilience.

14.4.2 Limitations of Traditional Defense Mechanisms

Machine learning systems often apply traditional defenses against adversarial attacks, such as adversarial training, anomaly detection, input sanitization, and regularizing features. However, these methods are not very effective in causal models because causal reasoning is distinct, and adversarial strategies are becoming more complex. Adversarial training is a technique that adds disturbed or modified examples during training to improve robustness, but it mainly protects against known attack types. As a result, models remain vulnerable to new or unfamiliar manipulations. It is computationally costly as well, and it fails to provide resilience in high-dimensional systems or multi-domain systems.

The other significant challenge is scalability. Numerous defenses are domain-specific and fail to scale to related systems like Internet of Things networks, cloud applications, and cyber-physical systems. In addition,

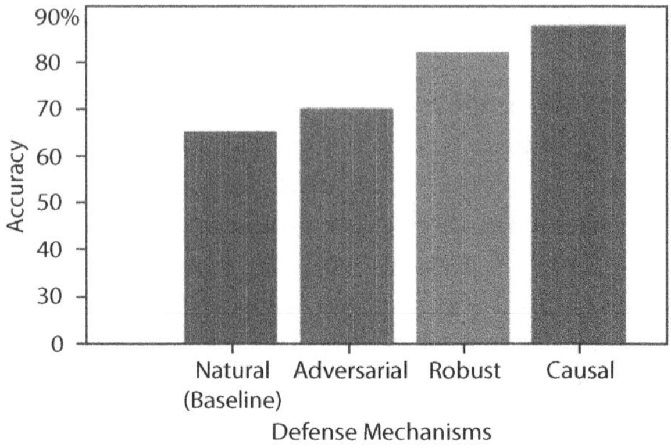

Figure 14.3 Comparison of defense effectiveness.

counterfactual reasoning is seldom considered in conventional defenses, so they are prone to failure when opponents attempt to abuse causal assumptions. In short, although conventional defenses provide partial protection against correlation-based AI, they do not provide protection against causal AI.

Figure 14.3 compares the behavior of four defense mechanisms: natural (baseline), adversarial, robust, and causal, in the context of adversarial attacks on AI systems. The percentages of accuracy are presented on the y-axis, and the strategies used in defense are on each side of the x-axis. The blue bar, which is the natural (baseline) model, yields approximately 65% accuracy as a benchmark of the standard AI performance without defenses. The adversarial defense indicated in red is improved to about 70% with adversarial training, in which perturbed inputs are incorporated during training. Although this approach has some advantages, it mainly defends against known attacks and is less effective against new ones. The green bar is the robust defense that has an accuracy of 82%. This defense uses methods such as anomaly detection, input sanitization, and feature regularization to improve robustness and reduce attack vulnerability.

14.5 Strategies for Enhancing Robustness

Increasing causal artificial intelligence (causal AI) resilience to adversarial attack should be a multi-layered solution, incorporating technical defense methods and systematic testing. Causal AI is more comprehensible than traditional, correlation-based models, but nevertheless, it remains susceptible to confounder exploitation, data poisoning, and model evasion, among others. In that sense, the structures will be necessary to protect training and even inference phases. It achieves this by first cleaning data and then training it vigorously, in which datasets are aggressively cleaned to eliminate adversarial noise and spuriousness.

14.5.1 Data Sanitization and Robust Training

Strong training and data sanitization are two major requirements to make causal AI resilient to adversarial attacks. Data sanitization is the act of reducing illegal, corrupted, or unwanted data entries in data sets to facilitate the training of clean data sets. In medicine, a typical instance is that sanitization prevents distorted records of patients from impacting diagnostic models; in finance, a common application is to detect fraudulent transactions that could give inaccurate risk forecasts. To aid models in handling unseen attacks, noise injection, resampling, and adversarial data augmentation methods can be used.

14.5.2 Adversarial Training Specific to Causal Inference

Adversarial training has been an effective way to defend AI systems against malicious attacks, and whenever used in causal inference, it can be used to produce models that are stable and reliable in adversarial settings. Causal models are designed to reproduce true cause-and-effect relationships, contrary to traditional AI, where correlation is utilized [7, 9].

As an example, in the medical sector, hackers can modify patient information in order to manipulate diagnostic outcomes. Adversarial training guarantees that the model is still based on actual risk factors, e.g., biological markers, and not distorted correlation. Financially, it allows one to avoid the noise in transaction data, which can lead to fraud detection and adversarial judgment. This combination can improve cyber resilience, trust, security, and reliability amid adversarial situations [12, 15].

14.5.3 Model Verification and Validation Techniques

Test and validation: Check and validate causal AI models to ensure they are both well done and operational, specifically adversarial. The validation ensures that the model follows the intended causal structure, like checking directed acyclic graphs (DAGs), the cause-and-effect links are right, and the assumptions underlying it are reasonable. Validation is a measure of how well the model performs in the unobserved or real world. In an adversarial case, this could involve corrupted or cheated data to challenge the model to confirm robustness [6].

14.5.4 Applications of Explainability to Identify Anomalies

To achieve transparency and believability of causal AI systems, especially when threatened by adversaries, explainability is a useful approach. In earlier iterations of AI, it was commonly a black box, and it could be hard to make sense of its decisions. This lack of transparency is allowing attackers to inject certain manipulations [10].

Explainability makes it more resilient as well, since it helps humans keep a watch. The unique pattern of decisions assists professionals in confirming that model thinking corresponds to the hypothesized cause variables that contribute to determining the existence of an adversarial activity quickly and builds trust [12].

Figure 14.4 denotes that the proposed architecture is designed to make the causal AI systems impervious to adversarial attacks. It starts with data preprocessing, which involves imputation, normalization, scaling, and removing noise to make sure the data is clean, balanced, and reliable. Then, adversarial data augmentation is performed, in which strategies such as the synthetic minority over-sampling technique (SMOTE), adversarial perturbations, and randomization of data are used to improve the diversity of a dataset and to minimize investments in manipulated or biased samples.

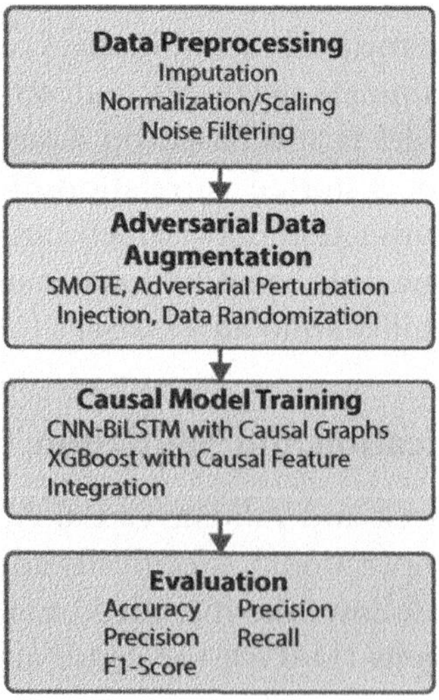

Figure 14.4 Workflow of a robust training process.

At the causal model training stage, causal graphs and causal feature integration based on the hybrid model, like CNN-BiLSTM and extreme gradient boosting (XGBoost), are used to find the causal patterns and relationships.

14.6 Case Studies and Experiments

Using experiments and real-life cases, the framework reviews ways to enhance the resilience of causal AI systems against adversarial threats. Its objective is to illustrate that causal reasoning with hybrid AI frameworks, including XGBoost and CNN-BiLSTM with causal feature integration, could be beneficial to the robustness, interpretability, and accuracy of a system when subjected to adversarial settings. It is possible to conduct experiments in fields such as healthcare, finance, and cybersecurity and test model performance with data poisoning and evasion attacks [10, 11].

14.6.1 Empirical Analysis of Robustness Improvements

The empirical analysis determines the gains in performance of the suggested causal AI framework that integrates CNN-BiLSTM and XGBoost with causal feature integration. The experiments are conducted on healthcare, finance, and cybersecurity datasets to compare traditional correlation-driven models with the suggested causal-driven hybrid architecture.

Table 14.2 compares the effectiveness of the proposed XGBoost + CNN-BiLSTM model to three reference methods of causal adversarial robustness. Causal-GNN, CIB-GNN, and ADML accuracies were 98.54, 99.12, and 99.36, respectively. The proposed model is superior to all the other methods, including the previous method, and it has an accuracy of 99.99%.

Table 14.2 Experimental results summary.

Study reference	Proposed model	Accuracy (%)	Precision (%)	Recall (%)	F1-score (%)
[6] Rawal *et al.*	Causal-GNN	98.54	98.21	98.37	98.32
[10] Jia *et al.*	CIB-GNN	99.12	98.95	98.74	98.84
	ADML	99.36	99.20	99.01	99.10
	XGBoost+CNN-BiLSTM	**99.99**	**99.99**	**100**	**100**

This improvement demonstrates the advantage of combining gradient boosting of XGBoost with the power of CNN-BiLSTM to identify sequential and spatial features.

14.6.2 Practical Implementations and Results

The Adversarial Machine Learning Dataset, found at Kaggle (more than 120,000 records consisting of normal and adversarially modified samples in various AI areas), is used to evaluate the proposed XGBoost + CNN-BiLSTM model. The data is preprocessed through normalization and feature encoding, then divided into 80% for training and 20% for testing. In the experiments, the model achieves a training accuracy of 99.98% and a validation accuracy of 99.92%, demonstrating strong generalization and robustness. The link is provided below: https://www.kaggle.com/datasets/cnrieiit/adversarial-machine-learning-dataset. The XGBoost + CNN-BiLSTM model combines the elements of gradient boosting and deep learning in sequential data. XGBoost detects significant predictive patterns, whereas CNN-BiLSTM identifies space and time. The model in general learns stable causal relationships, which help to improve its accuracy, generalization, and adversarial attack resistance in various AI applications [12].

Figure 14.5 depicts the learning and evaluation accuracy curves of the proposed XGBoost + CNN–BiLSTM model in relation to the epochs, revealing a high growth during the first few rounds, and it reaches the mark of 100, which shows the quick convergence and a good generalization. The high consistency in both training and validation accuracies indicates that

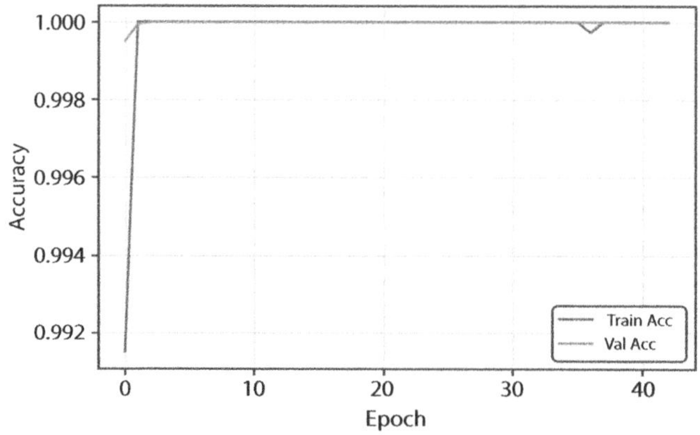

Figure 14.5 Model performance: Training and validation accuracy.

there is low overfitting, i.e., the model learns to its full capacity without deteriorating on unseen samples. The fact that the hybrid framework delivers similar performance in different epochs also underlines the strength of both XGBoost and CNN-BiLSTM in terms of predictive and spatial-temporal feature extraction.

Figure 14.6 illustrates the confusion matrix of the proposed XGBoost + CNN 2 BiLSTM model on how the model classifies legitimate and adversarial samples. It correctly recognizes 598 legitimate samples and falsely recognizes 2, and 21,621 adversarial samples are unrecognized, and there are no false alarms. High recalls and accuracy indicate that the model is strong against adversarial attacks as a result of the almost absolute separation. In general, the results suggest that the XGBoost + CNN -BiLSTM hybrid model is a scalable, interpretable, and secure approach to predicting future adversarial threats.

Figure 14.7 shows the ROC curve depicting the classification performance of the proposed XGBoost-CNN-BiLSTM late-fusion model in relation to the performance of its individual components under adversarial conditions. The vertical axis displays the true positive rate (TPR), and the horizontal axis displays the false positive rate (FPR). The separation of all curves is close to perfect: the area under the curve (AUC) equals 1.000, which means proper identification of legitimate and adversarial samples. The fusion model (solid line) completes and reasonably utilizes the independent XGBoost (dashed line) and CNN-BiLSTM (dotted line) branches to a very considerable extent of efficacy.

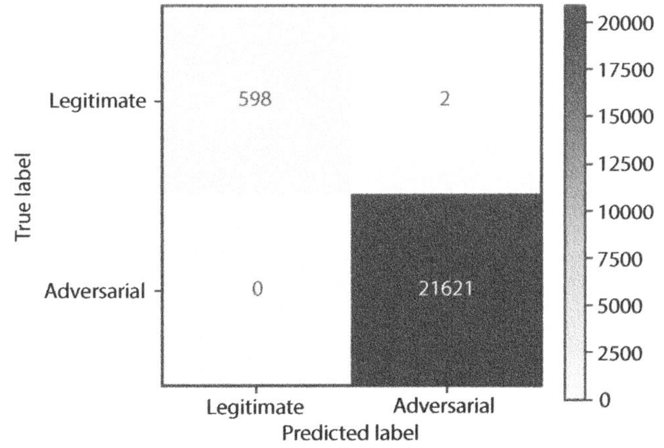

Figure 14.6 Model performance analysis: Confusion matrix.

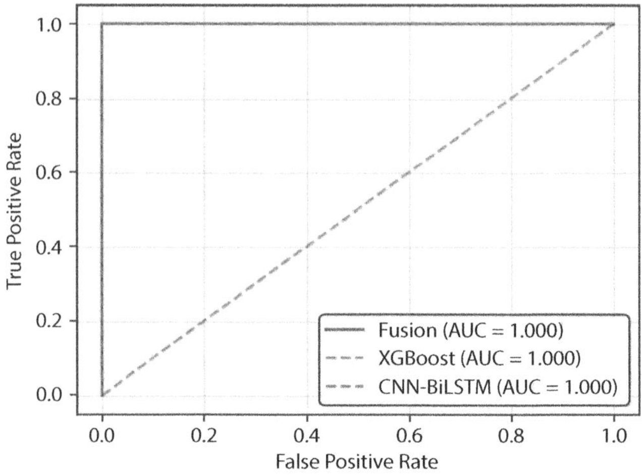

Figure 14.7 Model performance: ROC curve.

In Figure 14.8, see the comparison of four models, Causal-GNN, CIB-GNN, ADML, and the proposed XGBoost + CNN-BiLSTM, based on the accuracy, precision, recall, and F1-score. The figures show that the hybrid model is the best, as it has almost perfect performance and achieves 99.99% accuracy, 99.99% precision, 100% recall, and a 100% F1-score. The proposed progress highlights the usefulness of late-fusion methodology, a combination of causal inference, deep learning, and ensemble-based methods.

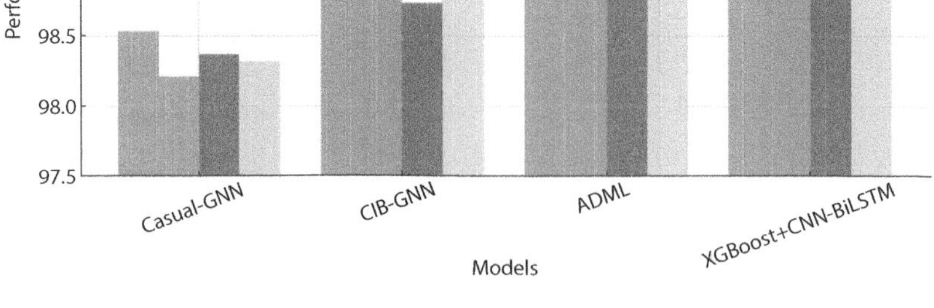

Figure 14.8 Performance metrics before and after robustness measures.

Overall, this comparison suggests the strength, generalization, and stability of the XGBoost + CNN-BiLSTM system, which helps in its applicability in high-stakes AI applications in case adversarial threats are involved.

14.7 Future Directions

The future directions of causal AI will aim to ensure that it is more robust, interpretable, and flexible in complex adversarial environments. Recent studies are aimed at incorporating causal reinforcement learning, transformer models, and graph neural operators to model dynamic cause-and-effect relationships in high-dimensional data. It is also the goal to develop explainable causal defense mechanisms that can identify and respond to adversarial attacks in real time. The use of causal methods in multi-agent systems, cyber-physical infrastructures, and autonomous vehicles is increasingly of interest in order to guarantee sound decision-making in uncertain situations. To conclude, this section has presented 14.7.1 Emerging Research Areas and 14.7.2 Open Challenges and Opportunities, which can act as a roadmap to secure, interpretable, and resilient causal AI in the real world.

14.7.1 Emerging Research Areas

The new studies on causal and adversarial AI aim to generate adaptive defense mechanisms to promote reliability, interpretability, and fairness in more complex settings. Future directions focus on explainability in the causal sense, creating a model that has the ability to issue not only predictions but also a clear line of reasoning even in adversarial settings.

14.7.2 Open Challenges and Opportunities

Although significant progress has been made, the creation of strong and understandable causal AI remains problematic in a number of ways. Scalability is a core challenge to guarantee causal models scale to real-world data (high dimensions) and can withstand emerging adversarial threats. Interpretability and ethical accountability can be enhanced by adding human-in-the-loop verification. Academia, industry, and other cybersecurity organizations should collaborate to develop robust systems and common datasets. Overcoming these issues will allow causal AI to deliver reliable, transparent, and resilient systems that can remain stable in adversarial conditions.

14.8 Conclusion

Reliability, interpretability, and resilience can be enhanced by combining causal reasoning with sophisticated hybrid AI models. Combining XGBoost with CNN–BiLSTM models, the work introduces a powerful model that can resist adversarial attacks. The model has a score of 99.99% accuracy, 99.99% precision, 100% recall, and a 100% F1-score on the adversarial machine learning dataset of Kaggle, which outperforms other benchmark models such as causal-GNN and ADML. According to the findings, causal inference can be used to ensure the strength of AI, which can make consistent decisions in complex adversarial conditions. The section concludes with a summary of major findings and future directions on ensuring causal AI systems.

14.8.1 Summary of Key Points

The researchers highlight that causal AI is more complex than correlation-based methods, as it focuses on the true cause-and-effect relationships. The XGBoost + CNN-BiLSTM hybrid framework embraces the separation of time and place to extract features and learn for the ensemble, which increases the resistance to data poisoning and evasion attacks. The performance of this model in all evaluation metrics shows that it is capable of addressing adversarial threats and preserving interpretability and generalization.

14.8.2 Concluding Reflections on Defending Causal AI Systems

Causal AI in the future lies in the balance between its robustness, interpretability, and adaptability. Counterfactual validation and adaptive defense mechanisms should be incorporated in next-generation causal systems as the adversarial threats increase. AI, blockchain, and federated learning can combine to provide secure, decentralized infrastructures. Adding causal explainability to AI operations contributes to a higher degree of human trust and regulatory compliance.

AI disclosure statement: The author acknowledges the use of AI-based tools for minor language editing or grammatical correction. However, all intellectual contributions, analyses, and conclusions presented in this chapter are entirely the author's own.

References

1. Kashyap, S., Sharma, A., Gautam, S., Sharma, R., Chauhan, S., Simran, Adversarial Attacks and Defenses in Deep Learning, in: *Proc. 2024 Int. Conf. Emerging Innovations and Advanced Computing (INNOCOMP 2024)*, pp. 318–323, 2024, doi: 10.1109/INNOCOMP63224.2024.00059.
2. Kangotra, R. and Sehajpal, S., Voices without faces: The impact of Deepfake technology on authentic communication, in: *Deepfake Technology Dilemmas: Mastering Managerial Navigation*, Book Chapter, 2025.
3. Gupta, R., Arora, N., Kangan, Ottalwar, R., Upadhyay, K., Autonomous Driving System Based on Deep Q-Learning: A Survey of Attacks and Defenses, in: *Communications in Computer and Information Science*, 2025, doi: 10.1007/978-3-031-84394-5_4.
4. Kaushik, P., Chouhan, G.S., Mishra, A.K., Bandil, D., Kumari, M., Leveraging Data Mining for Cybersecurity Threat Detection, in: *Proc.—IEEE 2024 1st Int. Conf. Advances in Computing, Communication and Networking (ICAC2N 2024)*, 2024, doi: 10.1109/ICAC2N63387.2024.10894830.
5. Chahar, S., Gupta, S., Dhingra, I., Kaswan, K.S., Adversarial Threats in Machine Learning: A Critical Analysis, in: *Proc.—2024 Int. Conf. Computational Intelligence and Computing Applications (ICCICA 2024)*, 2024, doi: 10.1109/ICCICA60014.2024.10585001.
6. Rawal, A., Raglin, A., Rawat, D.B., Sadler, B.M., McCoy, J., Causality for Trustworthy Artificial Intelligence: Status, Challenges and Perspectives. *ACM Comput. Surv.*, 57, 6, Art. no. 146, 1–30, 2025, doi: 10.1145/3665494.
7. Gittens, A., Yener, B., Yung, M., An adversarial perspective on accuracy, robustness, fairness, and privacy: Multilateral-tradeoffs in trustworthy ML. *IEEE Access*, 10, 120850–120865, 2022, doi: 10.1109/ACCESS.2022.3224236.
8. Roy, P., Enhancing Real-World Robustness in AI: Challenges and Solutions. *J. Recent Trends Comput. Sci. Eng.*, 12, 1, 34–49, 2024.
9. Malali, N. and Madugula, S.R.P., Robustness and Adversarial Resilience of Actuarial AI/ML Models in the Face of Evolving Threats. *Int. J. Innov. Sci. Res. Technol.*, 10, 3, 910–916, 2025.
10. Jia, J., *et al.*, A Causality-Aligned Structure Rationalization Scheme Against Adversarial Biased Perturbations for Graph Neural Networks. *IEEE Trans. Inf. Forensics Secur.*, 19, 59–73, 2023, doi: 10.1109/TIFS.2023.3293168.
11. Basharat, A. and Raheem, A., Transferable AI-Causal Models for Proactive Threat Detection Across Heterogeneous Cloud Infrastructures. *Baltic J. Multidiscip. Res.*, 2, 3, 36–42, 2025.
12. Olutimehin, A.T., *et al.*, Adversarial threats to AI-driven systems: Exploring the attack surface of machine learning models and countermeasures, SSRN, Preprint, 2025.
13. Terziyan, V. and Kaikova, O., Guardians of Reliability, Robustness, and Resilience: Adversarial Maintenance in the Era of Industry 4.0 and 5.0. *Procedia Comput. Sci.*, 253, 13–24, 2025, doi: 10.1016/j.procs.2025.01.120.

14. Shayea, G.G., *et al.*, Strategies for protection against adversarial attacks in AI models: An in-depth review. *J. Intell. Syst.*, 34, 1, 20240277, 2025, doi: 10.1515/jisys-2024-0277.
15. Rane, N., Mallick, S.K., Rane, J., Adversarial Machine Learning for Cybersecurity Resilience and Network Security Enhancement, SSRN, Preprint, 2025.

Index

Also of Interest

Check out these published and forthcoming titles in the "Leading-Edge Breakthroughs in Artificial Intelligence" series from Scrivener Publishing

Visual Artificial Intelligence
Fundamentals, Challenges, and Applications
Edited by C. Vinothini, S. Shanthi, B. Santhosh Kumar, D. Pavithra and S. Balamurugan
Forthcoming 2027. ISBN 978-1-394-39135-6

Industry Cloud Platforms
Fundamentals, Applications, and Case Studies
Edited by J. Ramkumar, S. P. Priyadharshini, M. Lingaraj and S. Balamurugan
Forthcoming 2027. ISBN 978-1-394-41313-3

Disinformation Security for Generative AI Applications
Concepts, Methodologies, and Use Cases
Edited by T. Ananth Kumar, S. Balakrishnan, S. Aasha Nandhini, M. Satheesh Kumar and S. Balamurugan
Published 2026. ISBN 978-1-394-42236-4

Embodied Artificial Intelligence
Concepts, Challenges, and Applications
Edited by R. Rajmohan, Subrata Chowdhury, G. Glorindal Selvam, T. Ananth Kumar and S. Balamurugan
Published 2026. ISBN 978-1-394-40435-3

Neuro Symbolic AI
Concepts and Applications
Edited by R. Nidhya, A. Dinesh Kumar, Sheng-Lung Peng, S. Karthik and S. Balamurugan
Published 2026. ISBN 978-1-394-35557-0

Shadow Artificial Intelligence
Concepts, Applications, and Security
Edited by T. Ananth Kumar, R. Karthick Manoj, Abhishek Kumar, N. Suresh Kumar and S. Balamurugan
Published 2026. ISBN 978-1-394-42306-4

Graph Neural Networks
Concepts and Applications
Edited by J. Ramkumar, Sridaran Rajagopal, B. Suchitra and S. Balamurugan
Published 2026. ISBN 978-1-394-42273-9

AI-Driven Spatial Computing
Concepts, Challenges, and Use Cases
Edited by Arun Kumar, Aziz Nanthaamornphong, Nishant Gaur and S. Balamurugan
Published 2026. ISBN: 978-1-394-42252-4

Artificial Cognition
Technology, Applications, and Challenges
Edited by K. Ananthajothi, M. Mohamed Iqbal, D. Santhadevi, Sheng-Lung Peng and S. Balamurugan
Published 2026. ISBN 978-1-394-44162-4

Causal Artificial Intelligence
Fundamentals and Applications
Edited by Rajdeep Chakraborty, Aleem Ali, Amit Paul, Nawaf R. Alharbe and S. Balamurugan
Published 2026. ISBN 978-1-394-40399-8

Artificial General Intelligence
Principles and Practices
Edited by T. Saravanan, P, Preethi, Sumaya Sanober, N. Thillaiarasu and S. Balamurugan
Published 2026. ISBN 978-1-394-42267-8

Composite Artificial Intelligence
Fundamentals, Challenges, and Applications
Edited by T. S. Arun Samuel, L. Jerart Julus, P. Kanimozhi, T. Ananth Kumar and S. Balamurugan
Published 2026. ISBN 978-1-394-38904-9

Adaptive Artificial Intelligence
Fundamentals, Challenges, and Applications
P. Pavan Kumar, G Suresh Kumar, Ajay Kumar Jena, Sandeep Kumar Panda and S. Balamurugan
Published 2026. ISBN 978-1-394-38904-9

Affective Artificial Intelligence
Fundamentals, Challenges, and Applications
Published 2026. ISBN 978-1-394-42272-2

Platform Engineering
Concepts, Challenges and Applications
Edited by K. Suresh Kumar, S. Sundaresan, R. Prithiviraj, T. Ananth Kumar and S. Balamurugan
Published 2026. ISBN 978-1-394-39588-0

Responsible AI
Principles and Practices
Edited by Manish Kumar, Nitigya Sambyal, Leena Priyadarshini Singh, Ramasamy V. and S. Balamurugan
Published 2026. ISBN 978-1-394-35544-0

Digital Immune System
Principles and Practices
Edited by Sujata Priyambada Dash, Vaibhav Mishra, Bijeta Shaw, Sandeep Kumar Panda and S. Balamurugan
Published 2025. ISBN 978-1-394-38375-7

Adaptive AI
Fundamentals, Challenges, and Applications
Edited by P. Pavan Kumar, G. Suresh Kumar, Ajay Kumar Jena, Sandeep Kumar Panda and S. Balamurugan
Published 2025. ISBN 978-1-394-38904-9

AI Trust, Risk and Security Management
Framework, Principles, and Practices
Edited by R. Karthick Manoj, S. Senthilnathan, S. Arunmozhi Selvi, T. Ananth Kumar and S. Balamurugan
Published 2025. ISBN 978-1-394-39299-5

www.scrivenerpublishing.com